Making Circles

MAKING CIRCLES

THE MEMOIR OF A COWBOY JOURNALIST

BARNEY NELSON

UNIVERSITY OF OKLAHOMA PRESS : NORMAN

Library of Congress Cataloging-in-Publication Data

Names: Nelson, Barney, 1947– author.
Title: Making circles : the memoir of a cowboy journalist / Barney Nelson.
Description: Norman : University of Oklahoma Press, 2021. | Includes bibliographical references. | Summary: "A philosophical tour de force through the working class cowboy's anything-but-simple lifestyle and lessons learned while freelancing as a photo-journalist for horse and ranching magazines"—Provided by publisher.
Identifiers: LCCN 2020032140 | ISBN 978-0-8061-6845-6 (paperback)
Subjects: LCSH: Nelson, Barney, 1947– | Photojournalists—United States—Biography. | Journalists—United States—Biography. | English teachers—United States—Biography. | College teachers—United States—Biography.
Classification: LCC TR140.N3127 A3 2020 | DDC 770.92 [B]—dc23
LC record available at https://lccn.loc.gov/2020032140

The paper in this book meets the guidelines for permanence and durability of the Committee on Production Guidelines for Book Longevity of the Council on Library Resources, Inc. ∞

To
Carla Grace Spencer
my daughter

Contents

Introduction
Coffee

"I don't know about truth, but I believe journalism can lead to a moment of real human connection between the reader and a world that they would not otherwise know."
—Adrian Nicole LeBlanc

I START MY DAY, every morning, with coffee. The chair where I drink it has wide wooden arms. A pen and pad of lined paper sit less than an arm's length away, and one thing seems to lead to another. So I will begin with coffee, as always, and a few rules about values, privacy, humor, art, and truth that I try to live by. I call myself a cowboy journalist, which probably sounds small town and rustic, but cowboys have inhabited every culture, continent, and century, from bedouins to Huns, samurai to *csikós*, Lakotas to *paniolos*; from Argentine gauchos to Kenyan Masai to Australian ringers; from Pegasus to Cervantes to Tolstoy and Shakespeare. Even Henry David Thoreau called himself a cowboy. We forget that almost everyone's ancestors once rode horses or drove some kind of vehicle pulled by horses.

My parents drank their coffee with milk, but not me. I acquired a taste for the real thing—no milk, no sugar, just hot and black. I got into a friendly argument once with a famous horseman over coffee grounds. He said one of his jobs as a kid was to keep the drains open, and every time he had to dig up drainpipes, they were full of coffee grounds. I said I'd always thought that coffee grounds would scratch out those pipes and keep the drains open and that I had stopped up a drain only once in my life. I think we both stuck to our guns, but for some reason, today I throw my coffee dregs on the ground or in the trash, not down the drain. Maybe coffee, the conversations that went with it, and my later reflection on those conversations helped me question my own stubborn opinions.

Coffee has probably saved my life on many occasions: boiling coffee from brackish or polluted water that was otherwise unsafe to drink, stopping for a wake-up cup on a long West Texas highway, or cradling a steaming cup in frozen hands. In tree forks near water I stashed empty coffee cans, matches, and cups, and of course ground coffee. In those places I could hobble my horse, build a fire, dip the coffee can full of water from a nearby source, and brew a cup. One morning with hoar frost an inch thick, I stopped near Barney's Tank in the top of a basin to start a fire right after one of the cowboys said, "I'd give a million bucks for a cup of coffee right now." Of course he didn't have a dime in his pocket, but he got some coffee. Wherever I've been and whoever dropped in on me unexpectedly, neither guest nor host has ever felt embarrassed or poor as long as we had coffee to offer or accept. I've had coffee served to me poolside by a uniformed maid out of a pot made of gold and out of a handleless saucepan that the owner had never washed, and I can't say it tasted any different. Coffee provided common ground.

While chasing stories, camped out in the hills of the West, the best parts of the days and nights have been spent around a fire cradling a cup of coffee. I've drunk coffee on the other side of a snowmelt-swollen creek in Wyoming. I've drunk coffee made from crick water near Oregon's Jordan Valley, out of a brackish Musselshell tributary in Montana, from cisterns in Paraguay's Gran Chaco, and from springs in Coahuila where bears had been bathing. Coffee accompanied conversations in the bottom of Arizona's Aravaipa and Blue River canyons, in the bottom of Texas's Dry, Horse Thief, and Palo Duro Canyons. My best interviews, my best photographs, my best ideas usually included a cup of coffee. Coffee and the water it came from made a writer out of me.

But writing is a lonely life. So, sometimes, when I felt lonesome, I'd head to a local coffee shop. Around here, we often use *coffee* as a verb, as in "Where do you coffee?" Mostly, I coffeed in Alpine and Marfa. In Alpine I was usually the first to arrive, so the other local coffee drinkers simply joined me. Perhaps because Alpine is a college town, the locals did not feel threatened by a damn writer, although that could have been my imagination. In Marfa, an old ranching town, it was harder to get up early enough to be the first to arrive. So I usually sat alone in a booth, near but not at the locals' table in Carmen's Café. I sat alone, not because I felt unwelcome but because it allowed me to eavesdrop and take notes without causing a stir. Rural coffee shops have rules, and a writer's presence affects those rules, but not as much as a stranger's presence. For instance, one morning a stranger walked up to the locals' table in Marfa and asked, "Does anyone here know Bill Shurley?"

Of course we all did, but nobody said a word. Suddenly everyone needed to either sip or stir their coffee.

Long silence.

Finally, Bill Shurley himself stood up from the circle of silent coffee drinkers, stuck out his hand, and said, "Yeah, I know him. I'm Bill Shurley. What can I do for you, Mister?"

If Bill hadn't stood, the stranger wouldn't have gotten an answer. Maybe eventually someone might have asked what the stranger wanted to see this fellow about, but probably not. If it was a bill collector or a jealous husband or even just some feed salesman, all of that would have been Bill's business, not ours—well, at least until Bill got up and left. We are not saints.

What they say about everybody knowing your business in small towns is true, so you better behave. Although even if you don't, we soon forgive and forget and move on to our next victim. We are our own favorite soap opera. The old adage "Sticks and stones can break my bones, but words can never hurt me" was probably coined in a small-town coffee shop.

We're friendly but not easy to get to know. So I often wonder what strangers might think when they overhear our coffee shop banter. For instance, one of the old men might bring up some female politician and claim that, by God, his own wife was home pregnant, barefoot, and washing dishes. The others would nod in agreement. One might chime in that, yes, by God, he doesn't tolerate any of that femi-nazi crap and beats his wife every night after supper just to keep her in line. Again everybody would nod agreement. Somebody else might add that, by God, every one of those damn Democrats should be shot.

Strangers who overheard this conversation might leave the coffee shop with their minds made up about rural men. But the strangers don't know, as we locals do, that the fellow whose wife is supposed to be home washing dishes is actually out horseback checking water on the ranch she owns and he married, or that the fellow who claims to beat those feminist ideas out of his wife is married to the town mayor, county judge, or school superintendent. The guy who made the crack about Democrats might have voted a straight Democratic ticket all his life while cussing big government and welfare with every other breath. He might even think that being a Democrat has something to do with *not* being a damn Yankee. Let the tenderfoot beware.

One morning, Billito Donnell opened Carmen's screen door, sat at the local's table, and ordered a bowl of menudo: a "real man's breakfast" and a recommended cure for a hangover. "Menudo for the *crudo*," we say. Billito usually coffees in the Alpine coffee shop but had obviously come to Marfa to check on his family ranch, which neighbored the ranch where I lived at the time. We use *neighbor* as a verb too. So I asked him what he was doing over here. Of course he knew I knew and didn't answer. Instead he asked me if I was staying warm out there on the Marfa flats. He quite well knew I was living in the coldest, windiest spot in Presidio County and that my hands had probably frozen to the metal gate latch when I opened it that morning to head to the coffee shop. So I didn't answer him either.

Next, a well-dressed, pretty lady in heels walked in, sat at the table of six men, and ordered French toast.

One of the men said, "Billito, you ever ate any French toast?"

Billito sipped his coffee. "You know," he finally said, "I got this friend over in Alpine—Joe Richardson—you know him. He likes to drink that cappuccino stuff, but he goes to the coffee shop real early so he can order it without anybody knowing he's drinking it."

Everybody laughed.

Now, what would a stranger get from overhearing that brief exchange? That none of us listened to or answered each other? Maybe that rural men were so judgmental and provincial that they forced each other to eat and drink only acceptable "manly" foods? My interpretation was that only Billito was a smooth enough politician to have wormed his way out of that corner. He had managed to defend the lady without sounding condescending and without embarrassing the guy who had unintentionally insulted her breakfast choice. At the same time, he avoided setting himself up for further teasing about menudo.

Of course Billito had used his friend Joe as a stalking horse. For just a second I thought, "Poor Joe!" But only for a second. I was pretty sure that at that very moment someone had just joined the locals' table at The Ponderosa in Alpine and said, "Where's Billito this morning?"

I could almost hear Billito's fellow coffee drinker Joe Richardson saying, "Oh, you know, every now and then Billito gets hungry for menudo and heads over to Carmen's so we can't accuse him of a hangover." Everybody would laugh.

I tell these stories to help establish my insider credentials. I have to be careful, though, because I live in a small rural community and hope to continue. A few of these people actually read what I write. Some of them are lawyers. All of them know lawyers. So occasionally I might be trying to protect someone—maybe me—or I might not be sure of my facts. When I name a name, you can bet on it. For instance the scene with Bill Shurley and the stranger did happen. The scene with Billito and the menudo and the French toast did happen, and Billito read it. What Joe Richardson might have been saying in Alpine, I'd have no way of knowing except through a long, teasing fifty-year acquaintance so familiar that I was willing to risk putting his name on my guess. If I was wrong, he'd get even. He also read it before he died. I might also add or delete a detail or two so the reader does not misunderstand. If I don't give a name or change one, then there is a reason. I will try to let you know when I do this. The husbands of the mayor, the county judge, and the female ranch owner were probably not all sitting in one particular coffee shop on one particular day; nor did they say those particular words in that particular order. None of them read this, but the banter, the rooster crowing, the humor, and saying the opposite of what they think are quite real and typical.

Humor helps us get along, but it's tricky. In my world, it's not okay to make fun of others unless we are sure they can take a joke and don't mind being the goat. We say that the joke should be *with* you not *at* you or *at* someone else. One of my favorite examples of good humor came one morning in an Alpine coffee shop when Rex Ivey joined us. His dad, also Rex, was one of the early settlers in the region and ran a trading post down on the Rio Grande during a time when Texas Rangers and cavalry still thought they could tame the Big Bend, the Big Empty, El Despoblado, or La Frontera—various names for Far West Texas through the years. The elder Rex seemed to be able to turn any situation into a laugh and so lived safely along our border with Mexico, selling coffee and buying furs from the bandits who lived on both sides of the shallow river, as well as the bandits wearing stars or stripes who chased them. His son was equally fearless and funny. The morning he joined our table, the talk had been running on midlife crisis. Rex the younger, probably in his early thirties at the time, was still struggling mightily to get past those hormone-filled, crazy teenage years—although some said he wasn't struggling enough.

"What's a midlife crisis?" he asked, setting himself up for a joke. Someone explained and he replied in mock horror, "You mean I have to go through all this again?" Everyone nearly fell out of their chairs laughing. Why was that so funny? According to rumor, eleven different women wept at his funeral after he crashed his helicopter while herding pronghorn antelope. Rumors run rampant around here. Usually they contain a grain of truth, but the grain is sometimes quite small. I'd say maybe only three women wept, but that might be a conservative guess. Neither of the Rexes read this for accuracy because both are dead, but they both loved a good joke, especially on themselves, so it feels like honoring their memory to write this.

Real journalists aren't supposed to let their subjects read their work before publication. I was told it's because the subjects might want the writer to make them look better than they are. That was never my experience. Other than correcting mistakes or misunderstandings, my subjects most often asked me to tone down anything that sounded like a compliment. If my subjects had faults, they were usually proud of them, but I had better get those faults right. I never thought I could write about anything without making a mistake, even if I had spent my entire life living it and writing about it. I wanted to get their stories straight, totally accurate, and never misunderstand or misrepresent. One of my favorite Charlie Russell paintings is a self-portrait where a real Indian in full regalia looks over Charlie's shoulder while he paints an Indian scene. Charlie wanted to preserve a vanishing way of life, and the Indian wanted to make sure the picture-maker got it right. Both knew how easy it could be to make a mistake and that portraying someone else's life should go beyond exotic costumes. Getting it right, to me, still involves the real deal looking over my shoulder.

I also usually wrote about the working class. Since cowboys often live in ranch housing and don't punch time clocks, the boundaries between their private lives and jobs can blur. They don't always think about what they blurt out until it's staring back at them in cold black ink. Cowboys are natural-born complainers, so they might call the ranch owner and her favorite grandson an ugly name or gripe about some of their duties and the poor skills of fellow employees. Even something as simple as preferring one of their personal horses over those the ranch raises might get them in trouble. Sometimes they might not realize that the boss doesn't want them riding outside horses for pay, or they might brag about placing at some roping when the boss thought they should have been working. So I wanted them to read my words both for accuracy and to make sure I didn't reveal anything they might lose their job over, although I think I was more conscious of the negative effects the spotlight could cause them than they were.

Something might be a "fact" but not the "truth" about who they were or what they believed, or might not even be relevant to the story. Some ranchers who fiercely protect their privacy might even feel justified in firing an employee who talked to the press at all.

As a journalist, I tell other people's stories, not my own, although those who read closely can probably find parallels between my own values and the people I choose to write about. I have always written in the *I/me/we* voice, but my *I* was a journalist's (I watched, I listened) and my *we* the voice of a culture (We rode out the gate and into the sunrise). I seldom wrote in the third-person "objective" voice. Third person is not objective. It's the voice of God. I'm not God. I'm a little mouse in the corner. I wish I didn't even need to capitalize that *I*. One good illustration happened in 2011. *Texas Monthly* magazine hosted a panel discussion in conjunction with the opening of a photography exhibit on the Texas Big Bend at the Wittliff Collections in San Marcos. The panel consisted of the moderator, *Texas Monthly* editor at the time Jake Silverstein, plus one of their regular writers, one of their regular photographers, me, and a recently retired longtime Big Bend park ranger, Marcos Paredes. Marcos and I spent several hours in the hotel coffee shop waiting for sunrise and then finally the time to head to the panel. He had me laughing so hard during coffee that I was peeing my pants and gasping for breath. After a life patrolling the Rio Grande along the Mexico border, often horseback, Marcos was full of stories. However, once we were seated on the panel, in a big fancy room and staring out at a bunch of *strangers*, Marcos clammed up. The other two panelists did most of the talking, until I started prodding Marcos, "Tell them about the time . . . tell them about . . . tell them . . ." Marcos finally got our audience belly laughing and seeing the Mexican border through his eyes. As the audience began to listen to the unfiltered real *borderisto* sitting right there in front of them, they forgot all about the professionals. My biggest contribution to the panel—as the journalistic mouse in the corner—was poking Marcos and telling the audience they "should have been at coffee!"

Author Jon Krakauer once said, "The journalist never has any intention of telling the story your subject wants told. Your job is to tell the story as you see it. Once a subject has talked to you, he has surrendered all control." That makes my blood boil. If a journalist wants to tell a story as the journalist sees it, then they should write an editorial, an opinion piece, or a memoir like this and not call it journalism. During the years when

I practiced cowboy journalism, people always knew when I was doing a story on them. They had plenty of chances to tell me what was on or off the record. If they had any secrets, I wanted to honor those secrets. This book is scarier because none of us knew I'd ever try to write my own story—although maybe I knew. Otherwise why did I take notes in coffee shops? Taking notes in secret is not the way an ethical journalist works. We are not spies. Unless we let our subject know they are being interviewed and that the conversation is on the record, we don't quote them. A memoir is different because it is about my own life, my own story. Evidently I started planning one many years ago.

Consequently, I want to be circumspect about my community's privacy yet still explain how I became a cowboy journalist and what I learned. This has been the most difficult project I have ever attempted, involving more than twelve years of starts and stops, revision and reorganization. I've finally settled on what cowboys call making circles. Every morning we head out to make a circle, sometimes horseback, sometimes in a pickup, sometimes on foot—this time through memories. Sometimes the circle is to gather cattle but more often to check water, pay close attention, and look for problems. Mostly we appreciate and admire whatever we see, but if we find a problem, we fix it, or find someone who can. In the first chapter I make a chronological circle around my immersion into both journalism and the cowboy world. In each chapter that follows, I make another circle, going back over that same ground, not always chronologically but focusing on how letters, horses, cattle, and various forms of education helped me pay attention, notice problems, try to fix them, or find someone who could. As a cowboy journalist, my circles gradually widened as I covered more country and tried to solve bigger problems, such as gender, poverty and wealth, defending cows, and living alone. At the end of each circle, I always came home.

Writing a memoir also brings up the subject of art, and I suppose this time I hope to produce some. The best conversation I ever had about art happened in an Alpine coffee shop several years ago while coffeeing with cowboy and western artist Gary Morton. Gary had been what we call "a real good hand" and the wagon boss for New Mexico's historic Bell Ranch in his youth. So his art was correct in every detail. He said he thought he had mastered both his subject and artistic techniques, but now he struggled with what to *say*. Did the world need just another realistic painting of a cowboy on horseback?

I said, as a writer, I knew exactly what he meant because I struggled with that too. I had mastered the rules of grammar (although that could be debated), learned vivid description, organization, development, dialogue—down to when to dot an *i* and use a comma, or not. But purpose was always the elephant in the room. Did we really need another story about spring branding or another photograph of some cowboy's spur? Gary and I both felt we had lived and studied the cowboy culture from every angle and had been deeply influenced by it, but what did we learn that jelled down to wisdom or something that should be preserved and passed on, possibly even to a wider audience? What was our purpose?

Gary and I talked about how message was different from story. The story was entertainment, but the message was the kernel of wisdom. We talked about how hard it was to make our message clear to the wide world and still pass muster within our own world, which didn't like the story faked, bragged, or watered down. We also worried about how different audiences could misinterpret our message—if we ever figured one out.

Another Russell painting *Jerked Down*, provides a quick example. The story is often misinterpreted as a cowboy trying to step off as his horse is about to be "jerked down" by a cow he has roped around the horns. The captured moment looks like everything is about to end in a big wreck. The message seems obvious—that reckless cowboys should be more careful. But that's neither the story nor the message.

The horse is just a colt and still in training. The roper has kicked loose the stirrup on the side of his saddle that will hit the ground, but he has hooked the spur on his stirrup-free boot around the cantle to keep his saddle from slipping. He is still hanging on to the other stirrup and his dallies. The roper has also thrown slack into his reins so that his young colt (still wearing a hackamore) can do what he needs to do to regain his balance. The colt still has one front foot braced. When he goes down, the roper in the jam has every intention of riding the colt down—if it comes to that—and back up on its feet. They'd welcome some help, but they're certainly not helpless. A colt doesn't become a seasoned working horse until he learns how to keep his balance and handle a rope, and the best and fastest lessons often come from wrecks.

To non-cowboys, the moment looks hopeless, but it's not. Instead, a second roper has also "jerked down" his rope. He's riding a more seasoned horse that is wearing a bridle. He's waiting for the bovine that has stepped over the rope to get out of the way. Once it passes, he plans to rope the cow, maybe by the head, front feet, or hind feet—whichever opportunity arises first. If time runs out or the second roper misses, the roper on the colt still has time to quickly pop his dallies and give the cow his rope—but nobody expects a miss. A third cowboy in the background has also "jerked down" his rope and is also racing to the scene with a loop built. It is sort of a perfect moment, with every member of the team doing exactly what they need to do in that split second. Five skilled members know exactly what to do; one is learning. It's a moment understood by cowboys but often misinterpreted by a wider audience. To me, Russell's purpose is to show the world what real teamwork looks like. We call that art.

Even if we risk being misunderstood, Gary and I talked about how important it was not to talk down to any audience but to assume that they would eventually understand and could then apply our message to their own world. Our job was not to preach but to remind. A good message should simply ring a bell. If the bell rings, we call it art. In great art or great literature we recognize ourselves and our own struggles in something created a thousand years ago in a place that speaks a language we've never heard. Three thousand years in the future, true Art, such as "Choose a job you love, and you will never have to work a day in your life" (Confucius, 470 B.C.), should still stir emotion, reveal beauty, reinforce values, question perspectives, or explain actions.

Even more important than art, to me, is truth. I consider myself an old-school journalist who believes that truth is stranger than fiction and more valuable. I'd rather have my hide tacked to the side of a barn than be accused of misrepresentation or elaboration. I don't even dye my gray hair or wear makeup, and I drink my coffee black. As an academic, I've read and heard all the modern arguments about truth: that you can't really get there and that memory is undependable. However, warts and all, I'm still gonna try to write this book because I had to teach myself how to write in a serious yet positive way. I believe we desperately need more cowboy journalism because truth can be positive as well as negative.

Of course, truth is not the same as memory. I learned some profound personal lessons about faulty memory. One of those occurred in a local coffee shop, and I'm still not sure what the truth is. One morning an old lion hunter and former wolf trapper joined us. He was a legend in our little town because he was an artist with hounds, scents, and tracks. None of the coffee drinkers at the table could do what he could do, and maybe no one else in the world could. Some secretly wondered if his mysterious skills were even real, but I believed. He was seldom in town, and when he was, he seldom joined the coffee drinkers. So when he sat down, I watched the interaction and listened carefully.

The morning's talk soon drifted to the government—what crooks they were, what they ought to be doing, all the time and money they waste, and on and on. Same ol', same ol'—the default rural coffee shop banter when no one can think of a more interesting topic. The old hunter just quietly sipped his coffee.

Then someone said, "I wish they'd just tell us the truth."

The old hunter stared into his cup thoughtfully for a long moment and finally said, "If they told you the truth, it would scare you to death." He drained his cup and left. Nobody spoke.

The old hunter's words echoed through the silence like one of those huge Buddhist temple bells had been struck. I remember the color and the shape of our coffee mugs, where we each sat, the big round table—every detail of the scene is recorded in my writer's brain like a sepia-toned black-and-white photograph. The moment etched itself into my memory like the moment I heard Kennedy had been shot, the *Challenger* had exploded, and the second tower had been hit.

Maybe the hunter's words struck me so powerfully because I knew he had been working either for or against, or testifying for or against, various government agencies worldwide all his life. He'd often mentioned their Machiavellian schemes involving funding. He had personally experienced the political cycles of extermination, endangered species, conservation, protection, live capture, captive breeding, inbreeding, reintroduction, overpopulation, and eminent domain. He was famous for telling the truth even when it went against the agency that had called him in as an expert witness. He fought for the animals being used as political pawns. He'd given those animals his youth, his loyalty, his health. He'd endured a life of hardships in their honor, living intimately with weather, mosquitoes, snakes, and spiders to be close to the animals he loved and sometimes killed.

I knew his deadly skills depended, like those of a baseball pitcher, on attraction and deception—that a wolf would discover the truth just one split second too late. I had often tried to write about him, but he never gave his permission, never wanted publicity or recognition, probably realizing that I did not and should not know enough about his life to write it accurately or truthfully. But I kept trying because his words didn't spring, like the rest of us, from ignorance and distance and media sound-bites. When someone like him spoke, I took notes. His sentence seared itself into my memory like a branding iron, and I never forgot.

Many years later, when I began writing this memoir, I ran into the old hunter again and reminded him of that long-ago coffee shop conversation. I said that his words had haunted me all these years, how I had often told that story and used his words of wisdom as a beacon when I struggled to tell my cowboy stories as true as I possibly could.

"I never said that," he said.

CHAPTER ONE

Immersed

"In my experience with native peoples . . . they are less and less interested in you the more and more interested you are in being like them—because they know you can never be like them. What they wish is that you would express, with the integrity of your own positions in a discussion or in the way you live, the best of what your culture represents. Then there is something to talk about."

—Barry Lopez

I OWE MY LIFE TO HORSES. In the earliest family photos of me as a toddler, I'm already wearing cowboy boots. According to old photographs, my great-grandmother Taylor's family raised horses to sell for farming, buggies, or riding. The Taylors were my dad's ancestors, but by the time I came along, all those horses were long gone and the bronc-riding Taylors had moved on to homestead in South Dakota. I learned to ride after we moved to my mother's farm in Jackson County, Iowa, where my widowed grandmother lived alone. Gram never learned to drive a car or a tractor, but she could do just about anything with teams of work horses. Her daughter, my mother, could drive both teams and tractors, and much preferred either over driving a car, which I never saw her do. Half of the farm's limestone bluff country was too rough and timbered for crops, so the family had always raised cattle, probably for thirteen generations since we've traced that side back to the *Mayflower*'s William Bradford.

When my little brother and I were about five and seven, he won a pony in a raffle at the local county fair, and soon we were feeding and attempting to ride three or four dang ponies. Ponies are the meanest toys ever given to kids because ponies are too small for adults to ride and school (we use *school* as a verb too). Consequently ponies have no manners. They do, however, provide young future cowboys with plenty of bad habits to practice on: runaways, raring up, bucking, biting, kicking, and refusing to obey all requests for cooperation. They say you can lead a horse to water, but you can't make him drink. Well, you can't always lead a Shetland pony to water.

There is an old Australian Aboriginal greeting: “From what water do you come?” Today most people, animals, and even wasps don’t know where their water comes from. I’ve always known painfully too well, and it was often at least partly my job to make sure the water came, not only for me but for anything else that needed a drink for a several-mile radius.

Back in the timber on the far south side of Gram’s farm, a small spring fed a small creek. The ponies and I drank from it often, so part of me comes from that spring. Our house and barns were on the far north side, so house and barn water was provided by a windmill and hand pump that brought up underground water from limestone caverns. Our cattle, ponies, pigs, chickens, and family all drank from that windmill.

When I was eleven, in 1958, we sold the farm and the ponies and moved to Arizona. My little brother never rode again, but I was hooked. Because I couldn’t afford to own a horse, I sold my soul to the devil to stay horseback, mostly exercising spoiled backyard horses for owners who didn’t or couldn’t ride them. My best friend, Boofer, half Apache, lived about a mile down a nearby irrigation canal and owned a scrufty barrel horse, so she taught me to barrel race. Our house water and the water all those horses drank came from rain caught behind dams in large reservoirs located in distant mountains, full of fish poop and guts, boat fuel, and no telling what else. I come from that water too.

About that same time I started writing for my junior high and high school newspapers, which is probably where horses and journalism started to get hopelessly tangled up. At the end of my senior year, 1965, I won a journalism award and a small scholarship to Eastern Arizona Community College in Thatcher, where I became the student newspaper editor. My small scholarship and two jobs—newspaper editor and student center manager—stretched only far enough for a five-day meal ticket. So unless I had a date, from Friday night supper until Monday morning breakfast, I didn’t eat.

I rode more borrowed horses there and made the rodeo team as a goat tier. I ran for rodeo queen (lost) and went home with ranch-owning friends to help gather cattle in some of Arizona’s roughest country: a ranch whose name I’ve forgotten in Aravaipa Canyon and the Triangle M Ranch at Mayer. At the end of one long, hot day, two cowboys at the Triangle M carried me kicking and screaming to the creek to baptize me as a cowboy complete with a new name, Jake. The name didn’t stick, but the baptism did.

My Hispanic roommate and I were the only white girls in our dorm, the rest being either Apaches or Navajos. One weekend I met Boofer at the San Carlos Reservation arena, where she helped me pass as Apache so we could both compete in the barrel racing at the all-Indian rodeo. I think I placed last. Tired of being hungry and broke, I quit school after that freshman year and kept riding borrowed horses while rambling around Arizona, working different jobs: legal secretary, tractor parts sales, bookkeeper. I rode pens for Producers Feedlot in Chandler, learned to team rope there (tied-on heeler), disastrously started a colt, and showed up at Cotton Rosser's PRCA rodeos to race around the arena carrying either the U.S. or Arizona flag in his grand entries. I ran for Phoenix PRCA rodeo queen and made it to top ten but didn't win. Just before the Fourth of July, I always dumped boyfriends in order to head to Prescott's rodeo and Whiskey Row to celebrate Independence Day. I seldom drank, but I loved to dance.

In 1968, now twenty-one, bored with my tractor parts job and in trouble with the Arizona Highway Patrol for speeding tickets, I called Sul Ross State University in Alpine, Texas, to ask if they needed a student newspaper editor. They did, so I headed back to college to try again. I wanted to be a veterinarian or at least a ranch manager, but reality kept intruding and my pen seemed to provide better access to the life I wanted to live. I tried to pick boyfriends who owned ranches and went home with one ideal prospect to work cattle on his big beautiful family ranch in northern New Mexico. I talked to the local high school there about teaching after graduation. He was even a great dancer. Sadly, our romance ended, but a later one with a recently returned Vietnam veteran began. We started dating in February 1971, and when I didn't break up with him to return to Prescott on the Fourth of July, I knew I was probably done with Whiskey Row. So in August, the day after my college graduation, I married a vet who didn't own either a horse or a single square foot of land and couldn't dance. We did hire on to a ranch job, though, and for most of the rest of my life, I lived in old Texas ranch houses where I helped tend water, helped pay the bills with my pen, and had plenty of horses to ride.

My new husband's mother was cooking for the Nail Ranch near Albany, Texas. She and his dad persuaded the ranch owners to hire us. We agreed to calve heifers and tend the remote 7W camp for the grand sum of $350 per month. A ranch camp, sometimes called a division, is part of a larger ranch. Some were originally smaller ranches bought by the larger ones. A camp usually includes a house of some kind, and whoever lives there is responsible for the several pastures surrounding it, especially the water. As a camp bride, I started marriage with one bedroll and two kerosene lamps, but we gradually fixed things up. We rode around holding hands for a while but soon got over that. As we rode, I did a lot of bragging about the superiority of Arizona cowboys and their methods over Texans, until my new spouse decided to leave me with my rope tied Arizona style—one end to my saddle horn and the other end to a big feral boar hog with long, sharp tushes that I had caught by only one hind foot. As he removed only his own rope and rode away, he said over his shoulder that he hoped some Arizona cowboy would come along to help me get loose. After that, I stopped bragging about Arizona, and our marriage survived for almost twenty more years.

Our house water at the 7W came several miles from the Clear Fork of the Brazos, which was far from clear. By the time it had been agitated and mixed with mud and fish poop, pumped up the riverbank to a holding tank that had never been cleaned, then sloshed through used oil-field pipe for several miles, it came out of my faucet black. We joked that our bathwater left a ring on us, and the toilet always looked like someone eating prunes had used it and hadn't flushed. Because the toilet was tricky to flush, that black water often flooded the bathroom and our only closet whenever a guest tried to use it. So I wrote a poem about how to flush it and kept the poem tacked on the wall above the toilet paper. Problem solved.

The underground water there and the Clear Fork had long ago been polluted by saltwater from the oil fields, which enabled the ranchers who hired us to stay in the cow business. Animals could still drink it, but not humans. So I caught drinking water off my tin roof, funneled it into a big tin cistern, and drew it by the pitcherful. A neighbor who lived about ten miles down the dirt road toward town was horrified that I would drink bird shit. Her water came from a brown muddy cow tank that turned green in the summer. Nobody ever got sick drinking after cows, she said, but birds she didn't quite trust. I agreed. Cow manure attracts flies, which attracts a lot of flycatchers. Flocks of deafening scissortails woke me up every morning long before daylight and, along with their numerous flycatcher cousins, pooped on my roof. Consequently, I drank recycled flies in bird-shit-laced cistern water while my neighbor drank recycled grass. As Montana rancher Wally McRae once said, cow shit is just grass and water. But flies and water? Yuck.

That tin roof also turned rain and hail into music, but lightning hit it regularly. Our bedroom was a screened-in porch. Many nights we'd holler at the frogs in the salty creek just down the hill to, please, go to sleep. Instead they'd croak, "Sex? Sex? Anybody want sex?" all night long. We slept under a canvas tarp bedspread that kept off the rain, on a mattress my mother-in-law made from handpicked cotton, and in an old iron bed I found in the pasture dump. Sometimes we had to hang on to the tarp if the wind got up or shake off frost in the morning. After the first six-inch snow, the foreman and two headquarters men four-wheeled it to our camp determined to move our bed into the house. I served them cake and coffee, but we didn't move the bed.

The living room had double windows on three sides, but our closest neighbor was several miles away so I didn't need curtains. We had an abundance of black water, so I planted flowers and raised a big garden. Anytime I wanted to fish, the creeks provided trophy-size bass, and I beat all the old men in a local stringer weight contest once. Wild plums for jelly seemed to grow on every hillside. I thought the 7W was the most beautiful place I'd ever seen and held fancy dinner parties on the lawn, once sending all my guests home with chiggers. Obviously, not everyone saw the 7W the way I did. In winter the north wind rippled under the worn linoleum on the floors and thousands of yellow jackets denned in the walls and attic. A warm day would cause the wasps in a sluggish stupor to drop down into the house, where they crawled into hair or down shirt collars. Rattlesnakes denned under the house and in summer I easily found one somewhere in the yard if I looked.

We started marriage with six bullets for a .270 rifle and made each one count. I think two went for deer meat because we wouldn't get free beef until we'd been on the payroll for a year. The other four probably collected bobcat or coyote furs to sell. We tried to rope feral hogs and fatten them up to sell or eat, but neither venture proved financially successful. We needed boots, a washing machine, some furniture, to pay back my college loans, and to start saving for doctor and hospital bills so we could start a family. Although cowboy injuries were usually covered by workmen's comp, pregnancy was not. So most cowboy spouses worked in town, partly for insurance. Small towns have limited job opportunities: teaching, parts man, store clerk, bookkeeper/secretary, and café staff. I already had or was willing to take on any of those jobs, but we lived eighteen miles down a dirt road that was often impassable with snow or mud, not a dependable commute. A few lucky spouses sometimes earned extra cash cooking or running a tractor during hay season, but our ranch already had a cook and didn't raise hay. Some extremely lucky spouses even got paid for their horseback work, but most don't, and on this ranch I didn't.

My fastest source of extra cash was publishing. I like to say I never wrote for the money, but I did need some. I had published my first magazine story while in college and had already figured out that *Western Horseman* paid on acceptance. I had no money to travel or develop film, so I used what I had: my family's old horse pictures or simply words. Even in later years, after I started traveling, I often wrote about practical solutions to my own problems, like how to make my own range teepee tent or how to prevent sore jaws on a colt by wrapping a rawhide hackamore with worn-out nylon panty hose. Those checks from livestock magazines seemed like a gold mine. All they cost was my time, and I had lots of time, especially after my daughter was born in 1973.

Another way I tried to earn money was by substitute teaching English at the local high school, and about 1974, when preparations for the Shackelford County Bicentennial rolled around, I volunteered to involve the high school kids by helping them produce a magazine. I got no salary, but it gave me a purpose, and I could take my baby along. Eighteen kids signed up. We had nothing but enthusiasm and needed a publisher, so the kids (with me tagging along) attacked the local newspaper. The editor/owner, James Lenamon, had been searching for a way to participate in the bicentennial. He loved our idea but didn't have time to supervise magazine production.

I had already been a newspaper editor in chief at two colleges. So I said I could teach the kids how to interview, write stories, set type, do hot-wax pasteups, photograph and use a darkroom, count headlines, design, and fit pages together. This was all before computers, when pasteups were created by hand. Would he trust us with his equipment? I also promised we would use his newsroom only after hours because this was not a school project and the kids and I would be working after school and on weekends. Somehow he agreed to all that, but he couldn't afford the coated paper we wanted.

So the kids marched across the street to attack the local bank, where the kids laid out a plan to borrow $1,000 for paper. If we printed 750 copies and sold them at $2.50 each, we could easily pay back the loan. That doesn't sound like much risk today, but in the early '70s, that was a lot of money, especially to me. But the banker looked at those earnest young faces (maybe also knowing their oil-producing parents) and agreed.

We patterned our magazine after *Foxfire*, which had started in Raburn Gap, Georgia, in 1966 and was later funded by the Smithsonian. *Foxfire* paired teen reporters with local old-timers to dig up history about people, events, and places. That pairing created magic because the elders were delighted to have young people really listen to their stories. In turn the teens were amazed by what they learned. Old family photos were dug out, keepsakes explained, and hikes taken to long-forgotten places. Sometimes the elders were the kids' own grandparents, sometimes total strangers.

We brainstormed open-ended (not yes/no) interview questions, looking for topics the kids were actually interested in: family and school, friendships, fun, overcoming troubles, how to do something. We talked about making sure there were ten times as many words from their subjects on their tape recorders as from themselves, and never to argue. I advised my young reporters against trying to be wise when interviewing and instead pretending to be a dumb ass, an unskilled greenhorn, a slow learner, or a naive student to get the best quotes. They were to be the foil against whom their subject's little grains of wisdom could shine. We practiced on each other how to pause (giving a subject time to think) and how to expand interesting answers with "How?" and "Why?"

The kids and I looked for good subjects by asking around. We found Jack Pate, an old cowboy, when local rancher Watt Matthews recommended him as the best he ever knew. I'm not sure who taught whom, but maybe I taught the kids how to summarize their long, rambling interviews into stories and to listen for magical sentences full of emotion, vivid description, or colorful language, like when Jack said, "I'd prowl them hills just like an old coyote." We listened for uncommon behavior that might provide insight, for example into friendship: "Anytime you see me picking on somebody, it's somebody I like. If it's some old boy I like, I might do anything to him; but if it's some old boy I don't know or somebody that might not take a joke right, I just leave them alone," said Jack. And we looked for sentences that illustrated unusual values: "We used to play poker for pecans a lot—we didn't have much money. I wound up with two big cake sacks full of pecans one time. But I never did win any money playing poker—I never did play poker for money."

Readers of the small college newspapers I had edited were interested in what the school was doing right, what problems we were solving, so I learned to dig for the good stuff, not for evil. I never learned the kind of exposé journalism that "real" journalists learn. My high school and college newspapers had been tools to increase school spirit, inspire students, and promote can-do attitudes. When we "spoke truth to power," it was always to give examples of how our small schools were succeeding in spite of the odds against us, how our teachers were making college graduates out of Apaches, Hispanics, and white trash kids from the lowest economic rungs on the ladder. Both as an editor and a substitute teacher, I had already discovered that we all learned better and faster when praised for what we did right instead of being criticized for what we did wrong. Instead of resentment, praise built a fire under us—as long as it was specific and deserved. Undeserved praise just sounded manipulative.

The town of Albany also wanted a positive magazine. Maybe because of *The Fandangle*, a historical musical produced there every summer, the town was very history oriented. *The Fandangle* opens with a small child sitting on the knee of an old-timer, who begins to tell the history of the area, which unfolds across the grassy stage, complete with singing, dancing, horses, and longhorn cattle. My daughter played that small child one year so that I could race across the grassy stage on a sidesaddle in the opening flag parade. Anyway, we named our magazine *The Old Timer* after that old storyteller in *The Fandangle*. Neither the kids nor their subjects, and especially not the readers, would have wanted the town's problems, evildoers, or bad habits as our focus. Why give away precious publicity to the bad guys? Instead, we focused on heritage and role models.

For design, we simply picked a very classy-looking magazine of the day, *Persimmon Hill*, published by the Cowboy Hall of Fame in Oklahoma City, and copied its layouts. Our finished magazine included articles about water cisterns, early sheriffs, an old card game, the first high school class, one very old home, tiny pasture graveyards, cock fighting, a bank robbery, an early schoolmarm, a ghost town, and many more. The kids did it all, from picking subjects to interviews to photos to production. They were quite proud of themselves and the talk of the town. That first issue sold completely out within days, and the kids headed back to the bank to finance our next issue. After the second issue, we no longer needed the bank, and *The Old Timer* was standing on its own feet.

Then, in 1975, I moved away, as cowboys often do, back to the Davis Mountains. The mom of one of my editors took over as adviser, and *The Old Timer* became a product of the high school English department. The students joined up with the Texas Junior Historians and produced six more issues. Two of our stories (one on an old oil pumper who lived near the 7W and one on Jack Pate the cowboy) were published by Doubleday in an anthology called *I Wish I Could Give My Son a Wild Raccoon.*

The Nail Ranch's 7W house doesn't exist anymore. The ranch bulldozed it off the face of the earth because no one but me ever wanted to live there. From the 7W, we moved back to Alpine, into another old ranch camp, and I took a full-time job as ag department secretary at Sul Ross. The old flat-roofed house on the Tippit Ranch in a canyon nestled below Mitre Peak provided my next unique and conversation-stimulating bathroom. The house had stood abandoned for more than thirty years before we moved in and stands abandoned now. To my knowledge, no one but my little family of three ever lived there in more than seventy years. The house water system was spring fed, so at least the water was sweet and clear. A little frog had evidently swum through the pipes as a tadpole and took up residency in the toilet. We'd flush him away but in a few seconds he'd pop back up. It was always fun to listen to guests shriek when they went in the bathroom and then holler, "Hey, there's a frog in the pot?!"

I'd holler back, "Yeah, I know. It's okay. He lives there."

I tried not to think about what he ate.

I often heard people complain about ranch living conditions. A friend, Lynne Baldwin, and I once reminisced about that. We had been young cowboy wives together, and between the two of us, we'd probably fixed up and made livable at least ten old ranch camps in the area. We'd learned to wallpaper, paint, sand wood floors, fix toilets; remove lime from windows that probably hadn't been washed in eighty years and strip sometimes eleven coats of paint from beautiful old oak. We patchwork carpeted kids' rooms with carpet samples that the furniture store was about to toss. We tacked silvery old barn wood over damaged walls and hung antiques, bridles, or Navajo rugs over holes. We replaced rotten floors with bricks and sand. With a houseplant scattered here and there, we entertained guests. We were rustic, recycled, DIY, and country before all that was cool. Maybe I wrote about my life to help other people who lived in similar ratty old ranch camps appreciate their lives and to encourage them to fix them up, not tear them down. My spouse and I spent a year fixing up that little house, then left mad with four of our own horses and my little daughter's potbellied pony to feed and had to figure out how to live in town.

Still another interesting bathroom was at the next old ranch camp we moved into after a couple of miserable years in town. I would live for thirteen years at Willow Springs on the 06 Ranch in a beautiful old adobe house that I still consider home. We moved in just before my daughter began kindergarten in 1977. Skunks denned under the hardwood floors and perfumed our clothes. The bathroom was rather boring in comparison to the 7W and Tippit, but it had its moments, like when I'd have a house full of company for a party. The toilet sat in the middle of a sixteen-by-sixteen-foot room and gave real meaning to the word *throne*. Three doors led into the throne room. One of the doors had the aggravating habit of coming unlatched and drifting open when someone sat on the toilet because the hardwood floors weren't quite stable. We killed a rattlesnake in there once. She had evidently crawled in under a screen door and hidden under a dirty towel. When I picked up the towel to wash it, there she coiled. We also killed one rattler on each screened-in porch and shot an especially angry big one in the living room. If I found rattlers in the pasture, I let them live—I liked to joke that they helped keep away tourists—but inside my house was crossing the line.

Nature wasn't "out there" to me but was part of my home, and sometimes right inside my bathroom. I've even found nature inside my typewriter. When my old IBM Correcting Selectric started getting sluggish, I took it to a repair shop. My reputation as a tidy housekeeper probably suffered at the coffee shop when the trouble turned out to be pecans, evidently stashed there by an enterprising packrat. The house was surrounded by ancient pecan trees, so those rattlesnakes were probably just after rats. Eventually I insisted that we fix the gaps under the screen doors. Consequently, I viewed nature with great respect, the way Thoreau found it on Mount Ktaadn, and not as idyllic like a manicured national park in summer.

Cowboy spouses must accept the living conditions going in, be willing to live without job security, health insurance, and retirement. They usually live with poverty, frequent moves, challenging roads, and the smells of manure and sweat. Sometimes they live with alcoholism, infidelity, and abuse. Anyone who imagines an idyllic life in a sprawling ranch home on a shaded creek, with a view of snowcapped peaks, will be quite disappointed in the rat-infested trailer house with rocks and tumbleweeds for a yard and a trickle of gyp water piped from a windmill ten miles distant that produces zero water pressure. Electricity, heat, and phone are luxuries, not necessities. Nobody will pick up the garbage, grade the roads, fix the frozen pipes, or unstop the drains. Nobody will bring the mail or a pizza. Someone must make the two-hour drive to take the kids to school every morning and pick them up at night—in spite of mud, swollen creeks, flat tires, and broken fan belts. The kids will probably get lice, pinkeye, scabies, and every kind of bug bite and injury imaginable. It's no Shangri-la—unless you make it one, and I tried to do that.

That Willow Springs bathroom also housed the world's most wonderful bathtub. It was one of those old cast-iron, footed tubs with a long comfortable backrest. It sat next to a window in a thick adobe wall where I could set a book, a mason jar "vase" full of wildflowers, and a glass of wine. I don't like to curtain windows, so in early spring I used to schedule my bath when the sun was at the right angle to strike the bathwater and me. The water would sparkle. In winter I'd snuggle down in a hot bubble bath and watch the snow fall. Twice a year, when the cattle roundup was camped at my house, I would bathe in the dark before sunrise, ducked down out of sight, and listen to the cowboys jingle the remuda of horses past my window. I feel sorry for people who have never lain naked in a tub of warm water, immersed in bubbles up to their neck, with their eyes closed, and listened to a hundred horses trot through the rocks less than ten feet away. The warm water trembled. I suppose most women would prefer normal bathrooms, but I always wondered what they'd write about.

I spent many wonderful idle hours looking out that bathtub window. I've identified many rare birds while soaking in that tub, from flycatchers and tanagers to painted buntings. I wrote about birds a lot, mostly in letters, and started publishing newspaper columns, starting one for a local small-town weekly. I called it "Switchin' Flies" after the habit horses have of pairing up and standing nose to tail to switch flies off each other's heads. I had read a lot of nature writers but usually felt those writers were just visitors, identifying plants and birds as they hiked along, getting their exercise in a scenic open-air gym. Instead, I tried to capture my deep relationship with nature. I never thought of nature as something fragile that I needed to protect but rather as a partner that I depended on and needed, sometimes just for friendship. In one guest column I wrote for the *Dallas Times Herald* about a vermillion flycatcher, I said that when the dry March winds began to blow, I sometimes felt sorry for myself and wondered what it would feel like to be a wealthy businessman's wife. But just in the nick of time, I would catch a glimpse of a little ball of red fire and realize that my friend "Vermie" was back from his winter vacation, and suddenly that drab Texas spring became beautiful.

Although I don't think I worked at it, I spent my entire life deeply immersed in nature. As a livestock journalist, following stories, I've taken outdoor baths in many rivers and creeks, the coldest in Yellowstone's Slough Creek, not long after snowmelt—always careful not to get soap in the water. My all-time favorite outdoor bathtubs were clean cement cattle troughs in a pasture somewhere. I'd grab a towel, hike out after the cows drank, and take an open-air bath late on summer evenings. Nothing is quite as soothing as soaking naked in sun-warmed water with a windmill turning in the breeze and pumping nearby. Depending on where a person is raised, I suppose water sounds different. Maybe it roars, crashes, tinkles, or slaps. To Norman MacLean, Montana's Big Blackfoot evidently babbles and speaks the words of God. To me water sounds like a windmill—*ca-ca-ca, ca-reeee, careeeecareeecareee.* Nobody's shelf of $30 candles with Vivaldi cranked on a stereo can compare. Nothing feels quite as sensual as a sundown breeze on wet skin with a poor-will calling in the distance. After those experiences, like Henry David Thoreau, I never valued sex much. I suppose if I worship anything, I worship water.

I once brought home a bob-tailed Australian shepherd puppy that we named Perro Pinto, meaning "spotted dog" in Spanish. His name honored a dessert of rice and raisins that our 06 Ranch roundup cook made. Perro was a real dog and far from perfect. He used to mark the cowboys' bedrolls when roundup moved into his territory. He never passed up the chance to aggravate a skunk and loved to roll in a dead one after it turned green and squishy. Another favorite pastime was to jump in the horses' water trough, get soaked, probably do what kids do in swimming pools, and then go roll in loose horse manure. He thought it made him a pretty dog. The only safe place to pet him was between his eyes. He also loved to chew on anything that smelled dead, especially thrushy horse-hoof pairings. Nobody ever allowed him to lick them in the face but once. He did not sleep with me.

After he was grown, one day Perro and I went for a little walk up an almost-dried-up creek. In this country, creeks with springs along them might run for a foot or a mile, then disappear underground and pop out again later. Sometimes those creeks roar after a rain and then gradually dry up, as this one was doing. On our walk, we found the last remaining puddle of stinky green water with a scum on top. The scum should have been a warning to me since I'd seen it before, but I sat down on a rock and Perro decided to take his version of a bath. We'd been there just long enough for both of us to drift off into another world when suddenly we had company. This was a favorite afternoon lie-around-in-the-puddle spot for a band of javelinas.

They bristled at the smell or sound of us. So Perro and I gave the javelina bathtub back to its original owners, on the run. Javelinas don't see well, so escape was easy. After my initial burst of adrenaline wore off, I stopped to pick up a couple of rocks, just in case the javelinas tried to follow. My good West Texas dog, deciding I was now ready to defend that water, as he thought we should, headed back to the puddle to pick a fight. I don't like to argue with hogs. But my dog was right: we should always fight for water. While the American thirst for creature comforts has increased by leaps and bounds, I felt content if I just had water, and it didn't have to be fancy. I wasn't much more particular than my dog. So I wrote about water a lot too.

In West Texas sometimes water comes out of the ground as a seep or *cienega*, which results in just wet ground and is undrinkable. We have a saying: either dig or climb for water. Cool, clear, drinkable springs are usually located high up, under a rocky rim where a clump of green can be seen. But after the strenuous climb, sometimes you find that the spring has been fouled into a seepy mud hole by javelinas, or has gone dry. If it's dry, look for a nearby *tinaja*. A tinaja is a deep bowl carved into rock by water falling from above. Both springs and tinajas usually occur along rims, with water for the tinaja pouring off the top, water for the spring percolating down through the rocks. It seems that quite often in desert country, a spring and a tinaja will be located quite close to one another, almost as backup systems. I wondered if Indians had helped carve the tinajas. I know of one where the air stays jacket cool all summer because the thermals rush wildly up the rock chute surrounding the tinaja on hot days. A breeze blows there constantly, straight up. It's an air-conditioned desert water hole with no Freon problems.

After a rain, a tinaja will have caught water, but sometimes it takes years for the same rain to percolate through the rocks and pop out somewhere in a spring. So a spring will sometimes be dry during a rainy year and wet in a dry year. Illogically, springs are more dependable than tinajas during drouths. One of the most haunting photographs I ever saw was of a drowned mountain lion floating in deep, sheer-sided Ernst Tinaja in Big Bend National Park. I imagined the lion stretching farther and farther for a precious sip as the water gradually evaporated, perhaps falling in and scrambling out a few times, until finally the rain came too late and the climb out was just one inch too far.

We call our more dependable underground water sources aquifers, but there is no underground lake or river. Rock wasn't laid down here in neat limestone layers pocked with water-catching caverns. What we have is more like multicolored, spongy rock pancakes stacked and slung around like a food fight between two mad volcanic *cocineros.* After the pancakes hardened, earthquakes, uplifts, and dropping fault blocks cracked them, toppled them, shifted them, heaved them up, smashed them, and in general created a geologist's dream or nightmare, depending on the geologist's tolerance for puzzles. Geologic maps of this area look like Monet paintings with irregular dots of color. In places where the pancakes cracked and grated against one another, rock crumbs might form a porous layer or fill a crack, which might hold a little water, sometimes at fifty feet, sometimes at fifteen hundred feet, sometimes one on top of the other, or maybe not. When water is sucked out of a mess like this, no one seems able to measure or even find water tables. Our underground water sources don't show their bathtub rings to the world like a lake or reservoir. No one is sure how much water they hold. So we worry.

The name for an underground messy, hidden, soggy place where unknown amounts of precious water congregate is a bolson, from the Spanish word for purse, which seems like the perfect metaphor. Finding these little purses full of junk and precious water in this maze of broken pancakes has proven almost impossible through gambling, science, or prayer. So most of the wells in West Texas have been witched. Lots of jokes are told about Law West of the Pecos, insinuating that we have none. And when it comes to water, that may be true. When you need water, you need water—no matter whose laws get broken or what happens to your soul. So although most of our water witches and their customers have been good, God-fearing people, they are more afraid of running out of water than of God. And if God remembers where he hid the water, he isn't telling. So witches walk the rocky ground with two pieces of wire, a forked stick, or brass rods until twitching or swaying or some kind of movement—at least in their imagination—indicates water. I tried to write about our best local water witch once—he even witched his first oil well! But he wanted me to take all that witchery stuff out of his story because his preacher didn't like it. I wasn't interested in how reformed or rich he'd gotten, so I never finished that story.

Through the years, our well drillers have carefully filled glass bottles with rock samples taken at drilling intervals: band after band of pink, green, white, gray, and black rock dust. Rainbows. Pretty curiosities. Crystal balls. Lined up next to one another, the bottles tell stories, sometimes fiction. After years of sinking wells and filling bottles with colored layers, the witches and the drillers and the colored dirt in the bottles have given geologists clues about where water might be hiding. But even today, if an old rancher runs out of water, he's still more likely to call a witch than a geologist.

Recharge is another desert water mystery. Although some were, most desert bolsons or even aquifers are not really ancient pools that once mined are gone forever. Rather they act more like underground cisterns—purses—catching and holding the rains that fall on their desert roofs. Rain in the desert does not run away to the sea. Instead it collects in low places or playas and evaporates, or it trickles and percolates down between cracks, disappearing into the ground. We know that rain refills our bolsons, but how long does that take? Sometimes it doesn't rain for years, and maybe some bolsons don't recharge, at least not fast enough. So we worry. Pressing questions among desert dwellers sharing an underground water source are how much population can it support, how many trees, how many golf courses and lawns, how many cars can it wash per week, how many loads of laundry, how many swimming pools, fountains, or flush toilets? Nobody seems to know. So we worry and try to spend the water collected in those purses very carefully.

What about pollution? Underground water can be contaminated by human error: leaking gasoline storage tanks, septic tanks, city dumps; runoff from chemicals used on golf courses, yards, and gardens. Deep wells are harder to pollute but not impossible. Oil fields are masters at polluting deep water wells with injection or fracking. But pollution can also be caused by nature. Some wells have naturally occurring elements such as mercury or arsenic. Sometimes the surrounding rock contains uranium and the water becomes radioactive.

Some wells naturally produce water too salty to drink, often within a few yards of sweet water wells. Most desert playas, places without drainage where water collects on the surface and evaporates, are salty. The flat desert country around the Pecos River was salty long before the first spade of earth was turned, long before the first farmer arrived. Big rains have always washed salt into the Pecos. Old-timers claim to remember tall grass along the river and the river running with sweet water, but the earliest wagon train diaries complain of the scant salt-stunted weeds and water too salty to drink. Old-timers sometimes "remember" things through rose-colored glasses. So I'm careful which old-timers I interview and pay attention when those I do interview range beyond their expertise. Water tales, especially, should always be suspect. For example, some old cooks in this country claim that the secret to their good pinto beans is the water. People often say that gringos are not supposed to drink the water in Mexico because once you do, you will always return. In Mexico, travelers are warned that drinking water north of the border will give them diarrhea. After spending most of my life on the U.S.–Mexico border and crossing it often, I think these warnings are true. But beware of claims about the gallons per minute that someone's well or spring will produce—especially if it's for sale.

No one permanently lived here until the coming of the windmill, which brought dependable deep, underground water to the surface. So the windmill has become the symbol of West Texas. Silhouetted against a sunset, surrounded by miles and miles of grass, it appears serene in paintings, sculpture, and photographs; on T-shirts, jewelry, calendars, and greeting cards—but don't be deceived. Someone has to mother those pretty windmills constantly. Someone has to climb the tower at least once every two years and risk life and limb to change the oil in the gearbox and tighten bolts. Someone has to check storage tanks, reservoirs, tubs, and pipelines daily to make sure a float hasn't been knocked loose, a riser hasn't become air-locked, or a leak hasn't started somewhere. Like horses, more things can go wrong with windmills and water systems than can be counted.

At Willow Springs, eventually I learned to tell by a drop in my kitchen water pressure when a leak had appeared on the long hidden pipelines that threaded through the pastures connecting my house well to storage tanks and water tubs on the 06 Ranch. A two-day leak can drain a storage tank, and a windmill might not catch enough wind to replace it during the hot, still months of summer. I had to fix leaks myself or quickly call for help when several hundred head of cattle, not to mention deer, antelope, coyotes, mountain lions, birds, wasps, and no telling what or who else were depending on me. Someone once asked author and Buddhist Gary Snyder what we should do for animals since they have been so good to us. Snyder recommended that we sing, pray, and dance for them. I suggest that we never let them run out of water.

Much of my time when living on ranches has been spent maintaining, checking on, and worrying about water. In the fall, I helped wrap windmill pipes from the "T" (where water comes out) to the "spider and dogs" (where the pipes meet the ground) with paper sacks and baling wire to keep the standpipe from freezing where it goes into the casing. Before cold, still nights, I drove around pulling wooden brake handles down to collapse the windmill tail against the fan, so it would not catch a breeze if the pipe froze. To save the gears if water freezes inside the standpipe, the wooden rub rod between the fan and the sucker rod is designed to break if the fan tries to turn. I've helped replace rub rods and pull shallow wells by hand, lifting a heavy string of plastic pipe full of water until the submerged parts came to the surface for repair. But when a real working windmill with fifteen hundred feet of steel sucker rod must be fixed, it takes a good windmiller and tons of rolling equipment.

Consequently, two of my best friends are Don and Linda Coleman. Don operates Coleman Well Service, tending windmills from north of Sierra Blanca to Dryden, from the New Mexico state line up around Mentone and Red Bluff all the way to the Rio Grande. He was a good cowboy and ranch manager, but when the old local windmill man retired, Don stepped up. Somebody had to. Don loves the big rugged country, but since the windmills are often located at the end of some of the longest, most torturous steep rocky roads in the world, he says he can't always tell his help where they are going until he gets them in the truck and gets it rolling. Even then, he says, "You better be going pretty fast or they'll jump out."

His massive hydraulic pulling rig weighs around twenty-four thousand pounds. It's stuffed full of spare parts: all sizes of cylinders, leathers, rods, and pipe—some in abnormal sizes, depending on where he is headed. He also carries elevators and dogs, bottles of gas, a welder, pipe threaders, windmill oil and parts, huge wrenches and tools, three or four sizes of control boxes, spare tires, and pipe burros. He throws up his hands, "Oh, God, if we went to listing everything we carry on that truck . . ." and trails off. Because of the remote locations, he tries to carry everything he might need for any situation. Last but not least, he begrudgingly carries a couple of items for human comfort: dented cans of Vienna sausages whose labels have worn off rolling around on the floorboard and a cell phone, although neither he nor West Texas has really bowed to the latter. He says, "We carry the phone so we can drive around looking for a spot where it will work. When it rings we don't answer. It's for my convenience, not theirs."

Windmilling is an art with a language all its own. Watching Don and a helper sling elevators around a coupling on a joint of sucker rod is pure poetry. Each joint of pipe must be lifted gently by the giant winch on the windmill truck, then uncoupled with twenty-inch wrenches, and the loose end walked out to waiting metal burros. A windmill tower has missing braces on one side, called a window, just tall enough to tail out rods and pipes if they are long and flexible enough to sag just a little. Once the leathers are replaced in the stuffing box and the top check is checked, the sucker rod is recoupled joint by joint and lowered back down into the hole to fish for the bottom check. Under several feet of water, fifteen hundred feet in the ground, rests a heavy brass cylinder with a three-inch fitting that the bottom of the string of sucker rod must carefully touch and thread into. A windmiller fishes for this bottom check by listening to the hole. Once it's fished, the sucker rod is again uncoupled, joint by joint, tailed back out to the burros, and the bottom check brought to the top. Once its leathers too have been replaced, or any other needed repairs have been made, the bottom check is simply dropped back into the well, and again the windmiller listens. Even I can hear the sound like fragile glass shattering when the brass bottom check breaks the surface of the well water, but I can't hear what the windmiller hears when the check hits bottom. Meanwhile, the sucker rod threads have been daubed with soft black grease and once again, joint by joint, beginning with the rod that holds the top check, the sucker rods are recoupled and fed back into the well.

Today the old windmill towers are disappearing, being replaced by solar, but all the underground sucker rods, pipes, and checks remain the same. Wells still need tending even without the towers. But I miss the towers and especially the fans and tails. I worry about what cowboys who don't know our big country will use for landmarks, how anyone broke down or lost and desperate for a drink will find water, and once Don retires, how the next generation will even find those wells to fix them. Solar panels don't silhouette themselves against the sky to help pilgrims find their way.

Don says the old windmill rub rods made of ash were the best but that today all the ash trees are located on some kind of protected ground. The new rub rods are pink, and he doesn't think they're made of real wood. He says that pink wood makes the water taste funny—all of which I think is a joke. He's been known to fill my rain gauge with used beer, so I never quite believe everything he says. Most people like his humor and his stories, but what he actually does, they find boring. Most people also like to romanticize cowboys, but cowboys romanticize windmillers. So I wrote about Don. I doubt a single mule deer or wasp knows or appreciates where its water comes from and who keeps it flowing. I don't believe a writer can really know a place or know where they are until they know where their water comes from.

One year I tried to get myself appointed to the Far West Texas Water Planning Group as the environmental representative. Even though I was not selected, I went to many of its meetings as a spy. Rural communities fear water "development" both by their own neighbors and by large cities. We know our underground water sources are limited, and we know that water often "flows uphill toward money." But nothing strikes fear into our hearts like the words "I'm from the government, and I'm here to help." So I tried to write about things we could either do without, do ourselves, or needed to fight for.

For instance, lots of people search for ways to produce electricity without harming the environment. I say just turn off the damn lights. I knew a do-gooder once who had been raised in the city and started badgering our small town to install streetlights along a dark street on the south side of the railroad tracks. He thought that part of town had been neglected because the people who lived there were poor. Personally, I had often lain in bed at night, sleepless, during hotel stays or the few times when I lived in town, wondering how much trouble I'd get in if I shot out the streetlight that shone in my bedroom window. The do-gooder finally surveyed the neighborhood to gain support for his idea and discovered that the elderly small-town people who lived on that dark street unanimously did *not* want any damn streetlights. As a journalist, instead of assuming everyone shared my values, I tried to remember to ask.

I have probably been more sensitive to light pollution issues than most because I've lived near one of the world's largest astronomy observatories for most of my life. When I would head home from rare city shopping three or four hours away, I gradually left well-lighted areas and headed into darker ones. When I finally dropped off the freeway headed south, it was like dropping into a black hole. No lights. If the stars and night sky are more beautiful anywhere else on earth, it must be in a darker, drier place. When they sing about the stars at night being big and bright in Texas, they are singing about us. I love star parties, either formal ones at the observatory or informal ones lying in a pickup bed, with my dog for a pillow. So I have always tried to keep my electricity footprint small.

I don't collect electric gadgets. I've never owned an electric clothes dryer and often wrote about my solar one, which sounds like I had bowed to electrified technology. But my solar dryer was just two long wires tied to two used pipes welded into a T shape and set in cement. I was not trying to save the world or reform my neighbors. I just personally liked the smell of sunshine and desert wind. My clothesline helped me notice things I would have normally missed and provided an endless supply of writing material. Trudging to the line and back, I noticed the progress or lack of it in filaree plants, spotted those weird red velvet mites that appear after a rain, or worried about the young vermillion flycatcher with only one leg. Most importantly, hanging out my laundry eventually made it rain. Making it rain was my contribution to recharging those precious underground bolsons upon which my entire world depended. If my neighbors preferred to spend small fortunes on electricity, shrink their clothes, have them smell like plastic flowers, and wear them out faster, that was their business. I just happened to like hanging laundry on a clothesline. I didn't beat them clean on a rock, though.

I also preferred open windows to air-conditioning, even in the desert. For music I listened to wind and birds or windmills and hail. For entertainment I watched clouds drifting, jumping spiders catching flies, or dung beetles rolling their balls of dung. For elegance, I lit kerosene lamps. Of course I did own an electric typewriter (now a computer) and a refrigerator, and I used a toaster every morning, but I consciously tried to find things I didn't need and deleted them. Should we all do that? I don't know. Some of my best friends sell electrically powered stuff. I don't want to put them out of jobs and businesses. I never wanted to own a TV or a stereo because I liked my house quiet so I could write, not because I felt morally superior to my neighbors. Although, to be honest, I've seldom had any neighbors whose lights I could see.

Ranch house lights are few and often miles between, but it's more than distance. There is an old cowboy saying: "Never go to work for a man who has lights at the barn." Plus, hardly anyone with any sense leaves a light on at night in rural areas because lights draw moths that sometimes arrive by the millions. I also wondered what Ernest Hemingway was really trying to say with his "clean, well-lighted" places. As a hunter, surely he knew that darkness offers safety. Lights simply create shadows for those who hide while those bathed in light become targets. If my house was dark inside, then the outside world, even at night, was lighter, and I could see anything moving around in my yard, from skunks to humans. Sometimes at night, as I sat reading, alone at Willow Springs, with my closest neighbor several miles away, my senses would jump to alert. Each uncurtained window was uncomfortably black as I strained to see out into the night. As soon as I snapped my reading light off, the hunting advantage reversed. Now the windows, I knew, appeared blackest from the outside. Looking out, as soon as my eyes adjusted, I could see. Why people feel safer bathed in light, I've never understood. People who feel most comfortable in well-lighted places have never been hunters or hunted.

I pointed a gun of any kind at a human only once. I know soldiers and law officers laugh when weapons are called guns, but a gun was never a weapon to me, protection maybe. That one particular night a cowboy had bucked off, lost his hat, broken some ribs, and been carted off to the hospital. When the doctor turned him loose, the boss sent the poor crippled-up guy to stay at my house until he could ride again. Only I didn't know any of that.

What I did know was that the sound of a car motor coming down my gravel road after dark woke me as I slept on the screened-in porch. When the car, not a pickup, topped the last hill where my Willow Springs house would be visible, the driver cut his lights and motor. While the car coasted silently around to the back gate, I snuck down the hall to meet the intruder. He crept up my sidewalk, holding something against his chest (actually his broken ribs), and eased open the back-porch door.

I waited silently on the other side of that porch, in the blacker shadows of the kitchen, both hands on my pistol, which was aimed at his chest, safety off, my index finger ready to slide to the trigger. My adrenaline was pumping. The only reason I hadn't already shot him was my dad's gun safety training: always be sure of your target. I hadn't noticed that my dog hadn't barked, although that was not unusual. Perro had always been a silent dog. If he treed a coon in a pecan tree at night, he'd bark once. Then he'd sit patiently under the tree until someone either came out to shoot the coon or morning, whichever came sooner. If one of his people appeared with a gun, Perro would glance toward the coon once. That was all the help he thought a proper hunter needed. If Perro decided to bite a prowler, he didn't warn them. Maybe I finally wondered if my dog might know this guy. Something got through my adrenaline in that last tenth of a second. He's still alive and I'm not in prison, but it was close.

He stammered, "Ah . . . ah . . . I guess I should have called first?"

A few deep breaths later, I told my new houseguest, several times loudly, exactly how to approach a ranch house at night: horn honking, lights blazing, and hollering, "It's me! It's me! Hello the camp!" I doubt he ever tried to avoid waking someone again. Lots of other writers wrote about him, but I never did until right now.

Those of us who lived at the end of long dirt roads also usually drove dirty vehicles because we didn't want to waste precious drinking water washing them. A friend stopped me at the post office one day during a rainy spell and pointed to our matching muddy pickups parked along the curb. "You need to write about that," she suggested. So I did.

Not long after writing optimistic words about how driving a muddy pickup was a small price to pay for living on a road with grass growing down the middle, my road became impassable. That would be no major problem except that school districts in rural areas don't send buses down long dirt roads after one kid, so when my daughter started to school, I either had to take her or homeschool her. At the time, since my day job as college ag department secretary and my daughter's school were both on the other side of the creek, we had to cross it. During that rainy spell, some ranch kids went to school via canoe, but I didn't own one and the water wasn't deep enough to float one, just a big mud hole, soft enough to bury a caterpillar. My daughter and I solved our problem by hiking between our stranded ranch pickup and our stranded town pickup, luckily stranded on opposite sides. A thin strip of higher ground bordered the quarter mile of deep, rocky mud.

Each morning we were pretty grumpy until we turned off the radio and the motor, pulled on our rubber boots and jackets, and started carrying a big box containing books, lunches, homework, and town shoes. For the first few steps, we heard only silence. Then we heard our legs sloshing through water. As our ears tuned in to a new frequency, the water came alive. Killdeer screeched at us for invading their domain. Somewhere in the dark, ducks muttered softly, sounding just like my dad used to when calling them down to our hidden duck blind on the edge of some Mississippi River slough. The air was cold and smelled like water, the sky just turning gray in the east. It was that time of day that belongs only to hunters, fishermen, and cowboys. My daughter and I laughed and talked easily to one another in hushed voices. So of course, I wrote about that too.

Besides weather, another inconvenience was locked gates. Even though I lived behind those gates, having a key was a privilege that I seldom asked for. So how did I get home? Cattle guards usually replaced gates on roads that employee families traveled regularly. Roads less traveled were kept locked, and only responsible people had keys. So if I needed to travel a road with a locked gate, I had to ask permission and borrow a key.

I considered permission a gift that I did not want to abuse. I believe in locked gates. I've seen the beer cans, trash, tire tracks through the grass, and dead hawks and owls that accumulate along public roads. I wrote once that the only way I knew to protect the environment was to give it to cranky old ranchers who kept their gates locked. I read an essay by Dan Flores where he "flipped off" the private property owners as he drove through the Davis Mountains of West Texas. I wanted to shake him to his senses. "Don't you realize," I wanted to explain, "these mountains would not be so beautiful if the gates were open." Prohibiting roads into roadless areas and providing only backpack access are just variations of locked gates but with different key holders: government employees, scientists, or the young and fit. Without limits, all trails and roads deepen and erode, gather trash and campfire ashes, and all water becomes unfit to drink. Even backpackers and scientists have to shit somewhere. Humans must be locked out, even me.

So I don't abuse the privilege, and I don't go often. But occasionally, I've been behind the locked gates to places not on maps. Some keys protect tinajas, unique water dogs, huge madrone trees, Montezuma quail, or springs dripping with maidenhair ferns, but their secrets are safe with me. I believe in keys.

Behind the fences and locked gates are my favorite flowers. I suppose I could pick any one of a multitude of showy desert flowers: esperanza, mountain laurel, desert willow, claret cup cactus. But the tiny orchids in shades of lime green, white, orange, yellow, and blood red, dangling from the seed heads of wild grasses, are my favorites. I haven't always known that grass blooms. I once took a very intense college class on grass identification and memorized the common and scientific names of one hundred species. Each grass we studied was pressed at a specific time in its life and suspended under glass, which was good for memorization but bad for real knowledge. We could see subtle differences in how the blades were joined to the stem, how the seed heads differed, which had tufts of fuzz at the whorl, which ones grew in clumps, which on rhizomes. But grass never looks quite that way in real life. It is always either just sprouting, broken by the wind, shriveled from drouth, grazed, immature, over-mature, or somehow unrecognizable. I learned a lot about grass in that class, but nobody ever said it bloomed until a cowboy brought me a bouquet of grasses with tiny, pendulous, orchid-like blossoms hanging from the seed heads. He's long gone, but I still love those grass blossoms, and I often wrote about grass.

When we had a good year with lots of rain, I sometimes made tiny grass bouquets in empty blackleg vaccine bottles by picking just one stem of each different grass while they bloomed. Cows, horses, birds, and insects also depended on that feast of grass seed, and I didn't want to short them. I also liked my grasses wild. I just never respected pampered green lawns. Mowed grass never moans or blooms. Mowed grass never spun a spur rowel. But if mowing must be done, then I preferred critters or wind and lightning. During lightning storms, 06 Ranch cowboys usually drove out on a hill and watched for smoke. Fire is good for grass, but the price is high, so in our pickup beds sloshed a feed tub full of tow sacks or worn-out Levi's soaking in water and a shovel or two. At the first puff of smoke, we'd head to the fire, grab a wet sack, and start walking safely inside the blackened burned area, never in front of the fire. We'd twirl the sack like the end of a rope, beating out fire on the downswing. We needed only enough water to keep our sacks from drying out and catching fire. Two people could put out a lot of fire by heading in opposite directions around the outside and gradually closing the circle. Everyone kept their livestock sprayers full of water, some owned water backpacks, but most agreed that wet tow sacks put out the most fire. Two people swinging soaked sacks or Levi's could put out a mile of fire just about as fast as they could walk if the grass had been grazed. In rough country where cattle couldn't graze, we'd lose ground when it burned quickly uphill but catch up when it headed downhill and slowed.

Local schools sometimes dismissed classes, especially for big fires, so students could help. Somebody would start a sandwich brigade. Seeing our neighbors and community show up to help was rejuvenating. Fires that broke out on windy days or in places with lots of brush and trees attracted lots of help. Before the days of bottled water, I remember dashing to town to buy cases of beer and sodas for the volunteers, mostly beer. Fires often turned into parties, maybe too much so.

Once the flames were out, we'd walk back around the edge of the burn with shovels, tossing smoldering cow pies or smoking yuccas far into the blackened area. Then we'd take turns babysitting it day and night for a couple more days to make sure a strong wind didn't stir some missed coals back into flame. I remember one year, maybe around 1979, when we fought eleven fires just on the 06 Ranch, not counting neighbors' fires. Several happened during roundup, and once a fire started, men, women, and kids fought it day and night until it was out. I remember one night, driving in the dark from one fire to the next, hearing a young cowboy (his second night without sleep) named David Alloway joke, "I shoulda brought a lantern instead of a bedroll." David later became sort of famous for a book he wrote about desert survival skills. I'm sure he learned some of those skills while fighting fires in the rocks in the dark.

Today hundreds of trained firefighters with tons of equipment rush to the scene, but the fires keep growing and costing millions. The professionals concentrate on protecting lives, homes, and towns—which is much appreciated—but meanwhile out where there's "nothing," flames destroy wildlife, birds, fences, grass, nests, trees, shade, erosion-controlling vegetation, and scenery that may take years to replace, if ever. So what happened? Maybe like me, the people who had those old firefighting skills got too old? Maybe overprotecting kids has raised a generation more susceptible to heatstroke? Maybe beer got too expensive? Maybe too many lawyers wearing liability suits moved in? Stumbling around in the soot and rocks, cowboys often wore out a pair of boots on a big fire, so when the price of cowboy boots jumped from $200 a pair to $2,000 a pair, maybe they couldn't afford to walk around in the soot anymore? Athletic shoes just melt. Maybe we turned our responsibility for fighting fires over to people who don't know our country and don't understand what's at stake out there where there's "nothing"? Or maybe we let them take it? Personally I don't relax until I know that our local windmiller and a handful of cowboys have showed up. So, of course, I wrote about how to fight grass fires.

Maybe I wrote to convince myself that all this hardship was fun. It always seemed that when I put pen to paper, no matter how sorry for myself I felt, no matter how tired, scared, or mad, after a few pages I began to see what my grandmother called "the silver lining in every cloud." She thought a person could be as happy as they made up their mind to be and should be thankful for whatever they had. Maybe because of her influence and my pilgrim heritage, Thanksgiving was always my favorite holiday, and I tried to celebrate it as intended: as a day to be thankful. So, of course, I wrote about the way I liked to spend it. Instead of crowding around a big dining table set with china and cloth napkins, I packed our turkey and fixin's into kitchen panniers, which I converted into a chuck box at our destination. We loaded the panniers onto the back of our most dependable horse. The pumpkin pie went on as the top load, packed in a plastic pie keeper with a paper plate upside down over it and napkins stuffed in the extra room between there and the lid to keep it from shifting. We headed out horseback, leading packhorses, to some remote scenic spot on the ranch and never broke the crust on that pie.

We packed bedrolls into one long pack, putting all the blankets and pillows at each end in even loads. Draped over a horse, the whole thing stayed put and balanced without a packsaddle. Well, usually. Sometimes it ended up under a horse's belly and had to be repacked. Anytime you mix cowboys, pack strings, and big country together, there will be an occasional wreck. One year the horses decided to leave us in the top of a high mountain basin. Two fellows beat them in a footrace to the last narrow spot in the trail and brought them back. One year we were enjoying predinner wine in cold tin cups when Montana cowboy Bob Blackwell surprised us by showing up with a bottle of whiskey wrapped in his slicker and tied behind his cantle. He was also driving our horses ahead of him. They had pawed open a gate and returned to headquarters, maybe five miles away, and had left us stranded. We didn't know they were gone. So we picketed one horse in case it happened again and opened Bob's bottle. One year when Mike and Anne Capron joined us, Mike's half-broke packhorse bucked off his pack three times. Luckily their dishes were tin, but their lantern wasn't.

On Thanksgiving morning, I would build a fire to heat boned and smoked turkey, sweet potatoes, and vegetables over coals while I stirred up biscuits and set water to boil for instant stuffing. Some years the menu was ham with raisin sauce and corn on the cob, but always served with cranberry sauce, olives, and of course a sack of oats. Instead of watching football games, we'd lie back against a warm rock in the November sunshine (if there was any) and watch the shadows change on the mountains. Sometimes we went for exploratory rides to learn new country. One year we flew a bandana-tailed kite off Barbara's Point, the highest, windiest rim on the ranch.

Some years the weather was bitter cold, sometimes foggy, snowing, or cold and sunny. Long johns, gloves, wool socks, extra blankets in the bedrolls, and lots of layers were always part of Thanksgiving. In spite of the challenges, it was always worth it to get out there and give thanks for the open space and sweaty horses that made the world worth living in.

Most words about cowboys have been written by professionals, scholars, and historians who "lived" with the cowboys for a few hours or weeks. I didn't write about this life as a voyeur who went home to the city and all its conveniences after a few hours or days of roughing it. I didn't consider my neighbors or myself colorful characters living a simple life. We understood and dealt with its complexity and problems. If the best reporters are those who immerse themselves longest and deepest, why not just report on your own life? So I did.

CHAPTER TWO

Letters

"Thus all wild creatures are shy—even the fiercest. They are reluctant to let themselves be seen. This is not fear of physical hurt, but fear of being known."

—D. H. Lawrence

One day while picking up my mail, I proudly showed a real handwritten letter to a post office employee and asked, "How long since you've seen one of these?" She laughed and said I should frame it. Nothing made me happier than finding a real letter, with familiar handwriting, in my usual stack of bills-to-pay or trash. Because I wrote letters, I got a few back. Writing a letter, whether I mailed it or not, always helped me sort through difficult feelings. It was hard to hold a grudge, deny guilt, or assume moral high ground when facing that big white page. My envy, show-offityness, insecurities, and righteous anger always looked embarrassing in ink.

I guess, to me, writing a letter was a prayer that got answered, usually before I sent it.

As a kid I wrote thank-you notes, letters to Santa, distant cousins, and adopted pen pals like Miguel in Mexico. After my family moved to Arizona, I wrote to friends and relatives left behind in Iowa. As a young woman, I traded a few loooove letters signed in x's and o's. As a young mother on a remote ranch camp, I struck up an adult pen pal exchange with a ranch wife in Australia whose life was quite similar to mine. Those letters helped me realize the power of the pen to begin friendships or keep them alive and the importance of being both interesting and clear. I'm sure the reward of getting a real letter in return intensified my love for writing and developed my nose for news. Writing those letters probably gave me the confidence to try journalism. I started writing a column for my high school newspaper called "Barney's Barnyard." The column seemed like writing a letter to my classmates. It gave me the freedom to ramble and try my hand at being funny or profound.

Probably the most difficult thing about living on a remote ranch camp is boredom. Boredom drove me crazy. So I tried lots of different things to entertain myself. I gardened and canned and cooked. I sewed and quilted and crocheted. I hunted and fished and butchered meat, inventing new recipes for wild game. I persuaded my husband to acquire a milk cow so I could make butter, ice cream, cottage cheese, and cheese. I decoupaged, oil painted, and threw a few clay pots on a wheel. I taught myself to tie a few fancy knots with strips of rawhide and to hitch horsehair. I joined a garden club and learned to arrange flowers, learned to ride sidesaddle, and, using my grandma's recipe, baked bread and beat all the little old ladies at the county fair. Mostly, though, I pushed a pen across paper.

I almost never kept a journal. That always seemed a little too much like navel-gazing to me. Most of my journal entries were about tending water. Not often, but sometimes, I thought about something else:

> I went for a walk this evening up to the site of an old dump. There were some broken bits of clear glass and some that had turned purple. There were some broken bits of brown pottery, glazed dark brown and shiny on the surface and red like porous brick on the inside. There was an old rock corral nearby. Also a piece of a dutchoven lid with the handle intact. Everything blended into the rocks and surroundings. It was a dump but it was not offensive and I knew how the people must have cooked. What will some hiker think of me? Pipe corrals, plastic milk jugs, thousands of cans, bottles, and containers—none that will ever turn purple or blend in with rocks. I'm ashamed of my dump!

There is way too much "there" there. When I wasn't writing a letter to a real person, I seemed to struggle with what to say and often soared way over my own head while trying to make my thoughts seem important. The voice in this undated entry sounds like I'm talking to a professor:

> Although Aldo Leopold liked to compare ecological systems to corporate systems, the great predator at the "apex" of his pyramid

> was actually no more important, maybe even less so, than the soil microbes at the "bottom" who transformed sterile bits of rock into soil which nourished plants, which fed animals that fertilized microbes. Life is a circle, not a pyramid. Perhaps if I knew more about corporate systems, they too would fit Mother Nature's plan instead of the one we like to imagine filled with top guns, top dogs, alpha males, editors, college and U.S. presidents who come and go without making much of a noise down here at the microbe level. And it's not a perfect circle. Mother Nature doesn't operate in a "balance," but more like a kid learning to drive. She veers to the left, overcorrects, lurches, dents a few fenders, and sometimes piles up cars on the Interstate for miles. Those species of megafauna that became extinct did so without the help of cows, humans, fossil fuels, or the U.S. defense industry. This is supposed to be a journal, but obviously I'm imagining publication.

I was also imagining that I knew a whole lot more about how Mother Nature and corporations operated than I actually did. I needed a real person on the other end of my writing to keep me honest. I needed the real audience that letters provided to keep the bullshit out. So I wrote letters instead of journals. Writing letters taught me to use the lingo, pay attention, think, and describe vividly and honestly.

I also come from a long line of people who saved letters. I have a copy of a letter written by my great-great-great-grandfather Sisler describing the Iowa timber he was planning to purchase in 1851. I never met him, but I can hear his "voice" on the page through all those generations. I have two letters written to my grandfather by a World War I soldier stationed at Camp Cody, New Mexico, describing the thousands of horses and mules under his care. I have the letter my dad wrote from the South Pacific during World War II to my grandmother when my mom's dad died. My parents eloped just before Dad shipped out because Mom's parents didn't approve of the marriage: a landowning farmer's daughter to an unemployed fisherman. I can hear my dad's voice in that letter: proud, angry, but stiffly offering to help his mother-in-law farm when he returned. My grandmother saved that letter until she died; then Mom saved it; now I have it.

It's probably in my blood to have saved almost every letter I ever received, and I have often wondered if anyone saved mine. I have one from a one-room-school classmate and several from legendary horseman Tom Dorrance. Some are filed by person, some by year; many are undated. However, keeping copies of my own letters seemed shallow. Was a letter a real gift if my motive for writing it was future publication? So only a few of my own survive. I also wanted to trust my brain to remember the important stuff and forget the trivia. That was a mistake. I should have kept copies of every letter I wrote as "journals." One survivor was written at Willow Springs on April 5, 1985, to Bill "Blackie" Black, at the time cowboss for the MC Ranch in Adel, Oregon:

> Dear Blackie: Our spring works is underway right now. . . . Sometimes I wish we were on a small outfit where I can work more—these big outfits are kind of hard on female cowboys. I did get to be a hero one day though. One of the men lost his war bag off the wagon (we are using a team-drawn bed wagon this year) coming across the country. They went out that night in pick-ups and the next morning looking for it but didn't find it. He had $500 in it and dozens of credit cards and all sorts of valuable gear. He was pretty upset. I had a horse in the pen, so after they went to work, I tracked the wagon back across the country and found it. Pretty tough to track—ground real hard here and the wagon has rubber tires set the same distance apart as pick-ups and they had crossed and recrossed the tracks a dozen times. But being real smart, I managed. So far they've had more than the usual share of bad luck—my favorite story is one of the guys who smokes Bull Durham. He likes to do everything the hard way and carries kitchen matches too. Well, he had a shirt pocket full, stepped on his horse and brushed the saddle horn somehow. Struck the matches and set himself on fire. Burned his pocket off and started a grass fire! He didn't think it was funny, but I thought it was hilarious. I got left with 26 of our own new weaned calves we just put out and two heifers about to calve. Had two major water leaks on the main big line that runs all the way through our biggest pasture—about 300 head on it. Fixed one but the other one is going to be a job. The pipeline goes through the middle of the tub, no cutoff except to cut off the whole line, and the leak is somewhere in the pipe crossing the tub. Decided it was over my head. Guess ya'll don't

> have to mess with waters. Some places here have a separate crew too, but this ranch has so much live water that there really isn't enough to keep a pipeline man busy. We call in a guy that does the windmill work, but the everyday water lining, the campmen have to keep up. Not much goes wrong until the cowboys ride over the hill.

I like the voice in this letter much better than the journal voice and am fascinated more by what I don't say than what I did, assuming my reader would know. For instance, Blackie would know that the guy who lost his war bag off the wagon was upset because he thought someone had stolen it and that my motivation to find it was to prove him wrong. We probably harbored a few drunks, a few guys who would cheat on their wives, and those with other miscellaneous faults—but no thieves. Blackie would know the guy was a visitor and not a cowboy for several reasons. For one, no real cowboy would own that many credit cards. Blackie would also know that for the war bag to fall out of the wagon, the guy had to have been the last one to get his shit together to throw it on and that he wasn't careful. So my letter is gossiping to an insider.

Since I was bragging (something I shouldn't do) about finding the war bag, I exaggerate my bragging, calling myself a hero and real smart, so Blackie knows I know and am properly ashamed, but I thought he might enjoy the story. I knew he'd love the story about the guy setting himself and the grass afire. My only other news was complaining about water troubles. Blackie worked in buckaroo country, where the big ranches seldom ask their horseback crews to work on foot. I gently tried to stick up for the necessity of looking after water in the desert but hid that by griping about it. I threw in a quick brag about the ranch having lots of live water but sandwiched that brag between saying the leak was "over my head" and that "not much goes wrong until the cowboys ride over the hill." As a buckaroo cowboss on a ranch where he had one of those "straight riding jobs," Blackie would probably not be the least interested in my water leak problem, but I was. I should have tried harder to make it interesting to him. I didn't say whether the twenty-six calves got weaned okay, the two heifers produced live calves, or the leak I couldn't handle got fixed because that would just be more bragging. Besides, he would know it got done. I also threw in a quick brag about using a team-drawn bed wagon because that might make Blackie jealous and maybe make up for the water lining.

If I have that elusive voice that writers themselves can't hear but others can, it developed while writing letters. Reading them helped me understand the letter writers and seemed to inspire intimate conversations. My closest friendships have developed over years of trading letters. Some of those letter writers know more about me than my daughter does. I'm convinced that pioneer families who never saw one another again after sons and daughters left home in covered wagons stayed closer through letters than it's possible to do today with all of our fancy telephones, technology, and transportation. My grandmother walked a mile to her rural route mailbox every day no matter the Iowa weather, just in case one of her sisters had sent a letter.

I received and saved hundreds of letters from cowboy friends through the years, enough to stuff two drawers in a metal file cabinet. Someday I might even write a book called *Letters from Cowboys.* They all seemed to have an eye for detail and, had they wanted to, could have been writers. The letters helped me study their likes and dislikes, vulnerabilities and dreams; figure out when they were being truthful or pulling my leg and get a feel for cowboy lingo. The letters were my bottomless source of inspiration for articles. If they mentioned a problem, I looked for an answer. If they already had an answer, I searched for a publisher.

I have not reread those two file drawers full of letters, which would take months if not years, but I randomly pulled a few. Unless the letters were previously published, I have deleted the names of the letter writers and changed the names of anyone mentioned in them, mostly because some of the friendships and marriages have since dissolved. Some writers may have changed their minds about what they wrote, and some would never want their words to appear in public. I've lost touch with some of the letter writers and some have died, so permission would also be difficult, and I'm not sure how copyright laws cover letters received. So I have changed the names and sometimes places to protect their privacy, but the words are true. My interpretations were at the subconscious level at the time but appear here bolstered maybe by my later academic training in "reading between the lines." My interpretations have not changed, but maybe I can put them into words better now.

Because I was a safely married female at the time, male letter writers sometimes shared news about their sometimes hilarious and sometimes sad attempts at hooking up with females, like this one, although I am sure he was lying and exaggerating:

> Today I made the biggest fool of myself. It was pathetic! . . . There was this girl with blue eyes, but they somehow looked snowy white. I don't want to get into detail, all I can say is that she was good looking anyhow. She was fixing to leave, and I asked her if she had a good time. I guess she didn't hear me because she went to where I was and asked me what I had said. She then asked me if I had or was having a good time. I tried to speak to her, but my lips just quivered. Smiling, she asked me if I wanted something to drink. After several attempts, I was successful enough to say, "No th-th-th-thaa-thanks!" I don't know. All I know is that I'm glad that she doesn't know me and that any of ya'll weren't present to witness the comedy. I've been going to Mr. B's on the week-ends. It's a pretty nice place to go because you get to meet all kinds of people, including bald, real bald-headed girls. My friends challenged me by giving me money to dance with one of them, but there was no possible way I could've. There was this girl/woman that I did ask and danced with. Hell! It was scary. Every time she spoke, her ribs shaked and I could feel that. Heck, I can't even explain it. All I know is that her voice made a horrible hoarse sound, so I stopped asking her questions in order to keep her from talking.

That letter writer liked to pull pranks on me—calling late at night and pretending to be the police or silently sneaking up behind me while I was typing until I got that eerie feeling of being watched and turned around. I'm sure his letter was intended for entertainment, not fact. I tried hard to learn who I could trust and when, and about which subjects. This letter also reminds me of a common cowboy trait: overly critical. When giving advice about romance, I would tell them they were culling too deep, that they needed to cull deep enough to get the best they could get but not so deep that they weren't being realistic. It was almost impossible for the real world to pass their close inspection. Bachelor cowboys are common at least partly because a girl's eyes might be too light blue or too dark brown, her voice too raspy or whiny, her legs too skinny or too fat, or they didn't like the way she cooked pinto beans. They were the same way toward bosses, each other, gates, pickups, saddles, even horses. I suppose I am just as guilty of being overly critical of the outsider writers and photographers who try to write about us.

This next letter comes from a cowboy working at the King Ranch in Texas, one of the few ranches that welcome tourists to come and watch their cowboys work. The letter writer was there starting colts for the horse division. I had evidently warned him that his young female horses (fillies) might get even with him for the female human hearts he liked to break. Since my letter had obviously used *fillies* as a metaphor, he might be doing the same with *candle*:

> Well, the other day I got bucked off. Barney you jinxed me, because I read your letter and you said that the fillies were going to throw me and the first one I got on that day, did. I got hung up for a minute, my foot was hung in the stirrup and I was trying to roll over on my belly, but she got her kick in before I could. Well, it's not the candle you have to watch out for on your buck, it's them damn back feet when you fall off. She got me right in the arm. It's been sore these last couple of days but I think that I'll live. We started four new studs Saturday and we got on them today. Mine just ran around and grabbed their ass. We had our first encounter with the tourists the other day, really pissed us off. This guy had to be a Yankee loud mouth. We had been on horses all day and he wanted us to get back on just so he could make grunting noises at us as we did. Everybody that was on the tour was really embarrassed. If everybody else wouldn't have been there, I would have probably done a number on that "old fart." Teach him a little respect. It has been raining here a lot, so it has really been a hassle to work the new ones in the mud and all. . . . P.S. I spelled cantle wrong on purpose just to make you proud!

In the middle of the letter he mentions "the candle," which should be spelled "cantle"—meaning the part of a saddle that acts sort of like the back of a chair. Some people think a high cantle will help them ride a bucking horse; others believe it can hurt the rider's back. He is humorously saying that the mare's hind feet are apt to be more dangerous than the cantle.

Mares often cripple studs by kicking them when the studs are just trying to do their reproductive jobs. He's probably reminding me that he's a stud. When he says the studs "grabbed their ass," that is cowboy lingo for one of the first moves a horse does when he is thinking about bucking: clasping his tail tight against his rear end. It's a sign of fear or surprise. The letter writer had probably "grabbed his ass" over my critique of his love life. He knew saying that I had jinxed him, gotten him bucked off and almost hung up would make me "grab my ass" with guilt. He was probably warning me to bug off about his love life.

The following letter gives a more serious side to cowboy problems with women. The writer is bragging about his swanky living conditions and wondering if maybe he is ready to find a female to join him:

> Well, I'm alive. I moved again, not far, just over a couple of divides. I'm a Padlock cowboy now. In a camp being my own boss. Sure do like it. Haven't been mad at the circle leader yet. But I suppose it's just a matter of time until he screws up. Got a two-room shack, gas lights, heat, cook stove, and refrige. A well outside the door. Six old saddle horses, a toothless dog, two colts of my own, and a team. Just ride is all I have to do. And they feed me and even give me money! Can't hardly beat that can you. I'm on the Connally Division in the PK camp. It's about six miles north and east of Crow Agency. Can't say as my cooking is any good, but I'm not losing any weight, so guess I'm doing alright. But if you run into any young female cooks who can stand me, send them this way or have them send a resume or whatever it is you use to apply for a job. Pay's not too good, but the company and scenery is bearable.

His humor needs some translation: He hasn't been mad at the circle leader yet because he is his own circle leader, meaning his own boss, but he knows he is so critical that he will eventually get mad even at himself. A well outside the door means he has access to water right outside the door. It also means, though, that his house has no running water inside: no toilet, no shower, no bathtub, no washing machine. He doesn't mention an outhouse, and there may not be one. Even if there is, it's probably "full" because anybody who is looking for a straight ridin' job is not going to shovel shit—not even his own.

"Gas lights" means no electricity, but the same propane gas that runs his lights can also run heating and cooking stoves and a gas refrigerator. He knows this is a camp few women would tolerate but jokes that so many will want to join him here that he better have them fill out résumés. This is especially funny because I'm sure he has never filled out a résumé or maybe even seen one. The kind of ranches he likes to work for do not hire via résumés. You show up so they can look you in the eye, ask a few questions, look over your gear, and maybe check out what kind of boots you're wearing. They say you can't judge a book by its cover, but that's not always true.

His dark humor about women is also more sad than funny. People who want straight riding jobs are often the handsomest, most physically fit, and the best hands. Yet they probably also understand better than anyone why pretty girls feel objectified. Lots of women want these good cowboys for temporary arm candy to impress friends or for fantasy sex, but none want to actually live the way he lives. Country songs sometimes get it right, like the song that asks the girl what she plans to do with the cowboy she's brought home if he doesn't get up and ride away. Because their letters so often mentioned romance trouble, I tried to find article subjects that suggested answers at least metaphorically. Often the horse and rider relationship served as an allegory for a human relationship. One of the best horsemen I ever knew said that horsemanship didn't work on people, but I wasn't sure even he believed that. So I kept my eyes and ears open and spent many years trying unsuccessfully to solve that problem.

Sometimes cowboy letters made me sad, especially news from young cowboys trying to get started who dreamed about but couldn't afford the tools they needed. The news here is about an intended big purchase:

> I've been thinking about ordering a new pair of boots from Wilson's Boot Co. in Montana. They sent me a brochure and I think that I am going to try and get a yellow top with black bottom, and have black stitching inside of gold. I figured that it would at least make the stitching stand out on top of the yellow. It's hard to pick two right colors that work good together and don't make me look like a dork. Of course people always said that I dressed funny. Then if I like them, I might send my Tony Lama's in to get them entirely rebuilt, if it isn't too much. So then I can have two pair of boots

and I don't always have to wear just one pair every day. Maybe they will last longer that way.

Only people who work outside understand how important quality foot gear can be. This young cowboy is struggling to afford his first pair of handmade boots and to repair a factory-made pair. Good boot makers pull their waxed-thread stitches tight enough to keep out water and dirt, and embed steel shanks in the arch area so the foot won't bend in the stirrup. Factories don't do that. Not being able to afford good boots makes an all-day ride painful. Wearing the same pair of boots day after day often results in pulling on a pair of boots still damp from the day before. People who work in their boots all day often come in at night wearing wet boots, having sweat them through from the inside. Sometimes they are also wet on the outside from riding in the rain, wading in muddy pens, or fixing a water leak. Both dampness and dryness will rot leather. Taking care of all the leather a cowboy uses is a daily chore and a major expense, so I found experts to explain how best to take care of leather.

Cheap boots wear out faster too. Added to that problem is urban cowboy fashion. When people with lots of money who wear boots only for dancing start discovering the good boot makers, prices rise. A good pair of handmade boots used to cost a month's wages. Today that price might be two or three months' wages, maybe more. The same is true for jeans, coats, hats, and saddles. The most well-crafted horse gear has become "art" and now hangs in museums and collectors' mansions—way out of the price range of working cowboys. With mixed emotions, I often wrote about craftsmen and helped raise their prices. Fashion and publicity are good for the makers but bad for those who really need quality tools. I once read that Amish quilt makers sometimes put a rope around their finished work, barring outsiders from purchasing, so that young Amish couples could afford quilts. I wish our cowboy craftsmen did the same. This young cowboy doesn't complain openly, but I hear his desire between the lines.

The letters often gossiped about the whereabouts of mutual friends. We called that news "the cowboy grapevine." It seemed to work pretty good until technology came along. Social media does not inspire truthfulness the way writing letters did. Social media seems to cause everyone to sensationalize their own lives, groom their public faces, and hide their real feelings and thoughts. People were more truthful in letters and sort of spread the word to trusted friends when they were unhappy in their jobs. Information about who was working where and how happy they were sometimes proved valuable to ranchers when the time came to hire extra help for spring branding and fall shipping. No one publishes their frustrations with their boss and willingness to change jobs for public view, so hiring is probably more complicated now that cowboys write fewer letters. I also think it might be more lonesome.

Today cowboys living sixty miles from town might post their job changes and current whereabouts on social media or maybe stick a newsletter that's been copied one hundred times into a Christmas card. Maybe they'll send a quick email or text, maybe a forwarded news article telling me who to vote for—none of which goes into any depth of thought aimed at helping either them or me think harder or solve our own real problems. The more real problems a human has, the more likely they are to try to solve problems a thousand miles away instead, like to save tigers or the rain forest. A few cowboys today even write blogs. Although the blogs have the feel of letter writing, the fact that the audience could be anyone from anywhere seems to tempt bloggers into wearing a "public face" and embellishing their stories. A lot of sappiness, crap, and bragging sneaks in when the audience widens from a trusted friend to the wide world. Missing is the painful honesty and careful thoughts found in those one-on-one handwritten letters, composed out on the porch or beside the fire after a long day of work.

Cowboy letters were nearly always full of news about nature: a rare sighting, unusual behavior or appearance. Unlike "long" scientific studies observing animals for several months in select areas, cowboy observations occurred all day, every day, over a lifetime and sometimes from Canada to Australia. Nature notes and sightings of wild animals were always cowboy news and reported factually, especially anything out of the ordinary, as with this letter dated August 13, 1984:

> Last weekend I talked to Jeff and they were salting in the pick-up last week and saw a mama bear and two cubs. I haven't seen him smile that wide with lit up eyes for quite a while. He said they stopped the truck to watch and take a few pictures when Ma barked and zip, zip up went the cubs into a pine tree leaving footprints

scratched all the way up and were peeking around to see the cause of all this. They went on salting the herd and were coming back about an hour later when they saw them bears again. This time all three ran up the tree with bark flyin! Black bears are pretty common up there. One cub, he said, had a white spot on his rump.

I always found it interesting how urban people worship wild places and absolutely believe in nature's ability to improve one's character—yet also believe that those who actually live and work outside in nature daily are somehow ruined by those same experiences. Every rancher, cowboy, and rural kid was shocked when environmentalists began attacking cattle and those who raise them as nature's supreme enemies. We don't just love and worship nature as a vacation spot or scenic gym; we have given our very lives for the privilege of living where we do. Cowboys are also keen observers who remember. In ten years, if this letter writer runs across a grown bear with an identical white spot in the same place on its rump, he'll remember just where he saw it as a cub. We all wrote about nature a lot.

Letters from cowboys, such as this one, usually contained useful knowledge and kernels of wisdom that helped point me toward new thinking that might become future articles:

> Dear Barney, I'm on "poacher patrol." It's hunting season and my duty for the next couple weeks is to catch poachers, sort of a "man-hunter" you might say. I've no earthly idea what I'm going to do if I catch one, maybe he'll just surrender. Right now I'm sittin among some rocks on a ridge scopin' out the country with Diana's "Leitz" binoculars. I've got Mike hobbled down in the brush. This isn't real exciting but it does allow for lots of reading time. I just started a book by John Muir called "Wilderness Essays." Evidently he is one of the founders of the Sierra Club. I figured before I started criticizing these folks, I better find out where they are coming from (there's a bee buzzing to get some sugar out of me . . . imagine that) anyway, who knows, we might have something in common. Wouldn't it be great if we all found out that we all wanted the same basic things, then even though we didn't see eye to eye on how to achieve those things, we might be a little more tolerant of one another. Well, the

> sun finally came out, there's a hawk on the bluff right behind me (redtail . . . maybe). I just heard a couple of shots to the North towards Santiago, too far to be on me. I think I'm pretty well hid. I've got rocks behind me, cholla to my left, catclaw and greasewood in front of me. There's a rock poking me in the butt, but I think I can live with that. Well I better go check on Mike. P.S. That bee didn't get any sugar out of me.

When I started getting involved with the growing controversy between ranchers and environmentalists, cowboys had been thinking about it for several years and through letters like that one preparing me to think about it. I carefully followed the advice this cowboy gave and tried to "find out where they are coming from" before I criticized these folks. I spent many years on that project and eventually even wrote about John Muir.

I wrote to Marie Sheather, a stockman's wife who lived on a remote ranch in Australia's outback. She had read one of my early *Western Horseman* articles and wanted to trade letters with me. We traded snake stories, gardening tips, and wildflower seeds. I sent her some Chihuahua spurs, and she sent me a book of outback poetry by Banjo Paterson and music by Slim Dusty. We compared different cowboy ways, such as roping in Texas instead of using a stockwhip as in Australia. When she offered to send an Australian stockwhip, I declined, saying we never used whips. "Don't use whips?" she wrote back. "What in the world do you do, yell?" And she sent one anyway, braided from kangaroo leather, with the end of the wooden handle carved into a fist. It took a few years before I recognized the stockwhip as news and the other gifts her letters had given me, but eventually I published "Of Stockwhips and Friends."

After the article, stockwhips were almost an immediate hit, fitting perfectly into the cowboy "less is more" philosophy. No more yelling. The more I thought about yelling, the less dignified it seemed. While learning to use whips, we suffered a few bloody ears (both human and horse), some welts across our backs or legs, and runaway horses who probably thought we'd lost our minds, but eventually we improved. The Aussies preferred kangaroo, but we don't raise many kangaroos in the American West. When one good braider started making whips out of rawhide, nobody was impressed at first. Leather, especially kangaroo, is supple. Rawhide is more like coiled tin. But when a visiting Aussie ringer was able to crack a "Sydney flash" with my rawhide whip, he proved to us skeptics that rawhide could be just as good as kangaroo in the right hands. Suddenly the demand for my rawhide whip maker's whips far exceeded supply. He wrote letters with such irony, sarcasm, and dry humor that I always struggled to catch his meaning, as in this letter about how his business was going:

> I have begun to weaken a little in my resolve to support myself as a whip maker. I had 15 orders when I got back to Montana after your works and set down to whittle out a few. I've used two hides up, been making whips as steadily as I can stand and only have 17 left to make. At present I'm out of hides but got one in the creek and as soon as we get a chinook strong enough to melt about 3 feet of ice, I'll be back in business.
>
> Every day spent around this sheep-shed operation makes a job on a steer outfit of any kind look just that much better. This outfit has about 650 cows to calve in the next 10 days. They are husbanded very intensely. Most of them, cows as well as heifers, will calve in box stalls. Each stall has a record book and pencil on a string attached to the door. Entries from last year read like this: No. 561—started calving at 4:06, pulled calf at 4:45, calf weak, cow won't claim, warm calf in shack, suckle calf at 6:30, etc. etc. I'm really glad that I can be here to help Joe out but I wouldn't have this job stuck up my nose if I had room for a sawmill. Well, I guess I better get out there and try to make a hand lickin' them new babies off. I have decided that if I was in charge of things, everything north of the Red River would be yearling and dry stock country, and you southerners could run the cow-calf end to keep the north stocked.

To translate just a little, notice that at the end of October he began with orders for fifteen whips and after at least three months of "hard work" still had seventeen to make—meaning that he was farther behind than when he started. He'd left one hide in the creek so long, waiting for the hair to slough, that it had frozen solid. Obviously his heart wasn't in making whips anymore. Lots of letters were written during calving season, a time when cowboys often sat around waiting for a calf to be born or its mother to need help to make that happen. Calving, a typical northern job during the winter/early spring months partly because of cold weather, kept cowboy families from starving to death, but few liked it because of the endless waiting and repetition. After calving four hundred or so, the romance wore off. The letter writer was sort of comparing the repetition of whip braiding to the repetition of calving.

Most northern cowboys complained humorously about winter weather, made fun of helpless cows, and complained especially about owners who wanted a bunch of record keeping done. Just about every calf born to a first-calf heifer arrives weak, and first-time mamas often hesitate to claim the slimy things. In humans we call it postpartum blues. Calves often need to be physically pulled out of these young heifers with some kind of leveraged puller. In real cold weather, nearly every calf needs help getting dry, warm, and that important first nursing done. The author was making fun of all those repetitive calving notes left by his predecessor because they were just silly and worthless. It would be like keeping detailed records on what time you started your vehicle on a cold morning, noting how long it took for the motor to warm up, what time you turned on the heater, and how long before the vehicle got warm. Just saying that he calved 650 cows in ten days covers the subject, maybe with one additional note about how many calves and heifers died. Zero losses was the goal but was almost impossible to achieve. He was probably juxtaposing these two stories so that I would know the same was true of making whip after whip after whip, probably for customers who didn't really need one, and then having to show them how to use it. Just like calving.

Many of these snowbound northern letter writers also poked fun at southern cowboys, probably because of jealousy over our milder winter weather. Teasing each other got meaner and meaner, until some journalists began to accept the humorous criticism as fact and young cowboys began to believe that these differences between North and South were serious. Eventually it almost drew a line in the sand between buckaroos and Texans. Humans seem determined to separate themselves into us-versus-them tribes, and cowboys are no exception. Luckily, the lines keep getting redrawn because the tribal members can't seem to get along with each other either. This letter writer had already drawn a line between cows and steers. He suggests that we southerners can mess with the cows and calves and then send our steers north, which is pretty much the way it was done historically. He may even be aware that trailing all those steers north, day after day, same ol same ol, might have gotten boring to cowboys who lived that life, just like whip making and calving. The grass is always greener on the other side of the divide, river, fence, or way of doing things. My job as I saw it was trying to help us understand each other and encourage one another to be the best we could be, not compete. I always imagined that my audience came from within this hard-to-please cowboy culture. I did not try to describe cowboys to city people. I simply wrote for and about a culture that is seldom understood today, sometimes even by its own members, maybe especially by its own members.

Living the cowboy dream got harder after marriage and children. Everyone struggles with their dreams at some point in life—either due to age, health, or family. Bachelor cowboys with riding jobs sometimes struggle to find work in winter, so they grubline. Grublining means moving around and staying with employed friends who can afford to feed them, then moving on to the next friend when or before they wear out their welcome. It's hard on anyone's pride. Usually grubliners were single and pitched in to share their host's workload by taking the night shift during calving season, starting a colt or two, and somehow trading their labor for food and shelter. Once marriage and children come along, grublining gets more complicated and embarrassing. Few ranch houses have extra bedrooms, more than one bathroom, or even just space and food for more than one family. The next letter writer is searching for balance between his idealized lifestyle and more security for his family.

> I don't know why it has become such a struggle to write lately. I think it may have to do with my attitude. The way we live hasn't really changed. We've had several different jobs in the last year, have moved three or four times, and been forced to grubline a considerable amount of time between jobs. That is no new story for us, although it's harder with a child. But it isn't being done because we want to live like that anymore, and that, I guess, is the problem. It seems the more our vision of what we want to do with our lives becomes clear, the more obstacles we run up against in pursuing that vision. As defining our goals gets easier, reaching them gets harder. The last couple of full-time jobs I've held have broke an egg in me. Working for wages will be a last resort solution from now on. I've been self-employed the last four months or so and am liking it lots. We have a little feeding/calving job to do this winter for a

> pill-happy hay farmer that I already know will have me grinding my teeth in frustration, but it will keep us fed while there aren't many horses to shoe. Maybe, God willing, we can show these folks some different angles too. They are kids that are just doing it like Dad always did (with just a few more shots, pills, eartags, etc.) and may be open to change. At any rate we have a house in a good spot year-round and are working on leasing some country in the vicinity. We think that if we can ever get hold of a little grass and some cows that the cows will pay their own way and enough extra to let us start owning a few more of them each year. Well, I've whined long enough. Sure hope this cheery little letter lifts your spirits. I've been reading a lot of history lately: Churchill's memoirs and his history of the English people, Bruce Catton's Civil War stuff, etc. Maybe it's all this reading about wars that has me depressed. If you have any suggestions for long winter evenings, feel free to make them. I'll try to write again within the next year or so.

Few people realize how unhappy cowboys can get, especially in winter, or how well read they often are. Many don't own TVs, and it can be a long time from dark to daylight, especially in winter. So they either need a hobby like twisting hair, hitching hair, leather braiding, building saddles, writing poetry, or playing an instrument or a lot of books to read. Because I owned a lot of books, my house was often a target for grubliners, which started to feel like freeloading after a few days, just like any company, especially when the grubliner starts trying to convince the hosts to "do things different." Cowboys hate bosses who tell them how to do something, and bosses don't much like cowboys telling them how to do things either.

A letter from one person sometimes seemed to offer a solution for a problem another was having. I kept my eyes and ears open for good jobs, good bosses, and good solutions, as given in this next letter from one of our wise elders. We paid lots of attention to his words about getting along with horses, but those words often applied just as well to almost any problem in life. Instead of a pen pal, I considered him a life coach or counselor.

> The longer I live, the more I realize the impact of attitude on life. Attitude, to me, is more important than facts. It is more important than the past, than education, than money, than circumstances,

than failures, than what other people think or say or do. It is more important than appearance, giftedness or skill. It will make or break a company, a church, a home, a family. The remarkable thing is we have a choice everyday regarding the attitude we will embrace for that day. We cannot change our past. We cannot change the fact that people will act in a certain way. We cannot change the inevitable. The only thing we can do is play on the string we have, and that is our attitude. I am convinced that life is 10 × what happens to me and 90 × how I react to it.

Many cowboys who became excellent horsemen could instill a great attitude in their animals but struggled to instill a great attitude within themselves. I spent a lot of time worrying about friends who seemed to be their own worst enemy, caught in limbo between dreaming up a utopia and living in reality. Some were such purists that they'd rather drive a truck than cowboy on an outfit that was "too modern" or "too stupid" or "too farmer" or whatever. I would write back and gently try to remind them that being horseback even once a week was better than never—wasn't it? Branding calves using a calf table was better than never branding calves—wasn't it? But then I would think about my own writing and how I detested editors who tried to change my style or subject. No, publishing wasn't worth writing for those editors. So I guess I understood, but I still spent time searching for ways to improve attitude.

Sometimes, believe it or not, cowboys even complained about riding horses, like this young cowboy writing from Hawaii. Most people ride horses someone else has trained, and he was obviously finding out how hard it is to teach horses when the trainer is still learning:

Sometimes it just feels like I'm overloading my mind with things. It is like I'm trying to go slow with these horses, but then it turns out that I'm not getting good results or the horses weren't progressing any. Some of these horses you can show them how to do something one day and then quit them when they're going pretty good, but then the next day it is like they didn't remember anything. Then the next day they do it ok. Sometimes I just get overloaded thinking about what to do since nothing else is working, then I just get so mad. I feel like just saying, "Whatever sounds good to you." That's probably what I would say or worse, and just come back home. Hell, I'm tired and it's late, so I'm going to just call it a night.

Although ranch people nearly always romanticize horses, they know their rose-colored view of them is just as false as the rose-colored view of their "perfect" spouse or the children they might dearly "love." My all-time favorite description of horses was surprisingly written by Owen Ulph in a little book he called *The Fiddleback: Lore of the Linecamp.* I say "surprisingly" because as an Englishman with a PhD and an undergrad degree from Stanford, he had no business writing about the American West, but he came pretty close to getting horses right: "The truth is that horses exhibit, in an exaggerated form, many of the worst characteristics of people. They are greedy, envious, spiteful, malicious, slothful, superstitious, and stupid. They are congenital hysterics and each one is, ominously, a prospective homicide. If horses could talk, they would lie!" Ulph died in 2003 and *The Fiddleback* is out of print, but used copies of his books pop up occasionally when someone dies and leaves uneducated heirs.

I also like and respect good cowboys no matter what color their hides are, just like horses. I didn't dream up those feelings; I inherited them from my culture and was reminded of them periodically in cowboy letters. Like horses, all people have faults, some worse than others. This cowboy struggles to put his thoughts about that into words:

> Dear Barney, People always say to me, "You live in a little Mexican town." Truth. Their perception of this is both truth and myth. I've got friends that can't speak English that have better manners and treat their families better than any family in any big town. Truth. There are also some Mexican people here that steal, lie, deceive, and are drunks, drug addicts, and everything that goes with that. Truth. We are what we perceive ourselves to be and are shaped by the way we live, our thought values, ethics, and our way of thinking. They're inseparable. Am I prejudiced? Yes. But I think not because of a person's color but for the above reasons. People are more or less people; the cultural images are the difference. This is probably why there is so much trouble in this world: People trying to enforce their cultural expectations on other people with different images and expectations. Pioneers conquering the West? I think it's

> going for that illusive dream that did the conquering. It seems a person is happiest when there is some type of struggle, sense of worth, independence, achievement. All of the different cultures—Irish, English, German, etc.—had one thing in common, the illusion of the golden opportunity in the west. That spirit and drive is what settled the west. I'm not so sure it has been conquered. Don't look at these subjects from anyone else's point of view. I'd like to hear yours. Don't lose your "cultural expectations" because if you do, you won't like it.

Like the letter writer, I am prejudiced too. Not about race, religion, class, or ethnicity but about behavior. I don't "like" or respect lazy people of any race, people who are drug addicts or sellers, people I can't trust, or those who beat their spouses and children. I do respect some of our hard-working smugglers, several recovering alcoholics, even some recovering lawyers. Some of the letters I've already quoted were written by full-bloods, half-breeds, and mixed-breeds of various races. Eventually I wrote about Native American ranchers and cowboys; Mexican silver and rawhide craftsmen, ranchers and vaqueros, and charros. I wrote about those who inspired me, who had a strong work ethic, who embraced the poverty often associated with living a life somehow connected to the world that I understood. Cowboys never hesitated to adopt good ideas no matter who found them or where.

The following letter is a good example of some good cowboys experimenting with their own adaptation of an idea that came out of Africa, the Savory grazing system. Allan Savory is a tracker from Zimbabwe who paid attention and noticed how huge African herds completely destroyed the country as they grazed across it. However, he also noticed that as those herds churned the surface, they also planted seeds, slowed runoff after a rain, and provided fertilizer with their manure. Places that these wandering herds did not "destroy" became more and more barren, but the "destroyed" areas quickly became lush after a rain.

Almost everyone whose livelihood depended on grass understood the logic in Savory's theory immediately, and most already practiced it to some degree. Anyone paying attention notices that mowing grass regularly does not destroy it. You can't over-mow a lawn if it is watered and fertilized—which is Mother Nature's whole theory behind grazing in the first place.

The same destruction/improvement cycle happened with American bison. Likewise, during spring branding and fall shipping, horses and cattle pounded vegetation inside corrals into powdered dust. After branding, cowboys turned the animals back out to pasture and closed the corral gates. By fall they often had to chop those gates open with machetes because vegetation inside the corrals was knee-high if not worse. What was new about Savory's idea was that intentional destruction could improve grasslands. His theory basically said that the American West suffered from being undergrazed, not overgrazed, because undergrazing allowed livestock to graze selectively, like picky shoppers in a grocery produce section.

Originally Savory suggested that ranchers cut their pastures into small pieces in order to concentrate livestock for intensive grazing to force "destructive" manuring and trampling. Cowboys, of course, hated that idea. Who wants to ride ten feet and open another damn gate? Eventually most of those who practiced the Savory system did it on foot, training their cattle to move through the small pastures and many gates with whistles—a good description of hell to a cowboy. Besides, as the cowboys argued correctly, bison and those African grazers traveled around without fences. The author of this letter, along with friends and family, wanted to figure out how to accomplish "destruction" for range improvement the cowboy way, with fewer fences and more time horseback. I knew this was big news. So I had already asked permission to come do an article.

> Well we made it. Got here the 25th and started feeding hay to these steers. Snowed the 28th and kept on snowing till we had half a foot. Cleared up finally and the snow left, so we went to grass with them about the 3rd of April. The first week or two of feeding wasn't much fun, but it's getting better. Everyone is in good spirits since we quit feeding. Our boss said the other day that we did wreck the bearings on a front wheel of that John Deere we were feeding with. Out of our element he said. Glad to hear it. This is shore nice country. We've all got about 4 head of horses apiece with a couple of floaters just in case. We've just been using one dirt tank here to water these steers with, but it has water running into it. We just keep these steers kinda tucked into a piece of country till they get the grass clipped off and before they can graze it to nothing, we drift them to another piece of country, and so on. We've been working this country for

> about 5 days now and got about 3 left until we move the whole works to another BLM lease and do the same. Lotsa country. I guess there is a lot of people keeping an eye on how this is gonna work. It sure makes a lot of sense to me and I sure hope people see that it works because it uses this country for what it was intended to be used for and it means more job security for people like us. We'll fill ya in better when ya get down here. Plenty of horses here so we'll put ya to work. Just write and tell us when you plan on coming and we'll see if we can't be at a good camp about then. Looking forward to seeing ya.

If it worked, this was new cowboy technology that could almost bring back much of the lifestyle of the trail-driving days. This crew lived in bedrolls and tents, cooked over a fire using a pot rack and chuckwagon, and stayed horseback from dawn to dusk. It seemed like what heaven might be like, even if it had to begin with a few weeks of using machinery to feed in the snow. The letter writer is proud of the fact that the owner thought they were morons about machinery. Sure enough, by the next year, this crew had traded the tractor for another team of horses and a feed wagon. Purists. However, to my knowledge, they practiced their system only two years. It was very labor intensive and kept them out in the weather day after day. I'm not sure why they stopped. Maybe like a lot of things, it sounded better in daydreams than in reality.

I could seldom find anyone who was comfortable with the serious conversations I wanted. Friends preferred jokes and sarcasm unless they held a pen. Then they seemed to take their thoughts and words more seriously. I think the people who wrote letters to me or became subjects of my interviews were hungry for serious conversations too, but none of us wanted to expose our inner feelings or vulnerabilities unless there was a damn good reason. Sometimes, maybe, the chance to write a letter provided that reason.

I have traded handwritten letters with one prolific and master letter writer, California buckaroo Rod Flournoy, for more than thirty years. He ranched in Northern California on private land and on BLM and Forest Service leases. An aspiring writer, he sometimes worried about his country-boy grammar and spelling (but more often defended it); I worried about making errors about ranching and livestock. So we edited each other's work.

Rod did not type but wrote in beautiful Spencerian script and often sent me copies of letters he had written to others. Some of the country he operated had been designated as wilderness area; some was a huge wetland. To say that he was in the middle of almost every environmental controversy was an understatement. To defend himself, he wrote to backpackers who complained about grazing along his streams or to those worried about sage hens, and he would send me copies. He wrote with such eloquence that I typed several of his letters and convinced him to publish them. He also might be the richest person I've ever known. His forty-niner family settled during the gold rush, and he had a barn full of restored Pierce-Arrows, but I was more interested in the pride he took in irrigating his own hay meadows and how he got down on his knees to teach employees how to sharpen their shovels. Almost every time I showed up to visit, he was wearing gum boots, and he carried a very shiny shovel over his shoulder. He was a role model in a world that often ranks jobs into skilled and unskilled, manual labor and brain labor. Even in the rural world, irrigation and irrigators often represent some form of low-class employment.

Irrigation has long been the black sheep of western ranching operations. But the art of spreading water can't be learned in a week, a summer, or even a lifetime and is often handed down from generation to generation. Rock dams have never enjoyed the same prestige as rope and saddle. Although Flournoy could hold his own horseback, he had probably put in more personal hours and years irrigating than at any other job on his wilderness ranch. He said that although most people like to call themselves buckaroos or cattle ranchers, they are actually grass farmers. The less grass they produce, the fewer calves they can market. I thought it was past time to celebrate those who could make water run uphill and repeatedly badgered him to write a letter about his irrigating experiences. When he finally did, I wrote a brief introduction for *Range* magazine, and then all I had to do was type his beautiful handwritten letter about his romance with green meadows. Here are a few excerpts:

> Dear Barney, I enjoy shoveling ditch with members of a crew who can handle a shovel pretty good or at least seem interested in learning. Last summer four Mexican fellers helped us here and in July a side-hill ditch needed cleaning and we tackled it. The sod was tough with wide blade water grass and very strong roots which

required a very sharp shovel to cut through. Those fellers could shovel pretty good, but none had learned how to file a shovel to make it razor sharp, which I helped them learn how to do.

Lots of people these days call a shovel a Mexican backhoe, which rather annoys me. The big majority of American people would be better off if they didn't think they were too good to take up a shovel and put it to good use. In all my years of observation I have only known less than a dozen men who used a shovel enough to make it shine. . . .

When I was about nine, I built a rock dam up above the house a-ways. I was big enough to use a shovel some and I thought beings I have backed the water up along the banks of the crick and it's just ready to spill out, I'd just as well dig a ditch and take the water to a dry spot. I worked at it during some spare time over the next few days. I had to dig about 50 feet of ditch along a natural slope on the south side of the crick to reach my dry area and then I spread the water across that uneven area by means of small lead ditches. I had gone irrigating with my Dad and the other men lots by that time, so knew the fundamentals of spreading water.

My dry spot was only about 50 feet square, so I soon had it wet. I was so pleased with my main ditch, I got the idea I could keep it in use by building a flume out of it, downstream a little from the main rock dam, and thus run water over top of the main crick and out the north side to a larger dry area. This flume I constructed by means of one long piece of tin bent in a half circle and supported by poles on the sides. I got a head of water out on the north side but my water hit a low spot and ran off back toward the crick. So a lot more shoveling was required and I got a levee built across it and made some lead ditches out of the pond I created in the low spot above my levee.

This all took several days maybe two weeks of part time work to construct. When I was not working on it, I would turn the water back down the crick. I recall I got my system all working, had taken most of the crick through my ditch and flume both, and was irrigating what seemed to me big time when my Dad and Levoy came up from the East crick field and said, "We are irrigating the haymeadow down there but have lost our head of water."

> I sheepishly showed 'em my project. Pa said, "If you are this interested in irrigating, we better get you to work on some of the established system." . . .
>
> I've always felt sure the pleasures I have gotten from irrigating were mine alone and could not be shared with anyone. Not because the feeling was too personal, but because no one I have ever visited with seemed to experience the same thing. So the most I might say when watching the water flow through a freshly shoveled ditch, with green grass on both sides out of which just the right amount of water spread was, "That shore looks good, don't it?"
>
> My hearer would look around, then look at me to see what I was lookin' at, and then say, "Well yes, I guess so."

His letter and the subsequent article included the history of several ditches, former family irrigators, his worst and easiest year, and his own development as an artist with a shovel. Irrigation is as old as the earliest Egyptian and Native American civilizations. Modern Arizona irrigation systems follow miles and miles of canals and ditches laid down by the vanished and ancient Hohokam tribe. Today what we often believe are "natural" streamside willows and cottonwoods were actually planted by Native people to slow the water's mad rush to the sea, raise a crop of wild rice or willows for baskets, and trap suspended silt for fertilizer. Many "natural" boulders were placed in streambeds by Native Americans or early Hispanic settlers as *huacas*, or water tamers. In *River of Traps,* William deBuys and Alex Harris quote a New Mexico irrigator: "You got to let the water show you. You take your time, and sooner or later the water will show you."

From books like *Cadillac Desert* to articles in *National Geographic*, irrigation has come under the environmental magnifying glass. Water is the lifeblood of the West, and every inch of what is available has been claimed. Therefore the only way new recreation facilities, housing developments, golf courses, or campgrounds can be built is by buying or taking water away from someone. The popular press gives strong hints about where developers plan to get that water. For instance, by saying that agriculture "takes" 80 percent of California's water and "leaves" domestic, industrial, and environmental interests to vie for the rest, writers are able to slant a reader's response. Environmentalists, many of whom are vegetarians, often fight against their own irrigated food supply. Water is always worth fighting for, and I wrote about water every chance I got.

Flournoy and many other letter writers often gave me personal advice. I was living in Nevada when the following letter came from a cowboy friend back home in Texas. I must have written an earlier letter about quitting a Christmas cooking job in tears because the ranch owner kept giving me suggestions for improvement and insisted that I cook without salt or pepper.

> Dear Barney, I hope by now you have settled down and recovered from your Christmas holiday. I wish I could have been there. He sounds like a sterling fellow, although I have reservations about a man that doesn't use salt and pepper. Obviously he has never had biscuits and gravy with Bill Applegate. Everything here is about the same, just drier. We were west of Marfa the other day on the Hip-O. Off to the west a couple of miles away you could see a stringer of dust rising. It was moving too slow for a pickup, too small for a gathered herd, and it was too still for wind. I kept watching it and it turned out to be 4 or 5 cows and an odd calf or two going to water, not trotting, just shuffling as undisturbed cattle will travel. Well, enough of this drivel, was real good to hear from you and good hunting on your search for the Holy Grail.

That brief letter told me several things. First, I was making a mountain out of a molehill about not being able to use salt and pepper. Bill Applegate absolutely blackened his biscuits and gravy with pepper. If I had been cooking for Applegate, I'd have needed to cook at the other extreme. My friend was trying to tell me, gently, that I needed to adjust to the likes and dislikes of the people who ate the food I cooked and not try to make them change their tastes. In the same way that as a journalist I needed to respect my audience and not insert my opinions, I needed to respect those who ate my cooking and let them decide how much salt and pepper they wanted, because spices are much harder to remove than to add. Juxtaposing his gentle reprimand with his description of the cattle going to water also reminded me what a real tragedy worth crying over looked like. His image helped me picture how hard the country at home was faring during still another heartbreaking drouth. When just a handful of cows can stir up that much dust, it means they must have been walking miles to find grass and miles back for a drink of water. Their water trails had turned to powder. I'm sure my friend's clothes were also hanging on him, as he always lost weight during drouths, trying to make sure those cattle always found the water they had walked so far to find.

Cowboy letters were full of masterfully handled description, imagery, and metaphor. After more than 40 years, I can still hear their voices on the page and still recognize their handwriting. The above letter made me stop and ask myself very seriously just what I was looking for and if I already knew where to find it—maybe in these letters.

Rachel Carson once said, "Only the person who knows and is not afraid of loneliness should aspire to be a writer." One of the few times I got lonesome was during holidays. Family celebrations were always too far, too expensive—and who would feed the livestock and tend the water? So Christmas cards, with a few scribbled words just to me, always held a special spot in my heart, and of course I wrote about them. I have always been sort of a loner, recluse, and introvert. I enjoy people, but in small doses with nice, relaxing stretches of time in between—as long as I get a few letters. The few I still get are some of my most treasured possessions and still result in kernels of wisdom I find worth pondering. Computers have ruined all this wonderful letter writing and even Christmas cards. Today even I mail a mass-produced Thanksgiving/Christmas letter to friends once a year. Even though it arrives typed, I create it as I would a handwritten letter, sitting in my favorite chair, probably drinking coffee and watching birds and critters come in for a drink. But I know it's not the same. It's not a personal letter.

CHAPTER THREE

School

"Basic SEAL training is six months of long torturous runs in the soft sand, midnight swims in the cold water off San Diego, obstacle courses, unending calisthenics, days without sleep and always being cold, wet and miserable. It is six months of being constantly harassed by professionally trained warriors who seek to find the weak of mind and body and eliminate them from ever becoming a Navy SEAL."

—Admiral William H. McRaven

I REMEMBER STANDING around a campfire one rainy morning while the o6 cowboy crew was cussing and discussing education. I complained that my writing students didn't come to class, didn't do their homework, and didn't listen. So one by one, the cowboys started telling stories about school. Most of them claimed they never went to class, never did their homework or listened to the teacher. I knew them. Some had more money than others, but they all had pretty good lives and it didn't seem related to how many years they spent in school. Some had quit college after the second day, some lasted almost a year, some seemed to have spent half their lives in college. Some were better hands, some had happier marriages, maybe better kids, maybe better health. But again, it had nothing to do with school.

If I remember correctly, two of us were doctors (one MD; one PhD), several hadn't finished high school, one had a forestry degree, two had law degrees. One was called a preacher and several eventually became one. Several had agriculture degrees, one a degree in dancing. Several were musicians or artists or owned their own businesses. Three of us spoke no English, at least three spoke no Spanish, and the one we all respected the most could neither read nor write nor speak correctly in any language. Two had ancestors on the *Mayflower*; two had ancestors who met the boat. Three were illegal immigrants, one of those from Canada. Two homeschooled their children; one sent them to a private school. Several didn't believe in children. One had everything he owned in a war bag that was sitting out there in the rain. One of us was probably worth several million dollars. One, we all agreed, was worth absolutely nothing.

Our religions ranged from fundamentalist Christian to atheist to Taoist, Mormon, Ghost Dancer, and luck. We were married, divorced, single, cohabiting, one-night-standing, and abstaining, either by choice or not. Three of us were alcoholic; two went to meetings and one didn't. One smoked pot. We ranged in age from seventy to ten, our politics from red or blue radical to who the hell cares? We were one Sioux, one Apache, one African American, one Australian, four Hispanics, one British-Irish-German-Scottish-French, and God only knows what else. Four of us were female. We were almost all wearing hats or caps, boots, spurs, and slickers in various stages of wear and tear and cleanliness. Hunkered down in our slicker collars with rain dripping off hat brims, the only points we all agreed on were that the rain was good and we didn't learn to do what we were doing in school.

One who had made it to graduation told a story on himself about feeling very smart after he came home from college. Now that he was the manager, he was not going to do things the way Grandpa did. One thing he had learned at school was to put bluestone in the water troughs to kill moss and keep the water clear and sparkling. At first the horses refused to drink it, but when they finally did, that pretty water made all the horses sick.

Everybody laughed.

The rain had stopped. The boss threw the last of his coffee on the ground and his tin cup in the galvanized dishpan. We followed his lead. We all stepped down off our high horses and scattered to mount our real ones and get back to work. In spite of our differences, we depended on each other, even though no two people rode the same way or possessed the same skills. A good team is not a bunch of clones. No—we definitely did not learn to do what we were doing in school.

I started school in one of those quintessential one-room country schools: thirteen kids, kindergarten through eighth grade. My little brother had no classmates. I had one, a girl named Pepper Merrick. Our school was a no-frills-but-sturdy, hand-sawn wooden schoolhouse painted white. A neighbor we called Grandpa Mack had probably sawn the lumber from trees cleared off the hilltop where it stood. We had two wooden outhouses and a potbellied cast-iron heating stove that burned wood someone chopped and split, although one classmate remembered that it burned coal. I remember drinking water from a bucket with a ladle. I'm not sure if that water came from a spring or well, but someone had to fetch it. I'm not sure if we had electricity, but we did have big glass windows to let in light and fresh air. We sat at iron/wooden desks nailed to the floor in rows. We had a chalkboard, chalk, erasers, and a few worn books. We did not have any playground equipment, so instead of going up and down, round and round, or back and forth, we explored nearby fields and timber, inventing games and observing nature up close (especially nettles, poison ivy, poison oak, and poison sumac). In the winter we had snow for sledding, playing fox and goose, making angels, and building forts for fighting wars. We had a flagpole for the big kids to persuade the little kids to stick their tongues on. We all walked to and from school, no matter the weather, in clothes lovingly handmade by our mothers and grandmothers. We carried yummy home-butchered, home-cooked, and garden-raised lunches in metal pails. When the weather was warm, we loved to go barefoot and picnic outside on the grass.

Our teacher's name was Lois Keeney. I don't remember any drills, assignments, or homework. Everything we did at school was fun. We read wonderful books about animals, got to draw numbers on the chalkboard, sometimes even with colored chalk, had Big Chief tablets to write our stories in and fat pencils to write with. I'm sure the first sentence I ever wrote with my fat pencil had something to do with agriculture.

We had recess whenever we got sleepy or fidgety. During recess, Mrs. Keeney's husband sometimes showed up to coach baseball. Our school owned one cracked bat that had been nailed or screwed back together. Someone had wrapped a rag around it so we wouldn't get splinters. Baseball turned out to be a very complicated game with too many rules. We preferred no rules. Plus, we didn't have enough kids for teams, just a batter and fielders. Batters could run the bases either forward or backward to keep the fielders guessing. The whole point was just to wake up and burn energy anyway. When we got hot and tired or cold and tired, we could go back to our cool building or warm stove and read books again. We all walked to school in black four-buckle overshoes, which we left in the mudroom because they smelled of manure and put on again during recess to keep our shoes dry. We usually got only one new pair of shoes a year.

When our little one-room school closed about 1954, we country kids were bused to a bigger school in town, where I became more and more ashamed of that one-room hick school, my hick overshoes full of manure, and being a hick farmer's kid. The girls at the town school all wore red overshoes with fur around the top. I would keep my four-buckles on until I got on the school bus and then kick them off and hide them under my seat. My feet got cold and wet on the playground, and I ruined my shoes.

One day many years later, on the University of Nevada–Reno campus while working toward a PhD, I found myself standing in library stacks where bound periodicals were housed, skimming yet another article, searching for I did not yet know what, when some words jumped off the page. The title was "First They Changed My Name." The author had been raised in Tumbling Creek, Tennessee, until she was "dragged, wailing and sobbing, onto the school bus" to begin her education. In first grade, the teacher told her she was mispronouncing and misspelling her name and "corrected" Caffilene to Kathleen. In second grade, the teacher said Kathleen had to add a middle name, so she chose Barbara. Her mother, whose own formal education had stopped at third grade, believed "teachers were the keepers of some noble and powerful system upon which our survival and well-being depended, and we would be nothing less than ungrateful fools if we questioned their sterling wisdom." By the fifth grade, an "increasingly ashamed" Kathleen "almost came to despise" her mother "for her manner and speech." Education she said, "taught me to hate my culture." Evidently, after her mother's death, Dr. Kathleen Allen realized what her education had done to her as well as for her and took back her name, Caffilene. The author's note at the bottom of the article said that Caffilene Allen, PhD, was teaching English at Georgia State University and was a program analyst with the U.S. Environmental Protection Agency.

Of all the things I had read up to that point in my own education, nothing else stands out before or since as so life changing. From that day onward, I never again felt ashamed of those four-buckle overshoes, that one-room school, or my rural roots. I wrote a letter to the editor of the newspaper nearest the Iowa town where I thought Mrs. Keeney probably still lived. Alongside my heartfelt thank-you letter, the editor included a note saying Mrs. Keeney had died two years prior.

A few years later, I read another memorable article, this time in the *Chronicle of Higher Education*, titled "Here's Smarty-Pants, Home for the Holidays." It described the frustrations that PhD candidates had with their families. A counselor recommended that students empathize with family members and said, "When you are more educated than your parents, there's going to be an element of insecurity that gets played out at family gatherings. There is a real fear that you're smarter, going to be more successful, leave them behind, stop visiting them . . . [and] you are becoming a person they can't connect with intellectually or financially." Basically, the article said that once a person becomes educated, they probably can't go back to their uneducated communities, can't ever go back home.

Well, I went home.

However, I certainly didn't find any cowboys displaying insecurities about me being smarter because of my degree. Nobody was intimidated. They simply changed all the Aggie, North Dakota, or blonde jokes they ever heard to PhD jokes. How many PhD's does it take to change a lightbulb? Nobody knows, but they have three committees working on it. They said PhD stood for "posthole digger" or "piled higher and deeper." I had to constantly prove I hadn't lost all the sense I might have once had. Cowboys also seemed to enjoy entertaining me with their personal versions of an old cowboy poem about a cowboy applying to college: The dean asked him how his grammar was, and he said, "She's dead." But the cowboy *did* know which end of a horse to put the bridle on. Even the late Charles Krauthammer warned against becoming a smarty-pants: "You don't want to talk in highfalutin', ridiculous abstractions that nobody understands."

I also started researching one-room schools. Old photographs supported authors' claims that the children were so poor that they often had no shoes, ate on the ground, and wore makeshift clothes. The books described the poverty, squalor, poor education, poor teachers, shoddy workmanship, lonely lives, substandard heating-cooling-lighting, unimproved roads, isolation, and barren-nonexistent playgrounds. The books claimed that the children had no playgrounds and no "decent" schools because the uneducated farmers did not value education. What? I was shocked at how deeply wrong "facts" about someone else's world could be. So I wrote about that.

Old maps show that schoolhouses were built at the same time the first log cabins were built. Periodically, farmers who had school-aged children met to decide everything, from hiring and how much to pay the next year's teacher to whose turn it was to clean the privy. They divided up the work and the costs. Every penny and every hour of labor came from the parents of the children. Those schools were completely self-supporting. I have an old notebook where one grandfather kept records of his school expenses. In my particular school we had around thirteen pupils from six different families, and none of us attended the same church. I'm not sure if costs were divided six equal ways, by number of acres owned, by number of children, or by voluntary contributions. Those neighbors had to decide. What modern parent cares that much about their child's education? Farmers wrote our constitution. We teach several of their journals and letters as "classic" American literature. As Thomas Jefferson once said, "Ours are the only farmers who can read Homer." I have never known an uneducated farmer or rancher. My family genealogy shows that at least one grandmother and one great-grandmother had been one-room-school teachers. More ancestors probably held that position too but we have no record.

People then and now like to stereotype farmers as dumb "hayseeds." In reality, people in agriculture have not only learned but can actually apply math, physics, chemistry, biology, zoology, psychology, economics, finance—you name it. Every pioneer Iowa farm boy who had been taught math by a girl often younger than he was could figure out in five seconds, without benefit of pencil and paper, how much it would cost and what kind of lumber would be needed to build a country school, thirty-two by twenty-two feet, with a belfry, a coat and mudroom, six windows, and a shingled roof. He wouldn't have enough scrap lumber left over to build a silly teeter-totter.

Authors of the books about rural schools said the farmers fought consolidation of their little schools because they did not want to lose their free child labor or control of their children's minds. Maybe that's half-right. Once the country schools closed, most Americans stopped respecting hard work and stopped treating children like future adults. But controlling our minds was not so easy—chuckle. My parents said nightly prayers to give strength to our country schoolteacher. If I got in trouble at school, I got in double trouble at home. Our little school was forced to close when I started fourth grade. By then, I could read almost anything, write in cursive, and do simple long division. I've taught many freshman college students, raised in urban areas where millions of taxpayer dollars had been spent on their schools and where teachers earned six-figure salaries, who could not do those three things.

The last of the one-room schools closed in Iowa in 1980. After it was too late, historians discovered that the perception of substandard learning and need for "reform" was simply not true. Since the first census, Iowa had consistently maintained the lowest level of illiteracy in the nation. By 1940 only 4 percent of Iowans had fewer than five years of schooling, compared to New England at 10 percent and the continental United States in general at 14 percent. According to a U.S. Department of Education document published in 1993, "Iowa students led the nation in terms of average ACT and SAT scores, a position Iowa has held every year save one since these test scores have been published." Those top scores were accumulated during the years when Iowa still held on to many of its rural one-room schools. Iowa has also posted the lowest percentage of illiterate residents in every U.S. census, except 1990 when it temporarily dropped to second. From 1870 to 1950, Iowa usually ranked among the top five states in percentage of school-age children enrolled in school. All this happened not in spite of but because of those one-room country schools and those "uneducated" farmers who didn't care about education. I think the same is true about those "crummy" one-newspaper towns. Growth for the sake of growth produces cancer, not improvements, and "rural" does not equal "uneducated."

Education in the rural world goes well beyond books and begins with observation. Once upon a time I thought I wanted to be an artist, but until an art teacher pointed it out, I had never noticed that the sky was lighter at the horizon than straight overhead, even though by that time I'd spent almost twenty years looking at that sky. In college, my range plant identification professor would ask, "Is that blue grama or black?" When someone asked me if a red-tailed hawk tail looked red from the top or the bottom, for many years it seemed that my end of conversations consisted of mostly, "I dunno."

Observation is the secret to being both a good writer and a good cowboy, but nobody knows just how deeply that runs. A good cowboy can make John McPhee and Henry Thoreau look like they stumbled around half-asleep. Cowboys are ruthless teachers. Since they don't like being told how to do something, they don't like to tell beginners how to do anything either. Besides, keen observation is the one thing a prospective cowboy needs above all else. Long after I thought I'd finally become at least a beginner cowboy, some steely-eyed man who didn't want women on the crew in the first place would ride up to me and ask, "How many was in that bunch you just brought in?"

"Er, ah . . . I dunno."

"How many calves?"

"Dunno."

"Did that cow you brought in with the yearling have a calf?"

"Dunno."

"Well, was she dry or wet?"

"Dunno."

"Where'd you pick her up?"

"Dunno."

He'd glare at me for a second and ride off. The next time, I'd pay better attention: look to see if cows and calves were paired up, remember where I found them, look to see if the cows had been sucked. I'd check the calves' genders, look for slicks, look for branded calves that were still bulls, estimate all their ages, estimate their weights, look for pinkeye or for white spots in an old cow's eye. I'd expect praise, but instead one of them would ride up and ask, "Was that windmill pumping?"

"Dunno."

"Had a vehicle been back there lately?"

"Dunno."

"Was that gate shut?"

"Dunno."

"Was there any feed left back in there?"

"Dunno."

He'd glare at me for a second and ride off. So the next time, I'd remember everything anyone could possibly want to know about the country I was working. I'd remember all the animals I was bringing in, every detail about the water system, fences, and roads. I'd note any wild animals that someone might want to hunt: where they were bedding down, their genders, general health, what they'd been eating, what trails they were using, where they were watering, whether their hair was straight or curly, what direction the wind was blowing, what direction they looked when they first noticed me, how many millimeters had been grazed off each blade of grass, and what the hell color the rocks were. I'd count flies and buzzards and filaree and coyote tracks until I had a headache.

Then one of them would ride up and ask, "Do you know your horse has throwed a shoe?" Or my favorite: "You better tighten that cinch."

Shit.

Cowboy school is mostly making mistakes, surviving, vowing never to do that again, and promising to pay better attention next time.

I made lots of mistakes and bucked off a lot of horses, who were also my teachers. I suppose I should talk about bucking off because I'm sure my teacher horses probably thought I was a very slow learner. I figured out several ways to get bucked off, but it seemed to happen mostly because of my bad habit of pulling up when things got fast. Cowboys are not supposed to pull up and horses don't like to be left behind, so quite often my horses just decided to go on without me. I remember once when I tried to get myself and three kids bucked off. We were moving one hundred or so remuda horses from one place to another, one of my favorite things to do as long as everything stayed under control. One hundred horses, strung out and trotting across rocky country, provide a beautiful sight and sound. The earth trembles.

Even better is to see them all stretched out and running, as long as I'm not in there among them, jumping brush or dodging rocks and holes in rotten ground. After a few moves from place to place, the horses usually establish their pecking order and settle down. Two horsemen can usually move them—one in front to hold the lead and set the pace, and one behind to bring up the lollygaggers. Even if the horses run, as long as the cowboy in the lead can ride fast enough to stay in front, the remuda will all gradually slow down when his lead horse slows down. So the secret is never to lose the lead. I panicked when things got fast, so obviously I never volunteered to point the remuda. Only once was I ever asked to do so by a boss, I'll call him Chris Lacy.

We were coming out of a big mountain horse pasture where the extra remuda horses had been turned out to graze and rest between spring and fall work, my first time to help gather them. As we climbed out on the trail to headquarters, the barefooted horses, somewhat sore-footed, trailed each other single file at a walk. Nice and slow, just like I like it. When we got to the last gate and the trail leading down to the shipping traps, the boss asked me to take the lead and hold them up. Taking the point was not usually a job anyone asked me to do. But I was riding a new custom-built saddle and wearing new custom-built Mercer boots and some chink leggings with twelve-inch fringe. I felt about as punchy as I looked. I was also feeling quite proud of myself because I hadn't gotten lost in the maze of canyons we'd just come out of, so I tightened the stampede string on my hat and took the lead like I knew what I was doing. Thinking back, my biggest wrecks in both the cowboy world and publishing usually followed close on the heels of feeling proud of myself and getting cocky.

Well, as we came down the side of the mountain and into the headquarters traps, the ground leveled out and the dirt deepened. Good ground, good running ground, even for sore-footed horses. The lead horses started picking up speed, so I trotted out ahead, holding the lead. They kept getting a little faster and spreading out, trying to pass me on both sides. Pretty soon the lead was fifty horses abreast and all of us running wide open. Too fast! I tried hard to pull my horse up. Luckily he was too busy running to buck me off. I looked back over my shoulder once and could see those big white Lacy teeth shining in the sun. Everybody but me knew that from that last gate on was a free-for-all. Nobody could hold those horses because they felt that soft ground and knew where they were going. So of course the cowboys all thought it was very funny. In the cowboy world, anything short of fatal is funny. Remember that.

Anyway, back to this other day moving horses with the kids. My little daughter and two of the boss's kids wanted to ride along as the remuda trotted across country to the next camp. The kids, ranging from four to six, were all good little riders, and the remuda had been handled several times lately with no running. Most kids raised on farms and ranches learn to be useful at very early ages—gathering eggs, feeding animals, cleaning pens—sometimes receiving small paychecks by the time they are five years old. But mostly what they earn is self-respect. Adults need and praise them, which is more important than wages. By the time they are thirteen, they have learned how to treat the boss and each other with respect and can be trusted with responsibility, and they might finally be worth some better wages. Are there risks? Of course. But it's not as risky as turning loose on the world a middle school dropout or a college graduate who has never held a job. It takes a village to raise a kid, no matter how old they are. So off we went, me and the kids riding drag. But the day was a little too cool. When the horses hit the flats and found some good running ground, they were off.

I started trying to pull up, thinking I could use the kids as an excuse and their kid horses as company for my horse. But when I looked around, the little brats were grinning and leaning forward, whipping and spurring their poor old lazy kid ponies for more speed. I could see the situation was hopeless, and since by this time I'd already been bucked off several times for trying to pull up, I just screwed down my hat and rode. After a few miles, the cowboy in the lead finally got hold of the horses again and we slowed back to a trot. The kids loved it. Even I smiled because the kids were still alive and my heart was still beating—I could hear it. And, as one old cowboy we called Uncle Arb always used to say, "And I thanked God that'n was over."

Another memorable runaway happened at night. I was tagging along, riding drag again, and got a taste of what it must have felt like to ride with a stampede. The last pasture we had to cross in the dark included an old dump. The horses knew they were almost home for the night and so took off across the dump in the pitch dark. My horse crashed through an old clay sewer drain and fell—falling is the main reason I don't like speed. Somehow I must have kicked out of the stirrups, landed on my feet, and started running toward the pens, trying to stay within shouting distance of the horses. I knew the others would see my saddled horse come through the gate, figure I was hurt, and make another wild ride across that treacherous pasture in the dark. I kept hollering that I was okay but knew they couldn't hear me over the thunder of running horses. Finally I heard someone shout my name when he saw my saddled horse with no rider. I hollered back and then of course the cowboys thought it was funny. I soon wished I had just hidden in the grass and let them look for me until daylight or until they all broke their damn necks, whichever came sooner. One of my great frustrations was that I always figured out what I should have done or said after it was too late.

Well, I promised I would write about bucking off and instead I've been writing about runaways. I'm getting there, but it is all related and hard to know where to begin because you need to know this background to understand why I kept bucking off and why the horses probably thought I was a slow learner. Okay. Here goes.

One time we were leaving the barn on a morning circle and my horse kept getting slower and slower, finally stretching out to pee. The rest of the cowboys kept trotting faster and faster, leaving us behind. By this time in my cowboy education, I knew I'd get bucked off if we got behind, so I spurred him to catch up. Well, I guess he really had to pee.

Another time I had a bunch of expensive camera equipment hanging around my neck and stuffed in vest pockets. We were heading out on a circle at a trot and my cameras were banging on my boobs, so I tried to pull old Serrucho up. When Serrucho went sailing by with my empty saddle, without turning around to even look, one of the cowboys in the lead hollered back, "Did your cameras break?"—hoping for a yes, I'm sure.

Another time we were gathering a trap close to the barn and the cattle were trotting off. My horse and I were getting behind, so I just let my horse start trotting too.

Another time we were just quietly leaving the barn, no cattle, no other horses.

Another time—oh well, you get the picture. My buck-off stories are pretty short and repetitive. It didn't seem to matter if I pulled up or spurred up or let him do what he wanted to do or did nothing. One jump—bam! It was over. I can't even make these moments into decent stories or even explain what happened because I never *knew* what happened. Cowboys, of course, don't have that problem. They can make a story out of nothing.

It is sort of an old cowboy saying that when a person bucks off (or falls off in my case), they "own" the piece of ground they land on. They "bought" it. Maybe the 06 Ranch owners were getting nervous about how much of the ranch their cowboys were starting to own, especially me, but in any event, Chris Lacy, our boss and great-grandson of the outfit, had heard stories about some horse trainer and brought him in to stop the cowboys from "buying" so much country. The boss's idea was about as popular as anything human resources departments bring in to "help" urban employees, so I didn't plan to go. However, one of the cowboys said that this trainer supposedly had the participants take the first ride with nothing on their colts' heads. No hackamore, no snaffle, no halter, no rope—nothing. It sounded like learning to drive a car without a steering wheel. Now *that* sounded like cowboy news. So I went.

That first time I watched and wrote about him, Ray Hunt was about fifty, sort of average tall, average weight, and average looking. He limped a little on a clubfoot he was born with. He stood in the middle of a round pen and talked briefly about the intelligence of the horse. He didn't tell us where he'd been, the horses he'd trained, the famous trainers he knew, or that his technique was better than ours, so I tried to write about him that way. He just said that this was "a colt-breaking clinic," but he didn't really like the word *breaking* and asked if we'd send our children to a "child breaker." He preferred to be called a teacher and quietly led a two-year-old filly into the round pen. Although he didn't pronounce or use all his words the way Webster would like, he turned out to be the best teacher I ever knew.

Leaning on the outside of the round pen were successful cutting horse trainers, horse breakers, sweet little old ladies, cowboys, ropers, pretty girls, and college horsemanship teachers. All had their own reasons for being there. Some came for the show, some because they had their arms twisted. A few had stayed up until 3 A.M. listening to a friend tell them about Ray's horse Barry. So I decided to write about Barry.

Through the morning, as bronc after bronc was roped, handled, saddled, and turned out to soak with the saddle, Barry never lost his patience. Ray would say, "You might not need your horse to take a step. Just lean to the right." Barry leaned to the right. "Or you might need him to lean to the left." Barry leaned left. "Or maybe lean back." Barry almost sat on his tail. "Or forward," and Barry leaned out over his nose. "You want your horse to be relaxed and soft," and Ray would pull Barry's head around into his lap, sliding one hand down the rein. "Now, you're probably thinking this ol' rubber-necked horse can't work, but he knows the difference between this"—he pulled Barry's head into his lap in the other direction—"and this"—he did something I couldn't even see and Barry became a spinning blur. The folks around the pen wondered who was really the colt breaker—or we should say teacher—Ray or Barry. The watchers constantly elbowed the person standing next to them: "Did you see that?!"

Ray Hunt didn't preach, condemn, embarrass, or correct. He was a teacher. He knew the folks standing outside the round pen were already pretty good hands or they wouldn't be there ready to climb on a bronc with no reins. Ray didn't tell anyone they had a long way to go, but by lunch break most were shaking their heads and saying it themselves. He punctuated his instruction with philosophy and humor. Leading a new bronc on a loose rope around the pen he might say, "I've had people tell me they don't know what's wrong with their stupid horse. They've even pulled him around with a tractor and he still doesn't lead." Everyone laughed, but the laughs were often guilty little self-conscious ones; mine was.

At no time did Ray and Barry confine or make the bronc accept anything. The bronc always had a choice between an escape route, a way to get away—which might involve running (work)—and a way to get immediate relief, an immediate reward (rest). "Make the wrong thing difficult and the right thing easy," Ray repeated over and over. His goal was an eager, willing student that was working his ears and watching, trying to understand, instead of a tense, frightened animal submitting.

When Ray Hunt went to feed his horses, ten to fifteen cowboys soon gathered around. If he went to wash his horses' backs, the same crowd showed up. Some probably followed him to the bathroom. Some "got religion" and would never ride another bronc with anything on its head for the first saddle. Maybe a few never tried it again. One thing I was certain of: none of the fifteen bronc riders and none of the spectators who watched Barry and Ray Hunt work together and saw how fast those colts learned would ever call another horse "stupid."

While Ray worked the colts in a round pen, he told stories to help us get the point he was trying to make. I especially liked his stories about school: "We don't learn to reason," said Ray. "We don't learn to compare. When a child gets up in the morning, we tell him to go wash his face, go comb his hair, sit down, eat his breakfast, put on his coat, go to school. When they get to school the teacher says, 'Color this little Indian here. Color the hair black, the moccasins buckskin. Make the feathers all different colors—this one's green, this one's blue, this one's red, this one's yellow.' We tell the child everything to do. So later on, when you ask the child what he wants to do, he says, 'I dunno.' We're born with this 'brain damage' Bill Cosby talks about. If a child was really working and hadn't wrote his name yet, but he was trying to, and the teacher slapped him upside the head and took that pencil away from him and said, 'Like this, dummy,' how many times do you think he'd want to come to school? Or if he was trying to spell a word and he was working at it and thinking about it and the teacher said, 'What the hell's the matter—you tongue-tied?' You think he's gonna want to spell?" I carried a tape recorder and have put quotation marks around Ray's words. I would not want to trust my memory. I knew I did not understand everything I was hearing or seeing, and I worked hard to report accurately without adding my own interpretations.

Ray was funny and we laughed a lot. But sometimes we didn't. Ray came from the old school of horse breakers who waded into a round corral, slung a rope around a bronc's neck, tied up a foot, rolled the son of a gun into a saddle, stepped aboard, and turned everything loose. He could ride as fast and as high as a horse could run or buck. Then one day, he said, he met a horse with more potential than he had ever felt, but his old methods would not work. Instead of creating a winner, he was creating a nervous wreck. So an old Oregon buckaroo, Tom Dorrance, introduced Ray to some gentler methods. But *gentle* isn't the right word, because sometimes, if a horse has been taught to disrespect humans and take over, those gentle methods might become very tough. When a horse has learned disrespect and bad habits, his next destination is usually dog food. Helping a spoiled horse that had no respect for humans sometimes involved blood, and Ray might ask the owner to price the horse. Ray wanted to buy it so that if the owner decided Ray was being too rough, the owner couldn't stop him. It was not a matter of pride. Ray knew he was that horse's last best chance. Through the years, I saw Ray hurt a few horses—I even saw him kill a horse once—but never from anger or for revenge, always while trying to help the horse become useful and save its life.

As a teacher, my classroom methods were also usually very gentle, but on those rare occasions when I used harsher methods, it was because I didn't know what else to do. I had already tried everything else. Running out of answers was never the reason Ray used harsher methods. He never wanted to start anything that he couldn't finish because if he did, that horse would be even worse for the next person who tried. The attitude behind a teacher's methods, whether gentle or rough, should always be communication—never punishment. If a horse bites or kicks me, according to Ray I should just bear the pain. Anything I do after it happens would be too late and would be punishment or retaliation instead of teaching. A good horse teacher should feel the horse preparing to bite or kick and head it off. That sounds easy to do, but every situation depends on being able to read and feel the circumstances accurately, being aware of one's own contribution to the situation or psychological projections, and then figuring out a solution. Ray was exactly the kind of teacher I wanted to be and the kind I wanted to write about.

Ray didn't like to "fix" a horse and then send it back to the owner. That wouldn't work any better than sending a kid to a rehabilitation center and then sending him home. Ray needed to watch both horse and rider, but he didn't act as a referee. Neither Ray nor Tom liked to give advice in a book or over the phone. What they tried to do, I think, was watch horse and rider try to work together, help them "listen to" (feel) each other better, help horse understand rider, help rider understand horse. Their goal was clear communication.

A few years later, Ray and Tom's method was called horse whispering and was made into a movie. But nobody whispered. That was a goofy Hollywood twist—not the real thing. The real thing is figuring out how to get just enough positive response to start building on, not doing too much and not doing too little or too late. Sometimes it takes less than a feather stroke. Sometimes it takes every muscle and maybe a two-by-four. If the horse teacher doesn't have much skill, knowledge, or know-how to teach it, then, as Ray Hunt would say, "Don't start nuthin' you can't finish."

That reminds me of a story an old friend told me once. I'll call him Wally. It's a funny story about what cowboy school looks like in real life. I love Wally's stories because he is never the hero. To the uninitiated, he never does anything right, never succeeds at anything. People who never make mistakes make me feel bad. So I like to stand next to Wally because he makes me feel competent. I tried hard to remember that as a journalist and as a teacher, my goal was to build my students' or readers' competence and confidence, not to prove my own smartness.

My favorite of Wally's quixotic misadventures concerns a spoiled red mule he was trying to retrain for Yellowstone National Park rangers. Whoever had started the red mule had failed to teach her how to lead properly, and as more people tried and failed, her habits had gotten very ingrained. Wally was an old-school buckaroo but had also been a devoted student of Ray Hunt for several years, so he had learned and mastered Ray's wiser methods. Wally would never claim to be a master, but some masters might bestow that title on him. I did.

Wally had been ordered to take five National Park Service secretaries out into the mountains on a pack trip and bring them back safely. While the girls sunbathed in their underwear, Wally decided he needed a distraction, so he and his saddle horse set out down a trail with the red mule following on the end of a halter rope. When they came to a spot where the trail crossed a four-inch-wide and four-inch-deep creek, the mule refused to cross. So the mule in the saddle stacked up about five dallies and started across. The halter rope snapped.

Next the mule in the saddle traded the halter for his fairly unbreakable nylon rope and rigged up a cowboy-style "war bridle"—a complicated way to place a nylon rope around an animal's head and nose to inflict discomfort, choke off some air, pinch, rub hair loose, and in general cause the animal to behave much worse than under any other circumstances. A cowboy using a war bridle has probably already lost his own temper, but in skilled hands, a war bridle prevents actual murder because if tied and used correctly, it can't completely cut off air and provides immediate relief as soon as the animal takes one step in the right direction. To the uninitiated the theory behind using one, probably seems to expose every nasty part of both rider and horse's personalities, find out that none of it works, eventually regain their lost tempers out of sheer exhaustion, come to some kind of stubborn truce, and go on with life as though nothing happened.

That may seem to be exactly what happened here, but neither Wally nor the red mule are in this book to tell their own story, so beware. Wally likes to tell his stories as though he doesn't know what he is doing, but he does. The listener needs to pay careful attention. Anyway, about an hour later, Wally said he had torn the little breast collar D-ring out of the front of his fairly new and very expensive buckaroo saddle, had totally skint up the red mule's head, and had sweat dripping off his own nose. When he stopped to breathe, he looked up to see the shining young faces of a band of Boy Scouts. The boys were patiently sitting on a rock, watching to see what they could learn from Uncle Wally. Since Uncle Wally, his trusty steed, and the red mule had been all over the trail, the scouts had been unable to pass but had been quite able to watch and listen. So Uncle Wally sheepishly got out of their way.

I'm sure those Boy Scouts learned some new words that day, witnessed firsthand the dark side of cowboy temperament, vowed never to get close to a mule or a cowboy ever again, and had probably taken some great snapshots to sell to animal rights activists.

Did Wally succeed in his quest and get the red mule to lead better? Of course! As Ray Hunt would say, Wally wears a big hat and makes a lot of noise when he walks. If Wally starts something, he will finish it. The red mule kept its nose right in the tail of Wally's horse all the way home, eventually stepping on the heels of Wally's horse and pulling off a shoe. That's probably the funniest story I ever heard because he did too good of a job. It's always hard to know when enough is enough. So I wrote about Wally and the red mule in my little local newspaper column.

Many cowboy stories are funny, so most people think storytelling is a time for socialization and laughter. Not for me. I'm in school, although school doesn't have to be serious all the time. I might tell a story and then listen very carefully to the stories told in return. As Ray would say, making good decisions comes from experience and experience comes from making poor decisions. Cowboys especially like to tell stories about their poor decisions. They don't like to give advice openly, but they might trade screw-up stories with me, and if I paid close attention, I might avoid having to make the same mistakes they had already made. That's the reason I tell the stories I do in this book.

Another of my master teachers was an "uneducated" old camp cook, Ramón Hartnett. He hitched his chuckwagon to a pickup, but otherwise he operated like the old traditional pot rack and Dutch oven wagon cooks who went up the trail, just the way cowboys like it. As a young man he had apprenticed under Gavino Romero. Ramón considered himself fluently bilingual, speaking both English and Spanish. However, the rest of the world kinda considered him no-lingual since he butchered both languages—although nobody was ever brave enough to tell him. By the time I started hanging around, he was already past the age when most men retire.

Ramón became my role model partly because he did a job none of the cowboys wanted to do—cook. He also took it upon his shoulders to teach wagon etiquette to greenhorns. I had already decided that the best way to start worming my way into tagging along was to make friends with the cook and to take on jobs that nobody else wanted to do. That was the way I got most of the jobs I ever had. Another job none of the cowboys wanted was fetching groceries for the cook. Ramón never learned to read or write, so he couldn't write down a grocery list. Someone had to write one for him as he shook spice cans and smelled them or peered into the nooks and crannies of his chuck box to figure out what was missing or running low. Most people, including bosses and owners, walked on eggshells around an old master chuckwagon cook. Good wagon cooks who produced great meals were bulletproof when it came to firing. A wagon outfit can't operate without a cook, and cowboys refuse to work for an outfit that skimps on food.

So Ramón was the most valuable member of the crew and drew the highest wages, and if he quit—well, where were we gonna find another one? He couldn't be replaced. Women who think cooks get no respect have never hung out around a chuckwagon.

This is the way I remember an early conversation between us when I first started learning to be his grocery fetcher. I'm sure he did not look forward to having to communicate with a dang gringa.

"The boss says you need groceries?" I say and then stand there smiling with my pen and notebook poised.

Ramón turns to the chuck box and starts looking and naming items, sometimes in Spanish, while I write them down. "Papas."

"Okay, potatoes, right?"

"Yes."

And I write down potatoes, probably twenty pounds.

"Manteca."

"Lard?"

The cook responds by showing me an almost empty twenty-five-pound can and says, "Ketchum."

I chuckle. "Okay, I know that is Ramónese for ketchup."

Ramón doesn't laugh, shakes a spice can that is almost empty, smells it, and shows me the can so that I can read "cinnamon." He shakes another, smells it, and says, "Pepper." Then he says, "Zapharinos."

I frown and say, "No savvy *zapharinos*."

Ramón frowns and says, "Curds."

"Curds? No savvy *curds*?"

Ramón is getting irritated. This is the reason none of the cowboys want to fetch groceries for him. Nobody wants to get on the wrong side of the cook. He says "curds" louder, like English speakers do to those who can't speak English. Maybe louder again. I'm getting nervous but shrug my shoulders and gesture that I still don't understand. Ramón impatiently makes a motion like pulling taffy between his two hands and says, "Curds! For *ensalada*."

"Cheese? For a salad?"

"No! Aieee!" Ramón is getting mad at me. "Yellow curds!" He makes the stretching motion again.

"Marshmallows?" (That's not as dumb as it sounds because he used marshmallows in one of his salads.)

"No!"

"Parsnips?"

"No! Curds! Yellow curds!"

"Yellow . . . hmmm . . . do you mean *amarillo*?"

"No! *Naranja*!"

"No savvy *naranja*."

"Aiee, Chihuahua!" and the cook rattles off something under his breath that it was probably best I did not understand.

I know I'm about to get fired, but I try one last idea: "Carrots?"

Ramón throws up his hands, "Yes, curds!" He thought that was what he had been saying all along. I did not correct his pronunciation and did not laugh.

The rest of the grocery list went about like that. But we got through it. By the time we reached his last item, we were both in a better humor. He said finally, "Suckers," and he laughed.

I laughed too. What would Hollywood movie producers think of a ranch that furnished Tootsie Pops or Dum Dums to its cowboys? When they sat around horseback holding herd for the cutters after lunch, their jaws were puffed up with little white sucker stems sticking out of each mouth. They looked ridiculous. The 06 didn't believe in furnishing tobacco and hardly anyone smoked, but we did furnish suckers.

Instead of figuring out what to cook before each meal, Ramón had a system that followed the perishable rate of his groceries. The first night after groceries had been delivered, he'd make a salad. After a new hind quarter of beef was delivered, he'd saw off rib eyes. He'd follow the meat down to stews and hash (which he called "hatch") and then start over when the next quarter of beef arrived. After a few roundups, the cowboys knew exactly what would be served at each meal and place. Always menudo here, always spinach with hard-boiled eggs there, always powdered-sugar donuts here, always perro pinto (rice and raisins) at the camp where Perro Pinto the dog lived. Always camp bread and beans and papas every meal. Mistakes didn't happen often, but once at a remote cow camp, the beans must have spoiled and the outhouse got a real workout for a couple of days. Since the outhouse didn't have a door, everyone was nervous when I showed up to get groceries for the cook. Ramón's list was short, and I didn't stay long.

Finally, on the last day of roundup, after he'd used the last sliver of meat from the last quarter of beef, he'd finish up with red enchiladas. The crew would be camped close to the highway, so his wife, Consuelo, would make and bring the red sauce. One of the cowboys once asked her if Ramón did all the cooking at home. She faked being horrified and insulted, "Not in *my* kitchen! He tries to cook there just like he does here. He thinks my floor is dirt." She mimicked him cleaning flour off his hands by brushing them together and letting the flour hit the ground. "And he throws salt at the stove." She mimicked him throwing salt at his skillets. Ramón just looked off in the distance like he was not listening. The cowboys all laughed. Consuelo once brought me a birthday cake when we were camped close to the highway after I had given her lots of pictures of Ramón. I still have some of those grocery lists Ramón and I struggled through together.

Because of the wagon and scenic country, the 06 Ranch often hosted movie crews, artists, and visitors of various stripes. So the cook and his helpers often had to work around someone standing in their way. Especially on cold mornings, when everyone wanted to warm up, the fire was just not big enough, so one or two visitors would stand on Ramón's side of the fire. Ramón would elbow around past them and get a shovelful of coals. Then he'd casually stand behind one culprit and hold that shovelful of glowing coals right under their back pockets until they either felt the heat and moved or caught fire—he didn't much care which. Nobody laughed. After they jumped and moved, Ramón would calmly place his shovelful of coals under the flat piece of steel he used for a pancake griddle. I don't remember anyone dumb enough to need a second treatment. Those of us already trained kept one eye peeled for Ramón when we were near his fire.

He liked to give the cowboys nicknames and was very good at it. Like Rooster for a fancy dresser and Gran Dote for a big ol' guy. I also remember Weasel, Preacher, and Lamb Chop—hard to explain why those nicknames were so funny. Whether he was handing out names, cooking, joking, or silently smoking his evening cigarette, Ramón was always teaching someone something if they paid attention.

Eventually, after I thought I had learned enough to write about him, I did. In the article, I included several of his recipes: camp bread, pan dulce, cherry cobbler, hatch (hash), chili macho, chorizo Mexicano, frijoles con queso, and perro pinto. I watched his every move, photographed most of them, and eventually could cook most of his dishes—but not for twenty men, three meals a day, rain, shine, wind, or snow. The recipe I spent the most time watching was his camp bread, which he called *pan* (Spanish for "bread"). It was mostly one big buttermilk biscuit that he didn't divide into little balls. In the middle of a big dishpan of flour, he'd make a little low place and pour a cup of buttermilk or canned milk into it, one spoonful of salt, one spoonful of baking soda, and the ends of his fingers full of lard or shortening. He'd stir the stuff in the low place together with his hand, gradually flipping flour into it until it formed a soft ball on top of the rest of the flour. He'd lift out the ball and slap it into a hot Dutch oven. He'd pat it out to the edge of the oven like a fat tortilla with his knuckles.

Resting near the fire on a rock or stick of firewood to keep the inside clean, the lid would already be hot with a few coals on top. He'd lift the lid with his gonch hook, place it on the oven, grab the oven handle with the hook, set it on a few coals, and tamp the lid down tight with the hook. Depending on the weather, temperature, number of coals, how hot the coals were, how much the wind was blowing, and other variables, the circle of bread would be ready in just a few minutes, golden and crunchy (more so if he still had buttermilk) on both sides with a biscuit-like texture in the middle. He'd prop the lid back on the rock, tip the circle of hot bread onto a clean rag in his hand, and toss it into a metal bread keeper, usually breaking it at least in two. Then he'd make another batch until the bread box was full. When Ramón called them to eat, the cowboys would break off a chunk of warm camp bread just the size they wanted. The old cook would say mischievously, "Make it thin and they'll eat a lot. Make it thick and they won't eat so much." One of the old remuda horses used to come right into the fire area to beg for a piece of Ramón's pan.

It could have been my imagination, but it seemed like after I wrote about him, Dutch oven cooking went through a revival that's still building steam. So-called chuckwagon cooks and cast-iron cookware are almost common again. But nobody can learn to do what Ramón did by reading a book or following recipes. The food was only part of it.

I called Ramón my *tio* (Spanish for "uncle") and eventually loved him dearly. One Christmas I embroidered some new white aprons with "06 Cocinero" in red across the front. The best gift I ever gave him was a "new" old granite coffeepot I found in an antiques store in Montana. Ramón was in his seventies at the time. Both of his old coffeepots leaked, and he said he couldn't find replacements. I told him I'd give him the one I had found, on the condition that he'd keep cooking long enough to wear it out. He almost made it. When he retired, he gave me an old rolling pin that he had made by shoving a worn-out wooden rolling pin inside a section of gray PVC pipe. I treasured it for years and eventually passed it on to one of his granddaughters.

Ramón taught me to keep my head down, so once I got access to hanging around the wagon, I tried to be the last one to get a plate, in case the cooks ran out of cherry cobbler. The cooks always ate last, and I would have been happy to wait until they'd filled their plates too, but that would have gone against tradition. They wouldn't have liked that. I'm not even sure if my desire to eat last after the cowboys was a good idea. Traditionally cowboys ate first because they had been working. Guests came next and then the cooks. But our boss was a gentleman and expected the men he hired to be too, so I think they all hung back, wanting guests and especially women to eat first. Consequently, I might have unintentionally caused trouble by hanging back. Anyway, eventually we all got fed and got our plates scraped and thrown in the dishpan before dishwashing was over.

Like Ramón, I tried to do whatever job I was given without complaining or seeking attention. I tried to be useful and take the jobs nobody else wanted. A horse needs to go to the vet? Sure. Need a flat tire taken to town? Okay. Hurt cowboy needs a place to stay. Of course. Hold cuts? No problem. Hang back and ride with the kids? Got it. Heel calves? Nah, I'd rather flank. Cowboys love to rope, and in Arizona I did too, but I never learned to dally or teach a horse how to handle a tied-on rope. So I seldom even carried a rope. That way the cowboys could see at a glance that I was not going to want a turn at roping and spoil their fun. Instead I tried to add some fun—but not too much. Teasing and pranks got old quick, both for them and me.

Ramón also taught me to keep my head up. When roundup camped at my house, I sometimes bravely provided early evening "school." As soon as the sun went down, I'd set up my projector outside and project slides from my latest ranch visit onto the side of a shed or barn. The cowboys could learn about places and ways of doing things they'd never seen. I learned more too, as they pointed out details I had missed. They helped me choose slides and possible "news" for my next article. But I kept one eye on Ramón, careful to run out of slides when I saw him head to his camper for the night.

In 1982, when Ramón turned seventy, he and his apprentice finished cooking early and walked down to the branding pen to watch. The pen was small, so the calves had been separated from their mothers. Tommy Vaughn was riding a gentle colt and heeling calves, bringing them to the branding fire. He saw the cook and his apprentice leaning on the fence, rode over, stepped off, and offered his colt to Ramón. He said, "Here, Cookie, rope a few." Ramón handed his apron to his apprentice, climbed stiffly over the fence, and tightened the cinch. Tommy helped him mount. The two other cowboys who had been roping in the pen stopped, got off, and hobbled their horses outside the pen. Everyone was nervous. One said, "Cookie needs a hat, not that damn cap, just in case." Nobody else volunteered, so I offered Ramón my hat because it had a stampede string on it. Ramón reluctantly took it and tightened the stampede string at the insistence of the cowboys. They told him he couldn't rope without a "helmet." Then they all stood at ready alert to help the old cook. Ramón tied the rope hard and fast to the saddle horn—Arizona style. Being tied on seemed even more dangerous to the branding pen full of dally ropers, especially on a colt! So the cowboys became even more watchful, wondering if they should really let him do this.

Tommy said, "I've never tied on. Not sure what my colt will do."

Someone else said, "What if we kill the cook?"

Too late! Being tied to a colt that hadn't learned everything yet didn't bother Ramón. He had already headed toward the calves, swung his loop once, and dragged one to the fire by two feet. Perfect! The cowboys cheered and flanked his calf. As soon as a flanker threw his rope off the calf's heels, Ramón headed back in, brought out another, then another, then another.

Pretty soon Ramón had everyone scrambling to keep up. He had six sets of flankers holding calves on the ground. He had the brander, vaccinator, ear marker, dehorner, and castrator running and breathing hard. He was bringing in calves faster than the three ropers he had replaced. Once his rope was loose, Ramón quickly headed back into the herd for more.

Someone hollered, "Take care of the old cook, my ass!"

Someone else hollered, "Send that damn cook back to the kitchen before he kills us!"

Ramón flashed a big toothy grin. I ended up with dozens of photos of the old cook dragging calves and a great story, although I never published it until now. He was in every position in the saddle, sometimes pulled way off to one side and hanging onto a stirrup with just his toe. When I took copies of my photos to Consuelo, she looked at them, then at me probably recognizing my hat, and then at the pictures again. She did not approve of her seventy-year-old husband roping and finally said to Ramón, accusingly and worried, "That looks like you in the teeth?" Ramón laughed.

At the end of roundup, the ranch often had a wagon party with music and dancing at one of the barns closest to town. Ramón usually cooked for the party. One year, as the old cook was finishing his chores, I convinced him to polka with me when the band played "El Rancho Grande." He could still do a wild Norteña polka too. He completely wore out his gringa partner who was thirty-five years younger. I almost got fired over that first grocery list, but in the end, I could dance pretty good with the old cook. He never once stepped on my toes, and I never stepped on his.

Several years after Ramón died, my grandson Riley told me a story. Riley had been about six and with his dad, who was helping with the 06 roundup. While the cowboys gathered a rough pasture, the little boy stayed in camp with Ramón and his apprentice, Marcos Najera, who would take over when Ramón retired in 1991. Riley noticed the hose filling the first of two buckets with water to heat over the fire for dishes. The bucket was almost full, the other was empty, and Marcos had gone off to do something else. Riley understood what needed to be done. So he jumped up and grabbed the hose to switch buckets, but didn't kink it first like Marcos always did to stop the flow of water. Riley sprayed the fire, ashes billowed up, and he got himself and Marcos both wet and ashy before Marcos could kink the hose and get things back under control. Riley quickly went back to his chair. For several minutes, neither Ramón nor Marcos said anything. Maybe Ramón was thinking about his own childhood, when old Gavino had grabbed him by the ankles and turned him upside down, picking up goat head stickers with the top of his head.

Instead Ramón walked over and said to Riley, "You know, Marcos was just trying to help you. Maybe you should go thank him." Immediately Riley got up, walked over to Marcos, and said, "Thank you, Marcos, for helping me."

Had that little boy sprayed water to be funny or mean, I'm sure he would have gotten stickers in his hair, but because he was trying to be helpful, Ramón didn't want to kill that desire. Obviously Ramón was taking his job as teacher of the next generation—both future cooks and future cowboys—seriously. We like to say that kids learn slowly and by repetition, but by the time Riley told me the story, he had remembered that moment for eleven years.

Storytelling has always been an important part of cowboy school. Before each roundup, the 06 camp men provided huge stacks of live oak wood at each location where Ramón would cook, more wood than needed. Sometimes a norther would blow in, and the cowboys would burn that extra wood to stay warm. Of equal or maybe more importance, sometimes the night owls liked to stay up and burn wood while they told stories. Ramón called that extra wood "bullshit wood."

Cowboy storytelling is similar to Native American storytelling, a method of teaching, remembering, and passing cultural wisdom on to the next generations. Laguna writer Leslie Marmon Silko goes to great pains to explain that her books and words are the products of many voices. She says she merely told the stories; she did not make up the wisdom they might contain. National Book Award winner Barry Lopez says that the position of the storyteller in a community is "not to be the wise person, the person who speaks from his own wisdom but to create an atmosphere in which the wisdom of the world becomes apparent." Keith Basso, in *Wisdom Sits in Places: Landscape and Language among the Western Apache*, explains that stories were often tied to places or animals that tribal members would see repeatedly so that the stories would "stalk" them and their children. Sometimes just mentioning the name of the animal or place would be enough. Cowboy stories and poetry were sometimes used the same way. For instance, I was once chattering and joking in a crowded restaurant when a friend at the table asked me if I knew Bruce Kiskaddon's poem "Little Blue Roan." I quickly realized that I had not been "paying attention to my horse's ears" and my glib remarks could be heard by someone at a nearby table. So I reined in my tongue. As Apache Lola Machuse explains in Basso's book, we were "speaking with names," only in my case we were using the name of a poem instead of Apache place-names.

Most of our cowboy night owls traded stories; occasionally someone brought a guitar. Maybe we all owned a small collection of old poetry books written by and about cowboys: Badger Clark, S. Omar Barker, E. A. Brininstool, Bill Chittenden, Henry Herbert Knibbs, Curley Fletcher, and even Charlie Russell had published some poetry. Maybe on a wall somewhere we had all tacked up a page from an old *Western Livestock Journal* calendar where a favorite poem appeared, but I never heard a poem recited around a bullshit fire by the night owls until some northern cowboys joined the crew in 1983. In addition to new stories we hadn't heard before, they recited poems, several from the Australian poet Banjo Patterson and several from Bruce Kiskaddon. One of them pointed out a tiny half-inch notice in one of my magazines that advertised a cowboy poetry gathering to be held in a few months in Elko, Nevada. He said, "Let's go." He didn't, but I did.

Everyone loved those old poems. Favorites usually spoke through an anonymous voice representing the culture, usually as a character within the story but watching from the fringe of the action, like a traditional Indian storyteller—or a journalist. The voice was often breaking a law, bucking off, being made a fool of, or getting old, sometimes dead serious and sometimes hilariously funny. Through the voice we committed a justified murder ("The Dude Wrangler"), our horses warned us ("Little Blue Roan"), we aged and remembered mistakes ("The Old Nighthawk"), we bucked off ("The Strawberry Roan"), and we sometimes succumbed to a sinful show of pride ("New Boots"). In poems touching on religion, we were all sinners. Gail Gardner's "The Sierry Petes," better known as "Tying Knots in the Devil's Tail," simply points out the similarities between the devil and an old renegade steer: horns, cloven hooves, tail, and bad attitude—none of which were too dangerous even for sinful drunk cowboys to handle, especially if they teamed up. If we stuck together, we could somehow get through any wreck, even when tangling with the devil. If not, perhaps we could somehow use our trickster minds to get into heaven, maybe by solving a riddle, like picking out Adam from the look-alike old angels ("The Belly Button"—Adam didn't have one!). Or if rejected by Saint Peter, we might "accidentally" spur a horse in the shoulder so that when the horse quit "bucking" and the dust settled, we just happened to end up inside the pearly gates ("Stan from Brewery Gulch"). Another favorite, recited by one of the northern cowboys, "Judgement Day," compares that dreaded final settling of affairs to fall shipping. In the end, the Boss of Heaven judges us cowboys by our own book of rules—instead of the Ten Commandments—because, as an angel explains: "You can never judge a cowboy by another feller's laws." If going to heaven doesn't work out, we will simply wake up back in camp with frost on our bed tarps, wishing we hadn't been thrown out just for trying to seduce an angel ("A Cow Boy's Dream"). Both the poetry and stories were designed to teach, but not with didactic finger shaking in someone's face, and sometimes it took a lifetime to understand the message.

A classic example of the kind of poem that is important to keep remembering is "The Zebra Dun," which seems to be about a heroic dude embarrassing a bunch of cowboys by riding their rankest horse. According to early folklorist John Lomax, the poem was authored by a black cook working for the John Z. Means and George W. Evans Z Bar Ranch on the Pecos River in West Texas in the late 1800s, but no one really knows for sure.

In "The Zebra Dun," an anonymous cowboy voice tells the story to his fellow cowboys. A city slicker rides a worn-out horse into a cowboy wagon camp and asks to trade it for a fresh horse. They offer him food, and while eating, he brags and brags until the cowboys get irritated enough to provide a "rank" horse to teach him a lesson. But the dude miraculously rides the horse and impresses the boss, who offers him a job. On the surface, the poem addresses the issue of prejudice and being too quick to judge by surface appearances: maybe dress, physical fitness, skin color, or even gender. The moral seemed to be: "Don't judge a book by its cover." A modern audience would enjoy identifying with the dude because he is godlike, a superhero who rides the zebra dun.

However, that's not what the poem is about. Like a pool hall hustler, the stranger in the poem was no dude but a sly cowboy carefully orchestrating the drama. Cowboys have a reputation for putting greenhorns on bad horses as a joke, but in reality, they would not want to hurt someone who does not ride well. If that person somehow made them mad, which was exactly what the stranger was doing, then they might decide to teach a lesson. The stranger knew just how to irritate cowboys—by talking too much and using jaw-breaking words. His bragging finally made them "sick" and they "began to look around" for a way to play a trick on him. Basso explained a similar situation in the Apache culture: "Persons who speak too much insult the imaginative capabilities of other people, 'blocking their thinking' . . . and 'holding down their minds.'" Since Apaches began raising cattle and riding horses about the same time the trail drives sprang into being, it would be interesting, but probably impossible, to determine who might have influenced whom. Maybe cultural storytelling is just a good example of the universal wisdom of the world surfacing.

For modern readers, the zebra dun seems to stand in for an archetypical devil/dragon/monster. However, the fact that the horse stood perfectly still to be saddled was a sign that he was not the least afraid of humans, unschooled, or any kind of devil. The dun was a wise old working horse who didn't like nonsense, was probably just a little "cold backed," and could be counted on to scare a braggart dude. When the ride begins, Dunny rears up and seems about to go over backward, a trick that will sometimes scare and loosen even a good rider. He also seems to try to paw the bridle off to gain control: "A-pitching and a-squealing, a-having wall-eyed fits, / His hind feet perpendicular, his front ones in the bits." A squealing horse also sounded like he would be especially tough to ride. The cowboys had chosen the perfect ride for a bragging dude: a horse that seemed scary but really wasn't. If the stranger had really been a dude, he would have fallen or maybe even jumped off because of the squealing. No harm done; nobody hurt; lesson learned. The cowboys could have then given him some old worn-out, lame horse to ride away on. But none of this horse noise and nonsense bothered the stranger.

The tenth stanza contains a key word that is usually misspelled (maybe "fixed" by an editor) in modern reprints, such as in Hal Cannon's collection *Cowboy Poetry: A Gathering*, where we find, "He thumped him in the shoulders." The stranger did not *thump* the horse in the shoulders but *thumbed* him, as in this version published around 1910 by John A. Lomax in *Cowboy Songs, Ballads, and Cattle Calls from Texas:* "He thumbed him in the neck, and he spurred him as he whirled / To show us flunky punchers he was the wolf of the world." Jabbing a horse in the neck just in front of the shoulders with both thumbs and then running the thumbs up the neck is called thumbing. It must irritate or tickle horses, usually causing even a gentle horse to buck. Maybe the horse thinks he has a cougar on his back. By thumbing the horse, the stranger was asking the horse to buck harder. With this word (if not before), the cowboys would realize they had been fooled. This stranger was no dude. He was a disguised cowboy who knew that a cold-backed but otherwise broke horse would put on a better show if thumbed. The stranger needed a fresh horse, not a worn-out old kid horse. But that was not the only purpose for his dude disguise.

Within the old traditional cowboy culture, a good cowboy never wanted to have to ask for a job; the boss should offer. Neither employer nor employee wanted to be turned down or judged as not good enough. Like Arthurian knights, a good crew consisted of more than just a bunch of employees; they were a closely knit, efficient team. Hiring was done carefully. So the stranger was actually a good hand who tricked the crew into letting him show his abilities. If the boss didn't offer a job, no problem. He'd had a little breakfast, played a good trick, gotten himself a decent fresh horse, and was now ready to ride on to the next wagon to try for a job again.

In retrospect, only a good hand would have been confident enough to go looking for a job dressed like a dude. Only a good hand would have been able to eat breakfast, knowing he was going to have to prove himself. Only someone who regularly ate at a cowboy wagon would choose coffee, a biscuit, and beans. Those items would always be available and easy for the cook to spare. The one person the voice in the poem did not dare fool was the cook, especially since the author was supposedly a cook. Even the first time this poem was told around a bullshit fire, the cook would get the first hint that this stranger was no dude.

Finally, only a good hand would use this method to apply for a job, which both complimented the crew and provided a good laugh. The stranger knew that if irritated enough, the cowboys would give him a horse that would buck a little but not one of their really tough horses. If he had asked for and ridden their toughest horse, the crew would have labeled him a showboat and the boss would have sent him on his way. He didn't want to show off or beat anyone; he just needed a job and hoped the boss would offer one. The poem models complicated human behavior that helps form friendships, trust, and respect.

The voice in the poem also softens his trick by exaggerating: "The stranger sat upon him and curled his black mustache, / Just like a summer boarder waiting for his hash." Anyone who has ever ridden a bucking horse knows that the jerking and snapping would cause even a good rider to pull his mustache out, unless the horse was a pretty easy bucker. This excessive bragging calls attention to the fact that a little joke has been played, but not too much of a joke. Anyone who missed the obvious hints that the dude was actually a disguised cowboy might be somewhat embarrassed, but not too much. And the author/cook might even be adding a bit of a jab at his cowboys, since wagon cooks were expected to have food hot and ready as soon as starving cowboys stepped off their horses. No patient waiting for hash (hatch) around this wagon!

The voice also made sure the stranger remained a common cowboy, enjoying the easy ride he tricked the crew into giving him. He even missed a loop occasionally, as he was able only to "catch them feet nine out of ten." The stranger was good enough to be equal but was no hero. A poem like this was often used the same way Native American storytellers "stalked" a target: to teach a young person how to apply for a job, to remind someone about the finer points of friendship, to chastise a braggart, or to help a newcomer feel welcome—an endless list.

Traditional cowboy poetry is often criticized for its singsong rhyming; defenders claim that rhyme is used primarily to aid memory. However, because rhyme is so obviously different from normal speech, rhyme and rhythm conjure another time and place. This is similar to the traditional opening *Humma-hah* (meaning "Long, long ago") with which, Silko says, Pueblo storytellers begin their stories or to the traditional opening of a fairy tale: "Once upon a time." Thus, even though a rhymed poem is probably being recited around the fire for the same reason stories are told—to illuminate a current situation and maybe teach a lesson—the rhyme adds distance to any chastisement or compliment. Only the target should feel the arrow strike. I wrote several articles trying to explain cowboy stories and poems to both insider and outsider audiences. As I said, we didn't learn how to do what we were doing in school.

Teachers, poets, journalists—any of those who take on the mantle of storyteller—carry tremendous responsibility on their shoulders. Storytellers use entertainment to attract and keep an audience interested, but their purpose is more serious, or at least should be. Storytellers are the keepers of the code, the glue that holds communities together, and every listener or reader shares in that responsibility. Native Americans all had the responsibility to tell, listen to, and correct their tribe's stories. They were all participants. As one modern-day chief of the Onondaga tribe, Irvin Powless Jr., said, "If it were up to us, we wouldn't have written a Bill of Rights without a Bill of Responsibilities." Storytelling was and is a conversation—not a lecture, not a debate, not a competition. Every member was supposed to speak up when they disagreed, remembered the story differently, or had a different perspective. Journalism is a form of storytelling. It determines how we see ourselves, what we remember and pass on to future generations. If journalism tells only our negative stories, it's no wonder that our citizens drop out, commit suicide, and turn to mind-numbing drugs or alcohol. Journalists are modern-day storytellers. We have responsibilities, not just rights.

In the end, though, Ramón was right. Most of what got shared while burning bullshit wood was just that: bullshit. One old funny cowboy poem says it well: "Till by the time the fire goes down, / And all hands hit the straw, / They've rode more broncs and kissed more gals / Than a cowboy ever saw!"

In the cowboy world, where anything short of fatal is funny, humor plays an important role in stories, poems, and conversation. We don't usually just tell each other jokes, though. I remember standing next to Tom Dorrance once at a horsemanship clinic that he and Ray Hunt were giving in Colorado Springs. A black bronc mule was tied to the fence, and one of my old bachelor cowboy teachers, Bob Blackwell, stood next to the mule. I'm not sure what Tom and I had been talking about—maybe how being kicked by a mule had provided Tom with a lesson that he never forgot. At that exact moment Tom said that mules had a sense of humor. I laughed. Then I looked at that black mule and then at Bob in his black cowboy hat and black mustache and then back at that mule and thought to myself, "Wait a minute . . ."

Two or three of Bob's one-sentence "jokes" have also stuck in my memory. I once asked how he could be such a terrible person and I could be such a great person, but I lost friends and he kept them. He said he lost them too, but he'd just show up again on their doorstep. I laughed.

Another time when one of Bob's "jokes" kicked me happened just before I watched my eighteen-year-old daughter drive off to work on a dude ranch in Montana, where she would be loosely supervised by "Uncle" Bob and "Uncle" Wally, who both lived just across a mountain range. I think it was some kind of final exam to see if she was ready to be turned loose on the world. It takes a village to raise a kid and sometimes the cowboy village stretches across thousands of miles.

Anyway, Bob and I were having a semi-serious conversation about raising children and sending them to cowboy school. I said that my philosophy was to let my daughter make as many decisions as possible but if the situation became life threatening, then I'd step in.

Bob said, "When it really is life threatening, you ain't gonna be there."

I laughed. He didn't.

CHAPTER FOUR

Class

"My Uncle Bailie, the eldest son, had been brought up on what might be termed luxury, for he had a pony to ride."
—Andrew Carnegie

PART OF THE ROMANCE in riding out horseback just before dawn with a good crew is the music. There's the percussion of steel-shod hooves striking rocks with horses grunting, farting, groaning, snorting, and blowing rollers as their bodies and attitudes adjust to carrying weight on their backs. Horses with crickets in their bits play ratchet music with their tongues. Cold leather creaks and groans as saddles warm up. There's the swish of fringe on fringe and the flag-like snap of wildrags in the wind. Surrounding it all is the tinkle of bells. If there are buckaroos on the crew, actual tiny brass or silver bells chime as they swing from bridle throat latches, the bottom of stirrups, and cinch-to-flank-strap hobbles. Mostly the sound of bells comes from the *ching, ching, ching* of spurs and jingle-bobs ringing with every step the horses take. The sweeter the music, the classier the crew.

When the rest of the world talks about class, they mean a ranking based on money. When cowboys talk about class, they mean earned pride. So the theme for several of my articles was how to show pride without money—how to fancy up a saddle by using old Mexican silver coins for conchos or how to turn horsehair and dead cowhides into art. Cowboys like one-of-a-kind gear, but how to afford it? Some readers might put into practice one of my articles about making fancy bit hangers and bridle buckles out of Grandma's silver spoons or identify with one about an uncommonly good brush hand's austere, all leather, Zen-like outfit.

"Cowboy Customized Spurs" is a good example of an early how-to article about improving gear without money. I combined techniques from several cowboys to describe removing, replacing, and jazzing up spurs, especially for sound. Heating the rowels on a cookstove or campfire to red hot and quickly dipping them into water tempers the steel, causing the rowels to ring like a wind chime. The real purpose of a spur is music, not pain. One of our good local cowboys, Tommy Vaughn, used to say, "If it don't ring, it ain't a spur."

My accompanying photos showed spurs in various stages of customization, with captions such as, "These Crockett spurs have been customized by their owner over the past twelve years until their original design is no longer recognizable. The chrome plating was filed off, and the shanks shortened and reshaped. These rowels (the sixth pair) were changed from twenty points to ten and highly tempered. The rowel pins have been substituted with small hinge pins, to which jinglebobs were attached." One photo showed an off-the-shelf spur in original condition and its mate transformed. Another showed a name punched into the spur band with metal alphabet stamps, the punched letters inlaid with brass brazing rod.

I ended the article by saying, "Of course, next winter, when cabin fever again sets in, the cowboy may decide to take it all off, fill the holes with a rivet or epoxy, and grind it smooth." I suppose that sounded fairly boring unless you were a young, broke cowboy who wanted to show he had some pride in himself. Anything mass-produced that could be bought off a shelf, no matter the price, screamed amateur. These telltale signs of making do, pride, and skills were what wise old ranchers looked for when hiring. We called that class.

When cowboys complimented some young craftsman, I would arrange to do a profile. One of those was "Mark Dahl: Self-Made Silversmith." Mark's engraving seemed to sparkle, even when dirty. He'd never taken lessons, never seen anyone engrave. He made many of his own tools and came up with unusual combinations of lines, swirls, and even squares. "What worked I did again," he said, "and what didn't work, I didn't do again."

Mark spent his early years as a buckaroo and like most tried the old cowboy dream of owning his own cows. "I'd always wanted a few cows and some ground of my own," he said, "but when I finally got them, I couldn't make a living on them. I drove a truck for a little while, but that didn't work. I wrecked a couple of those. So I just decided on silversmithing." Mark kept his first pieces and hid them. As his skills grew, his circle of customers widened from family to some of the best buckaroos in the West. I mentioned a few names of customers, such as Bill "Blackie" Black, Joe Wolter, Steve Dorrance, Bryan Neubert, and Jerry Pardue, so that readers who knew their sterling reputations and picky taste would know that Mark was more than some reporter's idea of a fine silversmith.

One of his innovations was to place conchos on the cheek pieces of his bits so that when horses rolled their crickets, the conchos would ring like tiny bells. Another was brazing silver: "I melt sterling silver in like brazing rod. It becomes part of the metal. It is welded in. I do it on spurs, for instance, when the bands are flat and then bend them afterward and the silver just stays. It is part of it. It helps strengthen the piece, and I use my own scraps. When I first started, I couldn't get the silver to flow. It took a lot of experimenting with luck and temperature."

I didn't ask but wondered if Mark had read my article on customizing spurs from five years earlier. Obviously, he had solved some of the problems and improved on some of the techniques I had mentioned. Brazed silver inlay would be a huge improvement over brass inlay and the additional sound would be especially popular with the music makers. He became one of the West's premier bit and spur makers, his work now hanging in museums and art galleries. I worried that the publicity I provided to craftsmen quickly put their work out of a working cowboy's price range, but Mark had kids to support too. Besides, for most cowboys, buying someone else's art was not as classy as making their own.

Also, every time a horse fell or an auction gavel dropped, a new craftsman might need to be born. Learning a craft is a form of financial security for someone with a job that can be risky and seasonal, but it's more than that. Cowboys move around a lot from one ranch to another, sometimes because of personality conflicts, sometimes hunting that "perfect" boss or situation, and sometimes simply to ride different horses and see new country. So between jobs—while injuries mend, maybe while serving jail or prison time, or especially after the years and injuries start to take a physical toll—crafts can become a lifeline. Aging cowboys of both genders often become artists in welding, cooking, making saddles, twisting horsehair mecates; hitching horsehair belts, bridles, or jewelry; engraving and inlaying silver; or braiding rawhide or leather reins and romals, reatas, bosals, quirts, hobbles, and whips—maybe writing. If they haven't taught themselves a craft, maybe they become truck drivers, mechanics, handymen, or gardeners. Usually they need some kind of real work until the day they die.

They can't feel useful and stay happy if they sit down, turn on the TV, and live off a pension. Once they are no longer physically able to cowboy, crafts can provide both a purpose and self-respect, as well as keep them socializing in the cowboy world. The lucky ones stay horseback until they die, but few cowboys are lucky.

Eventually I discovered a fine line between instilling pride to inspire being the best you can be and instilling ego, which caused competition, jealousy, and insecurity that could wreck marriages and friendships. Few spouses approve when their partner drops a thousand bucks on a silver bit for the sake of ego when the kids need shoes. Pride needs to be tempered, sometimes with levity, sometimes with fire, a hammer, and water—or sometimes by boiling in oil. For instance, my old slicker probably hadn't been used but once or twice because it seldom rains in the desert. Desert cowboys joke about their slickers dry-rotting, but mine had simply gotten so hot from being carried around in the sun that the waterproofing had melted out of the seams. I had fixed it with clumpy white bathtub caulk. Catclaw and mesquite thorns had shredded its edges and ripped several three-cornered tears. It was not a pretty slicker, but it kept me somewhat drier than nothing. I was always quite proud of that slicker because it represented making do and self-sufficiency, but I wouldn't call it class.

Instilling pride seems to depend on what writers and storytellers romanticize. *Romanticism* is one of those often totally misunderstood words. The way I'm using it doesn't mean "looove." It means elevating something to ideal, seeing only the good (through rose-colored glasses) and ignoring the bad. Anything can be romanticized, from death to taxes. Landownership has been through several cycles of romance. We look back and romanticize the precontact American continent as a Garden of Eden. Our historians and journalists have convinced their readers, including modern Native Americans, that the first people never "owned" land but somehow lived innocently and happily (romantically) in a socialistic communal paradise, where they shared everything, loved one another, and never harmed plant, animal, or bird. In truth they defended their hunting and farming territories with blood, lots of blood. When nobody owns it, everybody fights over it.

Eventually reservations were "owned" by tribes, and almost all reservation land was used to raise food, usually livestock, historically bison and today cattle. Between 1900 and 1920, the Allotment Act divided reservations into 160-acre plots, finally providing individual Indians with land ownership titles. Perhaps because romanticism had convinced them that non-ownership was their utopian tradition, many sold their new allotments almost immediately, sometimes back to the tribe, more often to non-Indians for higher prices. Although modern maps still show reservation boundaries intact, most are at best a checkerboard of Indian/non-Indian land ownership. Each tribe is a sovereign nation with its own laws and government, and each rancher has a unique situation. So I traveled to the Crow and Northern Cheyenne Reservations to interview Indian ranchers and cowboys. Some owned their own land and had successfully acquired more. Some leased their land from either the tribe, tribal landowners, or non-Indians who owned land within the reservation. Those who leased tribal-owned land complained about tribe members camping near livestock water and leaving gates open. Tribal members who didn't ranch complained that the ranchers imposed too many restrictions on "their" land. Nobody seemed to know or care when they were on private or public property. In short, Indian ranchers had the same problems as all ranchers, especially those who lease "public" land from the U.S. government and own the land surrounding the water source.

One of the Northern Cheyenne ranchers I interviewed wore a bald eagle feather in his black cowboy hat. I went to a branding, ate buffalo, traded jokes and stories, drank coffee, met wives and kids, and got taken to grave sites for children killed in car accidents. We cussed the government, environmentalists, and reintroduction of wolves. He was involved with the traditional Cheyenne religion and served on both the tribal council and the cattlemen's board. One of his goals was to create difficult jobs for Indian youths to keep them away from boredom and the bottle. He saw ranching as one of those difficult jobs and similar to the traditional Cheyenne horseback lifestyle. He was fighting with tribal members who spent their time dreaming of a return to their old ways—a romanticized utopia that never existed.

"Well, we can't," he said. "For one thing, we can't feed the people. It's my job to get up every morning and go out here and do something because I've got to feed sixty people today, and I've got to feed them tomorrow. That's part of the responsibility I took on when I went into ranching. I have a responsibility to make sure my people get fed." He considered the grazing land he operated a responsibility and a place to produce food, not a sign of wealth.

He was also fighting with his tribe over its desire to sell mineral rights and water rights along Rosebud Creek. He said, "I keep telling them it doesn't matter how much money we're offered; how can we live without our water? It is the same deal as selling Long Island for colored beads."

Knowing it would be easy for a white reporter to make mistakes, I nervously asked him what he preferred to be called: First Nation? Native American? Northern Cheyenne? Indian?

He said, "When people ask my nationality, I say cowboy. But you can call me anything you want. Just don't call me a Crow."

His tribe had some history with the neighboring Crow tribe since the Crow had been General Custer's friendly scouts, while the Northern Cheyennes, Lakotas, and Arapahos had joined together to wipe Custer and his army off the face of the earth. However, he was even more ashamed of his Crow neighbors for selling their land than for being Custer's scouts. At the time of my interviews, more than half of the 2.5 million–acre Crow Reservation had been sold or leased to non-Indians, while 90 percent of the smaller 0.5 million–acre Northern Cheyenne Reservation was still owned and run by Cheyennes. Then I went to interview Crow ranchers for their side of the story.

So in a two-part article for *Western Horseman* ("Ranching on the Reservation"), I tried to romanticize land ownership enough that tribal members would value and operate their remaining land but not so much that they would consider their land to be wealth or would judge each other's worth by acres owned. I wish someone had been around to encourage my own family to hang on to the land they once owned. Unfortunately, my ancestors too, every generation, sold out for "colored beads," and I'm ashamed of them for that. Colored beads represent everything advertisers convince us is more necessary than land—a bigger house, faster car, another boat, more jewelry. Sadly, sometimes colored beads can be alcohol and drugs.

Even sadder is when land is not sold but simply taken, as happened in Mexico during a redistribution of wealth called "agrarian reform," and again romanticism might be to blame. Although too complicated to simplify here, the reform seemed to have been caused by romanticizing land ownership to the point that "the public" became convinced that the large ranch owners were an "elite class" and that landless cowboys had been "driven" to sell their labor to the haciendas. Needless to say, Mexican cowboys did not see themselves that way, maybe due to their stories and *corridos*. But owning land became so romanticized in Mexico that the urban poor were convinced that taking and dividing the haciendas would remedy their problems. Once the land was divided, the resulting *ejidos* were too small for anyone to make even a meager living on, especially in desert areas. The new owners did not have ranching or farming skills; nor could they afford to hire the now jobless cowboys. Consequently all that beautiful grassland soon turned to dust and the new landowners soon wanted to move back to the city.

I found and wrote about a legendary cowboy (on both sides of the border) who had personally experienced the results of Mexico's agrarian reform: "Carlos Ochoa: Today's Mexican Rancher." His ancestors had owned ranches in northern Mexico since coming from Spain. After the Mexican government took his family's ranches, young Carlos crossed the border and cowboyed for two large New Mexico ranches: the Ladder Ranch at Truth or Consequences and Bill Munday at Chama. When he returned to Mexico, the Almeida family hired him to run a five thousand–head operation. Then the Almeida Ranch was also taken and split up, and Carlos was again out of a job. "I ran it for seven years. It was a good time in my life, but the land is in pieces now," he said.

Luckily, at about that time, the Cattle Growers Association of Chihuahua decided to start an auction and offered Carlos the job of organizing and running it. "I guess somebody told them I needed a job," he said. He contacted U.S. friends to find out how auction sales worked and sent employees to auctioneer school in the United States. His new job provided a good salary and commission, so he started buying agrarian reform land as the disillusioned *ejido* owners returned to the cities. At the time I interviewed him, Carlos had a good start on putting together a cattle ranch again. "That sounds like I'm a rich son of a gun," he laughed, "but I'm really working for the bank."

He also said, "We have a lot of poor people in Mexico, but the cowboys are the only ones who are proud of what they are. But you don't find the pride in the new cowboys that you found in the old ones. The good cowboys send their children to town to get an education, and they get easier jobs. Progress is killing them."

A few years later, a young Elmer Ochoa turned up in one of my college classes. I think he was having trouble passing English and thought maybe he'd do better in my class since I knew his family. He passed, and I even published one of his essays in the university literary magazine that I sponsored at the time. I also entered it in a statewide Texas Intercollegiate Press Association writing contest, where he won honorable mention even though his English still showed a few rough edges. He called his essay "Don't Drink the Water." It was a tribute to the taste of the water from wells on his family's Mexico ranch. He explained that people who hadn't grown up drinking that water couldn't stand the taste; even his mom took bottled water when she went to the ranch. "But my dad, my brother, and me," he wrote, "love to drink the water from our place. When I go to the ranch, the first thing I do is have a big drink of Santa Rita water." That may sound like romanticizing bad water, but he's romanticizing the taste, not a health risk. Elmer simply had a deep sense of place and had learned to love the taste of home. I hoped his taste for that water would eventually send him back to operate the ranch after college, not as wealth but as a good purpose for his life.

I always wrote a little poetry, not trying to be a poet but just because I couldn't leave paper and pen alone. So I once wrote a poem against romanticizing landownership as wealth. Instead I tried to romanticize the skills needed to take care of it. I used an old and difficult-to-translate Spanish word: *jinete.* Spanish has several words for "cowboy" and each has a different meaning: *vaquero, caballero, charro,* and probably more. As I understand it, *jinete* described an excellent horseman who came from the lowest economic class; was at least part Aztec, Tarahumara, or Apache; and could ride horses no one else could handle. Not only could a *jinete* ride them, but he made those horses shine. A true *jinete* felt no envy toward anyone. I also tried to capture the feelings of both Mexico's cowboys and its landowners about agrarian reform, maybe even hoped it would be a deterrent to the old cowboy dream (romanticism again) of owning some cows of their own.

Jinete

The first time I saw you,
You rode a dancing black stallion.
You and he were one.
You looked down your dark Indian nose at me,
Spun your horse in a silver spade,
And galloped away.

Because I couldn't ride like you,
I built a rancho.
I bought your children shoes,
Just so I could watch you ride.

From out there in the rain,
You looked in my window,
Saw me warm and comfortable.
Your black eyes flashed with envy.
You were strong and fast,
Myself fat and slow.
So, you took my ranch.

Now I'm out here in the rain.
You sit by the fire warm and fat.
You buy my children shoes.

Ah, but look up, *Jinete,*
I'm riding your horse!

"You shouldn't romanticize poverty," said a Hispanic colleague at the university where I taught. "Working conditions for agriculture are terrible."

"I don't think we should romanticize us either," I said. "Look at us. If we are supposed to be teaching our youth how to be good people, we are pathetic role models. We call ourselves colleagues but we don't work well together. We compete fiercely and dishonestly over budgets. Most of us are bored with our subjects, hate teaching, hate research, and hate our administrators. We either hate our students or exploit them. Faculty members are almost all divorced, childless, or never married. Those of us with children or grandchildren seldom get to see them. We've nearly all got serious health problems caused by our stressful and sedentary lifestyle. We sit in air-conditioned offices all day and half the night putting on weight and die young . . . or we work a second 'job' in some gym after hours to fight it. We diet constantly. People with physical agriculture jobs often work side by side with their families every day, go home and grill steaks, relax, and drink a beer or two. We need to romanticize work, real work, skills that take a lifetime to master not just four years of partying at some expensive university."

I did not change his mind, and he did not change mine.

No job is easy, although many appear to be from outside. I've sat in cushy offices watching desk-bound executives struggling through mounds of paperwork. Looking out their windows, they notice the groundskeepers laughing and "leaning on their shovels." The executives said, "Those guys do more fooling around than working, but I wouldn't do what they do for any amount of money." I've also hung out with groundskeepers as they watched executives strolling to a meeting. The groundskeepers said, "Those guys do more fooling around than working, but I wouldn't do what they do for any amount of money." These different perspectives come from values, and values come from stories. The groundskeepers had obviously listened to stories that romanticized physical labor. The meeting-goers had listened to stories that romanticized salary to the point that most people today measure their own worth based on their wages. We say the rich are "worth" some amount of money. That is no way to measure a human being's worth. Every wealthy person I know struggles to find meaningful work as a purpose for their life.

So I looked for and wrote stories aimed at both a landowning and a cowboy audience, hoping to help them understand one another, their mutual dependence, and their need for mutual respect. Maybe every article I wrote dealt with wealth and poverty in various ways and through various eyes: laborer, landowner, customer, craftsman. I didn't try to prove who was right or wrong—just that how we feel about each other, about our work, and what makes a good life depends on what our storytellers choose to romanticize.

I remember one creative writing student who was trying to write about his job and his life as a cowboy. His fellow students hammered him for being too romantic, too full of sunshine and good news, too positive. He finally looked to me, the teacher, and said something like, "Okay. I love this desert country. I love my job. I love weather. I love horses. I have a great family. I'm young and strong and happy. So I can't be a writer because I have nothing to gripe about?"

I don't remember how I answered, but I knew exactly how he felt. I had spent my entire writing life trying to figure out a serious way to tell positive stories because I believed the world needed them. How many wise sayings are there? Carlos Ruiz Zafón: "Making money isn't hard in itself. . . . What's hard is to earn it doing something worth devoting one's life to."

Epictetus: “Wealth consists not in having great possessions, but in having few wants.” Voltaire: “Don’t think money does everything or you are going to end up doing everything for money.” Theodore Roosevelt: “Far and away the best prize that life offers is the chance to work hard at work worth doing.” Dodie Smith: “No bathroom on earth will make up for marrying a man you hate.” I don’t know who Dodie was, but she was one smart lady. Every philosopher, every ethnicity, every world religion sings a similar song. The words “Too many people spend money they haven’t earned to buy things they don’t want to impress people they don’t like” have been credited to at least eleven different people, most often to Will Rogers. So if romanticizing poverty is wrong, then that student and I are in good company. Today we have demonized positive stories, but I think they are the key to our future. We just need to recognize what and who we are romanticizing and the consequences.

I considered it my responsibility as a cowboy journalist to romanticize work and skill. When we journalists glorify and romanticize work, people love their work. When we glorify and romanticize leisure, people hate their work. Most journalists write about work as though it is slavery and equate leisure with freedom. Someday we may look back on million-dollar athletes as bought and sold, owned and driven to physical and mental exhaustion and injury. Future generations may condemn us for forcing our children to “play” sports. We may someday hang people who chain their fellow humans to desk jobs where they receive no sunlight, fresh air, or proper exercise and consider it cruelty.

Although our news and history are full of stories about the tragic lives of the very wealthy, we have romanticized wealth to the point that most people believe money is the root of all happiness, and the higher the wages, the better the job. At least ideally and philosophically, the cowboy is an exception. I vaguely remember an old conversation about cowboy wages. An heir to a large local ranch operation explained tearfully that she didn’t think her family had been paying their cowboys enough. “Do we?” she asked.

Since there was no one else around, I tried to answer. Although I may view the working-class cowboy life through rose-colored glasses, I did actually live that life. I have put in lots of miles horseback, calved lots of heifers, flanked lots of calves, and kept tabs on lots of water, but I was seldom ever paid for any of it. My personal self-respect comes from trying real hard to maintain a balance between what I'm worth and my wages. Pay me too much and I feel guilty and get defensive. Since I was usually free help as a cowboy, I can truthfully and proudly say that I was always worth every single penny I was ever paid—although a few cowboys and bosses did joke that when I showed up to "help," it was like two good men riding off. (Or at least I pretended they were joking.)

However, the ranch usually furnished my house, utilities, water, horses to ride, hunting, fishing, beef, and scenery. I never came close to earning all that, so I found it difficult to keep my score with the ranch owners even and be able to look myself in the eye. I personally never wanted charity. To me, happiness comes, if it ever does, from taking care of myself. So as a totally unauthorized, self-appointed representative of the cowboy culture—at least the bill-paying side—I took her question seriously. I'm still trying to dig deep enough to answer her truthfully.

Spanish-speaking ranch employees sometimes call the ranch owner *patrón* or *patróna. Patrón* doesn't translate easily. Spanish has several words for "boss" or "landowner" that get all mixed up: *jefe* (boss), *dueño* (owner), *cacique* (a boss/owner to whom political loyalty is also pledged), *mayordomo* (employer), *corporal* (foreman), *merogallo* (head rooster), *segundo* (second in command), *ganadero* (cattleman), and *patrón,* which is the hardest to define. Although *patrón* comes from the same Latin root as *patronizing,* it doesn't imply a condescending relationship when used by a ranch employee. *Patrón* sort of means all the other words combined with a bit of patron saint mixed in and indicates a sacred version of respect, gratefulness, defending, and caretaking, both given and received, and especially earned by both employee and employer.

I found a story about one of our "rich" local ranchers that illustrated this fragile partnership between cowboys and ranchers. The story began in 1874 with Bug Means's father. Instead of taking his wages in money, Bug's father traded his labor for cattle. Once he had put a small herd together, he and his wife, with a baby in arms, drove their herd toward West Texas. While stopping for the night and to water the cattle in the Pecos River before crossing, they woke up surrounded by thirty-five Comanches who wanted their herd, either peacefully or by force. Bug's father wisely chose peace, loaded up his little family, and turned around to start over. Ten years later, they tried again and this time succeeded. Bug's father used to say that all he wanted was West Texas to run his cows and New Mexico to run his steers.

Eventually the Means family nearly fulfilled that old family dream, operating several large ranches in both West Texas and New Mexico. One day during the 1930s drouth, a destitute nineteen-year-old cowboy rode in horseback and asked Bug for a job. Bug had plenty of work but no money to pay wages. No problem. The young cowboy was hungry and offered his labor if the ranch would just feed him. They struck a deal. The young cowboy did a good job breaking several rank horses, so when it came time for him to leave, Bug Means, by this time one of the largest ranchers in West Texas, said, "Here. I have twelve sacks of Bull Durham tobacco and eight cents. That's all the money I've got in this house. You take half the tobacco and all the money."

Before I published Bug's story as a chapter in a book (*Cowboys Who Rode Proudly*) the Means family wanted me to check it for accuracy with that young cowboy, James Kinney, who had since become a famous Texas cutting horse trainer. Kinney corrected the details to six sacks of Bull Durham and eighty cents. Both men told that story over and over until they died. Those who know the Means family and James Kinney call them classy people. Journalists today strive to prove that every wealthy person is evil. I never found that to be even close to the truth and tried hard to keep ranch owners and working-class cowboys respecting each other instead of working against each other. If journalists are to give voice to the voiceless and act as watchdogs over the powerful, I would argue that today's "rich" ranchers are voiceless and powerless against the hordes of urban voters and urban-biased journalists who now control our democracy. Rural votes hardly represent a single raindrop during a drouth, and "rich" ranchers can't outvote even the tiniest nearby town.

If a ranch tried to match worth with salary, then no ranch and maybe no business could ever pay a really good hand what he or she is actually worth, no more than a newspaper, magazine, or book publisher could ever afford to pay its best writers what they are worth. We writers try not to complain because we know we practice the best part of the publishing business. Those of us who love what we do want the business side to succeed so we can continue to do what we do, as do cowboys. I have written a column for the *Mountain Dispatch* on and off for almost forty years—without pay—at least partly because I don't want our community to lose that little weekly paper.

I don't believe anyone decides to work as a cowboy or a writer just for the money. Few writers want to be editors; even fewer want to be publishers.

Editors and publishers might be paid more and wield more power, but we writers feel no envy. Like writing, cowboying is a skill, a lifework, often beginning with picking up the rhythm of a horse by riding around in a horseback mom's womb, roping the dog while still in diapers, and that first "real job" (unpaid) at maybe five years old carrying the *juevos* bucket during branding. Cowboying is one of the hardest professions in the world to become really good at. For many years a wannabe is simply allowed to tag along and work from daylight to dark—for nothing—enduring constant teasing and abuse because that's exactly what they are worth. The teasing weeds out the weak and toughens the hides of the stayers. We call it paying dues, but it's no labor union. Maybe elsewhere respect can be bought or maybe negotiated, but it's not the same kind of respect that comes from earning it.

Ranching is not romance. In reality, it's a business, and I am concerned about the future of ranching. Less and less land is actually being grazed—thus more grass fires. More and more ranches are being sold—thus more subdivisions and "nature preserves" (in my opinion just tax-free fronts to accumulate prime real estate). Owners of all those miles and miles of Texas are imagined as very rich, and they might be if they sold out or struck an oil well or two. But those who don't have oil or don't want to sell walk a tightrope to stay in the cattle business. There's an old joke: "If I had a million dollars, I'd keep right on ranching until it was all gone."

Take a thousand-head West Texas cow/calf operation for example. To keep the math easy, say each cow had a calf and it lived until shipping time. Assume every calf weighed five hundred pounds by shipping time and sold for $2 per pound. In real life, prices for calves rise and fall, and ranchers never receive the high prices for beef on the hoof that consumers pay in the grocery stores. Every cow does not raise a calf for various reasons, some female calves must be kept each year to replace aging cows, and those replacement heifers don't earn a dime for three or four years. All calves don't weigh the same. But again to keep the math easy, we will say our income is $1,000 per calf, or $1 million per year, which would be unrealistically high.

Now deduct income taxes, land taxes, payroll taxes, insurance, and winter feed; a salary for the owner and at least one full-time employee, and day wages for several temporary employees during branding and shipping.

Ranchers also furnish themselves and their full-time employees with houses, utilities, one beef per year, and a pickup and trailer with inspections, insurance, licenses, repairs, tires, and gas. Maybe one way to think about this list is that in 1950, a pickup truck cost about eight steers. Today that truck costs forty steers or more.

Water needs to be checked daily. Our hypothetical ranch has five windmills pumping water through scattered pipelines to water troughs. Some ranches have thirty to one hundred windmills. Calling in a windmill man might cost more than $1,000 per visit, depending on the depth of the well, distance, problem, or what parts need replacing. The ranch usually furnishes horses and pays for their food and upkeep. This may include a band of good mares and a very expensive stud (or maybe several bands and studs, depending on the number of horses needed), a bunch of weaned colts, two-year-olds needing to be schooled, and enough fresh and extra horses to get the work done. New bulls need to be purchased regularly to prevent inbreeding, at least one bull for every ten to thirty cows, depending on the country, fences, water, breed, and whether or not the cowboys notice and go hunt up a bull when cows are riding each other. Bull prices sometimes reach into the thousands or tens of thousands of dollars. Add veterinarian bills, hiring cattle trucks—the list is endless.

During a drouth, winter feed expenses accumulate all year, and some drouths last for years. After a grass fire, sometimes cattle must be sold or fed hay until new grass grows, and miles and miles of burned fences must be replaced at about $10,000 to $20,000 per mile, depending on rocks, steep terrain, and accessibility. After a deep cold snap, miles of pipeline may need repair or replacing. After a good rain, roads need grading and water gaps must be fixed. I'm not sure how good the average reader might be with math, but that imaginary $1 million annual income just doesn't come close to covering all these expenses. So during a crisis, ranchers borrow money, hoping for a better year next year. Ranch owners might also have to prepare their children to pay a death tax before they can inherit the ranch. Heirs often have to begin and succeed at another business—or several—to pay that tax. The most common reason ranches go under or split up and sell is the inability of heirs to pay all those taxes or the heirs' lack of desire to do the hard work of ranching that land. Another common way ranches go under is when banks get nervous about excessive debt and call in the loans or decide the tied-up money could make more if invested some other way. Once a rancher slips deep enough into debt, he or she is actually working for the bank and helpless to fight the bankers' decisions.

I remember one sobering assignment when I was a senior ag major in college. We students were "given" one hundred imaginary sections (one hundred square miles) of land. All we had to do was stock it, fence it, water it, and keep it running. The whole point of the assignment was to show us it couldn't be done even if the land was totally free. Enough ranch land to support even one hundred cows can sell for millions or even billions of dollars. Paying for the land from the cattle business is impossible. Ranchers in business today either inherited their land and pinch every penny, pay expensive grazing leases, or have an outside source of wealth such as oil.

So I found and wrote about Bob Eidson, whose cowboy father had worked like a slave for twenty years on a ranch owned by a distant cousin. When young Bob returned from World War II, he hired on to cowboy with his father. He explained, "I've been here ever since. I always did what nobody else wanted to do for thirty years. I rode all the broncs. The other boys picked what they wanted and I got what was left." He once told the landowner that he "just couldn't work for $100 a month and needed a raise. He said, 'I'll tell you something about these dang buttons [young cowboys], the more you pay them, the sorrier hands they are!' I had five daughters at the time, so I couldn't afford to quit. Nobody else would have fed us for what I could do."

When the landowner died, he left the ranch to his son, but just nine years later, that son died of a massive heart attack, probably from stress. The next day, when the will was read, Bob Eidson, the bronc rider and handyman, found himself sole heir to the land, cattle, and oil—with the government giving him six months to come up with the inheritance taxes, things he only vaguely knew existed the day before. I wrote a two-part article on him: "Bob Eidson: Cowboy, Cowman" for *Western Horseman.* At the time the Eidson Ranch included eighty sections in New Mexico and fifty sections near Penwell, Texas. A section is one square mile, with 640 acres in a section. So the Eidson Ranch covered 130 square miles, or 83,200 acres, with oil under almost every inch of it in both states.

For a while paying the taxes and keeping the ranch going woke Bob up at night and kept him awake. "It's no disgrace to inherit something like this," he said, "but it's a danged disgrace not to do something with it and make it work." Did the inheritance change him? When I interviewed him, he was sixty, still riding young horses, flanking calves during branding, fixing windmills and fences, and doing anything that needed doing and that nobody else wanted to do. During spring branding and fall shipping, his wife, Juandell, washed nearly every dish used for cooking and eating by the often seventeen-man crew. She waited quietly to eat with the other wives after the men finished. Their home, like those of all Eidson Ranch employees, was spotless and comfortable but no fancier.

Because of the oil, in addition to a salary, the ranch furnished everything for its employees, from the cup towels on up. Anything they needed or wanted was charged to the ranch with no questions asked. "I've had people tell me they wouldn't trust anybody with their credit like that," said Bob. "But I think if you can't trust them, you better get rid of them."

Through the years I've known of several cowboys who inherited the ranches they worked for. I also know one bachelor rancher who has been searching for the right heir for half his life. He's still not sure he's found someone who will keep the land and ranch it instead of selling out. The land might be worth a fortune, but to stay in the ranching business is another story. As Henry Thoreau said, "I see young men, my townsmen, whose misfortune it is to have inherited farms, houses, barns, cattle, and farming tools; for these are more easily acquired than got rid of." That is especially true when you care more about stewardship, about taking care of the land and animals and the employees who are counting on you for a job, than the money or the colored beads the land might sell for. Of course if I had looked, I could have found greed, dishonesty, and all the evils of the world, but I chose to look for and give publicity to the people who deserved it.

People are happier if they choose their life's work for greater reasons than wealth or salary. Life should be about how we spend our time, not how much money we spend. Spending precious time just trying to make money is no way to spend a life. However, I have also listened to a few cowboys lament that they had risked and dedicated their own and their family's lives while learning skills the ranch owners didn't appreciate or even recognize. Like the code of Arthurian knights, the cowboy code insists on loyalty to the brand, but the brand's owner is supposed to repay that loyalty with respect, trust, and appreciation. Of course this reciprocity didn't and doesn't always happen. I have also heard a few cowboys say that they quit some ranch because it didn't pay enough, but I never totally believed them. I don't think I ever heard any disagreement with the statement that a ranch didn't have to pay as well if it "did things right." Maybe I listened to too many idealists, although it seemed to me that most cowboys were idealists. If they weren't, they'd be doing something else.

Through the years, from Montana to Mexico, I interviewed hundreds of cowboys and read in their letters, "I'd rather drive a potato chip truck than work for an outfit that uses a calf table." That statement almost seemed like a rallying cry, a parable, or a pledge of allegiance. When a ranch "modernizes," it often loses the loyalty of those who love the traditional work. A calf table is often a metaphor for this modernization. It's basically a mechanical tilting metal squeeze chute. Calves are separated from their mothers and crowded into small pens and then down alleys that lead to the calf table. Once a calf is poked into it, someone pulls a lever to catch the calf's head, squeeze its body like a piece of toast in a toaster, and tilt it onto its side, where it can be vaccinated, dehorned, castrated, earmarked, branded, or whatever. Some believe a calf table is easier on calves and employees, especially if employees are unskilled.

Skilled cowboys, however, prefer to quietly sneak up horseback beside a calf standing with its mother and rope it. They believe a metal calf table is much more traumatic on the calves. Pipe and steel are not as soft as ropes, powdered dirt, and human hands. Skilled ropers can flip a loop softly over a calf's hip and under its flank, the loop standing up in front of its hind legs like a trap for it to step into. After both feet step inside the loop, the roper quickly snugs it tight ("jerks his slack") and quietly but quickly brings the calf out of the herd, dragging it up close to the branding fire, ideally while the calf remains standing and dragging on its front feet. Flanking crews work in pairs, one standing to each side of the approaching horse. One of them will grab the rope and pull one direction while the other grabs the calf's tail and pulls the opposite direction, laying the calf down on its side, always with the side where the brand will go facing up. They remove the rope and secure the calf's legs and feet with their own hands and legs. Sometimes one roper ropes the head; another ropes the heels. Sometimes the heeler continues to hold the heels with his rope. Sometimes the crew uses pickets with inner tubes or various other inventions to hold the heels in order to turn the roper loose, especially when working short-handed. I wrote about any new ideas for "doing it right" that I witnessed.

If the branding area is large enough, a cow can follow her roped calf and stand nearby, ready to stick a horn in the ribs of anyone who upsets her baby too much. Once the ordeal is over, usually in less than a minute, the calf immediately rejoins Mama for a warm milk snack and licked sympathy. Good cowboys believe that roping is faster, safer, easier on animals, and of course much more fun. Working around a calf table is miserable: pinching fingers, delivering bruises, and breaking bones. So cowboys expect higher wages if one is used, even though they consider it very low-skilled labor. Banging metal also grates on tempers and nerves. By the end of the day, everyone has a headache, whether human or animal. Calves might be separated from their mothers for hours. Calf tables are just one example of numerous modern methods that idealistic skilled cowboys hate. The further an owner gets from "right," the more the wages matter, and the highest-skilled idealists will avoid those places like the plague no matter the wages. Good bosses know the likes and dislikes of their employees and struggle to maintain mutual respect and preferred working conditions. The others have a lot of trouble hiring and keeping help—unless they pay a lot, and then they get only what they pay for.

As an academic, I heard and read a lot about class based on money. In the horse world, that kind of class often showed up among horse breeders. Expensive Arabian show horses, for example, would rank as "high class," while cowboys and their sweaty working horses would rank as "low class." However, my definition of class is based on skill, not wealth. I also believe that beauty is in the eye of the beholder, and in the cowboy world, any skilled horse is beautiful, no matter how ugly. So I tackled this high/low class division with "Hothouse Flowers to Texas Bluebonnets" and sent it to the top Arabian magazine, *Arabian Horse World*. My goal was mutual respect, not changing minds. So I used flowers as metaphors for class—maybe even a layered metaphor, since the horses were also metaphors for class divisions. I suppose since the horse owners also represented white- and blue-collar working classes, they were some kind of metaphor too—and no telling what else. Hopefully, my article was not just a confusing and messy jumble of mixed metaphors.

Tony Allen, a hardworking fourth-generation (on both sides) Texas rancher, married a sophisticated lady raised in New York City, San Francisco, Washington, D.C., and Houston. His new bride, Lee, spoke Russian and Japanese and regularly won regional and national awards with her fancy-dancy Arabian horses. Cowboys call them A-rabs. Tony spoke Tex-Mex Spanish and raised sheep, angora goats, and cattle on forty-five thousand acres of brush and limestone hill country near Ozona. He needed tough, hardworking quarter horses and used them as partners in his business. Lee was a confirmed career woman with an exciting executive job. She was into travel, entertaining, legal matters, marketing, network design, and engineering—but still single. Once again set up on still another blind date, she vividly remembered "opening my front door and there, on my front porch, stood the Marlboro Man in his hat and boots. I knew I was in trouble." And so was Tony. When he asked, she said yes.

His ranch employees thought the fancy lady and her fancy horses would be nothing but trouble, and for a while the new couple seemed hopelessly mismatched. Tony expected horses to stand out in the rain like wildflowers and jumped them already saddled into crowded trailers, no leg wraps, no padded partitions between them. Lee imagined her horses saying, "Please tell this oaf we just don't do things this way!"

Tony said he "felt like I was raising hothouse flowers and wondered if I had a snowball's chance." (He liked lots of metaphors too.) Their situation was typical for any couple that crossed cultural boundaries.

Trying to remain optimistic, Lee set about learning her husband's business. She had proven herself before in a man's world, but on Lee's first sheep roundup, Tony sent her around the outside fence so she wouldn't get lost. As he rode off into the wind, he hollered back over his shoulder, "And don't just ride down the road. Get out in the brush and look for sheep." All Lee heard was, "Just ride down the road."

She took off in a happy canter down the road, around the outside fence, just as she thought she had been told. Soon Tony rode back within hollering distance and reinstructed his new wife, this time with an edge to his voice and again into the wind. All she heard was, "Just ride down the road, dammit!"

By the third time he rode over to give her instructions, his jaw was set. Lee, tired of being treated like an imbecile, had an Arabian arch in her neck and a brilliance in her eye. The honeymoon was deteriorating.

By the time I interviewed the Allens, Lee and Tony worked together like a team and Tony was riding a magnificent animal, a four-year-old A-rab stallion named High Copper, born the year Tony and Lee were married.

High Copper's potential as a sire was obvious, and he was beginning to feel his oats. He had to be kept in a box stall for his own protection. What once represented the best of care to Lee now represented imprisonment, and she was struggling with whether to geld him or not so he could join the other saddle horses in the pasture.

Watching Copper, I wondered what his choice would be if he could vote. His beautiful hocks were skinned from sliding down rocks, his flowing mane was tangled, and white sweat caked around the breast collar on Tony's saddle. But after two deep breaths, Copper was ready for more. The hard-riding rancher couldn't wear him down.

Which legacy would Copper's grandpa Serafix be more proud of? Would he rather see his grandson sire more beautiful show horses? Or would he rather see him become a legend of his own in a country where a horse stands on his own merit, not on his pedigree? Would Copper prefer the respect of the judges at the nationals or the respect of Tony Allen?

Notice I didn't send the cowboy and one of his non-Arabians to town to compete in a horse show and heroically win a trophy. That would only reinforce the class divisions I wanted to bridge. Instead I bragged about Lee and her show horses making good hands on the ranch, romanticizing class as ability. Since in the end, the show horses and fancy lady did measure up, my final article didn't create a win/lose situation but hopefully just built some mutual respect. Respect should not be a contest. Bloodlines and beauty don't count for much when horses are judged by what they can actually do. Race, show, rodeo, cutting, ranch, and pulling horses come in all colors. Breeding for a certain color rather than more important characteristics, such as stamina or intelligence, is almost considered racism in the horse world, except of course among those who breed for color, such as paint, pinto, palomino or Appaloosa breeders. Almost all horse breeders make fun of each other's breeds. Even cowboys joke about "Appaloosies" as the clown car on the bottom rung because they are bred for the spots on their butts, nothing else. The only breeders who object are, of course, Appaloosa breeders. And cowboys will proudly ride even a goofy-looking old Appy when they find a good one, maybe naming it after some guy who made the most fun of it.

Another place class sometimes showed up was between buckaroos who spent a fortune on fancy equipment and cowboys who didn't, even though they earned similar wages. Even in the cowboy world, we sometimes find ways to divide up into us versus them, and those two kinds of cowboys were about to come to blows—maybe a few did. It was a surface kind of hate that makes just about as much sense as ethnic or racial hate. So I wanted to try to fix that prejudice before it got worse. When two men showed up to work through our fall roundup, I thought maybe I'd found an answer. One was a sparkly buckaroo and one was a scuffed-up Texas brush popper. Both were good hands and had become great friends. They were even traveling together, but they picked on each other relentlessly. Their banter was hilarious. So I simply taped one of their heated arguments and published it like a drama. All I had to do was let them fight.

Most of their humor was only funny to those who knew how bad buckaroos hated cowboys, for what reasons, and vice versa. Anything they disagreed about was pretty much on the surface or connected to language. For instance, the Texan would call the extra horses a remuda, while the buckaroo would call them a cavvy. Somebody had to be wrong, right? Somebody needed a black eye, right? Humor, I've read, is very serious at some level or we wouldn't need the emotional release of laughter. I've also read that anything we laugh at we don't take quite as seriously the next time. I begin my article "The Odd Couple" by setting the stage and introducing the players for this drama.

Cotton Elliot's grandfather was a pioneer Texas rancher who also put in some cowboy years for the Hashknife, Swenson, and X Ranches. Cotton's father served fifteen years as a brand inspector for the Texas and Southwestern Cattle Raisers Association and proudly wore a diamond-studded stickpin with the 3 D's brand—a gift for ten years of service as a cowboy from the Waggoner Ranch in Vernon, Texas. So Cotton was as Texan as a Texan can get. He had also worked for the Pitchfork, Triangle, 06, and Muleshoe Ranches, and others in Texas. In New Mexico he had worked for the WS, UU Bar, and Turkey Track; and in Arizona for Babbitt, RO, Double O, Muleshoe, and others. He worked for Benny Binon in Montana and packed mules in California.

The buckaroo, a crabby guy who prefers that I don't use his name this second time around, was born in South Dakota. He worked at the Grapevine and Matador Ranches in Montana, for the Half Circle Cattle Company in Idaho, and for the IL, T Lazy S, and Squaw Valley in Nevada. In Wyoming he worked for the TR and Bob Douglas. He worked for the UU Bar in New Mexico and the 06 and Leoncita in Texas. His style was buckaroo from the tip of his rawhide romal to the three-inch silver conchos on his spur leathers. Cotton called them hubcaps.

I described their habits a little: Cotton appreciated a good salad, but the only green thing the buckaroo might eat was a little mold on his beef—that was about all they had in common. Then I just let them argue. Here are a few samples:

TEXAN: I ride a double-rigged saddle.

BUCKAROO: A wore-out one.

TEXAN: I ride a wore-out, double-rigged, Franklin-made saddle. It's flower stamped; or at least it was. Some parts are stamped; some parts just aren't there anymore. . . . I use thirty-five feet of nylon rope and the saddle's got a horn so I can dally or tie hard and fast. I do both, but I tie hard and fast most of the time. It depends on what I'm riding or what kind of country I'm in. If I'm riding a horse that's not very good, I tie so I know I'm gonna have whatever I rope. I've got him or he's got me.

BUCKAROO: He ties because he doesn't have enough rope.

TEXAN: The horn has a nylon rope wrap on it—just a strand out of a rope for a horn wrap. I can let my dallies run if I'm dallying on it. I don't like to use inner tube.

BUCKAROO: You aren't gonna run 'em far on twenty-eight feet of rope.

TEXAN: You've got a point there.

BUCKAROO: I ride a Franklin slick-fork, full-flower carved saddle with a five-eights-inch ring riggin', a four-and-a-half-inch cantle, and twenty-six-inch taps. It's got a dally horn wrapped with mule hide. I use sixty-five feet of nylon rope with a ring for a Honda. I dally.

TEXAN: He dallies because he's afraid to tie hard and fast. . . .

BUCKAROO: I use a snaffle bit. I grew up using one, and I can get better results out of it than I can with a hackamore. I've got three or four snaffles. My best one's got silver inlaid diamonds and stripes on the rings. The bridle's got an inch brow band with silver buckles on it and three-inch silver conchos, one-and-a-half-inch silver conchos where it connects the headstall to the bit, and one-and-a-half-inch silver conchos on the slobber leathers on my mane-hair McCarty.

TEXAN: And a set of Foster Grants to wear while he's using this gosh-awful getup.

I re-created their banter alike a drama for the entire article, using insider jokes to target the insider audience I wanted to reach. Once off the subject of gear, they agreed on the more important stuff, like the kind of ranches and bosses they wanted to work for:

TEXAN: Most bosses I've run into have been real good ones. A boss should be impartial, even tempered, and able to handle a bad situation without losing his head. He should be able to put his men where they need to be according to their capabilities, such as putting an older man next to a younger man who can be learning something while carrying a little more of the workload. I like a boss who knows how to place his horses properly. If he has some problem horses, he can place them with a fellow who can handle them instead of giving them to somebody who can't. . . .

BUCKAROO: I'd say Harold Smith, we called him Smitty, was probably the best cowboy I've ever been around. He's confident in his ability and can watch you make a mistake, just laugh about it, and go put the pieces back together—regather the herd, whatever. He doesn't get upset. He can get along with any kind of horse, and he knows cows. He likes to teach younger guys who are willing to learn. He knows several different styles of cowboying. . . .

TEXAN: I consider a good cowboy somebody who makes a hand in rough country, brush country, open country, on any kind of horse, and can work any breed of cattle. He stays awake around the herd and will be in the right place at the right time. He'll be good-humored. I don't like to work around somebody who's crabby all the time.

BUCKAROO: Whenever you start thinking you know everything, you quit learning. When you get to that one certain point where

> you think you know it all, you stay there the rest of your life. As far as punching cows, you could punch cows for a hundred years and still wouldn't know it all. There's something new every day. A good cowboy is somebody who can go to any man's country, do it his way, and make him a hand.

My original goal had been to describe the pros and cons of their differences. But their banter achieved that goal and more without much help from me. Eventually Cotton married a female veterinarian and became a Texas sheriff. The buckaroo remained a bachelor but did settle down on a good camp job where he is mostly his own boss. As far as I know, they're still friends, and I haven't heard much bickering between buckaroos and cowboys since our article came out. But I'm out of that big loop now, so I can only hope we made a difference.

Economic class differences continue today. Instead of romanticizing poverty or skill, we have chosen to demonize wealth to the point that people are pretending to be, if not poor, at least working class—like buying expensive sun-faded designer jeans with shredded holes and paint spatters. It should be no surprise that I consider "faded" denim silly, especially here in the desert, where just wearing jeans and hanging them on the clothesline results in the same faded blue after a week or two.

Because my family seemed to wear out jeans faster than I could patch them, I even went through a phase where I repurposed some into kitchen hot pads or Christmas stockings shaped like cowboy boots. One pair of my cutoff fishing shorts became an impromptu Halloween costume for my daughter just with the addition of colorful suspenders for a cute little rodeo bullfighter. My creativity, however, can't hold a candle to the stuff I find on the internet, like the legs of jeans attached to flip-flops to make "sandal boots" with scrunchy tops, which sort of look like you forgot to pull up your britches. Another genius cut the top off one pair of jeans, reattaching the two legs with garter clips. I'm not sure just where a person would wear either of those outfits—not around here.

Periodically, advertising or high fashion steals inspiration from cowboys, soldiers, sailors, farmers, cooks, and hunters. People seem starved for an identity. Who are we? What do we stand for? When the answer is "I dunno" or "Nothing," does a costume somehow help?

I find it hopeful that people still admire real work enough to at least pretend to be workers. Most people, no matter how rich, brag about how hard they work, how frugal they are, and what they do without. Politicians like to brag about their poverty-stricken roots. Authenticity and cultural appropriation are controversial, but when imposters haven't earned the calluses, those who have can't help but feel a little resentment at the posturing. But this is nothing new; even Tolstoy liked to dress like a peasant and hang out with his serfs. The world seems to need constant reminders that real work is more than "a look."

I'm not sure we have any idea what real poverty is either. In the United States, some sources define poverty as living on less than $24,000 a year, and only about 15 percent of U.S. citizens live below that level. The last time I checked numbers, world poverty is defined as living on less than $700 a year, which includes 22 percent of the world's population. No U.S. citizen, including cowboys, comes close to that level. Therefore, every U.S. citizen, no matter how poor, is probably part of the world's top 1 percent—even our homeless, even our cowboys.

Not long after China cracked open its door to Americans, the two governments sponsored some sort of cultural exchange. In 1982 several U.S. writers traveled to China to tour and talk to Chinese writers. Then several Chinese writers traveled to the United States. Pulitzer Prize–winning author Annie Dillard was in on both exchanges, first as guest, then as host, and wrote a little book called *Encounters with Chinese Writers.* In it she described the tremendous poverty she had witnessed. One vivid example was how China's clay soil retained fingerprints from the laborers who built with their hands the buildings, walls, windbreaks for crops, and every water-holding ring of earth surrounding every tree. She said the hosts tried to convince the Americans of China's modernization, but they knew that "no matter how many factories they show us, we will notice only the oxcarts and the fingerprints."

She said trees in China were very scarce and each was treated like a pet. Because of the scarcity of trees, paper was also very scarce and precious. Books were considered luxury items. At one point, the Chinese hosts opened their tiny notebooks to take tiny notes on thin, transparent pages and asked their guests which modern American authors should be translated into Chinese. Dillard said that while the Chinese waited with their pens poised, her group was suddenly struck dumb.

She said that the Chinese already held a low opinion of Americans—already believed from reading newspapers and magazines that Americans hated their own confusing form of government, that Americans did not live in harmony with each other, and that American children were spoiled delinquents. Dillard thought about the fingerprints, the hand-watered trees, and modern American literature: self-centered, materialistic, disgruntled, and sexually deviant. Which books should the American writers recommend for translation? Says Dillard, "Our six-person delegation of U.S. scholars, publishers, and writers cannot think of a blessed thing to say. . . . We appear never to have heard of any American writers in our lives."

We need to stop wasting trees by publishing trash.

America's storytellers, teachers, preachers, and writers seem to have forgotten their purpose and their responsibility. Instead they strive to write best sellers. I'm sure China has modernized since Dillard wrote, but in our own desert Southwest, our trees are still treated like pets and hand-watered. The water-holding rings around them and our adobe buildings often preserve our fingerprints. I too can't think of a single book I'd like to see waste one of our precious trees or be translated into Chinese, Spanish, Russian, Hindi, or any other world language—except maybe some old cowboy poetry. The best of the cowboy poets never quite gave up on those original American ideals of freedom, equality, and democracy. Maybe they even improved on some, like respect for genuine work and a better definition of class.

Working-class cowboys sifted and saved the best of the old poems, memorized them, preserved them, and passed them on. Although the traditional poems stressed non-capitalistic values, they did not idealize any form of socialism; nor did they encourage a class war based on economics between landowner and working stiff. Poems written by and for working cowboys simply warned against trading the pleasures of living a free life close to nature for collecting possessions and chasing less satisfying but higher-paying jobs. The old poets knew their responsibility went far beyond entertainment. Who, for example, would not catch a second wind after reading just these two lines from Badger Clark: "Rest to your souls, if they care to rest / Or else fresh horses beyond the crest." I can feel the surge of that fresh horse in those lines. I would translate every word Badger Clark ever wrote into Chinese.

The old poetry stressed the struggle between the lure of sinful bright lights and the quiet cowboy life, the choice between good work well done and a life of laziness, the choice between riding out toward the sunrise with bells ringing or being trapped inside a building, the choice between coyote songs and honky-tonks. It stressed making the right choices by embracing all the freedom that poverty provides. Poet Bruce Kiskaddon wrote, "I'll be poor of course, but a-stride a horse, / And breathing the western air." Early in life, Kiskaddon worked as a cowboy. In 1926, probably because of a taste for alcohol, he gave up the saddle for higher wages as a Hollywood film extra during the heyday of cowboy movies. After the movie money dried up, he spent the rest of his life as a bellhop, carrying suitcases for the stars and writing poems to encourage the friends he left behind to treasure the life he had thrown away. Kiskaddon was a classic example of realizing too late what bright lights and colored beads had really cost. I would translate his poetry into Chinese.

I believe throughout the world, people are tired of posturing. We all yearn for honesty and sincerity in our religion, our government, and our personal lives. People are hungry for real conversations with real people who aren't hiding behind masks and costumes, who aren't trying to manipulate them or turn them into victims. I think we may even be getting sick of collecting possessions and yearn for genuine mutual respect for who we are and what we can do, not what we own. Maybe the initial popularity of memoir and reality TV signaled that our love of phoniness was finally fading. Sadly, however, this hunger for the real and the publicity that goes with it seems to eventually turn the real into the phony.

After my articles about the first two Elko cowboy poetry gatherings appeared in *Western Horseman,* I felt responsible for helping to ruin that poetry. The gatherings and poets were inundated with national publicity. Although this attention gave cowboy poetry wide exposure, even groupies, the gatherings changed the audience. The old poetry had been aimed at people the poets worked with every day. When the audience changed from fellow cowboys to "visitors," the poetry changed. The old storyteller's humble "we" changed to a heroic "I." The new "I" wanted to impress the visitors, educate the ignorant, or shame and save the sinners.

The media, myself included, also encouraged entertainment, celebrities, and showmanship. Reducing any form of poetry or storytelling to entertainment is, in my mind, a tragedy if not a sacrilege. Certainly a campfire reciter did not seek to be a "celebrity" among the crew. I heard one campfire reciter mock such a desire by saying, "I worked so hard at being humble until dang if I didn't get proud of being humble!" For the next few years after the poetry gatherings began, while I was still lucky enough to have a good reason to hang out around a working campfire, I never heard another poem recited there. Most of the campfire reciters either stopped reciting immediately or soon after. Many became ashamed to admit that they ever memorized or wrote a single poem. Even cowboy storytellers and their stories change when the audience changes.

Once strangers composed the audience, performing poets became ashamed of their reputation for poor grammar and reached for twenty-dollar words. I could feel those old campfire storytellers turning in their graves. In the old poems, examples of the poorest grammar (I like to call it "rebel grammar" or what Henry Thoreau called "tawny grammar") often came from the pens of college graduates such as Gail Gardner (Dartmouth) or John A. Lomax (Harvard) as they tried to make sure they did not offend their listeners with jaw-breaking words. Even modern linguists agree that a change in language represents a change in values.

Over and over, the traditional poems attempted to inspire cowboys to continue to live in the country, patch their jeans, and eat those beans and tortillas. Although the world thinks the "last cowboy" has ridden off into the sunset, there are probably just as many today, maybe more, than there were one hundred years ago. Someone horseback looks after the water and animals who graze all that "empty" space lining interstate highways from San Antonio to Los Angeles, from the Yuma River to the Mississippi, Seattle to El Paso. Modern cowboy poetry has gotten almost completely away from the subject of good work, mutual respect, and our own better definition of class.

The best of the new cowboy poetry stays true to the old audience and old values. Former rodeo bareback rider Paul Zarzyski writes mostly in free verse. In "The Hand," Zarzyski tells a modern story of a cowboy watching TV. He sees a white South African aristocrat grab a black field worker's wrist to show their hands side by side to the camera. The aristocrat wants viewers to see the obvious difference between his own hand and the black man's hand. Zarzyski's cowboy, traditionally watching from the sidelines, does indeed notice a difference between the aristocrat's "tissue-paper appendage" and the working man's calloused hand. Zarzyski combines cowboy definitions of the word *hand* (a highly skilled cowboy) with landscape imagery to admire the "buttes and mesas" of honest labor eroded into the working hand. Highly skilled cowboys are called hands or top hands or good hands. Both skilled horses and skilled cowboys are called handy. Traditional cowboy poetry emphasized equality based on work, elevating and celebrating skills and values. Although the aristocrat thinks the world will admire his white manicured hand, Zarzyski's cowboy bestows his admiration on the calloused hand. I call that class and would translate this modern poem into Chinese. Those who consider wealth the measure of their worth can't understand those who value the work over the wages. Those who want power can't understand those who prefer responsibility. I participated as a cowboy poet from the first Elko gathering in 1985 until 1990 and served on the board of directors in its third year of existence. I founded the Texas Cowboy Poetry Gathering in Alpine in 1986 and served as its director until 1990. I published an anthology of old Texas cowboy poetry and numerous articles about cowboy poetry in academic journals such as *Western American Literature* and *Heritage of the Great Plains*. I wrote chapters for a Blackwell companion, *Contemporary Literary Criticism*, and the *Princeton Encyclopedia of Poetry and Poetics*. I considered all of this to be cowboy journalism because my purpose was the same: to help us understand ourselves, notice and appreciate the best parts, and give precious publicity to the good guys.

I humbly titled one article "Dana Gioia Is Wrong about Cowboy Poetry." Gioia had predicted the "death of the text" because of the popularity of rap, poetry slams, and performance poetry. I said the "death of the text" was a myth, similar to the myth of "the dying cowboy." Gioia also said that the public yawned at academic poetry as taught in literature and creative writing classes and that through oral performance, the working classes had wrestled poetry from the clutches of the academic elite. I said he was correct about the boredom and rebellion but wrong about the working class as the modern audience, at least for cowboy poetry. I said urban spectators were now influencing the voices and themes in cowboy poetry instead of its traditional working-class audience. Gioia was at the time George W. Bush's appointee heading the National Endowment for the Arts, so I was getting quite brave for a small-town journalist—or possibly reckless.

Eventually I taught a college class in cowboy poetry, maybe the only one ever taught. Just as my cowboy life provided a foundation for my journalism, my academic training and scholarship deepened and enhanced my cowboy journalism and helped me speak truth to power when I thought power was wrong. I deeply regretted contributing to the publicity that changed cowboy poetry and spilled lots of ink trying to correct that mistake.

I haven't seen Elko's founders, Hal Cannon and Meg Glaser, in years, so I'm not sure how they feel today, but we all struggled with the tragic side of cowboy poetry's popularity. The last time I went to Elko, I remember standing out at the end of the sidewalk in the cold in front of the Elko Convention Center. I was lost in guilty thoughts of loss and disappointment and only vaguely aware that someone had walked up beside me. We were both waiting for a shuttle bus that carried the poets back and forth to our rooms at The Stockman. The crowds that year had swelled way beyond capacity, and it was almost impossible to squeeze through to get from one session to the next. It also seemed that each one of those thousands of people wanted autographs. While frantically trying to battle my way through the crowd to the room where I was scheduled to "perform," if I told someone I didn't have time to sign their program or hat, they might get mad. "Fans" interrupted conversations and followed us to the bathroom. It was a zoo, and I knew exactly how a zoo animal must feel.

So there I stood on the curb, under a snowy Nevada sky, soaking up the silence. I knew I was done and would never come back. I was afraid to look to see who stood beside me for fear it would be another autograph seeker. Eventually he spoke. It was Hank Real Bird, a Crow Indian cowboy poet. He said something like, "Fantasy is not for us." I don't think I answered as we both stood there with our heads down and our shoulders drooping like hawks with broken wings. I think Hank still participates. Maybe after a couple of deep breaths he went back to fight for the best of the old values, but I never set foot in that building or on any other stage ever again. Our intentions were good, but the results were heartbreaking. Through the years, periodically the cowboy rises again as a possible role model—Will Rogers, Roy Rogers and Dale Evans, Arnold Rojas, John Wayne, Modoc/Navajo Sonny Jim, Ray Hunt, western novels, cowboy poetry—but nothing works. Before long it's all phony again and the cowboy hat becomes a symbol for over-the-top attention seeking.

Several years ago, during my college's ten-year accreditation review, I invited a distinguished African American female to speak to our faculty. Although a college president, she was afraid to travel alone in West Texas.

So someone volunteered to fetch her from the El Paso airport, and I volunteered to drive her back. My daughter decided to help me drive the eight-hour round-trip to the airport, and my son-in-law, dressed as he normally does, came to see us off and pick up my grandchildren. When my guest speaker saw him, her eyes got big and she stammered, "Is he . . . is he a . . . is he a . . . ?"

The only word I could think of that she couldn't seem to bring herself to say was *cowboy*. So I said, "Cowboy?"

She looked at me and asked sincerely, "And he doesn't mind being called that?"

Now I understood her reluctance to drive alone in West Texas and her reluctance to say the C-word. Where she came from, the C-word stood for lawlessness, violence, dishonesty, ignorance, or, at best, slapstick humor. Historically, cowboy culture has roots in Mexico, Spain, and the Middle East—even North America if you count harvesting bison from horseback, which I do. Cowboys of all ethnicities, including black ones, rose to fame as American laborers who got to do what only the very wealthy got to do in Europe: ride horses!

Newly freed slaves found employment as cowboys, went up the trail from Texas to Montana, and competed in early rodeos. One invented rodeo bulldogging, and some became outstanding bronc riders. The most famous post–Civil War Indian fighters were the horseback black soldiers of the Fighting Eighth and Ninth Cavalry stationed right here in West Texas, riding circles on the same ground I did. But their descendants certainly don't brag about that heritage or about their reputations for getting along good with mules. Some seem to be totally ashamed of their deep roots in agriculture; maybe because to them that work now seems dirty and low class. I once asked a local black athlete why he didn't like cowboys, and his answer shocked me: "Because they're so dirty." Today black cowboys are quite rare. That sometimes gets blamed on racism, which for some reason reminds me of a joke my dad used to tell: A wife was complaining to her husband that the romance had died in their marriage, and she used as an example the fact that she no longer sat cozied up to him when he drove. He said, "Well, Dear, I haven't moved." Although I looked, I never found a black cowboy to interview. So I understand the black lady's reluctance to use the C-word.

Through the years, the authors of dime novels and B movies created characters far removed from genuine working-class cowboys. The C-word became a stereotype for a white, independent, lone wolf lawbreaker, a drunk brawler who loved and left women and often rode horses into bars, either before or after he shot up the town. Cowboys were stereotyped as impatient, argumentative, selfish, ill-mannered liars with hearts of stone. The C-word stood for animal cruelty, especially toward horses, cattle, and dogs. Those who wore the C-word brand were adrenaline junkies who shot first and asked questions later. They were stupid corny hicks and poor dancers who yelled and stomped, kicked up their heels, and slung their bewildered partners around the dance floor. There might be a grain of truth in all that, but just a grain.

Today a "cowboy" businessman is dishonest, ruthless, risky, and a braggart. A "cowboy" politician is corrupt and disrespectful, and always arrives late and unprepared. The "cowboy" is bossy, fake, and flamboyant, always playing a role and acting like a poppa or mama bear. "Cowboys" throw around the word *freedom* as though it means the right to break laws instead of being responsible for their own lives. A "cowboy" construction contractor exhibits sloppy workmanship and operates in an irresponsible and destructive manner. A "cowboy" chef is dirty, slings hash, and serves up huge portions of unhealthy food. The "cowboy" idea of education is to get on and buck off until you die.

Cowboys are about the only group we can still make fun of. Children's books can't poke fun at animals without animal rights groups coming to the rescue. Wildlife lovers are offended by the cruelty of the Big Bad Wolf or the stupidity of Wile E. Coyote. Even the Peter Rabbit stories have come under fire for violence—a mean ol' gardener shooting bunnies. Children's books also have to be careful how they portray women: no more Miss Muffets scared of spiders, helpless Cinderellas needing godmothers, Snow Whites waiting for a kiss, or Gretels stupid enough to stick their heads in a witch's oven. Ethnic characters must now speak in correct English. The only characters still allowed to use poor grammar in children's books are cowboys—thankfully.

We can still be called names like "kicker" or "redneck" or "rodeo bum." We even have our music segregated into special sections in the music store; a common joke is that "country music" is an oxymoron.

The C-word also stands for anything that is washed up, out of date, and irrelevant. Cowboys have no future and are of no use to this modern world. It's over. It seems like almost every book, song, or movie about them is called something like *The Last Cowboy.*

Never mind that the "real cowboys" most people meet are all hat and no cows: movie stars, singers, football players, barstool sitters, or gay New Yorkers. If the average person today ranks journalists at the bottom of the social class ladder, it's easy to imagine where a C-word journalist would rank.

So I wasn't surprised that the educated black lady from the East didn't want to use the C-word. But I have often wondered what she thought of my response. I said, "No, he doesn't mind being called a cowboy. None of us do. We are all very proud of being called cowboys. If anything, we wonder if we are good enough to accept the label."

I once stood beside a cowboy friend, Bob Blackwell, while we both listened to our favorite cowboy horseman insult cowboy horsemanship and explain how cowboys like to "make a lot of noise when they walk."

"He sure doesn't cut cowboys any slack," I whispered.

Bob said, "We don't need any."

I call that class, another C-word.

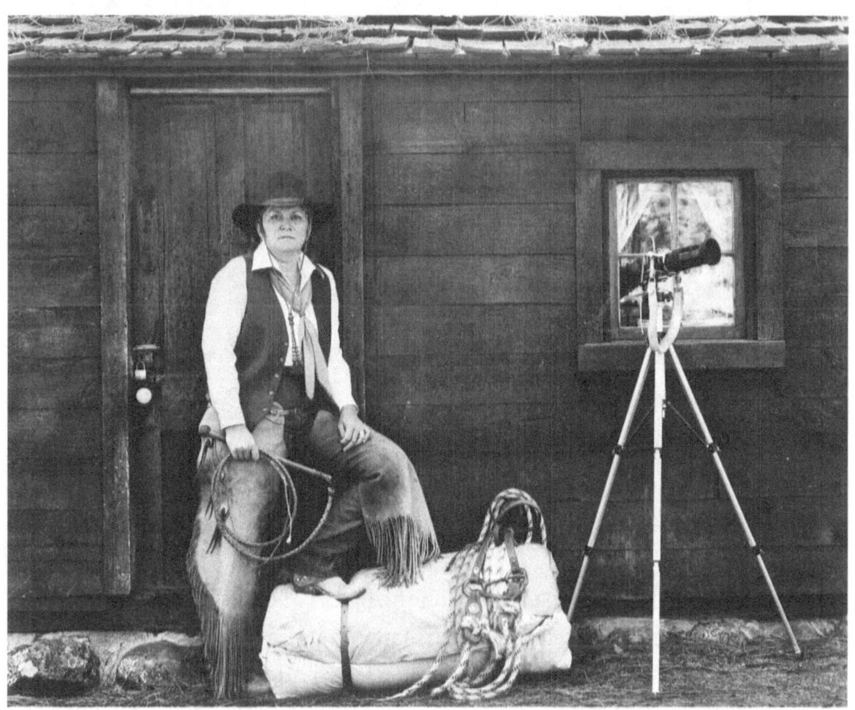

I traveled the western United States and Mexico while chasing stories as a cowboy journalist. I would check my bedroll as baggage, but I'd have to carry my gear and wear my boots and hat. This shot was taken by one of my hero photographers, Jay Dusard, in Flagstaff, Arizona. The photo is full of circles: the camera lens, rawhide stockwhip, bedroll, snaffle bit, spur rowels, buttons, ferules, and wildrag knot. It seems to represent all the circles I made chasing stories, riding in pastures, surviving various forms of education, accumulating philosophy, and doing my own thinking. Photo by Jay Dusard

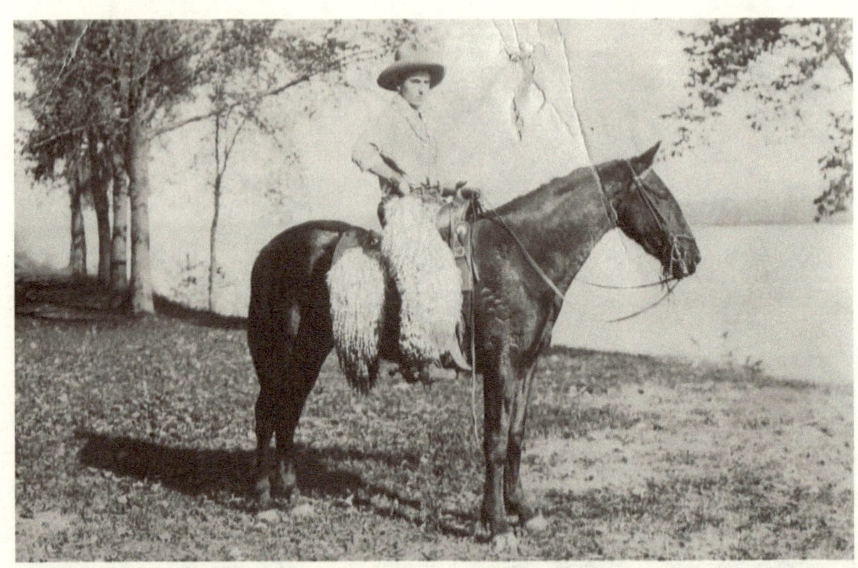

My Grandpa Bill DeGear (1895–1967) on the banks of either the Missouri River or the Mississippi River before 1916. His father's side of the family was French river rat, probably illiterate trappers, hunters, and professional fishermen. His mother's (Taylor) side raised and sold horses for both work and transportation. My Taylor great-great-grandparents left Iowa to homestead in South Dakota in 1907. So Grandpa may have been visiting his grandparents and uncles. This photo was one of many postcards that I inherited and was probably made to advertise the Taylor horses. Family collection

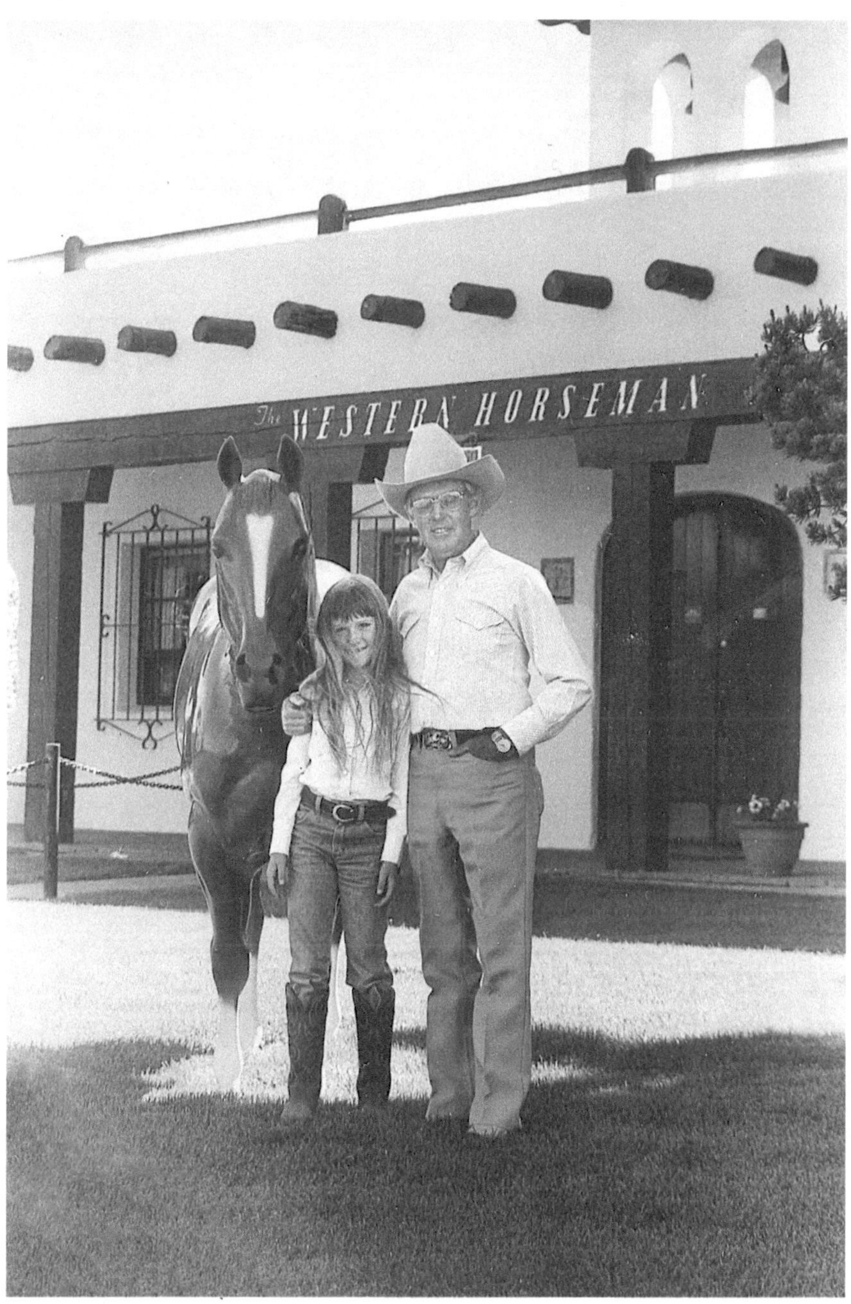

My daughter, Carla, with editor Chan Bergen at *Western Horseman* headquarters in Colorado Springs, around 1983. We had stopped by to meet the man who had done so much for my early career and published more than eighty-six of my articles. Photo by Barney Nelson

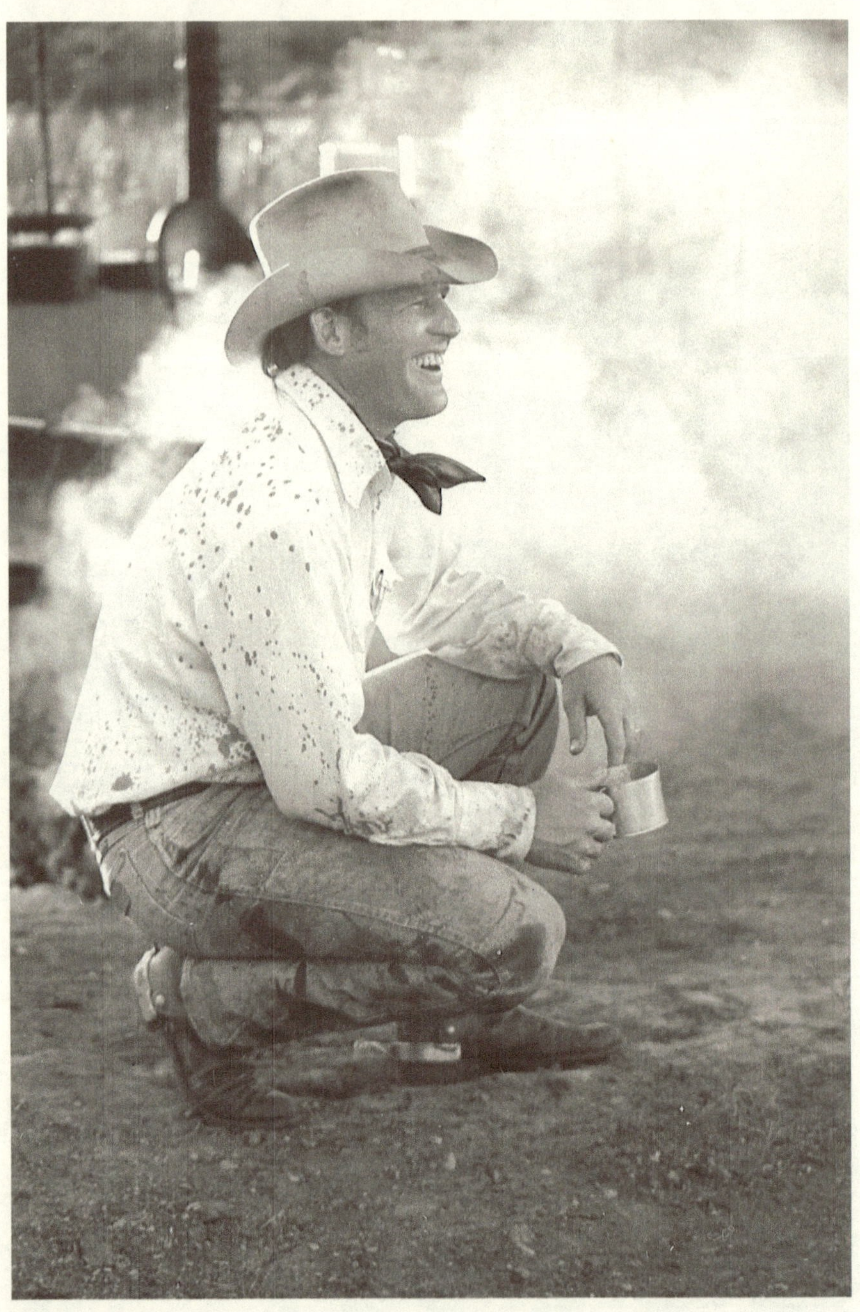

One of my favorite portraits of Chris Lacy, longtime boss and great-grandson of 06 Ranch founder H. L. Kokernot Sr. Chris is enjoying a cup of coffee and stories at Ramón's cook fire at Willow Springs during branding. Chris was the best cowboss I was ever around, and I watched, rode with, and interviewed a lot of them. Photo by Barney Nelson

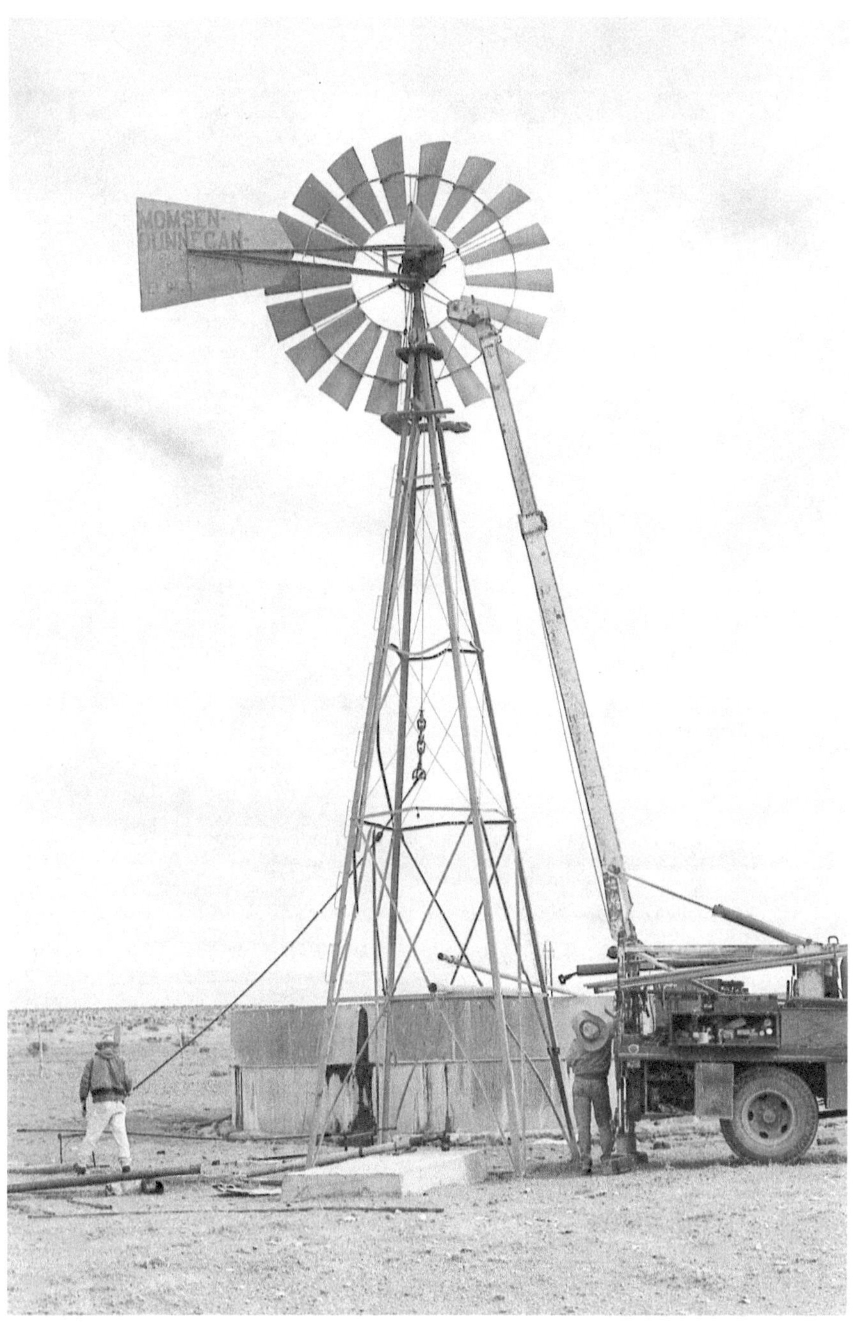

Don Coleman, owner and operator of Coleman Well Service, walks out a joint of sucker rod to waiting pipe burros while working on one of the windmills on the Catto-Gage Ranch in Marfa, Texas, where I was living alone at the time. His helper at the time, Cullen Jones, controls the hydraulics. Photo by Barney Nelson

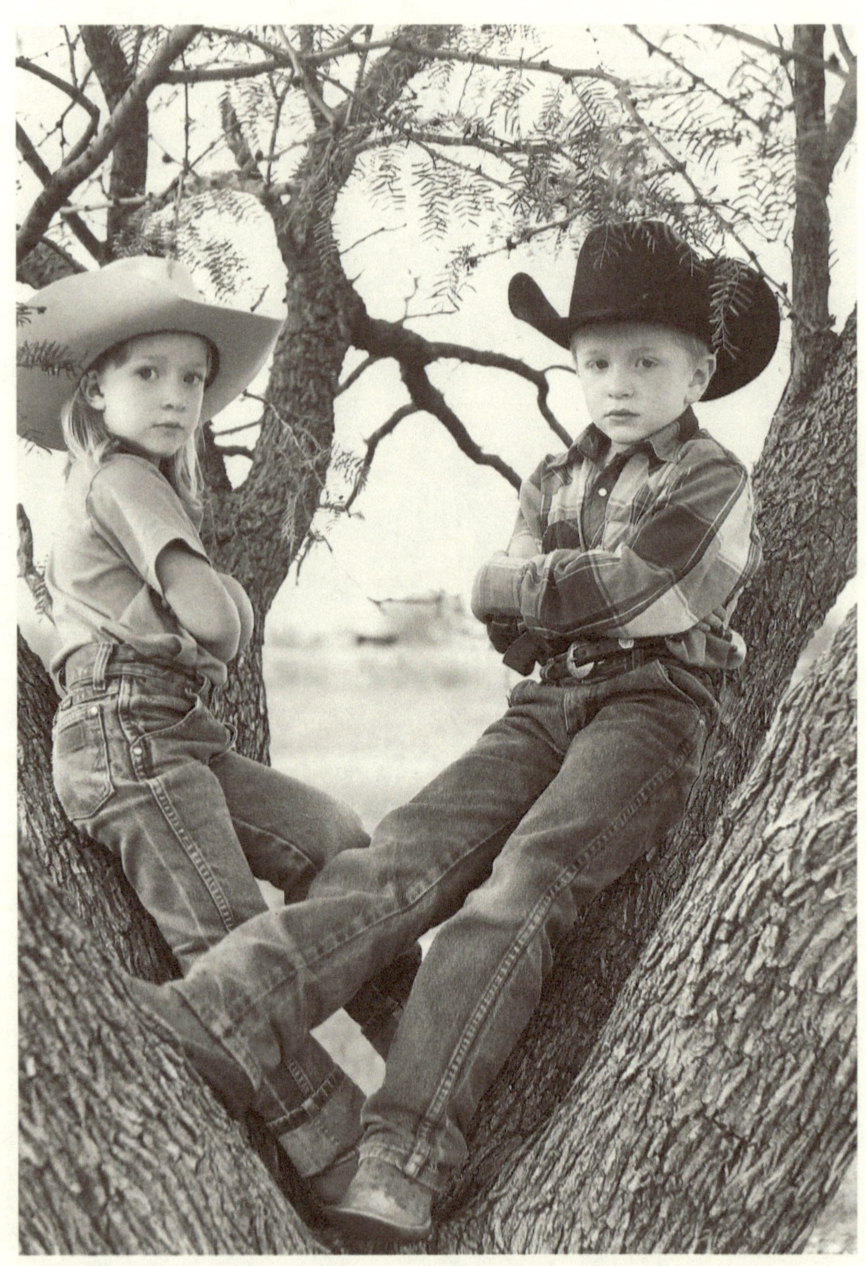

My redneck grandchildren, Jorey and Riley Spencer, already several years into cowboy school on a ranch near Kent, Texas, around 2006. The cowboy is not a dying breed. We are busy raising the generation that will replace us. Photo by Carla Spencer

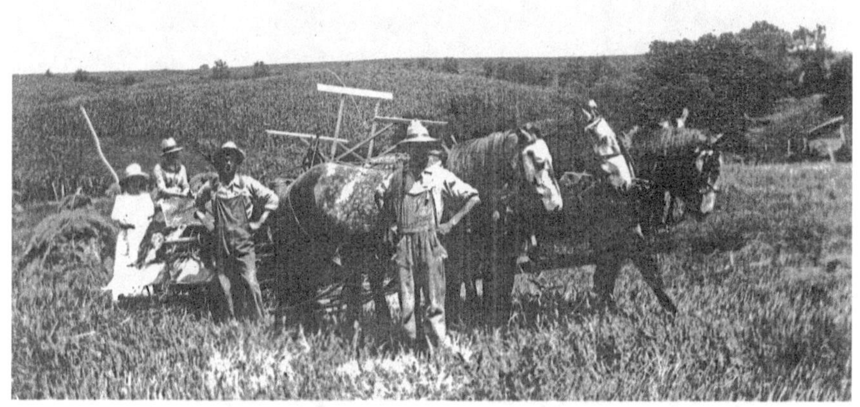

The other side of my family descends from pioneer farmers who trace back to the *Mayflower*'s William Bradford. This photo was taken around 1930 on the Iowa farm where I grew up. It shows my grandmother (*in white*), my mother (*driving a team*), my grandfather, and a hired man. Their horses may have been purchased from the Taylors. Family collection

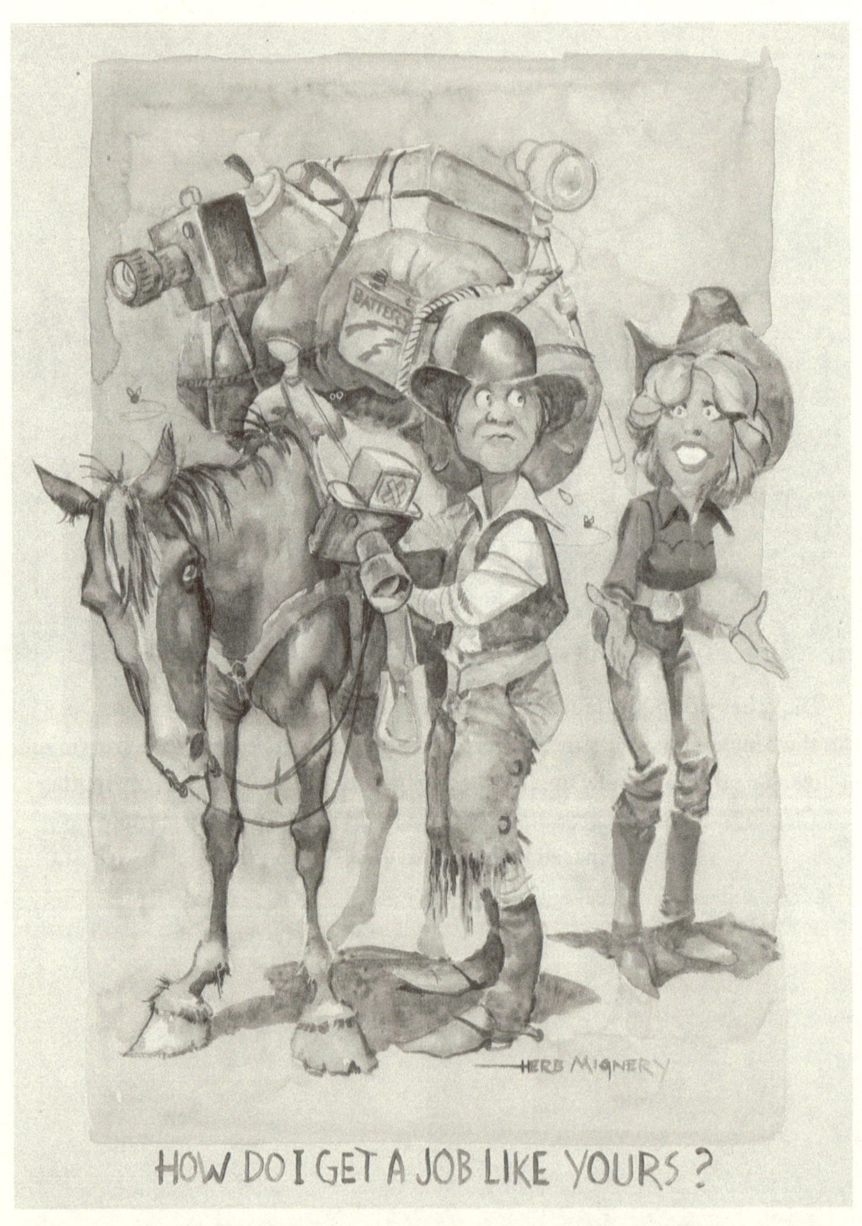

Herb Mignery drew this cartoon of me at work to illustrate my 1988 *Western Horseman* article about freelancing for horse magazines. Many years later, when he was an emeritus artist of the Cowboy Artists of America, he sent me the original cartoon. Courtesy of Herb Mignery; used with permission

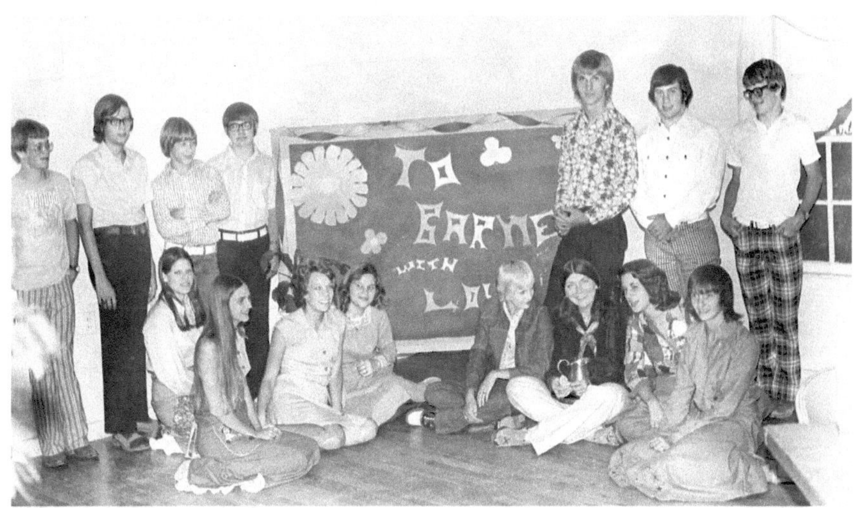

In Albany, Texas, I volunteered to help high school kids produce a Foxfire-style oral history magazine called *The Old Timer.* This photo was taken in 1975 at a going-away party given by the students for me (*in white pants*). My little family of three was leaving a camp job on Nail Ranch to manage the Tippit Ranch near Mitre Peak in Jeff Davis County, Texas. Family collection

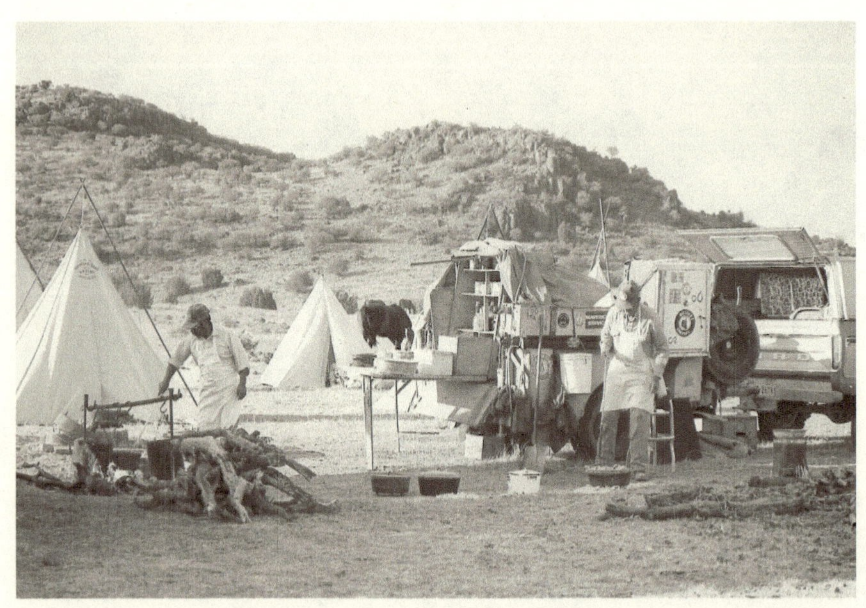

Longtime Kokernot 06 Ranch cook Ramón Hartnett (*right*), baking bread (*pan*) at the #5 camp on the 06 Ranch. His apprentice at the time and now the cook, Marcos Najera, is tending French-fried papas on the fire.
Photo by Barney Nelson

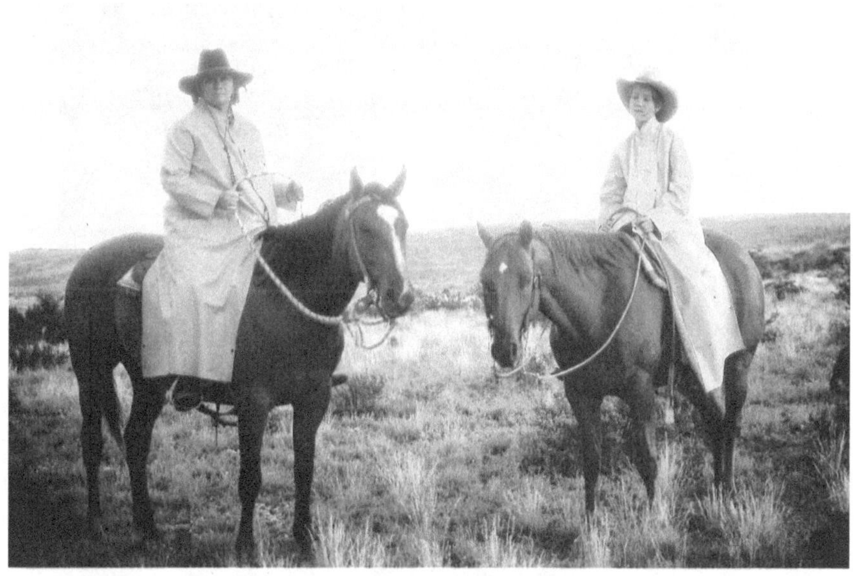

My daughter, Carla, and I had just ridden back in the rain from the East Pruitt windmill on the 06 Ranch, around 1983. I'm riding Secretariat (Sec) and Carla is riding Little Red. Family collection

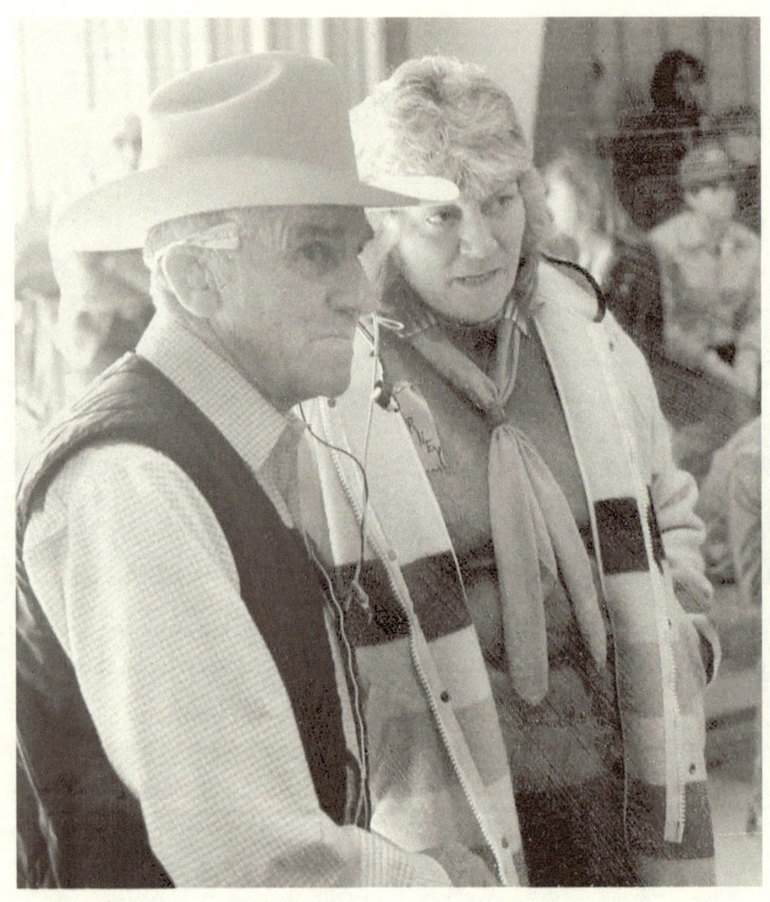

I'm watching Ray Hunt with horseman Tom Dorrance (*wearing a mic*) at an invitation-only clinic the two put on in Colorado Springs, around 1987. Ray always credited horses as his best teachers after Tom had shown him the way. This might be the moment when Tom and I were talking about the black mule. He and I traded lots of serious letters too. I wrote more than eleven articles about Ray Hunt, although everything I wrote after I met him in 1983 was influenced by him and Tom. Family collection; photo by Candi Cowden

CHAPTER FIVE

Practice

"The mystery of human existence lies not in just staying alive, but in finding something to live for."
—Fyodor Dostoyevsky

ONE OF THE THINGS I admire about Far Eastern cultures is their deep respect for masters. Zen, to me, but maybe because I don't understand it, is sort of the idea that everything and anything can become art: serving tea, raking sand, planting rice, sweeping sidewalks, disposing of trash, or washing dishes. To "practice" Zen, you pick something you love to do or at least don't mind doing and look for ways to do it better, more enjoyably, more deeply, until you "master" it. The Zen "trick" is that you can never master anything, but the more you learn, the more you enjoy the impossible journey. In the first magazine article I ever published, a middle-aged horseshoer said about his occupation: "It's an art. It's somethin' that not ever'body can do." I've known a couple of fishermen, farmers, rock layers, windmillers, and hunters who took their practice to art.

I have known lots of cowboys who strove for art in their horsemanship and cattle handling. There is no better place to practice meditation than while sitting (on a horse), and cowboys probably spend as much time alone in nature as any monk. To those who knew him, it should be no surprise that Ray Hunt, a master horseman, once appeared on the cover of the Buddhist magazine *Shambhala Sun*. Ray always claimed that the more he learned, the more he realized there was to learn. He also seemed happy to know he would never master the art of horsemanship.

I knew a Zen janitor once, Marcelo Galindo. Everyone who entered the building where he practiced noticed the shine. I met a black shoe-shiner in the Reno airport once who had also raised his "lowly" job to art. I was traveling hard at the time and noticed that my boots were dry and needed some leather care, so I stepped up on his stand. As soon as he cuffed my pant leg, he recognized the brand of boots I wore—Mercer—which shocked me. I was about two thousand miles from the dusty little boot shop on South Chadbourne Street in San Angelo, Texas, where Mr. Weaver took my measurements and Mr. Lopez put the boots together by hand. "How did you know?" I asked. He said he didn't make a living off people who wore store-bought shoes. He used the best leather products he could find and treated my boots like newborn babies. I sat there and pondered how we were the only two people in that crowd who knew that this dusty lady was probably wearing the most expensive footgear in that airport. I thought it was funny how few people really know quality when they see it and how a little pride can transform a laborer into a craftsman—although *funny* is not the right word. I published his story as the introduction to the "Craftsmen" section of my cowboy photography book *Voices and Visions of the American West*. That shine happened almost forty years ago. I'm sure Mr. Weaver and Mr. Lopez are dead. I'm sure the old shoe-shine man is dead, but they all found a good way to spend their lives. J. L. Mercer & Sons Boots in San Angelo still makes boots, and I'm sure someone still shines them. I hope they all still strive to be masters.

I've tried to follow my lowly practice of cowboy journalism to art too, but I often wonder: Why me? I can think of hundreds of cowboys who might have told their own stories, but they wouldn't or couldn't. Some were great storytellers around a campfire, a pot of coffee, or a beer, but working cowboys don't usually spend much time learning to write. Most thought writing was a lazy person's job. And maybe that's true. Yet when given a choice between writing and sweating, even the laziest of them preferred to sweat. They considered anything done in a chair tedious and draining. So do I. Nobel Prize–winning German novelist Thomas Mann once said, "A writer is someone for whom writing is more difficult than it is for other people." It's the hardest work I've ever done, and it seemed to become more difficult as I progressed rather than easier. Cowboys should understand because any dude can "ride" a horse, but for cowboys, riding a horse is much more difficult. I knew a few wannabe cowboys who wanted to wear the uniform but didn't really like the work, the weather, or dealing with horses and cattle. They weren't looking for a practice. Of course, I have also run across young wannabe writers who think that writers are rock stars, attending endless rounds of cocktail and autograph parties and raking in millions. They wanted to *be* writers, but they didn't really like to write. They weren't looking for a practice either. I'd show those wannabe rock stars one of my royalty statements for minus $7.47, which meant that I owed the publisher for books purchased by bookstores that were later returned unsold. I just loved to write and couldn't seem to stop, reward or not.

I've been pushing a pen across paper since signing on with my junior high newspaper, *Small Talk*. My only formal journalism class was in high school: who/what/when/where/why/how, inverted pyramid, accurate quotes, and facts. I'm so old I can probably still set hot lead type upside down and backward. I never thought about college until I won a high school journalism award and was offered a small scholarship and a paying job as editor of the Eastern Arizona Junior College newspaper in Thatcher. My dad did not approve of his daughter going to college, but I was eighteen and went anyway. When the school found out I was getting no assistance from home, they gave me a second paying job as afternoon manager of the student center. Even with both jobs, I could afford only a five-day meal ticket. So from Friday night supper until Monday morning breakfast, I subsisted on apples and crackers that we were allowed to take back to our dorms as snacks—or nothing. I made my grades and never missed a newspaper deadline, but that year took a toll. Skinny and worn out, I gave up on school and decided to get a real job.

I went to work first as a legal secretary and then in the parts department for a Case tractor dealership, which paid less than the lawyers but our customers were much less dangerous. I went shopping one day for a used pickup and somehow came home with a brand-new 1967 yellow Camaro with a black leather interior and four-on-the-floor. Soon my brother installed an eight track. That car was my undoing, or possibly doing, as I racked up one speeding ticket after another. Even though I was very cute and sweet at the time, Arizona Highway Patrol officers are heartless beasts, so when it looked like my next ticket was going to land me in jail, I called a small college in West Texas and asked if they needed a newspaper editor. They did. I sold my race car and went back to college. I like to claim that I headed to the Texas–Mexico border from Arizona because I was running from the law. There is a grain of truth in that.

While editor in chief of two college newspapers, I made plenty of mistakes; maybe my worst was a misspelled word in a banner headline on the front page of one of those college newspapers. That was probably my first hint that editing would not be my cup of tea. But I dusted myself off and got back on.

My first published magazine article was a college writing assignment. We were told to look for a problem and write about a solution. As a first-generation, at-risk, very broke student, the biggest problem in my world was how we students could somehow afford to get the college education that everyone seemed to think we needed. A graduating senior at the time, I was now working twenty hours a week as a student secretary and living on less than $100 a month. For the assignment, I wrote about an older student in one of my ag classes who had started a small business by shoeing horses between classes. I called it "Goin' to College on an Anvil." Part of our assignment was actually sending our articles to a magazine. I chose *Western Horseman*, sort of the equivalent in my world of a college student mailing off a class assignment to the *Atlantic*. When I got a big fat $90 check from *Western Horseman* instead of a rejection, my professor and I were speechless.

So I started trying to figure out how I could do that again. Cowboy and livestock magazines don't publish dirt, scandal, murder, porn, muckraking, activism, politics, soul-bearing confessions, or titillation; nor do they seek to expose the edgy, dark side of human nature. Consequently, I had to teach myself to write for magazines that wanted problems solved, ways to cope, trails to follow, new ideas, hope. I believe that when you look for evil, you will find it. If you look for answers, you might find them. You can't find what you don't look for. Today's journalists are masters at ferreting out freak shows and corruption. Mainstream writers and photographers often mine our "local color" for the odd, the violent, and the angry, and they present that as normal. To me, the only time odd was interesting was when it solved a problem in a particular situation. Why give publicity to people with no answers? Why lionize the corrupt, the druggies, the dishonest, and the murderers and make them famous? Why give Pulitzer Prizes to bring down a president or destroy the reputation of our military? To me, journalists have become wannabe detectives, prosecutors, judges, and traitors. Evil is not truth—not even a half-truth. But nobody seemed to be teaching young journalists how to find and write about anything except evil. They can't seem to find answers or write about anything positive, unless it's sappy stuff about someone leaving a waitress a thousand-dollar tip. That stuff reads like fluff. Serious positive is the hardest to find and to write. Cowboy and livestock magazines don't publish stories about people who murder and steal horses or about their corrupt owners. Nor do they publish stuff on petting horses and feeding them sugar lumps.

Gradually I tackled harder and harder subjects, usually not looking for *the* answer but at least for a different perspective, another choice. I don't mean that I photographed through rose-colored lenses or gave my articles false happy endings. What I looked for was: Had a ninety-year-old cowboy learned anything that was worth a twenty-year-old cowboy's time? Did a Brangus breeder have anything to say to Hereford breeders? Could irrigators begin to think of their work as art? Could a friendship between a buckaroo and a Texas brush popper give any insights into prejudice? If my subject was divorced, alcoholic, and abusive, I ignored that part and looked for a bit of wisdom. The dirt was usually in plain sight, so I didn't need to expose it. Instead I tried to dig for the silver and expose that. However, my best subjects usually preferred the dirt. If I made them sound heroic or larger than life, they were embarrassed, not flattered, and worried what their neighbors would think. So I tried to be as true to real as possible. I didn't write fiction. I wanted to find answers, and wrapping serious subjects in fiction just seemed to make it harder to believe and consequently learn from. My goal was to be useful.

As I began to identify myself as a cowboy journalist, I went through a stage of thinking I had to become a master horseman to write about horsemen. Eventually, I decided that made about as much sense as needing to eat oats and grass and to sleep standing up to ride a horse. Mostly I just needed to learn to write. Besides, as Will Rogers once said, "We can't all be heroes because somebody has to sit on the curb and applaud when they go by." So I chose the curb and a pen.

Almost everyone connected to ranching specializes in some aspect: A veterinarian knows the physiology and diseases of livestock better; any rancher knows the production side better. Most horse riders can outride me, most photographers can outshoot me, and most professors can outlecture me. But I'm not sure anyone else has made a practice and life's work in as many different directions or made as many circles writing about the cowboy world as I have. Writing about cowboys was a lot like being a cowboy—I knew I would never master it, and I didn't do it for the money. I did it because it was a good way to spend my life.

Finding those whose story needed to be told was probably the most difficult part. It seemed that the first person willing to talk to the press was the last person who should. Even sensible people turn into idiots when someone shows up with a notebook or tape recorder. They will say things to a microphone that they would never say to a neighbor. One author writing about Europe said that a foolproof way of knowing whether or not one was dealing with true Gypsies was to find a place that seemed deserted and to spin a gold coin in the air. If the silence deepened, there might be real Gypsies around. But if you were immediately surrounded by a clamoring throng of old and young, fighting to sell you something or to elbow others away from the central position of your camera, you were not dealing with true Gypsies. I always thought the same was true of cowboys. So a case can be made for silence. Traditionally, the first sign of a hopeless greenhorn was how much he talked, and the best bosses always spoke the least. Cowboys don't want to explain things to a kid they are trying to teach. It is taboo to brag. The crew in Andy Adams's cow camp never forgave the cowboy who interrupted another man's story. Charlie Siringo writes vividly about all the women who didn't like him—the ones who threw ears of corn at him, the ones whose parents wouldn't let him in the yard. But about the woman he quits the cattle trails for—nothing, not even the color of her hair.

Some of the taboos about interviewing ranchers—never ask how many acres or how many cows—are silly. The number of acres is public information if you know where to look. How many cows is probably coffee shop knowledge because the person who sells blackleg vaccine knows, the feed store guy knows, cattle buyers know, all the cowboys who ever helped brand or ship know, the cattle trucking company knows, neighbors know, the windmill man knows, as does the bank and the tax office. Maybe they don't know if the ranch runs exactly 98 cows or 105, but they know it is about 100. The only people who don't know include some out-of-town reporter. But I usually tried to respect the taboos and used my photographs to let readers estimate herd sizes or worded descriptions in such a way to give a sense of scope. Exact numbers weren't usually important anyway, but whether this was a one-person lease or a twenty-man roundup crew sometimes mattered. The smaller operators were usually the most sensitive about size unless they were cowboys trying to get a start. Then they were damn proud to own twenty head.

Teresa Jordan, author of several books about women in the West, once said, "The ranching world is a very private world: you don't complain and you don't tell anybody your secrets." As to complaining, I don't know any people who do more of it than cowboys and ranchers. Most cowboys threaten to quit at least once a day, and the owner of one ranch I lived on even complained when he got a good spring rain. He said it would bring on the "weeds," his word for wildflowers. And no culture harbors more gossips. Keeping secrets might be true about Jordan's family, but I come from one of the most sparsely settled places in the world. We West Texas *borderistos* are supposed to be especially close-mouthed to protect our "health," yet the books, articles, newspaper columns, plays, radio shows, poems, and movies written by and about ranchers and cowboys from this area number into the hundreds, maybe thousands. I once gave a program for the Texas and Southwestern Cattle Raisers Association about all their fellow local ranchers who had been writers. I would say we are not secretive, just careful. I don't know anyone who has ever undergone an interview who didn't feel misquoted, misunderstood, and patronized. We are always a "dying breed" living a "simple" life that's no longer relevant. Maybe we want to tell our stories ourselves. Maybe we are more likely to give interviews to someone writing for horse and cattle magazines, even though a lot of nonsense gets published there too.

I started publishing during the years when Chan Bergen was editor of *Western Horseman*. I imagined the magazine's audience as hard-to-please cowboys and horsemen who already knew more than I ever would about the subject, so I worked hard to find and interview people who knew even more or at least just as much as my readers. My fellow cowboy journalists, in my humble opinion, were seldom part of our culture, so instead of being influenced by them, I usually tried to correct them—humbly. I thought one of Bergen's staff writers was leading young cowboys astray by romanticizing their poor horsemanship and disloyalty to the ranches they worked for. He portrayed the cowboy culture as the "last of the buckaroos." Horses that bucked and had bad habits were romanticized as the proper mount for a good hand. He glamorized both men and horses who had chips on their shoulders. So I decided to help Bergen out, and he seemed to give me an absolute free rein. If any changes were made to my articles, it must have been spelling and commas, as I never noticed a single changed word. We developed a great editor–writer relationship, and I sometimes sent the magazine an article a month over a fifteen-year span. They often gave me two-part, full-color, several-page spreads. I was so grateful for Chan's encouragement that I dedicated my first book to him.

The people I interviewed as a journalist weren't usually talking to me but through me, and the writer behind the pen often disappeared completely. I accepted that, even desired that, but subjects who approached me sometimes had a motivation and an imaginary audience that I should have been more aware of. The most vivid example came while I was working on my first book. I knew my subject only as a board member at the bank where I had borrowed money. When he approached me about writing his life story, I jumped at the opportunity. I always preferred to choose my own subjects, but he had come to West Texas as a young man with nothing but a saddle and a bedroll. He had worked his way up through the ranks from day-working cowboy to full-time to camp man to wagon boss to ranch manager to leasing bigger and bigger ranches. He had been able not only to own some cows but also to buy his own ranch. As we progressed through taping his life story, I realized the book was headed toward a subject close to my heart: how a cowboy, or anyone, could achieve their dreams.

He was a coffee shop regular and master storyteller. He had told his stories so often that I was able to transcribe his taped words almost straight into text. He also knew just which stories to tell and just how to tell them so that he came out the hero. The subjects I picked myself didn't like to present themselves that way. He was equally good at creating villains—such as the owner of one ranch where he had once been the manager. The portrait he painted was not the same rancher I knew, but it was my subject's opinion. I struggled mightily between telling *his* truth and telling *the* truth as I saw it. I was young and unsure of how much control I should take. So I asked the grandson of the criticized ranch owner to read the manuscript before I published it, hoping he'd ask for corrections or deletions, as a fact checker would. But he didn't. He said basically that the ranch appreciated my subject's hard work while he was employed there, that the ranch had broad shoulders, and that it wouldn't be the first or probably the last time it would face criticism. His response made me feel even worse. Unfortunately, my name would go on the book, along with the reputation I had so carefully been building.

In the end, I structured the book chapters as half biography, where I set the stage in my words, and half oral history/autobiography, where my subject told stories in his own voice. I tried to separate his opinions from "fact" by dividing each chapter into my part and his part. The book remains his story of chasing a dream, but his dream was simply to become wealthy. That was never my dream—nor anything I thought worthy of becoming either a dream or a book. So I was especially careful about how I ended the book. In the end, as he shakes hands with the cook and drives away from the chuckwagon, a careful reader will hopefully realize that although this man had achieved his dream, he would never again have the privilege of sharing a campfire with real cowboys. Depending on your values, that is either a happy or a heartbreaking ending. To me it was heartbreaking, and I titled the book "The Last Campfire."

Eventually I disappeared so completely to him that he traveled around the country accepting awards and giving autograph sessions for "his" book. He even asked me for the copyright, which I declined. Unfortunately, the book became fairly popular and so far has gone through three printings. Too late I realized that my subject was talking through me to an audience I did not know. I wish I'd have had the knowledge and courage to take more control. I've been approached for a movie contract on the book but so far haven't signed anything. The movie people back off when I explain how much control I want. The money doesn't matter. It never did. By the way, it was *his* last campfire but not the last one for that ranch. Some of the West's best cowboys still hang out around that wagon and its campfires today.

The next person who asked me to write a book was a Texan who went to Australia and created maybe the biggest ranch in the world. I knew that his idea of success and mine were different and that he'd want me to make him a hero, so I turned that opportunity down. Although I later published six more books, I always felt more proud of being a journalist than of being an author. Journalists, like good cowboys, should just disappear. The best cowboys aren't the ones making wild, photogenic bronc rides or racing through the rocks to head off three hundred running heifers. The good ones ride good horses that quietly slip into the right spot at the right time in order for everything to move along smoothly like water. That was my goal as a writer, but I'm still trying to get there.

Through the years I adopted my own system. Finding news is like fishing or hunting. Since it worked the first time, I usually hunted for a problem and then fished for answers. Journalism gave me a reason to look closely, to ask questions, but I didn't usually go in with a list of questions. I wanted to respect my subjects enough to consider myself a "student" of each person I interviewed. My final question was often, "What have I not asked? What do you want to tell the world?" They would usually shrug. I found very few people who didn't have a story if I listened carefully. I never paid for an interview but almost always sent subjects copies of photos and tear sheets. Sometimes craftsmen sent me a piece of their work after an article ran, but gifts were never part of our deal.

I often used a tape recorder. Some subjects were nervous about that, but looking them in the eye instead of looking down while taking notes seemed like the only way I could pay enough attention to carry on a conversation. Sometimes it started out rough. I remember one dark night in Nevada, beginning to interview a glowering seven-foot Shoshone-Paiute. As I switched on my tape recorder, my first nervous question was, "What's your name?"

"Barney Nelson," he answered, and he crossed his arms.

But we soon both forgot the tape recorder was on. Any notes I wrote down were things I wanted to come back to later without interrupting our conversation. Jon Krakauer once said, "Do an interview in which you simultaneously use a tape recorder and take notes by hand. Then transcribe your tapes and compare this to the handwritten record. I bet you'll find that you got many of the quotes wrong in your handwritten notes. . . . Quotes not based on a taped interview often sound more like the writer than the interview subject." I agree. I always transcribed all my own tapes and heard many details on the tape that I had missed during the interview. I wanted real voices, true words. I did clean their quotes up a little by taking out the *ah*'s and *um*'s. People often start a sentence, stop, start again, stop, and eventually get to their point. To make a sentence that made sense, I would sometimes pair their best beginning with their best ending. Poor grammar can easily be used as a weapon to make someone sound stupid when they are not. So I tried to leave the flavor of their language, word choices, and syntax but cleaned up the grammar enough to give a more honest reflection of their intelligence.

I call my first draft "throwing up on paper." I never know where I'm headed. Sometimes, in magical moments, the piece almost writes itself, but usually I struggle through draft after draft. Sometimes, as with this book,

I agonize for years over drafts too numerous to count. I always begin with a lined pad and a pen. For me, magic happens with those flowing, curling, endless swirls of real ink. I can't think on a computer. My writing seemed to flow better before computers. When my handwritten or hand-corrected drafts got too messy to follow, I would stop and type. When those got too messy again, I'd retype. Now I do a lot of print, cut, rearrange, paste, repeat. I cut and tape, make notes along the edges, insert additional scraps of paper, make lists, look for related stuff, group, cut, and tape. I can't seem to do an outline until after I figure out what I want to say. I write with a pen and outline with scissors and tape. To me, outlining belongs in the organization phase, not the thinking and writing phase. With this book, for example, first I tried to organize it chronologically. Then I tried organizing it around water, with each chapter representing a different water source as a source of inspiration. Then I tried arranging it around each of the different magazines I wrote for. I'd get a chapter or two that worked; then it would all fall apart. With the system I have now, making circles, I seem to have written my way all the way to an ending.

Ideally, every book, every chapter, every article, as well as every paragraph and sentence, has a lead and a punch at the end. I aspire to literary journalism, I suppose, meaning that metaphors happen, tension appears between juxtaposed perspectives, and hopefully meaning goes beyond literal. Good quotes help produce that literary quality I'm after, but I don't embellish the "facts" or the "truth" to get there. (I use quotation marks around those two words because I'm not sure what they mean or even if they are the words I want.)

I like to read drafts to friends, mostly to keep me honest. It seems to work the way writing letters used to. Reading out loud helps me find mistakes, such as too-long sentences or repetition, but I quickly run out of friends. It's hard to find good critics: friends want to be supportive. My brother is honest but brutal. Truthfully, I guess I need both. Constructive criticism should be an editor's job, but I never found editors especially helpful until after I had finished a piece. The hardest parts—the message, organization, and art, if any appears—are up to me. Writer Richard Preston once said, "I made the mistake, a long time ago, of believing that editors can take draft material and make it better. They cannot. When I have shown my drafts to editors they tend to panic." As a teacher, I tried to do for students what I thought I wanted from editors, but maybe it's not possible to give good advice. My students would tell me that my suggestions changed their meaning, that I wanted them to write a different story, that I wanted them to write my story instead of their own.

Probably the most important embarrassing mistake I almost made was found by my students. I used one of my own pieces of writing as a guinea pig to introduce peer critique. I'd just finished the introduction to a book and had used stories about washing dishes to establish my rural authenticity. One story was about my college roommate, who threw a birthday party at our rental house for her cowboy boyfriend. Her contribution to the party was to entertain him and the guests by singing and playing her guitar around a backyard campfire. I didn't have a boyfriend, so my contribution had been behind the scenes: cooking and cleaning up. When the party ended, my pretty blonde roomie took her boyfriend home and came back in tears. She said he didn't speak to her all the way home, and when she let him out at the ranch, all he said was, "Who washed the dishes?"

One student asked, "So, did you start dating him?"

What?!

They heard my story as the boyfriend noticing me and wondering who I was. But he was an old friend. What I meant to say was that he was disappointed with my roommate because he thought, as the host of the party, she should have done more work and less socializing. For sure, she should have at least washed the dishes. Needless to say, I reworded that part to make my meaning clearer. Instead of "Who [was that cute girl who] washed the dishes?" I needed to figure out a way to make sure the reader heard instead, "If you're gonna host a party for a cowboy, you better do the most work. You better at least wash those dishes." I would have never found that error without those students; nor would an editor.

When I think a piece is close to done, I want my subject to read it. The statement "I don't let anyone vet a quote" is just arrogance to me. Even the venerable John McPhee said, "It's a journalistic custom—essentially a rule—that you don't show a manuscript to the subject. In many situations ego is too likely to spoil the transaction, not to mention a subject's attempts to massage the text. But science, for me, is the exception that proves the rule. I have never published anything in a science that has not been vetted by the scientists involved." I think that just shows his deep respect for scientists, a respect I believe cowboys also deserve. I've never known a single scientist who can properly cut pairs from a herd or teach a horse to keep a rope just tight enough. I believe it is the writers' egos that prevent them from allowing their subjects to find and correct errors.

I wanted absolute accuracy because I didn't have the distance and anonymity that reporters from outside the culture enjoy, and most of the magazines and newspapers I wrote for depended on me for fact checking. My subjects and their family and friends, my family and friends, everyone we all knew might read my words. If I made a mistake, someone would know. I also knew my readers were grandparents, teens, men, and women who made their living connected to livestock. I did not want to lead anyone astray or ruin lives or reputations. The same magazine editors who don't want their writers to let subjects read articles employ fact checkers to go over every quote and detail with the subject. How is that different from me getting it right in the first place? And where are they gonna find a fact checker who knows enough about the cowboy world? I also wanted my subject to read it in order to know what I had sent to the magazine, in case an editor made changes. I always honored requests for "off the record," but sometimes that meant I never finished the story. If something didn't feel right to the subject, I tried to get a better explanation in case I had misunderstood. I welcomed clarity. In nothing I ever wrote did I change any names, except in this book. A few subjects have read pieces of this book, but not all of it. So mistakes might be lurking. If so, I'm sorry.

Although I made a few enemies in life, I don't think I ever made one because of my writing, except once. In my local newspaper column I once wrote about how widespread some recent wonderful rains had been. I mentioned how much rain one friend got, but he was serious about his privacy and I lost a thirty-year friendship over a good rain. Maybe we will get past it, but I'm not sure. I'm sort of equally offended that he doesn't value what I do. I want to give respect, but I also want to receive it. Trust, respect, and friendship are all two-way streets.

I seldom pitched stories but preferred to write articles or books first and then look for the right publisher. Each magazine connected to livestock production had its own flavor. When I found a subject that didn't quite fit *Western Horseman*, it usually fit somewhere else: *Arabian Horse World*, *Quarter Horse Journal*, *Ranch*, *Country People*, *Art West*, *Horseman*, or *Equus*. *Horse and Rider* magazine was published in California, and in my mind at least, it seemed interested in a new age, touchy-feely horsemanship.

I did several articles for them on Ray Hunt. I thought his methods would appeal to their mind-set, but I tried to help them see the reality behind what might seem "spiritual." I'm not sure how successful I was in understanding how Californians think or in keeping my own feet on the ground when I wrote about Ray.

The *Cattleman*, a magazine published by the Texas and Southwestern Cattle Raisers Association, preferred serious pieces about cattle production. They often used my photos for covers or for creating ads, and I wrote profiles on ranchers, about new ideas for poisonous plant control, or about marketing methods dreamed up by producer associations. One profile was a tribute to Elmer Kelton, longtime editor of *Livestock Weekly*, a marketing newspaper out of San Angelo. Kelton was one of the few editors who helped me become a better writer. Texas A&M Press chose him as one of the reviewers for my first book. He carefully explained what I needed to do to improve and even rewrote one paragraph so I could see what he meant. I had a passive voice/"to be" verb wordiness habit that no one up until then had ever pointed out. Even though I had to completely rewrite every sentence, I was so grateful that I asked him to write an introduction for a later book.

Another magazine, *Persimmon Hill*, published by the Cowboy Hall of Fame in Oklahoma City, was interested in the historical and legendary. Their idea of who and what belonged in the Cowboy Hall of Fame and mine almost never meshed. Their inductees were usually either "cowboy" movie stars, singers, or donors. But I did publish two profiles in their magazine: one on historical West Texas photographer W. D. Smithers and one on legendary rodeo cowboy Harley May. I was never interested in "stars" until they got old, such as a rodeo cowboy who won numerous world championships and shaped the sport. Even then, I was more interested in how changing the heels on the boots Harley wore made all the difference in his bulldogging than in the list of championships he had won. I tried to write my first book about him but ended up with boxes of mixed-up transcribed tapes that I couldn't untangle. Eventually, I did eke out a magazine article, and those boxes of transcriptions reside in the Archives of the Big Bend waiting for a better author.

I described freelancing for horse magazines almost thirty years ago in an article for *Western Horseman*, and I guess I haven't learned much since because the process still seems to apply. I explained my methods, joys, and frustrations and used a little story about an incident that happened in Oregon for the lead:

> I was lugging my camera bag through the dusty parking lot of the Jordan Valley, Oregon, Big Loop Rodeo grounds. My back ached, my head ached, and sweat trickled in places I couldn't scratch in public. My eyes burned and the old familiar blister was stinging my middle finger where it gripped the edge of my camera. I was trying to get a story on the Big Loop when a young, pretty girl approached me and asked, "How do I get a job like yours?"
>
> I looked behind me. No one there—she must be talking to me.
>
> Job? I had borrowed $1,500 from my banker, who foolishly seems to have faith in me, to make this trip. I had myself scheduled from daylight to dark every day for two weeks, during which time I would need to be storing photographs and information to somehow sell between five and ten articles when I got home just to break even. I was camping in a canvas range teepee tent I'd made myself, sleeping in my bedroll on the ground, and making coffee and toast on a sagebrush fire for my meals—when I had time. I'd taken a bath that morning in the iciest creek I'd ever stuck a toe into. The only guarantee of a paycheck I had when it was all over was my own, also foolish, belief in myself—I freelance.

That banker's name was David A. Moore, and I don't think I ever properly thanked him for making all this practice possible. Along with the article, *Western Horseman*'s editors called me "one of the best in the business" and illustrated it with a cartoon by Herb Mignery, who was working for them at the time and later became an emeritus artist of the Cowboy Artists of America. Mignery pictured me as a serious reporter strapping piles of equipment on a pack horse, my graying hair stuffed haphazardly under an old work hat. Beside me stood a pretty blonde, obviously asking, "How can I get a job like yours?" She did not have a notebook or a pen, just a nice figure. I loved the illustration and felt it captured the essence of the difference between me and the girls who seemed interested in doing what I did for the purpose of access to cowboys rather than the purpose of journalism. I told a few stories about mistakes editors caused as well as a few about when they saved my neck. I called the article "Free-Lancing for Horse Magazines." Rereading it today, I sound a little egotistical and idealistic. I think I'm humbler now, but maybe still idealistic. I've also been haunted by that young woman. Maybe she was sincere? If so, then this book is my apology and a serious attempt at a better answer.

Most of my freelancing was done before computers and digital cameras. My photos were all created on film, which had to be developed and printed, and this kind of photography had a steep learning curve. One of my pet peeves was having someone admire a photograph I'd taken and ask, "What kind of camera do you use?" To me, that was no different than asking what kind of pen I use or what kind of bit. All my cowboy photographs came from a very un-prestigious Pentax manual camera. Eventually I carried two cameras—both Pentaxes—one filled with black-and-white film and one with color. A camera simply opens a shutter. What you get on film depends on what you see and how hard you are willing to work to get in tune with both your equipment and your subject.

I owned three lenses, a 50 mm, a wide angle, and a telephoto that I bought used from fellow local photographer Barbara Richerson. Mostly I used Barbara's old telephoto. I never used a motor drive—don't think they'd been invented yet. I couldn't have afforded one anyway or to develop that much film. In order to afford to keep taking pictures and give a few away, I had to make money. I had to be careful. I never "sold my pen" to the highest bidder but probably claimed I did so I could sound more like a serious businessperson. Maybe I was more of a businessperson when it came to photography since it was the expensive part of my practice, but I also made more money as a photographer. A million how-to books have been written about the art of photography, the business side, and all the legal problems surrounding copyright, permissions, and advertising. I won't repeat that information here; I'll stay focused on cowboy photography. A few additional tips: When shooting horses head-on, be sure to use a telephoto lens or their heads will look too big and long; a telephoto also keeps the mountains from going flat; never ask anyone to tip their hat brim up so you can see their eyes; carry some toilet paper in your pocket and a plastic baggie to pack the used paper to a trash can.

I began my photography career by publishing family photos; we just happened to be cowboys. I could sell more articles to magazines if I could provide both the photographs and the writing. So I practiced photojournalism, but I always considered myself a journalist first and a photographer second. A photo might be worth one thousand words, but that depends on the words, and photos can be misleading.

Once though, if it hadn't been for photography, I would have totally wasted an expensive trip. In Guadalajara I found a third-generation Mexican charro, Ricardo Zermeño, at the time president of Asociacion Hacienda Santa Cruz del Valle. My Spanish can get me fed, watered, and to a bathroom, but it's not even close to interview level. So while making arrangements, I asked for an interpreter, which his people agreed to supply. It turned out that the interpreter's English was about as good as my Spanish. I would ask a long, detailed, multilevel question, and she'd turn to him and say five words. He'd give a long, detailed, arm-waving, smiling, frowning, answer, and she'd turn to me and say, "Yes."

Okay, I'm exaggerating, but I understood only one sentence well enough to quote him. When he showed me his grandfathers' portraits, he said almost reverently, "I didn't become a charro; I was born a charro." I used that sentence as my ending and "Born a Charro" as my title. Instead of my subject's words, I had to rely mostly on a charro rule book and my photographs to tell his story. His family owned three city blocks, all walled and enclosing an arena, barns, gardens, and several homes. Everything was beautiful, immaculate, and dripping with flowering vines, luckily the perfect place to rely on description instead of interview. Here are a few paragraphs that show the complete absence of quotes and the abundance of visual description in my article:

> The entrance hall of the main Zermeño house is lined with charro trophies. Many are works of art in themselves, adorned with silver sculptures of competing and saluting charros. Overhead are chandeliers made from deer antlers. On the walls are braided rawhide gear and branding irons inlaid with the *corazon*, or heart, brand of grandfather Ignacio Zermeño. Chair seats, table, jackets, pistol handles—everything proudly carries the *corazon*. On the walls are photographs of charros, on the dining table are place mats of charro events, in the office are bronzes of charros, and over the fireplace are the wedding photos of the four sons—charro weddings, of course.
>
> One room is filled with a collection of antique and new saddles, each draped with its own matching headstall, quirt, leggings, spurs, and

> serape or blanket rolled behind the cantle. Some saddles are adorned with carved cow horn conchos, some with embroidery an inch thick, and some with twenty pounds of old silver. The wooden horn, fork, and cantle of one are entirely inlaid with a mother-of-pearl design outlined with gold. On many saddles was the *corazon* brand, either in tooled leather, raised red-and-black chenille, or embroidery.

I managed to provide thirty-two column inches like this, describing his saddle collection, bridles, stables, and guns enough to fill a four-page spread.

I watched a groom saddle a handsome black stallion for Ricardo and watched as Ricardo spun a dozen intricate rope loops on, over, and under his horse. But I could not ask a single question about that horse or his roping. I wrote a separate article on Ricardo's sister, Victoria, who performed in a women's horsemanship group as part of her brother's team. The women rode sidesaddles, wearing yards and yards of petticoats and lace, and raced into the round charro arena to slide their horses to a wild stop and to perform intricate riding patterns called *escaramusa*. Again I depended on photos and the charro rule book. Sadly, although the Vermeño horses were beautiful, athletic, and exceptionally well trained and well bred, and the horse was the centerpiece of the *charreada*, the language barrier prevented hardly any mention of them. That was the most money I ever spent and the farthest I ever traveled without being able to ask my subjects a single coherent question. The photography saved my bacon, but it couldn't provide the deeper kind of story that I and I'm sure the Zermeños wanted to tell.

Mostly I used photographs for note taking, as they helped me describe more vividly later. I also liked to take photographs of funny things, such as a spotless bedroll lying in the grass with airline baggage claim tickets flapping in the wind. Photos like that helped me worm my way into cowboy hearts with slide shows, sometimes projected against the side of some barn once the sun went down. I might not always understand what they found so fascinating or funny, but they could study photographs of a Paraguayan cowboy's saddle for hours. When I saw something different, I could snap a picture and try to figure out the significance when I got home, where cowboys could give me a lot of help. In order to be tolerated by them, I preferred to provide entertaining slide shows rather than be the target of their pranks—although I usually suffered both.

Photography also helped me get permission to watch and ride along. I helped if I could but preferred not to help if I was seriously after photos. My subjects seemed to like it better that way too. If I was part of the crew, they depended on me. If I was just a dang photographer, they could ignore or taunt me. With a few exceptions, my subjects usually trusted me and were flattered to be the target of my pen or camera. Photography helped me make friends with people who can be shy, antisocial, and difficult—but not always. I remember one who absolutely didn't want me to take his photo. He said he thought it would capture his soul. I honored his request and tried hard to avoid him even in the background. He does appear in one slide sent to me by a visiting artist. It is actually a photo of me vaccinating calves, with the guy who didn't want his picture taken working in the background. I treasure it just to remember him.

A few others did not want their photos taken—sometimes because of religion, sometimes because they were unsure of their own skills and feared I would capture a bad moment, or maybe because they thought I was stealing their images and stories for my own benefit. Sometimes I did my best to honor all reservations, and sometimes I ignored them. Maybe someone initially wanted attention but later, perhaps after being ridiculed, decided I had been out of line. Those things I couldn't fix. And one of those who cussed me the loudest and longest, I'll call him Ty Holland, has since come around hat in hand to ask, "Hey, do you have any pictures of me riding ol' Punkin'? He's dead now, you know." Most are real glad today that I froze them in amber when their mustaches were still black, their backs were still straight, and their stomachs still fit behind a saddle horn. The son of one cowboy recently contacted me for pictures of his now-deceased dad. "Shed a few tears," he said. "You are an angel. Thank you so much."

Like journalists, good photographers disappear, but I seem to have been especially good at it. I have a lot of pictures of weather. People like my shot of a lightning bolt striking the ground behind a cowboy in a slicker crossing a creek. I took it while sitting on top of the cab of a pickup truck. "Damn," they'll say, "that guy must have been crazy to be out in weather like that." Today's computer-savvy photographers can simply add a lightning bolt to a photograph without risking their lives to get it. Or I'll show people a photograph of a cowboy and his dog plowing through snowdrifts, and they'll say, "Nobody gets out in that kind of weather except cowboys and dogs." In truth, that cowboy and that dog would not have been out there at all if the photographer hadn't needed some good snow pictures for calendars.

I've stumbled around in the dark in rattlesnake country, stepped in fire ant hills, been wrapped in spiderwebs, been bonked by numerous tree limbs, and been awakened from a photographer's concentration by an on-the-fight sharp-horned maverick bull crashing against the post where I'd been steadying my camera. Cowboys love opportunities to teach photographers to pay better attention. I also found it humorous when people used one of my photographs to "prove" that women weren't allowed in the pastures of certain ranches because there were no women in my pictures. Swedish author Margareta Magnusson wrote recently that it was nice to sit and "browse through a photo album . . . and perhaps also think about the one who held the camera. That is like the backside of the picture that you cannot see."

I remember once disappearing completely while swimming my horse across a deep Montana creek. I never accepted pay to do a story, but I did sometimes accept a trade, like when H. A. Moore, a young upstart guide and packer, offered to take me and my family on a five-day pack trip into Yellowstone National Park in exchange for a story. We'd ride up Slough Creek in the spring, right after snowmelt, when the grizzlies had just crawled out of their dens hungry and cranky. I told him it would cost me a lot of money to get my family from Texas to northern Wyoming, but I'd trade my financial risk in exchange for his offer of a family pack trip. I said I couldn't guarantee that I'd write anything at the end and even if I did, I couldn't guarantee it would get published because I freelanced. We both agreed to gamble. He turned out to be terrific and often said my article made his business. I think I was paid $250, which didn't come close to paying for the travel, but I have no regrets.

My favorite story from the finished article was when H. A. told about an old packer who had helped teach him the ropes. The old packer was "sitting on the porch smoking his pipe. One of the guests came up and started talking to him. After a bit the guest asked, 'Jack, do you ever feel like you've kind of wasted your life?' Jack didn't say anything and the guest went on, 'All you've got to show for seventy years is that old pickup.' Jack just sat there and puffed on that pipe. Finally he said, 'Mister, all my life I've done for a living what you save up all year to do in two weeks.'" H. A. said he never forgot that, and neither have I. I can't imagine anyone who makes their living horseback paying for the privilege of spending their vacation sitting behind some executive's desk pretending to be one. Can you?

To get one photograph for that article, I had to swim my horse across a deep creek that was running over its banks. H. A. said we had to cross Slough Creek to reach his favorite campground, and to get across we would have to swim the horses and the heavily packed mules, something I had never done before. Just before he stepped his horse into the roiling fast water, I heard my desert rat, chickenhearted self say, "Wait! Let me go first so I can take your picture swimming the pack string across."

I knew how to swim, but not with a horse or loaded down with boots, spurs, leggings, cameras, and film. My photography equipment was wrapped in plastic and then packed in two small, custom-made leather saddle pouches that fit over the front of my A-fork saddle. I wanted to be able to work out of them, so I preferred my saddlebags to ride in front of my legs instead of behind the cantle. Luckily that also allowed them to ride a little higher and maybe not get wet. H. A. pointed to where he thought the crossing should be and explained that although the water would probably get thigh-deep on me, my horse would need only a few strokes of actual swimming before he'd be able to find his footing again. But if my horse started floundering, he said, I should slip out of the saddle and grab onto his tail—if I could. Or fend for myself and swim. I had crossed enough shin-deep creeks while fishing to know how tough it is to stay on your feet in fast water. I'd grown up on the Mississippi, a slow old river that engineers claimed had been tamed, but we fishermen knew hadn't been. I respected slow water and feared fast water, but I had to go first if I wanted the photograph.

My photo tells H. A.'s story but not my own. I've actually had college-educated people look at that photograph and say, "Damn, I hope you didn't have to cross that river too."

Slough Creek wasn't really that dangerous. I've interviewed Nebraska cowboys who swam flooded rivers to rescue cattle stranded on islands, and I've photographed Oregon buckaroos racing through irrigated hay fields. All of them were in much greater danger than I was, but on a scale of 0 to 10, crossing Slough Creek in early spring should rate at least a 2. Beyond the creek were deep bogs and downed timber, all new to me and terrifying hazards that I had never dealt with before. I tried to quit him once, but H. A. got us all safely to camp and back.

I never seek adventure or thrills. Once, heading to Montana again, I made the pilot of my small chartered plane sit us down and wait for a storm to pass over the Billings airport, my destination. I'd previously been caught in a storm in a small plane returning from doing a story on the College National Finals Rodeo in Bozeman. We all thought we were going down, including the pilot. I didn't want to fly into anymore storm clouds.

Photographing for horse and cattle magazines can be hazardous but maybe not as much as taking pictures for *National Geographic* or covering wars. The biggest danger for cowboy photographers was probably the romance. And by that I don't mean love; I mean viewing the cowboy as larger than life. However, without the media, cowboys and the big outfits might have faded into obscurity one hundred years ago. It seems like every few years someone has to prove again that we are still out here. So cowboy photographers such as Bank Langmore, Kurt Markus, William Allard, Jay Dusard, and I made circles around the West and each other bringing romantic cowboy images back into the public focus. We followed the trails of earlier photographers, such as Erwin E. Smith, Edward S. Curtis, W. D. Smithers, and Dorothea Lange. I believe each generation of photographers helps inspire at least a few young men and women to follow the cowboy occupation. A few ranchers might also have been persuaded by the photographs to practice the old methods that drew those idealistic young workers, who were willing to trade their hard-earned skills for lower and lower wages as long as the ranch still ran a wagon and kept their cowboys horseback.

But creating myths carries responsibility. Some photographers romanticized and glorified bad attitudes, huge mustaches, and uncommonly handsome subjects. Some glorified horsemanship skills over cattle handling or range management. Some glorified what they thought was horsemanship by photographing those whose horses had big problems instead of those whose horses were well schooled. I was sometimes just as guilty. I often kept women and kids out of my photographs, even my own hardworking daughter, because I thought photos of all-male crews sold better. Sometimes when I did try to include families, it seemed like every cowboy couple I photographed ended up divorced and then one or the other did not want me to use those photos anymore. I also avoided taking pictures of what I considered goofy, such as fifteen or so cowboys holding herd with Tootsie Pops sticking out of their mouths, because that sure wouldn't sell. But now I'd trade all my slides for that one shot I never took because of the memories it would bring back.

Ranchers also sometimes appreciated and needed publicity to sell bulls, sell horses, or recruit help, especially those who hired a big crew for a month or more during spring branding and fall shipping. Most cowboys thought a ranch should be able to attract help based on reputation and considered any ranch that had to advertise as probably a poor place to work. Photos showed the country, the horses, the cattle, the methods, and crew members more honestly and were more effective than any paid ad in a livestock publication. I knew both cowboys and ranchers depended on their reputations, so I was careful and honest.

Journalists work hard for access and guard it jealously; photographers even more so. I can't count the number of times I've been asked to provide contact information for various ranches or to suggest photogenic cowboys of both genders for other writers and photographers, advertisers, and filmmakers. Photographers, especially those from urban areas, mined one another's books and magazine articles for the names of prospective locations and subjects. Consequently, some places and cowboys appeared in almost every book. Western artists also mined articles and photography books to find subjects. At one time so many photographers were coming to the 06 Ranch that local cowboys working on other ranches and not getting as much attention came up with a joke. It was based on the old tradition that some ranches paid a little extra if a cowboy furnished his own horses: "Have you heard? The 06 is paying $100 a day or $150 if you bring your own camera." We didn't think that was funny.

Although I tried to maintain privacy with an unlisted phone number, people still tracked me down. A few years ago, Bank Langmore's son, I guess representing the next generation of cowboy photographers, left a message asking for help finding sources. I paused and thought to myself, "Should I help him or not?" I suppose I should feel ashamed that I refused to share my sources, but I'm not—and I didn't, but I should have. I think he did okay without me anyway. Cowboys move around a lot, so I started writing down the phone numbers for the various camps. Then, when I heard someone had moved there, I could call and surprise them. Although I have no idea who is there today, I still have phone numbers for the shoeing barn at Yellowstone, the King Ranch horse office, Grapevine, Yolo, RO, and the Old Saloon at Emigrant, Montana. I still have a few combinations to gate locks.

Because I could do most of the work myself to some degree and had carefully studied what I couldn't do, I caught moments that most photographers did not. I knew where and when to be, which horse or rider or cow to watch in certain circumstances. I knew the subtle differences between bridles and saddles and gear and the kind of results those who used them preferred. Horses and dogs were not pets but working partners who had their own finesse and expressed their own emotions. I still don't believe the best New York photographer can take photos or write about cowboys as well as someone who lives or has lived that life, and I don't think the best cowboy journalist could go to some big city and photograph or write about that city with any depth either. Maybe there are perspectives only an outsider can see, but there are also perspectives only an insider can see.

Photos taken on a real ranch with real employees doing real work have a different feel than those staged with models in phony situations. I remember once showing the cowboys a full-page boot ad I had found, with the spur buckled on upside down. Also, because I lived out there every day, I had access to weather, changing seasons, unusual cloud formations, grass fires, and moments that revealed personalities. In today's world, Photoshop makes stealing easy. Everyone from T-shirt manufacturers to artists simply copy the best photos, maybe change the shirt color, and swap heads, mustaches, hat creases, gear, mountains, or clouds. Even advertisers can get by without paying the original photographer as long as the final product is a "composite." It's flagrant plagiarism, an unethical and even illegal practice when copyright is involved, but it's usually too expensive to pursue in court. It's all about access.

Wildlife photographers have established rules for taking ethical photos. They don't place wildlife in harm's way; no zoo animals or game farms, no baiting, no changing brown bears to white. Contest judges and editors are fully aware of the magical corruption Photoshop has had on all types of photographs, especially of wildlife. Digital photography has created a glut of photographers while enhancement software makes everyone a pro. Color saturation, blemish deletions, even moving an animal from a zoo to a wild background is easily done today by any amateur. Famous outdoor photographer George Lepp says, "Just because you can, doesn't mean you should." I believe all the ethical rules that wildlife photographers have adopted should be adopted by cowboy photographers. In my day, excess manipulation was not a problem. Instead I wonder how many thousands of slides I threw away because of some defect that could now be easily fixed in Photoshop.

I was always torn between getting the great shot and being in the way. I never did quite stand in a gate while a crew was trying to pen cattle through it, but almost. I have one photo of a guy driving a loose horned bull into a stock trailer that seems to be taken from inside the trailer. Nobody has ever asked me how I did it. I always appreciated one particular boss's comment. As I was giving my opening token speech about hoping not to get in their way, he said loud enough for everyone to hear, "If I've got anybody on this crew who can't push cattle past a damn photographer, then I want to know it." After that not-so-subtle challenge, his crew would have pushed cattle through the middle of a rock band with dancing girls and barking dogs. So I got some great shots there. I have one photo shot inside a corral looking through the legs of loose horses. It seems like I must have been lying under the bellies of the milling horses shooting toward a roper who was catching the morning mounts. Nobody has ever asked me how I got that one either.

An advertising company once hired me to create photographs that were completely black at the top. It wanted to place its customer's boots and words against a black background that would seamlessly blend into the photograph below. The idea was to use black to subliminally join the product with a scene of boots at work. No one I photographed wore that brand of boots, but they paid $1,000 per photo and I paid my "models" 10 percent. We all liked that easy money.

So I looked for scenes with black at the top. I noticed that if I was inside a saddle house, a cowboy stepping out while reaching for a bridle hanging on the open door was surrounded by black. I noticed the same phenomenon while looking out of a hay barn with the hay lit golden by morning sun and a cowboy tossing out flakes of hay toward the sunrise. Another moment came inside an old log saddle shed with a cowboy carrying his saddle out the door. Sunlight streamed between the logs, framing him in strips of black. All these were gifts from blackness, not light. At night a lantern lit up only the chuck box while cowboys stepped in and out of the black night to get sugar for their coffee or to smear peanut butter on a piece of camp bread. Canvas teepee tents lit from within by lanterns glowed yellow against the night. Cowboys lit by the red glow of campfire light were also surrounded by black night. Even an ugly old dirt water tank suddenly became breathtaking as the water reflected a golden sundown while a silhouetted rider let his horse drink. The reflection on the water started out yellow, then turned pink, then lavender, then deep purple as the sun set. I could easily block out the sky by cropping through the mountains and surround the reflective water with black. Riding through backlit fall leaves against dark shadows or cowboys taking a break in the dense shade of a live oak tree that had been browsed by deer—all began to catch my eye. The list went on and on for twelve lucrative months.

It wasn't until several years after the boot company's checks stopped coming that I looked back to discover that the gift of black had advanced my photography miles down the road because I had learned to look for black, not just light. Black helped even the palest colors catch fire. Eventually I tried to teach my college photography students to look for black to save themselves years of shooting mediocre photos. Another goal of Zen is for the student to surpass the teacher, and mine will.

My all-time favorite photo, which I consider the best of my career, is of a loose remuda of one hundred horses trotting toward me as the sun sets. Not one of those horses, which might have shied at a piece of paper, has "throwed down" on me as a booger—meaning not one horse's eye or ear is pointed in my direction. I was on foot, standing in the middle of their favorite trail, totally unconcealed. Yet every one of those one hundred horses, as well as the lone cowboy in their lead, had stopped worrying about me. They just went about their business and flowed around me like water. I consider being totally ignored that day the highest compliment I was ever paid. I used that photo often. Now it also represents my greatest tragedy, partly because the original slide was lost by a printer who was trying to produce an oversize advertising calendar for Big Bend Saddlery, where my daughter was a part owner for several years.

My second favorite compliment was being noticed by famous New York photographer William Allard. I had never met him but hated him; I'm not sure why, other than jealousy. I was in the Stockman Bar in Elko, Nevada, when someone introduced us at his request. He said something like, "I'm really impressed with your work. I thought I knew what was going on, but I never heard of you until I saw your book *Voices and Visions of the American West.* The rest of us are portraying the cowboy culture as though it's dying—but you bring it to life." I don't remember what I said in reply or if I replied at all. It seemed that while the cowboys cussed me for tagging along and taking pictures, they clamored to appear in the more famous photographers' books. They seemed to like being portrayed as the "last of a dying breed," even though we were all working hard to teach our kids and grandkids how to ride and work around a herd of cattle. So I had a bit of a chip on my shoulder at the time.

I mentioned Allard in one of my local small-town newspaper columns when I recounted one of my almost big-deal photography coups. *Life* magazine had called asking for possible cover shots, which I scrambled to provide—but they chose one of Bill Allard's instead. Anything short of fatal is funny, right? So I turned it into humor by comparing *Life* to life (as in if *Life* ever calls, give it your best shot) and ended maturely by saying, "And if Bill Allard ever tries to talk to me in a bar in Elko, Nevada, again, I plan to say, 'What a nice surprise. I thought you were *dead*.'"

In spite of losing out on *Life*, I did publish covers on many other magazines, such as *Texas Monthly*, *Cattleman*, *Cowboy*, *Arabian Horse World*, *Horse and Rider*, *Texas Hereford Journal*, *American Hereford Journal*, *Southwest Hotel/Motel Review*, and *Towns West*. In Europe I published in *GEO*, *Merian*, and *L'Espresso*. My New York–based agent at one time was Black Star, so there could be more that I don't know about. Eventually I sold one tiny two-inch-square slide to Marlboro for $6,000. For a while, all that probably went to my head, and I even tried making a living as a full-time freelancer. But I soon ran out of ideas and started feeling like I was exploiting my family and friends, maybe even selling my soul by helping to convince people to smoke cigarettes. I needed a purpose, not a "career." And soon I went back to a full-time job to relieve the pressure.

Another important aspect of Zen is supposed to be peacefulness: serenity, simplicity, and humility. Anyone who has found their life's "practice" should not be dashing around, sweating and swearing and pumping iron to get better faster or else! They should simply be doing what they enjoy and notice tiny moments of grace that help make what they do even more enjoyable. The goal with Zen is never a contest, never to beat someone else, never to become rich and famous or "the best." The goal is just a good way to spend a life. Zen is like the cowboy habit of making circles. You start out every morning on a circle to see what's out there, maybe fix something, maybe just admire it. The next day, you make another circle.

However, practice is never as smooth and serene as it looks, especially in hindsight. I had a complicated relationship with *Texas Monthly*. I'm pretty sure I'm the only person who wrote a cover story for them, furnished the photography for another cover story (including the cover), and appeared as a subject in still another cover story. Although they pay extremely well, this magazine likes edgy Texas and to cover rural subjects from an urban perspective—thus the complication. Few people living west of the Pecos River trust them. My cover shot and inside eleven photographs were for an article called "The Last Roundup." (Notice it was the *last* even though more than thirty years later that same roundup still happens every spring and fall.) When one of their most notorious "edgy" writers wanted permission to come to the o6 Ranch to do a story on traditional ranching, our boss, Chris Lacy, reluctantly agreed—*if* they would use my photographs instead of sending a photographer. I think he hoped people would just look at my pictures and skip reading the words. I felt very trusted. Unknown to us at the time, the writer had also gotten permission to visit a neighboring ranch whose ranching style was quite different. One of the photos from that ranch showed its cowboy-boot-shaped swimming pool. During the interviews, the writer often played dumb and asked us how our operations differed from, say, the way our neighbor operated. The writer did the same with our neighbor. The finished article reads like a range war between neighbors. In my opinion, that's not journalism. I'm not sure what that is—maybe entrapment.

The *Texas Monthly* article in which I appeared as a subject consisted mostly of cowgirl portraits and a quote or two from those pictured, maybe trying to reconstruct the style of my book *Voices and Visions of the American West*, which *Texas Monthly*'s book division had published a year earlier. In that book, the photos and those photographed spoke for themselves. For the cowgirl article, I was photographed clutching my rawhide stock whip, paired with this quote: "Modern ranching has gotten to where they like to do things with smaller pastures, drive a pickup, and call the cattle up with a feed sack. My feeling is that you lose all the skills that make life worth living if you do it that way. The only reason I like to take care of cows is because I can do it horseback, and the only reason I like to be horseback is to take care of cows." The article was titled "In Praise of Cowgirls: The Blues Ain't Got 'em Yet." Notice the poor grammar in the title and that we evidently all had the blues.

Then *Texas Monthly* changed editors. The new guy had humbly begun his journalism career as a reporter for Marfa's tiny *Big Bend Sentinel*. He invited me to submit a new article on cowgirls ("Cowgirl Up") and asked me to suggest subjects to be photographed to illustrate it. He made a good impression, and his offer sounded good, so I agreed. In the article I tried to explain why some female cowboys and ranch women hate the word *cowgirl* and reached back in history to show that women had always been working side by side with their fathers, husbands, brothers, and sons. Somehow it still turned out with an urban spin, maybe my own fault for struggling to educate an urban audience. Several of the women I suggested had "cleaned up" for the photographer instead of wearing their working clothes, so they didn't look authentic. Everything changes when the audience changes. The article never said what I wanted to say, so maybe I'm trying again with this book.

One paragraph that I was not particularly proud of reads: "Frances Octavia Smith, better known as Dale Evans, once said, 'Cowgirl is an attitude, really. A pioneer spirit, a special American brand of courage. The cowgirl faces life head-on, lives by her own lights and makes no excuses.' Of course, Dale Evans herself bears some responsibility for rhinestoning the cowgirl, but she appears to have understood that there's more to being one than simply wearing a hat and boots." I am complaining about the stereotyping here, but what bothers me now is that dang word *rhinestoning*. It is the perfect word to use in that spot, but it wasn't *my* word. The editor inserted it there. I don't like to take credit for someone else's talent. To me that word sticks out like a diamond in a goat's butt.

I later did another article for *Texas Monthly*, a portrait of Wayne Baize, native Texan, rancher, and past president of the Cowboy Artists of America. I was a fan of Wayne's peaceful and authentic art and of him as a person, as was the *Texas Monthly* art editor at the time. Yet the finished article caused me to regret doing it—maybe all three of us regretted it. The magazine's new editor eventually moved on, and so did I.

In *Texas Monthly*'s defense, the book press editor I worked with on *Voices and Visions of the American West* was perfect. My text for *Voices and Visions* came from my cowboy journalism, where the intended audience had been cowboys, not the general public. I simply picked quotes and photos, and organized them. In that book I was actually able to disappear both as a photographer and a writer and let my subjects' words and photographs speak for themselves. My editor, Kathy Marcus, asked to change only one word in my entire text: "sitting a horse" to "sitting *on* a horse." When I carefully explained that a sack of potatoes could sit *on* a horse but only a good rider can "sit a horse" properly, she understood and agreed. I'm very proud of that book and grateful to Kathy for indulging my prickliness. The book sold out almost immediately, but the book press closed its doors at about the same time, so it was never reprinted.

Another complicated publishing relationship was with *Range* magazine. For twenty or so years, I struggled through a love/hate relationship with its editor/publisher, C. J. Hadley. I thought that instead of trying to solve problems as she claimed, she kept stoking the fires between rural people and environmentalists to sell more magazines. I thought she was too damn radical, and she thought I was too damn academic. While in Nevada working on my PhD, I worked for her one stormy year as managing editor of the University of Nevada–Reno alumni magazine, *Silver & Blue*, which she was also producing at the time. I desperately needed the job and couldn't quit. So I also moonlighted (and I mean that literally) for her when a new edition of *Range* was in production. She was a procrastinator, and just before deadlines, everyone under her thumb had to drop PhD papers, tests, food, even bathroom breaks, come hell or high water, and get it done. C. J. drove me crazy, but I also thought she was the finest editor I ever wrote for. When she wasn't being political or trying to squeeze in shorter and shorter articles to sell more magazines, she thickened my skin and sharpened my pencil. Through the years, I sent her numerous articles defending grazing and deconstructing the wild–domestic dichotomy (okay, that does sound academic) and book reviews exposing the clay feet of nature writers or drawing them into "our" circle. I also recruited other writers for the magazine, such as ranchers Rodney Flournoy of California and Mike Cade of Florida, and helped them figure out how to work with her.

Our final falling out occurred after she had been listing me as her "environmental editor" for fifteen years. (Maybe she still does.) I had spent weeks on what I considered the most important article I had ever done for her, about a co-op capturing pronghorn antelope on irrigated Panhandle fields, where they were considered pests, and releasing them on West Texas ranches, where they were becoming scarce. I had interviewed ranchers, scientists, graduate students, activists, and Texas Parks and Wildlife personnel who were all working together. It was just the kind of article she claimed to want and a win/win for all concerned, especially the pronghorns. To raise money for the project, ranchers had cooked and served several barbecues and held blind auctions. I had collected photos taken by ranchers and scientists of capture and radio collaring, of sedated and blindfolded pronghorns traveling in horse trailers and helicopters, and of pronghorns cradled in careful arms. C. J.'s response? "It's too long. Cut it." Instead, I cut *Range* magazine, a lose/lose for us both, and probably the pronghorns.

Maybe because of my practice, I became embedded more deeply into the cowboy culture than the cowboys themselves, for the same reason that a scholar/teacher/writer knows books at a much deeper level than the average reader or even writer. I've observed the culture of agriculture from lots of angles—as a descendant, granddaughter, daughter, wife, parent, employee, and producer.

When I started college, my major was agriculture. Then I fell more deeply in love with the pen and switched to English, but I earned a bachelor of science, not arts, with ag as my minor. When I went on to a master's degree in English, my thesis was on Shakespeare's horses and horsemanship. My dissertation for a PhD investigated the way wild and domestic animals have been misrepresented in our stories. As an academic, my research and teaching interests have all centered on livestock or the animals and plants connected to them. I studied and taught the authors who wrote books about agriculture. When I presented papers at academic conferences or published in professional journals, my subjects were cattle and sheep; Ansel Adams's photos of cattle, their pastures, and rural roads; or Gretel Ehrlich's Zenish cowboys. Themes for my English classes centered on endangered species, wolves, and cowboy poetry. I never chase rabbits. Everything I do or have ever done, every friend I made or make, takes me deeper down my chosen path, my chosen practice.

I have picked the brains of hundreds of cowboys who have never met one another. From ranch to ranch, I kept making circles as a cowboy journalist. Mostly on weekends, on holidays, or during summers, briefly as a full-time journalist, I kept practicing, even though I knew I would never master it. I spent thousands of hours studying horses and cattle from all angles, places, and periods—horses of the Middle Ages, horses and cattle worldwide, through science, history, and psychology. I asked questions. I went to bed thinking about it and woke up thinking about it. I traveled the West and beyond, into Mexico, South America, and Iowa looking for new ideas, listening to stories. I found universal "cowboys" historically in Paraguay's barefoot soldiers and in today's barefoot Cayman Island sailors.

Through books, I traveled vicariously to Australia, Scotland, Russia, China, and Africa, looking at the ways people there raised and related to livestock. I read about cowboys, talked about cowboys, thought about cowboys, and wrote letters to and about them. Periodically, I pulled my thoughts together, ordered them, questioned them, polished them, and published them. My family and most of my friends were and are in the livestock business or closely connected to it. I've turned the subject that I probably wrote my very first sentence about in that one-room school into a life.

I practice every day.

CHAPTER SIX

Gender

"There's no crying in journalism."
—Mollie Hemingway

SOMETIME IN THE LATE SEVENTIES or early eighties, my spouse and I bought a horse from Apache Adams. Apache had a reputation for being able to ride anything with hair on it. So if you bought one of his "gentle" horses, you might be taking a chance. We named our new horse Apache but called him Patch. If I remember right, he was a stout little bay with no white markings and could do anything. When first saddled, though, he usually had to buck a few kinks out. Cowboys call that "cold backed." He bucked real straight and not real hard, and when he was done, he was done for the day. So even I could and did ride him. The first morning I was allowed to ride with a big outfit crew, we saddled up in a big pen and I stepped on Patch. He blew up in the middle of the fifteen or so cowboys and horses, but I didn't buck off. The boss's wife thought he was one of their horses and asked, "What horse was *that*?" So real fast it went from, "Oh, hell, another damn female," to grins and slapping me on the back. So if you're a damn female and want to go along, I recommend riding a cold-backed horse the first morning. It's even better if you can also say, "He's mine—bought him from Apache Adams."

For years, I defiantly drove a very dirty red-and-white Ford super-cab pickup truck back and forth between the ranch and my job in town. Across the tailgate was plastered a big bumper sticker that read, "A Woman's Place Is on a Horse." But I never considered myself a feminist. I was raised by a father who taught me to hunt, fish, and drive a tractor but believed that females didn't need to go to college and said I couldn't go. I should have obeyed my father, but he didn't raise no victim. I always treated patriarchy and my father as interesting challenges. I've had a lot more trouble getting along with and competing successfully with other women than with men. I did need a sense of humor though.

Cowboy humor usually draws blood and leaves a scar. Probably the most difficult logistic for both genders while trying to cowboy together is bathroom breaks. We don't fight over whose name goes on the door because there's seldom a door, a building, or even anything to either sit or leave the seat up on. In pastures without many trees, an all-male crew can just step off their horses to pee. If there's a female around, the men have to ride off far enough from what they are doing to pretend to adjust a cinch and turn their backs. It's even worse for a woman because she has to find a place to hide other than behind her horse. It's worse for both if they need to do more than pee. A good example: Once, while working a pasture without even a bush in sight, I had to pee. Luckily, though, an old, almost dry creek ran through it. As I left my duties and rode past the *segundo*—I'll call him Jack—I said softly, "I'll be right back." He, of course, knew exactly what I was riding off to do. I should have known better than to draw his attention because Jack always overdid teasing. We also had a new teenage boy on the crew. He'd been raised on a remote New Mexico ranch and was very bashful, just the kind of a kid that Jack liked to pick on. Whenever anyone mentioned girls, the kid's face turned red, so naturally Jack had been turning the talk to women as often as possible.

Anyway, I loped to the creek, hobbled my horse, and slid quickly down the creek bank. No sooner had I gotten my britches down and squatted than the kid raced up, calling my name. Poor kid, I thought, he's really going to be embarrassed when he sees my naked butt. "Get out of here," I said calmly, but my words must have caught in the creek bank. If I stood to pull my britches up, I'd only make matters worse, so I held my ground.

"Jack sent me to help you. Where's the calf?" he asked, straining to see what I was doing.

By this time the dirt between my boots had turned a nice chocolate brown. It reminded me of being a young bride when my husband used to entertain us by writing his name in the snow and persuaded me to try. The best I ever mustered was a very blotched *B* before I tipped over in the snow. Ha-ha.

"Get out of here," I said again. This time I was careful to turn my head up so that my voice would carry better. He finally got the message and almost jerked his poor horse over backward when he realized what I was actually doing.

It seems that as soon as I rode off, Jack told him I had tied down a calf in the creek bed, to go help me, and to hurry. Tied-down calves have a tendency to die in hot weather if they don't get back on their feet quickly. So instead of being a hero and helping a female in distress, the kid became the laughingstock once again, and soon even I was teasing him.

I suppose that could be called bullying, but the way cowboys start a young horse is to gradually expose it to more and more of whatever scares it until it ain't scared of nuthin. They tend to do the same with each other. That kid grew up to be a real good hand, married, and produced kids, so I guess the exposure worked.

After I had told this story a dozen times as an example of what I had put up with as a female, I realized that I had been exposed too. Cowboys had done their best to either break or train me. Like a colt, they had sacked me out and toughened up my hide so that I could make mistake after mistake and keep right on going. As a reporter for the *St. Louis Tribune* once said, "I've been a soldier, cop, journalist, and the father of three teenage girls. I don't have any feelings left to hurt." Through the years I have watched talented people who wanted to write avoid publishing, frozen with fear that they might make an error. On good days, I grudgingly thank God that cowboys embarrassed me so often that being the target of jokes or making mistakes lost its terror. I stopped minding their sick humor, except when it was happening.

Although I did a little teasing, I was more often the target of humor—like the time at a party when I noticed an elderly man's zipper was down. I'll call him George. George lived on a nearby ranch and I knew he'd be embarrassed, so I tried to think of a way to discreetly let him know. I happened to be standing next to Jack—remember Jack? I knew Jack, knew him well, so I'll never know why on earth I was stupid enough to lean over and whisper to him of all people that George's pants were unzipped and to please pull him aside when he got a chance and tell him.

Jack sort of waited until there was a lull in the noisy party conversation and then announced in a loud voice, "Hey, George, Barney wants me to tell you that your pants are unzipped. And, say, Barney what were you doing looking down there anyway?"

Everybody laughed, including me and George. What else could we do?

Even cowboys I didn't know seemed to feel a responsibility to add to my training. As a journalist/photographer, I parasitized their lives and they knew it. So in trade, I had to provide something—entertainment if nothing else. My goals were higher: truth, enlightenment, art. But entertainment was better than nothing, so I took their teasing in stride—most of the time. They especially liked to watch me struggle to get horseback—tall horse, tight britches. They'd make farting noises, grunts, or pants-ripping sounds. They liked to leave me holding herd with my stomach growling while they rode to the wagon for lunch. Teasing and harassment are just part of cowboy school. It has nothing to do with gender. Nobody is safe. Even bosses had to endure a few pranks and teasing, especially new bosses.

Even my sweet little daughter occasionally added to my humility. We stopped at a little store once, and while I was paying, my daughter and her father started walking back to the truck. They met Jack at the door, and he started to tell a hilarious story about a bull that had "ass-holed" a local cowboy out of a tree. Seems the bull took the cowboy's horse away first. After the cowboy climbed a tree, the bull stuck a horn in the seat of his pants and hooked him down. The cowboy lived, so it was funny. Anyway, as soon as Jack said the word *asshole*, he noticed my cute little five-year-old daughter with ribbons in her twin pony tails and started apologizing for his language.

She looked up at him with a big smile and said, "Oh, that's okay. Mama calls Daddy that all the time." Jack could do a lot with material like that.

But I was also quite able to embarrass myself without any help. One article I wrote for the *Cattleman* magazine stands out in my memory. In it I gave wise advice to new cowboy brides, such as never wear a new bra. Bras used to be very uncomfortable and prone to chafing until they were well broken in. Bras have improved since then, or at least the ones I wear. Anyway, my so-called humor managed to make all women and especially myself sound like airheads. I'm sorry.

More seriously, I also understood that sometimes bosses didn't want to include women because men sometimes gave females too much attention and some women invited that attention. Men can act like idiots when they awkwardly struggle with their competitiveness, flirtatiousness, anger, jealousy, chivalry, or protectiveness while trying to impress or harass a woman. Consequently, their minds are not on getting the work done as smoothly and easily as possible. Wrecks seem to happen more often, and women who are easily offended scare everyone.

Misunderstandings are common, and when I found one, I tried to fix it. I once wrote about a female horseshoer who said, "I guess I catch more flak from old-timers than anyone else. The ranching tradition doesn't quite go hand in hand with a lady shoeing horses." She thought the old-timers didn't trust her to shoe their horses, but I thought they were just embarrassed that they had gotten so feeble and worthless. They didn't like paying someone else to do work they used to be able to do. Old men were usually also quite chivalrous and didn't think a lady should ever have to shoe her own horses. Men were supposed to open the doors, carry the heavy stuff, and shoe the horses. Their resentment was toward their own aging, not toward a female horseshoer.

Granted, I met some men who didn't want to work alongside women for various reasons, but I never met a cowboy who didn't respect a good hand. Most problems arose when the female couldn't really do the job but just wanted the "right" to go along. Cowboys of both genders and all ages almost unanimously objected to "visitors," myself included. Most females were visitors. During my years of "visiting" ranches all over the West, I met only two or three women who deserved full pay as a cowboy, and when I found one, I wrote about her. Most of us could fill a hole if things didn't get too rough, but we couldn't completely do the job. Some man shod our horses and roped the bulls, and that was okay with me. I was willing to trade a pan of biscuits for a shod horse any day. I also wanted to be able to chicken out when it was time to ride a horse that flipped over backward. Male cowboys, even the young ones, usually didn't get that choice unless they worked for a good boss.

Women who want to cowboy also need to learn to stay humble and keep their heads down. As a female wannabe cowboy living on ranches, I was often used as a whipping boy. When I rode with the crew on a big circle and we came together with trotty cattle, the circle boss sometimes yelled at me across the herd, "Ride up, Barney." Sometimes maybe I deserved it, but more often my horse's nose was already buried in some horse's tail and the cowboy in front of me needed yelling at instead. But the "Code of the West" says a good boss never yells at his men. Women, greenhorns, children, and dogs, however, are fair game.

Occasionally, *segundo* Jack bragged on me to embarrass and teach the men, such as the day he singled me out for praise for "a nice piece of cow work"—which I liked much better than being yelled at. He went on to explain, in front of the men, what I had done so well while holding herd. At least a few of the men listening got the message that was really intended for them. Most of us hated Jack, and after he bragged on me, they hated me too. They much preferred the guy who yelled at me instead and liked me better when I got yelled at. Experiences like that taught me to avoid looking too good or sounding like a know-it-all and to avoid making my journalism subjects look or sound too good either. We all preferred to be the butt of a joke or the bad example. Nobody wanted to be singled out for praise. I did my best to take teasing and blame in stride and not mess up my privilege. When you care about something at a deep enough level and work as a team, it shouldn't matter who gets credit or blame.

Plus, once a female actually earns a reputation as a good cowboy, she can stick up for herself. I especially like one story about one of our best local female cowboys. She was on a crew penning some cattle and a few started to drift off. She was already headed around them when the old boss waiting at the pens in his pickup hollered something like, "Can one of you sons-a-bitches get around those cattle." Once the gate was closed, the old man apologized to the female for his language and she shot back, "I don't give a shit what any of you old sons-a-bitches call me." Everybody laughed.

Did I ever make it as a real cowboy? That's a hard question. I was probably better when I left Arizona than after slowing down to be a mom and then riding a desk job in town. I probably never got my mojo back, if I ever had any. I use *cowboy* as a verb instead of a noun. It is not how you dress but what you can do. I've known some who call themselves cowboys but sit a horse like sacks of potatoes, can't rope, never rode a fresh horse or a tired one, never started a colt (or created problems if they tried), never shod their own horses. Some might be pretty good at riding a horse but have never ridden on a ranch or around cattle. Some ride the same horse over and over. Some never use their horses to work cattle, certainly never several hundred head at one time. Some work too fast or too slow and are never in the right place at the right time. Some who own or whose families own ranches have never ridden anything but an old kid's horse or one some trainer spent years perfecting. Some raised on a ranch never rode anything but three- or four-wheelers. Many ranches are actually hobby ranches, not the real thing. The list goes on and on, and many just wear the uniform.

Journalism helped me get horseback all over the West, often on a big crew, often the only female. Of course I had to abide by the same rules any male would have to abide by. I never got to ride a cutting horse to sort a big herd, but neither have most cowboys. We were all just a bunch of lowlife herd holders; some of us even had to hold the cuts. I've gathered big open country. I've ridden lots of different horses, from colts to old remuda horses. I've often changed horses at noon when the first horse got tired and we all needed a fresh one to finish the day; a few times we needed a third horse. I've done every job in a branding pen. I can brand, castrate, dehorn, earmark, implant, vaccinate, or flank with a partner. I could probably still do any of those as an old lady except flank. I never claimed to be a roper, but I have dragged a few calves to the fire and caught a few heels in an arena. I know how, but I'm neither fast nor particularly accurate. I seldom even carried a rope because I didn't like to rope and preferred to carry cameras instead. I also worried about losing a finger. I wanted to type.

I can fit in, take orders, ride my country, and show up when and where I'm supposed to in places I've never been before. I can fill a hole if it's not too big or deep. I've clumsily picked out my own keeper heifers for my own small herd. According to a book called *Women of the Range: Women's Roles in the Texas Beef Cattle Industry*, most Texas cattle ranchers of any gender own fewer than fifty head. Since I once owned, all by myself, a few more than fifty, I guess that author would consider me one of Texas's big cattle operators. To me that title belongs to those with more than a thousand head.

I've hired my own cowboy crew and shipped my own cattle to market. I have cooked on the ground, using a wood fire, for a crew of twenty. I have found and trapped remnants by myself and moved three hundred heifers from a holding trap across another trap to a pasture and put them on water, by myself. I've worked with a wagon crew, eaten food prepared on a chuck box lid, and slept in a range teepee that I made myself. Although I've never received full-time wages from a ranch, I've been paid cowboy day wages. I've jingled horses and helped to move a remuda of one hundred horses running free across ten to fifteen miles, herding them along on horseback. I can catch my own horse with a hoolihan. If a horse bucked, I usually fell off, but not always. I still own a personal "outfit," from a slick-fork, three-quarter-rigged saddle on a Wade tree to boots, spurs, leggings, bridles, hackamores, bosals, snaffles, bits, hobbles, rope, stock whips, blankets, slicker, halters, curry comb and brushes, range teepee, canvas-covered bedroll, Dutch ovens, and chuck box. Periodically I dig out all my leather, wash and oil it, and polish the silver, or pay my granddaughter to do it. I've slept on the ground in rain, hail, sleet, and snow. I've helped pull a shallow windmill by hand, packed salt, cleaned out springs, fixed floats, pulled calves from first-calf heifers by myself, doctored wormies and cancer eyes. I've helped move or work large herds of cattle or horses in at least five states—Texas, Arizona, New Mexico, Montana, and Wyoming—on maybe twenty different ranches, although I've lost count. I've probably taken photographs on more than a hundred different ranches in most western states, plus Chihuahua and Coahuila, Mexico, and Paraguay's Dry Chaco. Once in a Northern California mountain blizzard, I drove a two-up team of Percherons hitched to a sled to feed hay to several hundred head of cattle.

I can use an Australian-style stock whip to sting and turn a cranky bull, but I never learned to "crack" one very well. I rodeoed a little, team roped a little, but never came close to claiming any championships except that I might have washed more dishes under worse conditions in hunting camps, sheep camps, cow camps, farmhouses, and cookshacks—until my hands bled in more buckets, tin pans, galvanized tubs, or dry sinks, using water from more rivers, creeks, stock tanks, windmills, springs, tinajas, wells, cisterns, and rain barrels, in more hail, sleet, snow, and blowing dust—than any other human.

Yet I'm still hesitant to call myself a cowboy because I've known those of both genders who have done everything I've done only a lot more of it and a lot better. They shod their own horses, started more colts, rode tougher horses, worked on more ranches, and were willing to rope grown cows or bulls. I'm not in their league. I've heard it said that a real cowboy can ride as fast as a horse can run. But I never could. As soon as the rocks started to blur, I started trying to slow things down. If I fell off when things were trotty, I figured I would survive. But if I fell off when things were fast—although I never did try it—I figured something would break, if not die. So I pulled up. Not good. Real cowboys don't pull up. Women who want to be real cowboys don't pull up either. So I don't call myself a cowboy. I have also been afoot now for almost thirty years. *Cowboy* is a verb. It's something you do not something you are.

I once thought maybe I could at least call myself a camp woman. I thought I could live in the middle of nowhere and take care of myself. But when that chance came, I soon realized I was not really capable of maintaining a water system by myself. Wise bosses always gave me jobs and put me in positions that I could handle without putting myself or someone else in danger, but sometimes they had more faith in me than I deserved. I do call myself a cowboy journalist because that is something I've done for fifty years and still do.

Freelancing for magazines gave me a reason to live the life, to tag along. Journalism made me sort of a freelance cowboy too. I worked when I wanted to, not because I had to. That sense of freedom was important. Since I wasn't on the payroll except on rare occasions, I didn't have to take any bad treatment—unless I wanted to. I could ride on the beautiful cool days and type on the hot or drizzly cold ones. I could eat supper at the wagon or go to town for pizza. I could sleep on the ground or go home. I could take their stupid teasing or ride off. Abuse is only abuse when you have no choice. If you decide to stay of your own free will, then it's not abuse but something else. If I chose to cook for fifteen men who stomped across my clean floors in shitty boots, refused to wash the dishes, and refused to let me tag along, and I still didn't cuss them in public, there must have been a reason.

Journalism got me onto crews and into situations and places where even the best cowboys of either gender have never been. Maybe I wrote for respect—at least it made me some kind of professional. Rural women have almost been forced to be professionals. This is the other side of the rural patriarchy coin. Seldom have we been encouraged or financially able to simply "stay home." The first place women got the vote was Wyoming, not Massachusetts. The entire West had granted women's suffrage before the East Coast started thinking about it seriously. Rural men have always relied on hardworking, responsible women. Women tend to run the businesses, govern the towns, teach school, and a million other things. The best example of a hardworking professional rural woman that I wrote about was Becky Terry in "Fighting Hell with a Bucket."

I began by trying to overwhelm the reader with her list of duties. Her days as National CattleWomen president in 1993 often began with a champagne breakfast speech before daylight, all-day meetings, all-day bus tours, luncheon speeches, cocktail hours, banquet speeches, and after-dinner dancing. The next day, she began again in another town, with another full schedule. During that year and more than forty others, she held numerous other offices and committee appointments. All those gala events seem like privilege until they start adding up to several in one day, day after day, night after night serving the cattle industry. I said that Becky

> attended conventions, beef roundups, beef cook-offs, award ceremonies, International Livestock Congresses, workshops, health fairs, ag seminars, thousands of meetings, short courses, fashion shows, ladies seminars, ag tours, unveilings, receptions, parades, youth stock shows, and trade shows; she judged cook-offs, meat identification contests, essay contests, and youth agriculture projects in every state and around the world; she cooked and served food for many of the same events plus bull sales, grocery store promotions, and hospitality suites; she planned and executed raffles, referendums, political lobbying, Texas Beef for Christmas Week, Beef for Father's Day, ag days, farm/city weeks, and beef education booths.
>
> She wrote newspaper and magazine articles, letters to editors, columns, brochures, agendas, minutes, budgets, bulletins, pamphlets, newsletters, financial statements—sometimes in languages ranging from Chinese to Spanish; she sent and received thousands of letters, telegrams, thank-you notes, and phone calls; she designed and had printed name tags, place mats, napkins, promotional packets, invitations, certificates, business cards, advertisements, and cookbooks; she raised and donated funds for scholarships, memorials, and youth stock shows; she gave hundreds of tedious and sometimes hostile interviews for all types of media, including TV and radio, in every state and around the world; she gave and received awards, hundreds of recipes, thousands of hugs, smiles, and handshakes.

She attended meetings with state ag commissioners and national secretaries of agriculture, went to state dinners with U.S. presidents and vice presidents, and called herself truthfully a "pretty good plumber too." Becky and her husband, King, stayed married for life. Maybe their secret was that they each had their own projects. The year Becky was national president, she was away from home 285 days. Someone once asked King what he had ever done for the cattle industry and he answered, "Why, I gave them Becky!"

One of my favorite stories she told about their marriage was that one day she walked into the room where her husband was reading and said, "King, I'm having an affair."

He said, "Oh? Who's catering it?"

When Becky laughed, the world laughed with her. It was her trademark, her best weapon against enemies of the livestock industry, and her best anecdote against despair within it, her laugh livening up the tiniest West Texas coffee shop during a drouth. Becky had such a distinctive laugh that I recognized it once in the Denver airport and followed it until I found her. That laugh probably contributed to her successful marriage too.

I never worked as hard for the livestock industry as Becky did, but I'm descended from a long line of capable rural women. My thirteenth great-grandmother was not the first Mrs. William Bradford, who sailed with her husband on the *Mayflower* and jumped or fell overboard before ever setting foot on the new continent, possibly committing suicide. My ancestor was the second Mrs. Bradford, Alice Carpenter Southworth, a widow who sailed alone into a future that looked impossible at the time. Generation after generation, my foremothers walked, rode in wagons or horseback, and rowed boats to the edges of civilization. While their husbands fought the wars, my grandmothers "stayed home" to raise the children and the food alone, often taking up arms to protect their homes, children, crops, and livestock while their husbands were away.

I always considered men partners, and although I did and still do love some of them, I have always been somewhat wary of romantic entanglements. My first "love" seems to have set the pattern for my romances and is captured in one of those vivid postcard memories forever framed in yellow. When I was about six years old, growing up on my grandmother's farm, I had a major crush on a neighbor boy. I'll call him Jerry. One early spring morning I dressed up in a new yellow blouse with a ruffle around the neck that Gram had just sewn for me. I had long, thick, dark brown hair that my mother always braided and tied up with ribbons into a big loop behind each of my ears. So Gram always made hair ribbons to match my clothes. She had starched and ironed both my new yellow blouse and my new yellow ribbons. I probably looked like a little sunflower. Since I thought I looked especially pretty, I walked down the hill to the neighbor boy's farm to show him.

A few years older, he was just hooking a tractor to a wagonload of manure that he'd shoveled out of the barn and was headed out to a field to spread it around. The wagon was an old manure spreader with a rotating column of tines at the back that flicked the manure out over the field in baseball- to basketball-size globs. When he saw me walking up, he drove off. I followed. So Jerry turned on the manure spreader.

They say we never get over some of our traumatic childhood experiences. I never got over that one. Everyone but me thinks it is hilariously funny, and throughout the rest of my life I seemed to be stuck in a replay of that moment. After I was grown, for example, while riding pens to find and doctor sick steers at a feedlot in Arizona, the cowboy assigned to partner with me refused by saying, "I'll be happy to go to bed with her, but I ain't riding with no woman." Needless to say, he got neither opportunity. So although I have always loved boys and later men, the most affection I've usually mustered toward them was guarded tolerance, and that was the most they usually mustered toward me. That about covers my sex life too, such as it was. I don't need to tell any more of my romance stories because we've read them over and over in women's magazines and novels. We've all been there, either as the one shedding tears or the one laughing, and probably both. It seemed that if I went to bed with a cowboy, he left. If I didn't, he left. If I agreed with him, he left; if I disagreed, he left. If I never cheated on him, he left. And if he didn't leave, I did. I never had much luck. Maybe I got interested a few times but usually nothing happened. The only thing that I have figured out for sure is that nothing works. So if the reader is hoping to discover a love story, this book will disappoint. If you like steamy love scenes or if you're a young woman reading this book intending to learn how to use journalism or photography to find the love of your life, I recommend *The Bridges of Madison County.* It's fiction.

In spite of all this, my published stories about cowboys evidently still made the life sound so romantic that at least once a year or so, some sincere, single female would ask me, "How can I meet a cowboy?" I'd take a deep breath, sigh, and give a different answer every time, depending on the mood I was in or which memory popped into my head at the moment. Sometimes I'd tell a story about one very eligible bachelor cowboy who owned a little house down on the Arizona–Mexico border not far from the New Mexico boot heel. One day he discovered a nest of baby skunks in his underwear drawer. I'd leave her standing there thinking about that.

Sometimes I just said that chasing cowboys was like a dog chasing cars. Male cowboys are just like other men once the boots and hats come off. Some beat their wives, some cheat, some drink too much, some recline on the couch and belch or worse, some are tolerable in small doses, and maybe rarely a good one comes along. They are all different. Meeting them involves the same complicated games that meeting any man involves, although sometimes they haven't been to town often enough to get over being nervous around women. They cover their nervousness in various ways: bravado, drunkenness, shyness, aggression, humor. They are sometimes skilled at being lured home from the bar to some girl's bedroom, but they often disappear before daylight because they don't know what should come next.

We think we have studied the lone male in American literature, but usually with the idea that this lone male was a man who hated women. Even in some of the best cowboy fiction, the bachelors seem to prize freedom: Elmer Kelton's protagonist in *The Good Old Boys*, Edward Abbey's Jack Burns, and J. P. S. Brown's Bert Sorrells. But, again, those men are fiction. The real bachelor cowboys I got to know deeply through their letters were more often victims of women. Few women are willing to embrace the solitude and poverty it takes to live the cowboy life, so most women stay around just long enough to break a heart. Cowboy bachelors know the true meaning behind the popular song lyrics "freedom's just another word for nothin' left to lose." Most bachelor cowboys have tried hard to find mates, but they had their hearts broken so badly or so often that they eventually gave up. Some, I'm sure, just prefer peaceful solitude, like me. Everybody is different.

Since married cowboys' homes are considered havens for out-of-work single cowboys, a cowboy's wife may find herself cooking for six extra bachelors at a moment's notice. Sometimes one will sleep on her couch or throw his bedroll on the porch for weeks or months while a broken bone mends or maybe just while waiting for spring. Bachelors tend to repay this stoic patience with lifelong friendship—or that's been my experience. Maybe because of journalism, I listened carefully to them and didn't make judgments. But even as a little girl, old bachelor farmers, bachelor uncles, and bachelor cousins seemed to like me best. A few finally married in their late thirties and forties, but some never did. Even my favorite dog, Perro Pinto, never had a girlfriend until late in life and sired only one litter of puppies. I never rode a mare or a stallion, just geldings, so my horses were all bachelors too. Eventually my closest friends turned out to be old cowboy bachelors that I often named a horse after. Something about me must have seemed unthreatening or comfortable. Maybe because they were not attracted to me nor I to them, we could consider each other just friends. Attraction eventually seems to cause trouble.

Cowboys and pretty girls have a lot in common, so they should understand each other better than they do. Some pretty girls complain that affairs of the heart are very complicated for them because men just want to use them for ego trips. The men, they explain, never bother to get to know the real person behind the face and just wanted to show them off to other men as arm candy. Some women who think they want a cowboy have similar motives. They want a date with the myth, not the man. They want to show him off to their friends—like a cute, unusual breed of dog. Pam Houston's narrator in *Cowboys Are My Weakness* describes her various affairs. I have heard academics describe Houston's narrator as a woman who loves too much. I would argue that her narrator doesn't love at all. She just falls in "love" with uniforms, hats, occupations, adventures, and scenery—not the men. Consequently the affairs are mostly sexual, stormy, and short. Seducers and victims come in both genders and all sexual preferences.

Through cowboy letters and personal experience, I had learned that affairs of the heart were a major problem, so eventually I tried to find answers. Most of the self-help relationship books were written by and for urban people, so I thought maybe rural people needed different advice. Although it did me no good personally, I guess I learned the most about love from studying horsemanship. As I leaned on the fence or on my saddle horn and listened to good horsemen explain how to get along with horses, I always had the strange feeling that they weren't just talking about horses and riders but about relationships in general.

My obsession with horsemanship as philosophy and my own relationship problems reached a peak about the time cowboy poetry gatherings began. The gatherings seemed to be straining marriages. The media was also making fun of cowboy lingo and portraying cowboys as uneducated, so I wanted to challenge that stereotype. I had often read about writers being surprised to find a shelf containing the Harvard Classics in some remote cow camp. I'd seen the same collection of classics, published in Spanish, deep in the heart of Mexico's Norteño ranching country in northern Coahuila. Perhaps a few ranch people and cowboys read

Louis L'Amour or Max Brand, although I don't personally know anyone who does. In my opinion, "westerns" were written by city people for city people, not for us.

What we actually read is very eclectic. I have one cowboy friend who reads classic texts from Eastern religions. Another reads a lot of Tolstoy; one likes Dostoevsky better; another likes Dickens. One who lived in the shadow of El Capitan in the Guadalupe Mountains read a lot of John McPhee; another read Charles Krauthammer. Several were also interested in classical poetry. One year for the Elko cowboy poetry gathering I decided to record friends reciting or reading their choices and to use my cowboy photography to help the poetry audience see what cowboys found in these classic poems. Don Coleman chose Longfellow's "From My Arm-Chair" and Roddy Schoenfeldt chose the prelude to Chaucer's *Canterbury Tales.* Rancher Gage Holland had an extensive leather-bound collection of Rudyard Kipling that would put most universities to shame. He chose Kipling's "If." Randy Glover recited Lewis Carroll's "Jabberwocky." Tommy Vaughn chose Shakespeare's Sonnet 87. He said he could read and understand Shakespeare because he'd been raised reading the King James version of the Bible. He said Sonnet 87 reminded him of Ray Hunt's style of horsemanship.

Tommy's statement popped like a flashbulb going off in my head. Of course! Suddenly I remembered lines and moments from Shakespeare's plays, such as Richard III's desperate plea "A horse! A horse! My kingdom for a horse!" From Bolingbroke to Hotspur, Prince Hal to Falstaff, Othello to Macbeth, Shakespeare's characters seemed to reveal their character or lack of it through their horsemanship. Tiny versions of Shakespeare's plays, distributed by the company that made Bull Durham tobacco, went up the trail in cowboy shirt pockets during the 1890s. One common cowboy saying, "Come on, we're burning daylight," comes from *Romeo and Juliet.* The word *horse* appears in Shakespeare's plays 247 times, with many more horse-related words, such as *saddle*, *booted*, *spurred*, *mare*, and *stallion*. At the time, I was writing about Ray Hunt every chance I got, tutoring freshman writing, and working on a master's degree. I was searching for a subject for my thesis research and Tommy handed me the ideal subject on a silver tray. It combined horsemanship, relationships, and classics into one bundle. How could I have missed it?

For two years, I blinded myself reading horsemanship books published during Shakespeare's day on microfilm: Thomas Blundeville (1560, 1565,

1580, 1594), Christopher Clifford (1585), T. Bedingfield (1584), John Astley (1584), Nicholas Morgan (1609), Browne (1610), Michaell Baret (1618). Several of the first books ever printed or translated from French, Italian, and Spanish into English were horsemanship books. This foreign-inspired horse training, called collectively "the manage," stressed elaborate costumes and refined, controlled movements. Manage trainers dug deep trenches in the ground to "teach" various maneuvers by repetitively riding horses around and around in those trenches. They embedded ground glass under the skin over a horse's ribs. When spurred on the ground glass, horses who had been slow to obey commands supposedly improved. Sometimes a hedgehog was tied in a lazy horse's tail. No surprise that the horses frequently ran away and couldn't be stopped. Runaway horses were hit in the face with cudgels or burning torches. Trainers taught studs to whoa on command by jerking on strings tied around their scrotums. Bits were often designed to cut a horse's tongue. Grooves were cut into the tongue and jaw, or teeth were pulled to make a bit "fit" better. An exceptionally cruel Spanish horse trainer named Prospero invented a very popular hinged metal noseband with teeth. He crossed the reins to use it like a vise and carried a hammer to occasionally rap the teeth deeper into a horse's tender nose. After discovering this horse trainer, I could never read Shakespeare's *The Tempest*, with its seemingly wise father figure named Prospero, quite the same way again. My professors eventually told me that I had ruined Shakespeare for them because after reading my thesis all they saw were horses too.

The horsemanship of Shakespeare's day astounded me in both its stupidity and its cruelty. One would think that people who used horses every day would be most in tune with them. Instead these riders were the furthest away from understanding horses, even during a historical period when horsemanship skills determined a monarch's popularity with the masses or a rider's ability to impress the opposite sex. I expected horsemanship to have gotten progressively worse as people traded horses for automobiles and their understanding of a horse's mind for a motor. But that is not what I found.

Throughout literature, from Greek myth to Chaucer to Freud, control of the horse has been used to mirror relationships between men and women, governing oneself, and the fitness to govern others. Since the horse is no respecter of rank, in the days of Plutarch (A.D. 46–120), princes were encouraged to learn to ride because "the sons of kings could not properly learn anything except the art of horsemanship" since everyone else flattered, humored, and agreed with them. But a horse, since it does not know whether its rider is a nobleman or a slave, rich or poor, queen or subject, treats all riders equally and honestly.

Just as there is rivalry today between various urban-based training styles and the country cowboy, so there was in Shakespeare's day. Eventually I found Gervase Markham's books (1593, 1599, 1605, 1607, 1615, and more). He wrote for the rural English hunter and found the cruelty as well as the dancing and prancing of the manage quite silly. Markham's methods were based on a genuine affection for the horse and a respect for its intelligence. He treated horses like fellow beings instead of pets or possessions. Because of this respect, Markham discouraged either cruelty or gentleness when training horses because horses were quite capable of learning foul habits and manipulation too. While manage riders tried to force or coax, Markham taught communication and mutual respect. Shakespeare might have influenced or been influenced by Markham and applied at least the philosophy to his human characters. Markham, of course, reminded me of Ray Hunt, and all this horse and rider stuff reminded me of human love and marriage. So I wrote about Shakespeare and horses, trying to find answers for cowboy romance.

During the Renaissance people were "trained" to be better soldiers, servants, wives, or children through methods similar to the cruel ones used on horses. Cranky women who talked too much were called shrews and forced to wear a "shrew's bridle," a device that fit over the head and contained a bit with knives designed to cut if her tongue moved. Husbands were amazed when this treatment did not produce a docile, loving wife but instead often resulted in their own cuckoldry.

Shakespeare is notorious among scholars for stealing material from other authors and then working his magic on it. The earliest source for one of his plays was probably an old poem, "A Merry Jest of a Shrewd and Curst Wife Lapped in Morel's Skin," which described how a henpecked husband trained his wife. He killed his old faithful horse, Morel, skinned him, and wrapped his wife in the raw hide. Then he waited for the hide to dry and shrink until his wife humbly submitted to her "master." Happy ending!

In Shakespeare's version, *The Taming of the Shrew*, a man (Petruchio) is looking for a wife and finds Kate, who is anything but gentle. Instead of wrapping her in rawhide or putting her in a shrew's bridle, Petruchio decides to marry Kate the shrew because he likes her spirit, finds her witty and fun to talk to. As a horseman, the only fault he can't fix is lameness, and he quickly tests Kate to see if she is lame. He concludes in front of her that she is quite sound, that "the world has talked amiss of her," and that she has simply been treated poorly by her father and her sweet, manipulative sisters. Kate hears real understanding for the first time.

In my master's thesis, I go through the play line by line, bringing out the constant references to horsemanship. When Petruchio shows up at the wedding wearing a ridiculous costume and riding a horse with diseases and injuries caused by neglect and misuse, he's not simply testing Kate's love. At his own expense, Petruchio is changing the town's attitude toward Kate. She suddenly finds herself surrounded by sympathetic, concerned neighbors ready to defend her against this "monster." Kate now feels sympathy for the first time.

Like a good horseman, Petruchio respects Kate's intelligence and wants to be her partner, not her master or her slave, as he applies Markham's sensible horsemanship methods. At the play's end, Kate meekly offers her hand to help her husband mount his horse, but only because she knows he doesn't need or want that. They are both just fooling party guests into believing that Kate has been "tamed" so they can win a bet. They are now partners. I think the sense and meaning of this play is confusing to many scholars because they don't understand horses, horsemanship, or women.

In spite of the fact that entire libraries have been written about Shakespeare, no one is even sure if William Shakespeare actually wrote the plays, and fewer than a handful of scholars have been fascinated by his almost constant use of horses and horsemanship. One popular legend, although evidently started by an "unreliable scholar," was that Shakespeare's first job in London was holding horses outside theaters. As the tale passed down through the ages, it expanded to include "facts" such as that Shakespeare was so good at holding horses that he couldn't keep up with demand. As his popularity and business grew, he trained young boys to help him. When gentlemen arrived to watch a play and asked for Shakespeare to tend their horses, these young boys would step up and say, "I am Shakespeare's boy, Sir." For many years, even after Shakespeare's death, so the story goes, the boys who held horses at London theaters were called Shakespeare's boys.

My own theory is that when he came of age, young Will rode horseback to the city to seek his fortune and chase girls. As often happens when a country boy who grew up horseback goes to town, where everyone is a wannabe horseman, his horse and horsemanship can get him noticed. Maybe while simply holding their horses, young Shakespeare was able to correct some of their horses' bad habits. Horsemanship was one of the arts every Renaissance nobleman wanted to master. Soldiers needed courageous, dependable horses for the wars, while courtiers and their ladies wanted horses that could dance and prance. Well-trained horses were needed for travel; for bearing burdens; pulling carts, coaches, and plows; or for racing, hunting, recreation, and simply exercise. Horses were also important to monarchs for riding in parades. So a member of the noble class might hire a country boy to start colts and train horses. To me this is a much more plausible basis for Shakespeare's eventual friendship with royalty than their recognition of his ability with a pen, especially during a time when writing a play and going to theaters ranked right up there with cockfighting.

Shakespeare, whoever he was, wrote for a world in which people lived in fear of their church, their government, their spouses, and their parents. His plays continue to appeal through the centuries because not much has changed. Shakespeare's suggestions for human relationships, as well as Markham's horsemanship methods, were quickly forgotten or ignored, maybe because they took too much time, thought, and effort. People preferred fear, punishment, and gadgets. It seems that horsemanship, like history, repeats itself. *The Taming of the Shrew* begins when Petruchio marries Kate. It ends when they become partners, but remaining partners will take constant work, honest communication, and practice. Unfortunately, although a wedding seems like a happy ending, it's only the beginning—on steroids. We think we understand. We think we've got it. From now on things are going to be wonderful, but even Shakespeare found no easy or permanent answers.

Cowboy spouses who imagine riding off into the sunset together on well-behaved horses will be shocked the first time their horse dumps them on the ground and their spouse continues on with the cattle, not even looking back. Females, especially those raised in the cowboy world, who might even be better hands than the men they marry, will be devastated to hear an edict from the boss that "women can't ride on this outfit." One said it well when I interviewed her for the article "Cowboy's Wife." She said, "Mom used to pack us in a salt pannier when we were about a month old. I started riding when I was about three, and Dad had us breaking colts when we were six. We all helped him ride and brand and break colts, and he taught us to rope when we were real young." Then she met a handsome cowboy, but he "used to tell me when I helped him that he didn't approve of women riding. When we got married, I told him that I rode and that's all I knew because that's how I was raised. I figured if he didn't like it, he'd get used to it. I just ignored him and rode anyway."

She fought the situation for several years through moves from ranch to ranch, searching for answers. The frustration in her voice broke my heart: "I've asked a lot of people and they always say that's just the way it's always been. They've never really given me any reason why. A lot of people say women get in the way, and I'm sure some women do. But I know a lot of men that get in the way too." At the end of my article, I said that maybe they had finally found an ideal job for them both, where the ranch "did things right" enough to suit her husband and where she could also ride. But they have since divorced and remarried. I also found after interviewing old-timers that banning women wasn't "the way it's always been." Whether or not women are welcome on a crew also seems to cycle through history—in favor then out again.

My own marriage also started out idyllic, riding every day on a remote camp beside my new spouse, calving heifers, roping wild hogs, and finding all the best spots where buckeyes, bluebells, and wild plums grew. Then I got pregnant. As my belly grew, I unzipped my jeans and held them up with suspenders under long shirts. We had a screwworm outbreak that summer, so we rode and roped, doctoring wormies every day. Screwworms are the most evil critters ever invented by Mother Nature. The female fly lays her eggs in living flesh, not dead flesh like most flies. When screwworm maggots hatch, they eat the host animal alive. Screwworms lay their eggs in any open wound: in a scratch from catclaw brush, in cancered eyes, in foreheads of fighting bulls, and in wounds caused during branding. Maybe their cruelest and favorite spot to lay those deadly flesh-eating eggs is in the navels of newborn calves and any other animal born alive. Eventually the USDA discovered that the females mated only once, so dropping millions of sterile males eventually eradicated them in the United States. That was one of the few government programs almost everyone loved—except maybe the cowboys who liked to rope. I believe the USDA has now pushed screwworms back to the Panama Canal. In the past, though, during wet years they sometimes reappeared in Texas, and even pregnant cowboys had to pick up a rope. My old country doctor at the time assured me that I couldn't unseat a healthy baby by doing things I'd always done, even horseback. But after about eight months, I couldn't pull myself into the saddle anymore, and my belly bumped uncomfortably on the saddle horn. Once our daughter was born, we tried to take turns packing her horseback in a backpack. She'd quickly fall asleep and hang like a dead weight. It was not only exhausting; it slowed us down too much.

Somebody was going to have to stay home more. Even after my little daughter started riding her own horse, somebody still had to hang back with her. Somebody would have to take her to school and get a job in town that offered insurance. I knew who that somebody had to be. But I was determined that my pretty little daughter would have little boots and spurs, little chaps, a little saddle and rope, a big hat with a big red-tailed hawk feather, a pony, and then a good kid horse named Boss. She rode with the men and got to be a real good hand, better than her mom. At four she asked our 06 boss, Chris Lacy, for a job during branding, and he gave her complete charge of the *tecole* bucket, painting a sticky smear on all the little calves' branding wounds and navels to make sure they didn't get screwworms. He wisely knew she'd be very conscientious and gentle with those baby calves. At six she got fighting mad when another cowboy rode in front of her, at eight she drew her first cowboy day wages, at nine she was dragging calves, at eleven she bossed a crew of grown men on a circle in rough country. She was the sweetheart of young cowboys from Montana to Texas.

An old cowboy friend once lamented that he'd spent his life flanking calves. When he was young, he said, it was always, "Let them old men rope so they can stay on their horses." When he got old, it was, "Let them young boys rope so they can learn." He said he was always the wrong age and just never did get to rope. For me, when I was young, it was, "Let them young girls wash the dishes." So I washed them. When I was old, it was, "Don't let them young girls wash the dishes—it will wreck their lives." So I kept washing the damn dishes while listening to the men out on the back porch telling my daughter stories and about how much they liked young pretty girls who were good hands.

I looked for and wrote about other idyllic cowboy marriages too. I wrote about ranches owned by women, female cowboys married to men who did not ride, and wives who didn't want to ride. Instead of hiring on with a good job only for the husband, where the ranch did things "right" but women and children weren't welcome, a few figured out how to beat the system. I wrote two articles about the "Dugan Wagon," couples with babies or young children and a bachelor or two who hired out as contract branding and summer grazing crews. They stretched a rope corral to catch horses with hoolihans, slept in range teepees, and cooked on a pot-rack over an open fire. If they breached any cowboy etiquette, I never found it, from their wood branding fire to their workhorse–drawn chuckwagon. Women and kids were treated as equals. Everyone roped; everyone rode. The adults took turns cooking, although the women still washed the dishes. They operated by the traditional cowboy code and were sort of the envy of every cowboy family. Unfortunately, one of them was pronounced brain-dead after a horse accident, never regained consciousness, and lingered in a coma on life support for many years. The others all divorced. Like Shakespeare, I found no answers to affairs of the heart.

When my own marriage deteriorated, I think I used journalism to escape. Mom duties were fading as my daughter grew up, and I wanted her to remember me for more than washing dishes. Although at the time, I was more worried about my own life than my legacy.

When feminist scholars began hunting for female or "cowgirl" writers and photographers, they never found me. At times those omissions hurt my feelings. Maybe my work was of no consequence or maybe my male-sounding pen/nickname, Barney, hid my gender from them. I'm not exactly sure where Barney came from. People assumed I adopted the name to hide the fact that I was a female while writing and photographing in a traditionally male domain. But I had the nickname long before I began freelancing for livestock magazines and long before gender became an issue. When I was a little girl, I was a tomboy and always at the barn, a little barn crazy, maybe a little barn-ey? Later I had a crush on a guy whose middle name was Barney and my high school friends thought it was cute, like matching shirts: Barney and Barney. Maybe part of it came from those same high school friends who thought I should have been a size 3 instead of a size 14. In any event, I preferred Barney over Barbara, a name that to me sounded too formal, or Barb, a name that probably fit my personality but sounded too much like my mother was calling me. The name Barney served me well, though. I think it helped me visit places and publish in venues where I might have run up against some resistance if they'd have known—before it was too late—that ol' Barney was a dang girl.

I never hid the fact that I was a female or wished otherwise. After I began to write seriously, I usually wrote in first person, so my gender should have been obvious. Still people seemed to read my articles as though I was a male, which sometimes caused awkward moments during the years when I was married. My spouse would turn livid when new acquaintances would call him Barney, assuming that he was the writer/photographer. After our divorce, he became somewhat of a celebrity, perhaps motivated at least partly to avoid ever again being mistaken for Barney Nelson. Although he was almost never around when I was doing interviews or photography, I thought a big part of my access to the cowboy world rested on the fact that I was married. When I divorced at forty-three and moved to town, I lost that access overnight—at least in my own mind.

I had the same knowledge and skills, but as a "single female, divorcée," I felt self-conscious. I wondered about my motives. Am I looking? Why did I pick this person to interview? Am I interested in more than a story? As long as I was married, I felt like "one of the boys." I could relax around them and get them to relax around me. But once I was single again, I avoided old and dear friends, thought there were places I dared not go, and missed opportunities I thought I had to turn down. Instead of the divorce giving me more freedom, I felt less. Pre-divorce I never got hit on while doing a story, except once on the Northern Cheyenne Reservation. Not by my subject but one of his friends asked me if I wanted to "do" a sweat lodge. When I said no, he never asked again. Maybe I misunderstood his intentions. Post-divorce, after one of the single coffee shop men asked me on a date, I never went to morning coffee again—but not because I felt harassed. I just did not want to be responsible for breaking any fragile hearts.

The one thing I'm sure changed was my journalism style. My subjects pre-divorce were often in-depth portraits based on interviews. I prided myself in getting normally private, taciturn people to open up and spill their guts. I believed that as a female, I could get material that men couldn't, because men seem to have trouble talking seriously to each other.

After divorce, my subjects were less personal (environmental issues, history, books) and based more on research than interview. Single, I couldn't take the heat of an intense personal interview without fearing for my sanity or starting something that I didn't want to finish. Even age doesn't help. Now an old granny in my seventies, I'm still a female, still single, still closing doors (and gates) on myself.

While trying to remember as honestly as selective memory, rationalization, and self-censorship will allow, I've been rereading old letters to piece together the truth. I found one letter where Ray and Carolyn Hunt had found a dream ranch job for me. I'd have a little cabin of my own alongside a trout stream, and the ranch would furnish split wood for winter. But after making a trip to look it over and finding out I would be working for a divorced and single man, I turned it down.

Then I found a letter to a married couple whom I considered confidants and to whom I worked hard to tell the truth. I had written that I was tired of cowboy journalism. That I'd been there, done that, and now was looking for a subject that mattered. So what is the truth?

CHAPTER SEVEN

Horses

"You obviously can't become a law professor or a scientist in order to write a story. So you have to trust your instincts. It's partly a matter of deciding which people actually know something about the subject."

—Calvin Trillin

I WISH I HAD KEPT track of the miles I rode horseback. Most years it probably wouldn't have been much, but there were a few when it might have been respectable. I think only once did I put in what might have been a sixty-mile day. That's a lot. One summer I rode every day, all day, picking up bulls in the big Willow Springs pastures. I also wish I had kept track of all the horses I rode. I can name a few: Secretariat, Jeff, The Grey, Serrucho, Boss, Nylon, Cade, Patch, Scottie, Lefty, Cinnamon, Dominoe, Little Streak, Copenhagen, Festus, Little Red, Redline, Nig, and Gabe. The rest have disappeared into the fog. I called them "the boys." They were not only my teachers; they were the best friends I ever had, even though several of them bucked me off from time to time.

A cowboy friend who was once temporarily trapped in country where fences were closer together than they are here in the desert said that although he liked the people he worked for, he was not happy. He struggled to explain that he was tired of pickups and trailers and paved roads, and he finally said, "I haven't ridden a tired horse since I've been here."

I knew what he meant. We save lots of time with our modern conveniences, but back in the days when tired horses took weeks to deliver letters, people actually wrote to each other. Technology makes communication immediate and constant—yet we don't really communicate. We drive cars but we don't have to learn to communicate with them. Technology also replaces more physical labor every day. As our lives get easier, our minds and bodies should get healthier. But they don't. We are not tired but rushed, stressed, frustrated, and grouchy—just like horses that don't end their days tired. Tired horses don't fidget, sling their heads, or chomp bits. They don't have nervous problems like pawing dirt or chewing boards and sucking wind. They are more honest, dependable, and seem actually happier than horses that don't go to bed tired. But there is a flip side. After a couple days of rest, tired horses become fresh horses. Because the hard labor makes them more physically and mentally fit, they can be a handful once rested. Riding a fresh horse is a different kind of challenge than riding a spoiled, cranky, hobby horse. Maybe it's sort of a power thing—like flying fighter jets when you're used to driving golf carts.

Anyway, here in West Texas, where we ride both tired and fresh horses, a horse ridden hard one morning might get rested for three days. Each full-time cowboy claims and rides several horses to keep them rotating and recovering. Those horses are called a string and more or less belong to the cowboy, even though they are probably owned by the ranch. Some ranches allow their full-time employees to ride horses that the cowboys actually own, and some ask them to furnish all their own horses. The 06 Ranch owned and furnished almost all horses, often raising them from at least one mare band and a stallion, sometimes several. During spring and fall roundups, these strings expanded to six or seven horses, maybe more. The full-time cowboys picked their extras from the remuda first, and then the boss, Chris Lacy, assigned strings from what was left by matching skill and personality between horse and rider.

Remuda horses ran loose in rough country for ten months of the year, only coming in to work during spring branding and fall shipping. Remuda horses were not pets; nor were they really what most people would consider "broke" horses. If you wanted to catch one, you'd better have a rope. They had been ridden maybe thirty days as colts and turned out. From then on, they were ridden only when their turn came during roundups, maybe four or five days in the spring and five or six days in the fall. A horse with a teeth-jarring trot, like old Serrucho (meaning "saw" in Spanish), might not get ridden at all unless some dang visitor wanted to go along bad enough to ride him. Some remuda horses could be eighteen years old and still not have had three months' worth of wet blankets pulled from their backs. Traditionally, a ranch that carried a remuda had such big pastures that the cowboys rode one horse down in the morning, regathered the remuda, and caught a fresh horse for the afternoon. After a rest, like a baseball pitcher, the tired horse would be ready to work again.

A remuda horse needed a job to do. You didn't want to give him time to think of something to do on his own. Remuda horses tolerated no nonsense except their own. Sometimes they were hard to get on; sometimes they didn't like ropes or spurs or being cinched up or being bridled. Some didn't like noisy nylon jackets, zippers (one cowboy even named a colt Zipper as a warning), flapping fringe, slickers, yellow highway stripes, or certain colors of prickly pear. Some would shy, walk sideways, and blow rollers out their noses at anything different, or even something they saw regularly, like a cow pie. Packing a human just made them nervous. Sometimes they refused to let certain other horses walk in front of them or behind them. These were all just bad habits that could have been corrected, but because they were ridden so seldom and we always had a job to do, nobody ever took the time to fix their idiosyncrasies. We called them alligators because if a day worker brought some of his own horses, he would have to throw them in with the remuda. There the alligators would pick on, kick, and chew on their withers and backs until the owner either rescued them and took them home or they learned to fight back. Turning an innocent young colt in with those old campaigners was almost a death sentence for him. Remuda horses probably invented bullying. They didn't like being petted or treated like sissies, didn't eat carrots or sugar.

In spite of their faults, each remuda horse also had some redeeming reason why he hadn't been sold for dog food. Maybe he was good in the rocks like Copenhagen, could take the jerk when a trotty bull needed roping like Redline, had a smooth trot like Nylon, or had the stamina to last and take the outside circle like The Grey. Or maybe he was so ornery that you just didn't care if you killed him and so saved him for those horse-killer circles when there was no chance to change horses at noon. A few were so lazy that they were allowed to live only as kids' horses, like poor ol' Peacho—if you call that living. I remember one cowboy who used to say that his idea of hell was to be reincarnated as a kid's horse.

Remuda horses were nearly always geldings, old bachelors, born not quite pretty enough to be used as studs or else just one of so many born that year that no more studs were needed. So they were castrated, usually as two-year-olds, and from then on they would keep their minds mostly on their work. I always considered remuda horses a little more romantic than my pet horses. I treated them with more respect and rode them more carefully. My dearest cowboy friends and the subjects of my best articles were cranky old remuda cowboys who showed up twice a year ready to work. I probably also considered a freelance writer sort of an old remuda horse—not totally broke, not very friendly, but ready to work.

Photographing working horses well was difficult and often a one-shot chance. My own worst tragedy happened one beautiful sundown evening in Mexico. Alberto "Beto" Muzquiz had flown his private plane across the border to pick me up and fly me to his ranch in Coahuila to do a story. A few ranches in Texas and Nevada practiced lining up horses for bridling, but the technique had begun in Mexico. I was interested in the history of the technique, which Beto knew firsthand, but the main reason for my trip was one single photograph. For several days before my visit, Beto's cowboys had been out gathering every stallion, mare, colt, gelding, and mule on his extensive ranch and throwing them into traps. The cowboys quickly lined up all the animals along a fence just before my arrival because I especially wanted a photograph with as many horses lined up as possible, and Beto raised lots of horses.

By this time in my career, *Western Horseman* was publishing everything I sent them, often giving me color, extra pages, and even two-part articles that continued from month to month. I did both the writing and my own photography, using two cameras: one loaded with Kodachrome 64 color slides and one with Kodak 125 for black and white, which I developed myself. Both were slow films but produced much richer color and finer-grained black and white than faster films. I had to be especially careful of camera shake while using a telephoto in low light, but hunting had given me a steady hand. Shooting a camera is similar to shooting a gun: brace against something solid, hold your breath, and squeeze slowly. Don't jerk. I had mastered my film, lighting, lenses, filters, aperture, and speed. I seldom produced a single frame that wasn't perfect. So I was ready.

Beto and I landed just when the sun started down, providing me with that perfect golden photographer's light, and it seemed Beto's lineup of horses and mules went on for miles, a once-in-a-lifetime sight. His horse customers liked color, so he raised horses in every shade, from white to grulla to palomino to black. All I had to do was step out of the plane and shoot. I decided to forgo black and white and concentrate on color since the light and horse colors were so perfect and fading fast. I had just enough time to shoot an entire thirty-six-frame roll of color film before the sun slipped too low for my film speed, but I knew I had the shot I had come for. Then his cowboys hurried to return the colorful, variously aged and gendered horses and mules back to their separate pastures before full dark.

When I started to rewind my film, the rewind lever spun too easily. I knew without looking that I had forgotten to put film in my camera. My knees buckled. I had never done that before, nor have I since, and I never told Beto what happened. If he were still alive, I wouldn't admit it now. The photos that appeared with the finished article ("Beto Muzquiz: Raising Horses in Mexico") I shot the next morning at first light, and they showed only the lined-up horses that were being used for that day's work. One showed four or five colts being trained to line up. I think I told Beto that the light had been too low and that the evening shots had come back from the lab out of focus—or something. I'm sure he was very disappointed in me but too much of a gentleman to complain. I should have either been shot or shot myself. In my mind's eye, I can see that beautiful sight of a hundred horses and mules lined up and vanishing down a fence line lit by the golden glow of sundown—but no photograph.

I never got over that missed opportunity but had to dust myself off and get back on. Deeper into Mexico, I interviewed silversmiths, saddle makers, and more ranchers. Beto had recommended the kind of sources I wanted and assured me that either side of the border, there was more to being a rancher than economics. He said, "Whether you're involved in ranching in the U.S. or Mexico, you do so for the way of life, not the economic rewards. I've never met a rich man who didn't want to be a cowboy or a rancher." So I interviewed several rich men who wanted to be cowboys or ranchers, poor vaqueros who took pride in their work, and the good charros who bought Beto's colorful horses.

Back in the United States, I wrote articles on ranches where the cowboys preferred to teach the horses to line up facing away from the roper and toward the corral fence, because the cowboys who worked there preferred to throw hoolihans. In Mexico, Beto's horses were trained to back up to the fence, facing the cowboys who walked up with halters or bridles. In Mexico each cowboy caught his own horse. North of the border, the boss usually caught horses, although sometimes everyone roped their own. And then there were places where the cowboys preferred letting the horses mill about so they could practice loops other than hoolihans, like one pitched underhanded to stand on its edge to catch a running horse. Both cowboys and horses are masters at breaking or inventing rules and have created lots of ways to do things. As a journalist, I tried never to take sides and preach that one way was correct and the rest wrong. I believed in diversity and found the different styles were usually adapted to and fit best in different situations. To photograph all those different styles, I also had to anticipate and be in the right place at the right time. I have seen only one good photograph of a horse running into a standing loop, for example, and it wasn't one of mine.

A photographer often needs several years of failure to be in the right place at the right time. A few years ago I was invited to eat lunch at the 06 wagon. A lady photographer was there to take pictures of the cowboys moving the remuda to a new location, always a beautiful sight. She was enjoying the wagon lunch and visiting. I heard the boss, Chris Lacy, point out to her the direction the horses would come from and that they'd go through the corrals, out the other side, and up the mountain. Then I watched several cowboys clean their plates, toss them in the wreck pan, and disappear. I knew they were headed to gather the horses. One went toward the corrals to open gates. The boss reminded her again which direction the horses would come from. The lady photographer nodded but kept talking and smiling. Suddenly we heard thunder. She raced for her cameras and reached her vehicle about the time the remuda hit the corrals and shot out the other side on a dead run. She started her vehicle and followed quickly, but I was pretty sure all she'd get, if anything, was horses' butts.

Putting horses into words was even harder than photographing them. Through the years, I wrote about horses from all angles, but always through the people who rode and cared for them: breeders, breakers, trainers, horseshoers, veterinarians, kids, cowboys, buckaroos, vaqueros, ranchers, teamsters, horse traders, packers, trail and reining competitors, rodeo cowboys, charros, saddle and gear makers, silversmiths, and artists. My articles were about the people, with the horses standing silently in the background. When the action turned to the horses, I switched to my subjects' own words. I tried to remain in the position of observer/tagalong, the rookie's-eye view.

Usually, when cowboys tried to explain anything about horses, they resorted to jokes or wrecks or heroic and tragic tales about their activities while horseback. About the horse, we got maybe its name or color and a quirk or two. When explaining their training techniques, the best horsemen usually relied on metaphors about school, operating machinery, or being chased by Indians. Sometimes it took hours to come up with enough quotes that I could string together to explain their methods. They also did not want to brag, so I had to find a way to convince the reader that my subjects knew what they were talking about. My own opinion didn't carry much weight, so I would look for someone the reader might trust, as in this example from "Breaking Colts with Donnie Slover." I quoted J. J. Gipson, manager of the Four Sixes Ranch at Guthrie, Texas, who said, "He's one of the finest I know."

Another trick was to refer to horses that already had a reputation, so I also quoted rancher John Birdwell of Whiteface, Texas, who said, "He's an extraordinarily good hand. He broke a bunch of four- to six-year-old Binion horses for me, and there were some mean horses in that bunch. Donnie's the only man I know who would have stayed with them. Yet he was easy with them, didn't abuse them, and treated each one like an individual."

I said that Donnie's style with horses was "loose" but otherwise made him sound very serious. When he was a kid, he and a friend used to go out to a Four Sixes fence that ran along a highway, where they hung upside down by their ankles from fence posts, pretending to be dead coyotes, trying to shock tourists. That story, which I didn't include, gives a truer picture of Donnie's personality, but "loose" was the best I could muster at the time. The horses also remained a ghostly presence unless you were familiar with Binion horses.

I got better, maybe, at characterizing people quickly, as in "Cody Crider, Colt Breaker." I said that after thirty days with Cody, a young horse had been to school, not just saddled and ridden. He was as ready as he could ever be to begin life with a new rider because Cody tried to anticipate anything one of his customers might do and tried to expose the colt to everything from dragging calves to waiting patiently in the trailer. I said that if the future rider "decides to suddenly drop the reins, rear back in the saddle, and play a few hot licks on an imaginary guitar along with Bon Jovi, Cody has already done it." Cowboys often rolled their eyes and shook their heads when they saw Cody hug some bronc and kiss it on the nose. But little girls often show affection to their horses, and Cody didn't want any little girl suffering a broken nose during her first kiss. Their scoffing didn't bother Cody either. When he took one of his colts to Texas cuttings, he usually kicked those eye-rollers' asses. I called him "The Code of the West," and he usually lived up to it. But I never said he kissed horses on the nose in the article and neither did he. I should have. Again though, I'm still writing about the human, not the horse.

The best horsemen I ever knew couldn't talk about horses, maybe because they cared so much that they didn't think anyone else would understand. Ronnie Scott struggled mightily to put anything into words, and his hands often shook when he tried. He was a bachelor at the time, and it seems to be a law of Mother Nature that you never get to be both a good horseman and a social butterfly. He wrote a few letters, but when I tried to read them, even the paper shook. I especially looked for subjects like Ronnie, who didn't seek publicity but knew something worth hearing. Ronnie would stumble around, start and stop, start over, change his mind, and get all tangled up. So for "New Mexico Horse Trainer: Ronnie Scott," I tried to untangle his words: "I can sit down to talk to somebody and I won't say ten words, but I get to talking about these horses and this attitude and this approach to life—that's what it is, an approach to life—and you can't shut me up. Sometimes maybe I think I'm talking to convince myself of some things that I'm not sure of. . . . Horses are not only a tool that I use in my work; they're good friends that I really respect." Although Ronnie and I tried to put that friendship and respect into words, my article was still more about Ronnie than the horses.

Because horses can't talk, I couldn't interview them and get their opinions about how well their riders were communicating. Without the horse, there would be no cowboys. Horses were partners, and I found it so unfair to tell only one side of the story. It took years to get to know a horse well enough to try to speak for him, and even then the human could be dead wrong. When writing about horses, I could let the rider tell his or her side of the story, but I couldn't tell the horse's side. Maybe that was best, because if horses could talk and tell the truth, it would probably scare us to death.

The deepest I got into the mind of any horse was when I wrote about my own horseback experiences while trying to apply what I thought I was learning from Ray Hunt. The best I could do was just let the reader see my thoughts as I tried to learn a few words of horse and teach my horse a few words of human—although *teach* is not the right word in my case. I found it easier to get obedience than genuine understanding. Ray always said the horse was the best teacher and claimed to search for horses that resisted obedience without trust and understanding, or at least that's what I think he said. Who knows what he meant.

Eventually I decided that writing about horses in general was like trying to write about people in general. I needed to get to know and write about individuals, and probably start at home. If a person rides many horses, eventually one will stand out as the horse against which all others are measured, and maybe they will get to know that horse well enough to write about him. That horse for me was a big, good-looking bay with a white foot and stocking on the right rear leg and a white star and blaze down his nose. I've never known for sure how to measure a horse, but my bay was taller than most tall horses—a challenge to get on. I never weighed him either, but if a big horse weighed eleven hundred pounds, then this horse weighed twelve hundred or thirteen hundred. He was named Secretariat, after the famous racehorse. He looked like a muscled-up racehorse and had a reputation as a runaway. So I figured his name was half compliment, half warning. I rode him from the mid-1970s until the late '80s, when he gradually became lame. I called him Sec.

I have never been a gambler or a fan of horse racing and have never owned a TV, so it seems almost eerie that I watched when my horse's namesake won the Triple Crown. I had gone to visit some friends, Bill and Martha Fowler, at their ranch camp on the old Ralph Merriweather Ranch, which has since become a subdivision. They answered the door in a rush: "Hurry. Come in. We can't talk. Come on in. We gotta watch this race." There, standing in their living room, I watched on a tiny black-and-white TV while Secretariat ran the horse race of all horse races, winning by thirty-one lengths.

My bay must have been born that year or soon after. In the cowboy culture, traditionally whoever starts a colt names him. Sometimes a piece of paper in a dusty file drawer somewhere includes a colt's official registered name, his date of birth, and a drawing of his markings. The ranch stud about the time Sec was born was Rey Jigs, out of a Shug McCue mare by the stud Joe Reed, but he could have been out of a Jigs predecessor, a stud one of the bronc riders at the time called an old remount stud. I'm not sure who Sec's mother was either—although most of the ranch's mares at the time traced back to that remount stud—nor do I know what his registered name was. Too many years have passed to find out, but he looked and acted like what cowboys called a "Hancock horse," at whose altar most working ranch cowboys worshiped: feet, speed, size, withers, bone, heart. Sec was good looking enough that on any other ranch he would have been left a stud, but here Jigs already had the job of chasing the ladies. Sec was simply born to keep the remuda supplied with new muscle and soon became a gelding. Once a colt is gelded, his papers are worthless and his bloodline doesn't matter much anymore—only what he can do. Most Hancock horses can do.

When the big bay was roped out of the remuda and handed to me to ride for the first time, and I heard his name called, I'm sure we both looked at each other with a little white around our eyes. I figured he got his name because he could run. Maybe because so many bronc riders are little and the ground is a long way down, sometimes big horses are not as disciplined as they should be, at least in my imagination. I've never been a little girl, so I always needed a big horse to pack me around. When Sec looked at me, he was probably thinking, "Oh, shit! My back hurts already." He had the size I needed, but I also knew that nothing was more dangerous to ride than a big, stout runaway. Although I didn't hunt for it, I didn't mind too much if a horse bucked me off, but I was terrified of a runaway. If I hit the ground on a buck-off, I figured I might break something, but I'd live. If I hit the rocks under a big horse falling at high speed, at least one of us would probably never get up.

The main reason I eventually trusted Sec and got along with him so well is that he didn't explode; he just slowly came to a boil. I could feel the bubbles percolating and had time to turn down the fire. He didn't pull surprises. His fuse was long and smoldering. He warned me way ahead of time that trouble was brewing. His reason was never stubbornness or anger or spoiled habits. It was always fear, most often when cattle or other horses got fast. Maybe he too was afraid of falling. His reactions didn't flash into "all of a sudden for no reason at all" but built up over several long minutes. I could feel it coming, although I'm not sure I can put into words how it felt. His muscles seemed to tighten, to bunch up, to sort of cock. He seemed to gather himself, like he was getting ready for something. His warnings started early and gave me time to fix whatever was making him nervous. If my first idea didn't work, I had time to try another. Sometimes simply a hand on his neck or rump would calm him, sometimes a few strokes of petting. Sometimes I could slide my hand down one rein and pull him into a circle and bring him back to me. My last resort was to step off. He was a calm gentleman on the end of a rein or a McCarty lead rope, never taking out the slack. If I started to step off, he never tried to break away and settled right down. I'd sit on a rock to let his fear subside. I'd remount and he'd stay relaxed for the rest of the day. Although every day I felt his power surging, in all the years I rode him, he never ran away with me. He never bucked, never ducked out from under me, never dumped me on the ground for any reason, never hurt me in any way. But I knew he could. I never totally relaxed on his back. He was the most trustworthy untrustworthy horse I ever rode. He was rock-solid nervous, a brave fearful horse, who thought long and hard before he let his fear overpower his common sense. He was deep running water, but we could both swim. I wondered often about his tendency to run. How did he get that way? Did someone whip him as a colt or was it just his personality? Was it in his blood? Or was it my own fear that he sensed?

I think part of the reason I liked to ride him was that he made me look like a good hand. I thought I looked almost pretty riding him. His powerful rear end made mine look smaller. He also forced me to pay attention, sit up straight, keep my mind on business. So on Sec I sat a horse like a horse should be sat. He was no kid horse, no sweet little lady's horse. No kid ever rode him and no other lady. You could tell by the look in his eye that he was a handful; he had that high-headed, solemn look of hawks and eagles.

Once, after I'd been riding him for several months and had gotten very attached to him, my heart caught in my throat when a potbellied cow buyer spotted Sec hobbled outside the corral and asked the *segundo* handling the shipping, "What'll ya take for that big bay?"

I called Sec "my" horse, but he never belonged to me. He belonged to the ranch. I claimed him only by right of tradition: when a horse was placed in a person's string, nobody else rode him without their permission. Sec was in my string, but I wasn't on the payroll and the ranch sold horses. I knew that if the *segundo* priced him and the cow buyer accepted, then Sec would go with the calves. I held my breath and waited—another long moment frozen in my memory.

The *segundo* glanced at Sec, then back at the cow buyer. Finally, he said, "Tell ya what. I'll price him if you can get on him."

I let out my breath. I figured Sec could handle the problem now all by himself.

Sec was standing calmly in my hobbles, one hip cocked, half-asleep in the sun, like a good-looking, well-broke ranch horse, the kind of horse the cow buyer knew would sell for big bucks through the sale ring. My bridle hung on the saddle horn, so the cow buyer took a step in Sec's direction. With each step, Sec grew a little taller. The closer the cow buyer came, the more Sec looked like he'd seen a ghost. Head up, eyes white, he started dancing sideways in his hobbles, blowing rollers out his nose like an old feather-hocked rodeo bronc. The cow buyer turned, grinned at the *segundo*, and headed back to the scales to weigh calves.

Up until that moment, I'd been working hard to help Sec get over his broncy habits, but never again. After that I tried not to let too many people watch me get on him. I'd lead Sec up alongside a cement water trough or tub, climb onto the cement, and then step over his back. If no water trough was around, my mounting was not pretty. My pants were always a little tight, so I'd get way back behind the cantle, out on the end of my McCarty lead line, with the same hand lift my leg up high enough for my foot to reach the stirrup, hop forward until I could grab the saddle horn, and pull myself up with both the saddle horn and cantle until I could swing my leg over. My foot always seemed to stall about halfway over his rump, and then I'd sort of grab and claw with a spur until I finally inched my leg over to the other side. Then I'd fish around for the stirrup, wiggle around to get my leggins straight, and finally remember to gather up my rein. Meanwhile, Sec was a rock. If anyone else walked up to him, he got nervous and started his side-stepping bronc act. A cowboy would just cheek his head around with the headstall, stand next to his neck in front of his shoulder, turn the stirrup, slip in a toe, and swing on low, fluid, and catlike. Sec didn't like that much, and I couldn't get on that way. So after I got him caught and saddled, I'd usually lead him off behind the barn or some bushes, like I was going to pee, so nobody would follow me. Then I'd come back mounted, the big bay dancing sideways, sometimes with a little help from my off spur.

He wasn't nearly as wild as I could make him look. But if things got strange or fast, Sec came untrained and reverted back to his original flight response. I never tried to move horses or yearlings on him. The ranch raised horned Herefords and liked to keep them trotty, so they would travel good. Once in a while, on cool mornings, those horned Herefords could get very fast. That's when Sec and I would sometimes have to stop to calm down, pretending one of us had to pee again. I'd step off and wait for his panic to pass. Once it did, we could lope to catch up. He had a nice rocking-chair lope as long as he kept his cool.

During the time I rode Sec, I started hanging out at Ray Hunt horse training clinics. I followed Ray around the country, from Montana to California, Wyoming to Idaho, Colorado to Fort Worth. He kept encouraging me, so I kept writing, eventually publishing more than eleven articles about him. Nearly everything I wrote after I met Ray in 1983 was at least influenced by him. Usually my freelance paycheck reached far enough to cover only travel and the price of watching from the fence, but since my articles were bringing him more business, Ray's wife, Carolyn, started waiving my watching fees. Once Ray even mounted me on someone else's problem horse so I could actually ride. Through the years, Sec and I gradually got to know one another, but he never got over his tendency to run.

Here is a description of a typical day from a letter I wrote to Ray Hunt on July 15, 1985: "Even me and Secretariat are finally making some tiny progress steps. We can sidepass all the way down the corral with no hassles, can back into a corner without rearing up, he stands perfectly still and horizontal with the saddle house to be brushed and saddled, doesn't get wild-eyed at me touching him anywhere, doesn't shy in the pasture any more . . . these are all things I've accomplished! Things still kind of fall apart when it gets faster than a lope, but I know it is just me now for sure. We kind of had a break through the other day when I was helping a cowboy trying to pen a crippled bull who had taken up housekeeping with an old crazy dry cow and there wasn't a bend in them anywhere. The cowboy shook down his stock whip to try to talk the bull into some bending. Well, he got some response from Sec—one of his old-fashioned stiff-necked runaways. There wasn't a soft spot in him from his stretched out nose to his laid back ears to his clamped tail. Of course, for a little while I forgot all I had ever tried to learn. After I got my heart swallowed again, I timidly reached out to see if I could bring his head around—I knew I couldn't. Well, Sec just melted and floated around in a pretty little arc and by the time he finished half a circle was down to a trot. I petted him and bragged on him and his ears even came forward. It didn't last real long because I had to job him with my spurs again and take off after the damn bull and a couple of hours and lots of bad language and 50 head of cows and calves later—when we finally got the bull penned, I had probably set

Sec back to six months ago. But maybe he will forgive me and I'll get better." I don't remember what Ray thought of my letter and wish I could find his response.

Eventually I managed to scrape together enough cash to ride Sec through a clinic in Fort Stockton, Texas, probably about 1986. Sec was wide-eyed and so was I. By this time I had discovered that I couldn't describe what Ray Hunt did because I didn't know; nor could I try to interpret what the other riders were thinking. I didn't know enough to even ask good questions. My best idea was pretending to be an idiot and to let the reader learn at my expense, and I didn't actually have to pretend. I just described my experience of riding Sec in that clinic for "A Day in the Saddle." I said, "Sec walked on eggs into the coliseum on day one, blowing rollers. There were metal gates banging, microphones blaring, strange people, kicking mares, little running kids, and a horse-eating tractor at one end of the arena. I wanted a different horse. But, good grief, I live on a big ranch, I dress like a good cowboy, I write for horse magazines—I couldn't let anyone know I was scared of my horse! So I threw slack in my reins, relaxed, and tried to act nonchalant. Sec dropped his head and cocked a hip. Hey, thought I, this is easy. I just Ray Hunted him! That was the last thing I did right—even by accident—for the next two miserable days."

Ray has been dead now for more than ten years, but not a day, not an hour goes by that I don't think about his teaching. Ray's picture has been on the cover of almost every existing horse magazine. Foreign governments imported him to hold clinics. He traveled almost constantly. He touched hundreds, maybe thousands, maybe millions of people who will not forget. I've read Ray's book, *Think Harmony with Horses*, dozens of times, but I don't think we can learn much from a book. Ray Hunt opened the horse to me so that I could recognize horsemanship as one of those things that can't ever be truly mastered. Although some people think they have learned to ride a horse once they stop falling off at a gallop, or even when they can take a colt and make a reining or a calf-roping horse, we haven't scratched the surface. That trail is endless. The secret to curing boredom and loneliness is to find something that can't be mastered. So God created horses and ink.

Horses are more sensitive than most people would ever dream. For instance, one time while I was just trying to brush Sec, I noticed that he kept moving, depending on where I touched him with the brush. I wanted him to stand still, but he thought I was giving him some sort of signal to move around with the brush. By this time, he knew I could speak a few words of horse and he could understand a few words of human, so maybe he had too much faith that everything I said had meaning. I couldn't seem to figure out how to let him know when I just wanted to brush him and when I was trying to get him to move. I didn't want him to lose faith in my ability to speak horse or his ability to speak human, but I hadn't yet learned the horse words for "Just joking" or "I'm sorry" or "That's not what I meant" or "Ignore that."

Every movement on my part could mean something. Leaning forward could mean speed up; leaning backward could mean stop. Or not. Every movement on his part could also mean something. Leaning toward me when I reached for the flank cinch could mean that he was trying to help me, or it could mean that he was about to step on my foot. Trying to speak horse was very similar to writing. It seems like the harder we try to understand each other, the more confused and distrustful we become. The harder I tried, the more my confidence eroded. Probably to compensate, I'd try to ride horses that bucked off good cowboys. I always hoped for respect and instead got irritation. "You're trying too hard," Ray Hunt would tell me when I struggled with a horse problem. It probably applied to my whole life, but I kept trying too hard. I'd collect cowboy sentences to prove Ray Hunt wrong: "He's a good horse. He's got lots of try." Or "Well, maybe I can't ride him but nobody can say I didn't try." Or "All you gotta do is try." Try seemed to be a good thing when displayed by dogs, horses, and children—but not when I did it? I never understood and still don't.

Sec and I both got nervous when we didn't understand. I would never intentionally hurt him, but I'm sure I did. I would never want to ask him to do anything that he couldn't or didn't yet know how to do, but I'm sure I did. Communication carries a heavy burden of responsibility. Is it better to never try or to try and fail a thousand times to gain one new word of horse? All my frustrations made great material for articles. I never tried to present myself as an expert or claim I had found any answers, because I hadn't. I just described my situation honestly and let readers see me struggle so they could figure out their own answers. I tried to show people *how* to think, not tell them *what* to think.

Sec's nervousness made him interesting, but he had another habit that made him aggravating. He was a pig. He loved to roll, especially in mud. So when it came time to ride him, I needed to start an hour early so I could scrape, curry, and brush him clean enough to saddle him. After a ride, I would hose the sweat off his back and brush him until he gleamed like a wet otter. In spite of his piggy habits, in the summer, when he had slicked off and his coat had been bleached a little by the sun, I could really put a shine on him. John Steinbeck called it bay light. Sec's bay light resembled the glow of a clean hardwood floor at sunrise and sundown, smelled like a horse, and felt like thick satin. As soon as I turned him loose, though, he'd find a deep pile of dry manure, roll, and come up looking like he was wearing a moth-eaten raccoon coat. In one of my favorite pictures of him, now that I no longer have to brush him clean, Sec is rising from a big puddle absolutely dripping with mud and unrecognizable except by habits. We were moving the remuda, and of course, no other horse in the strung-out parade of one hundred trotting geldings took time to roll in the mud—only Sec.

Sec was also a pig when it came to food. About an hour before sundown, he'd come thundering down the horse trap hill, several lengths ahead of the other geldings. He wanted to beat the others to the barn, where he knew a few flakes of alfalfa would magically appear from the sky over their heads and plop down on the ground at their feet (thrown from a hay loft balcony on the second floor of the barn). He knew that if he got there first, he'd have time to pick the biggest flake of hay, swallow it whole, and then chase another gelding or two off half of their own hay—even though he'd already been grazing all day. He'd sell his soul for a handful of oats or a two-inch cube of cottonseed cake. He'd try hard to resist, but if I waited, his appetite would overrule his better judgment and I could slip a rope around his neck. Once he felt the rope, he was caught. But I never got him over being hard to catch, even after all my years at Hunt clinics. If I wanted to ride him, I'd need a jingle horse and a rope, or patience and food, because Sec didn't pen simply by opening a gate. Inside a pen, I'd have to slap my leg with my lead rope before he'd stop, head up, and let me catch him. Even then I had to approach him just right, never head-on but from the shoulder, slipping a rein or a rope around his neck. Then I could slip a headstall over his ears if I didn't go too fast or too slow. He didn't like his ears messed with, didn't like someone standing directly in front of him. Never in our many years together did he ever just let me walk up and bridle him. It always took either a bribe or a threat. I claimed it was just his personality, but I should have been able to teach him better habits.

Sec never admitted to being tired or sore. He never groaned or complained about my weight in any way. He never ran out of "want to." Cowboys call it heart. So I'm sure Sec, like his namesake, had a huge heart. I almost killed us both one day because of it. During spring branding and fall shipping, my horses were needed to help supply the additional crew. I didn't like it, but I'd accept losing the others as long as Sec could stay with me. I didn't want anybody else riding that horse. So to justify leaving a good horse behind, one of the *segundos* usually gave me, or I came up with, a few jobs to do alone in the evenings when I got home from my town job or over a weekend. I picked up remnants, pushed cattle out of traps and into pastures, or checked water.

Once, the crew left about three hundred keeper heifers for me to push out of one trap, push across another trap, and then put on water in an adjoining pasture. Sec and I tackled the job one sweltering Saturday morning, not a wise choice, but the only one I had. I tried gathering the whole herd at once, but that wasn't working. So I'd peel off about ten head at a time and push them through one gate, then another gate, and then another, and on to the water trough about a half mile from the third gate. It was slow going and the sun kept climbing. Hot, humid, no breeze. I was anxious to get the job over with and go find a sweating can of iced tea. (I saved empty tomato cans for glasses.) Neither Sec nor I were enjoying ourselves. The heifers got harder and harder to handle as the day got hotter. We'd get a few head started toward the first gate and go back to get a few more. Meanwhile, the first bunch would turn around and head back toward the shade at the other side of the trap. I was cussing and concentrating, unaware of time passing. Shutting the pasture gate for about the eighth time, I looked down at my horse's neck. Sec was covered with white lather.

I had been interviewing a retired cowboy/rancher who had just told me about a good horse that he'd ridden to death. That horse too had been covered in white lather. The horse had died, never untracking from the spot where the cowboy had pulled off the saddle. I stepped off Sec immediately, loosened his girth, and lifted the saddle skirts and blankets off his back so he could feel a breeze, although none was blowing. I was terrified. I blew on his back.

I often rode horses until white lather formed around the edges of bridles or saddle girths. That was the salty sweat that left an outline of my bridles and saddle pads imprinted on a horse after I'd unsaddled. It was the stuff I'd wash off their backs and necks and faces after a ride, the stuff I had to wash out of my bridles and saddles, and then oil with neatsfoot to keep the leather from rotting. That was the stuff that made my boots wear out on the inside first, that destroyed hatbands and stained leather belts. But this was different. This lather was everywhere, not just along the edges. I knew Sec was in trouble. A water trough was only about two hundred yards away, so I led him slowly toward it. I let him take a few sips and then splashed water on him. Take a few sips. Splash water. He seemed to revive, so I looked toward the barn, maybe another quarter mile away, where we'd have shade and another water trough, and decided to try it. About halfway there, my own vision started to blur. I had been so concerned about Sec that I hadn't taken a drink myself or splashed any water on my own face. Now I was walking in the heat wearing heavy leggins and boots, long sleeves, long pants, and a dark hat. I was soaking up sun with no breeze. Now we were both in trouble.

Somehow we made it to the barn, and I immediately collapsed in the wooden feed bunk in the shade. The water trough was only about fifteen feet farther, but every time I raised my head to try to get there, the world spun. Sec had water, but he stood in the sun, still saddled, looking at me like his heart was breaking. *How can you just take a nap and let me stand here with the saddle on? Can't you see how miserable I am?* I felt terribly guilty but afraid to move. If I died, Sec would stand there in that pen with that saddle on his back and with no feed for days before anyone would check on us. I had to keep myself alive. Judging by the change in the shadows, I must have lain in the feed bunk for two or three hours before I got up the courage to try to make it to the water trough. I soaked my shirt down and peeled off my heavy leather leggins but did not drink.

I had no qualms about drinking from anything that held water, including tracks, on any ranch anywhere, but this one particular water trough was different. I knew too much about it. My Australian shepherd dog, who had worse cleanliness habits than Sec, would jump in there to cool off, float for a while, and I'm sure pee in the water. Then he'd jump out and go roll in a dead skunk and come back for another soak. The slimy green water stank, and foamy yellowish clumps of horse slobbers speckled with feathers and chicken lice floated on top. I knew too much history about that water to drink it.

I felt a little less shaky after wetting my shirt down. I went back and lay in the feed bunk, and the ground stopped spinning. Eventually I unsaddled Sec, lay down again, soaked myself again, lay down, and finally felt strong enough to try to make it to the house about another fifty yards away. Once there, I drank a cool glass of clean water, waited a half hour, drank another glass, waited, and then drank another. I ran myself a deep cool bath and soaked a while, sipping water. About sundown, I felt strong enough to walk out to feed Sec. He was coated in dry sweat, but I told him he'd have to give me until morning before he got a bath. We were alone, would be for several more days, and I didn't want to chance passing out. I knew we had both been very lucky. The next day, Sec got his bath, and we both took a few days off. The next weekend, we finished moving the rest of the heifers.

After I'd been to a few of Ray's horse clinics, I thought I had begun to understand how to communicate with horses and the kind of relationship that was possible between horse and rider. To test my understanding, I tried some crazy experiments, even selling *Horse and Rider* an article about sitting in that same feed bunk where I had almost died and watching flies land on a horse. I think it was Ray's favorite article. Most of my experiments were totally unsuccessful, like when I tried to teach a kitten to lead at the end of a leash. However, a few experiments with Sec did seem to work, at least in my own mind. Sec always seemed reluctant to go to work. He dutifully did anything he was asked, but he didn't really want to. He wasn't "ticking and grinning." So I decided to just try starting all over with him, just go with him anywhere he wanted to go and at whatever speed. He was a tad lazy, so unless he got upset about something, speed wasn't his natural goal. I'd leave the reins slack, with my hands anchored on the A-fork of my saddle to remind me not to direct him. I'd keep my legs relaxed and try not to even shift my weight—no cues, no clues. We'd go wherever he wanted to go. Quite often that would be an investigative half circle around the horse trap at a nice lively reaching walk that I could never get when I asked.

Then he'd head up on a ridge, where we discovered that a breeze kept the flies from bothering him. I watched a terrified horse once in California. His muscles stayed in a constant state of tension. Flies crawled all over his face, but he took no notice of them. The man I was there to write about said the flies weren't bothering him because the horse had worse trouble right now. He said that when the horse got happier, the flies would begin to bother him again. Sure enough, as the day went on and the horse improved under my friend's guidance, that horse started stomping at the flies and tossing his head. So when Sec would throw major fits over one little fly, I couldn't help but wonder if I had made him especially happy.

Anyway, we'd just sit there in the breeze and look around. He'd watch birds fly over or a bug crawling on the ground. He didn't miss much. It didn't take much to entertain him, and it did seem to lift his spirits. He started to stride out with me and his ears pricked up, like he was looking forward to the day. When I would direct him, he'd go, but he still felt just a little resistant. He felt so much smoother when he was calling the shots. So I tried to pick what mattered to me and let him decide the rest. I looked for chances to let him decide—where to cross a creek, which tire track to follow to a windmill. None of this was probably a great idea.

One day we were helping a cowboy sort two-year-old heifers. I don't remember exactly what we were doing, but the job was very repetitious. Sec and I would get behind the pen full of heifers and push them clockwise around the pen to the cowboy in the gate, who peeled off what he wanted. Maybe we were sorting off heavies, although this particular ranch let heifers calve on their own. The 06 didn't assist its heifers, so those that had trouble simply died. This gradually improved the genetics and weeded out calving problems, and we seldom ever found a dead heifer. It seemed like the perfect solution.

Anyway, I don't remember what we were doing, but Sec and I would make circle after circle. Eventually I stopped using my reins to see if Sec could make a circle on his own. He did. Then I stepped off and let him make one complete circle without me. Sec was teaching me to speak horse and I was listening. Then the cowboy hollered and asked what in the hell I was doing?

Annie Dillard tried to explain crossing that line once. She was busy with a book that was pushing her sanity, and she said that one day the floor moved and her typewriter blew up, spouting flames and sparks. She said she finally calmed the fire by opening her curtains and looking outside. She cleaned up the mess and threw away the shirt she had been wearing because it had gotten scorched. Her typewriter evidently still worked, but she treated it more cautiously because now she "knew it could happen." So I got back on my horse. Sec seemed as interested in my experiments as I was, but we didn't dare talk about them. So I wrote more articles. Obviously not here, not on this ranch, not in this little town, but somewhere out there, I hoped, were people who might understand.

As the years wore on, Sec meant more and more to me, although I rode him less and less. I had taken on other horses to ride and had less and less time to get them all ridden. Although part of that might have been denial. Even at a trot, Sec had a long-legged, smooth, flowing gait that made him a pleasure to ride. Too much of a pleasure. I loaned him out only twice that I remember. Once Sec carried country singer Charlie Daniels across the flats from my house, up the rimrock trail, and then across what we called "on top" to catch up with the wagon for a few days of branding between singing gigs. Charlie was a big man who needed a big horse that could pack him comfortably a long way and not leave him too sore to ride the next morning. Sec was the only logical option. Besides, most of the other horses were already up on top.

The second time I loaned him out might have been a little more tragic. One of the full-time cowboys wanted to borrow him because Sec was such a good traveling horse. He wanted to trot over to the neighboring Leoncita Ranch and visit a friend from Montana who was working at their wagon, eat some of Ramón's cooking, and then trot back, a round-trip of maybe twenty miles. No other horse in the trap was legged up for a long trot like that. The colts were all too soft. It was the kind of a ride through rocky country that could seriously hurt a young horse. Sec was in top condition at the time from packing around my extra weight. The cowboy and his saddle probably weighed at least seventy-five pounds less than my saddle and I. Sec could handle it, and I agreed that the ride might hurt one of the colts. I gave Sec a few days rest when he got back. But he was never quite the same horse. I didn't want to blame anyone, didn't want to complain, and especially didn't want anyone to know Sec might have a problem.

The next time I rode him, Sec stumbled, just a little, probably just a coincidence, probably nothing. He was usually very sure-footed in the rocks, but I didn't quite trust him from that day on. His stumbling wasn't often, but often enough. I refused to notice it though and never mentioned it to anyone for fear of what might happen to Sec. Old racehorses can still live long productive lives at stud once they start slowing down, but not old ranch geldings, not those on working ranches that carry one hundred–head remudas. Working ranches can't afford to be sentimental about their old horses or they'd soon be out of grass and out of business. Once a working horse outlives his usefulness, he climbs on a truck headed for a dog food factory. Although it broke my heart, I knew those horse slaughterhouses were good for old horses because death by old age is cruel. I loved horses too much to want them to suffer a "natural" death. But I buried those thoughts in the back of my mind and made up feeble excuses to ride other horses or not ride at all.

Then I began to notice Sec standing with his weight off his right front foot instead of hip-shot. He sort of kept that front foot stuck out in front of him a little. I tried not to notice, but sometimes when I rode him, his head seemed to bob just a little—*not much, not bad at all, probably nothing*—when he stepped with his weight onto that right front foot. I sank deeper into denial. *He must have bruised the frog, pulled a muscle; maybe his shoe is nailed on too tight. He'll get over it with a little rest. Maybe if I shift the way I ride and keep my weight off that foot when he sets it down. Maybe if I lose weight . . . if I cut my hair . . . if I wear my lucky shirt . . . if I start praying.*

Although I've always heard that white feet are vulnerable and break down sooner than dark feet, for Sec it was a dark hoof—right front—with navicular. A horseshoer diagnosed it and told me. So I researched and wrote about navicular, an incurable disease of a bone with the same name, shaped like a half moon, that fits inside a horse's hoof. The disease seems sort of like osteoporosis in people. A healthy navicular bone is dense but slightly porous, full of tiny holes, but with the onset of navicular, those holes begin to enlarge. They eventually look like lace, and the bone gets weak and painful. A horse that gets navicular is done. Nobody knows why it begins, but overuse is suspect.

I needed to come up with something fast—no more denial. At the next Hunt clinic, I ran into a friend who owned a ranch about two hundred miles northeast. I'd been to her place and knew she had a "pensioners pasture," where she kept old horses that she was too soft-hearted to sell. Her ranch raised a few "black cows" that grazed for "black gold" by bobbing their heads rhythmically up and down. Those black cows helped her afford to be a little sentimental toward old horses. I told her about my problem with Sec, and she offered to retire him for me. I knew I would eventually face the same problem when navicular made it too painful for him to graze or even stand, but I could give us (mostly me) a little more time.

All I had to do was figure out what canner horses were bringing, write an article or two to raise the money, and buy Sec from the ranch. When I got home from that clinic, Sec didn't come in for his supper, so I went looking. I couldn't find him and finally had to ask. My almost ex-spouse didn't look at me or answer, so I knew. Sec had been shipped while I was gone. I never got to say good-bye. I got over the marriage after a few years, but I'm still not over the horse.

Although my emotions were too tangled at the time, as the years passed, eventually I realized that my desire to protect Sec from slaughter was a selfish act. Death should be quick and painless instead of a long, slow, painful decline into starvation, the way many wild horses die. Mother Nature is a bitch. I've watched deer struck by cars, hungry and crawling on their broken legs, trying to graze until an animal control officer brings them the gift of a bullet. My father was an ethical hunter and we tracked our wounded animals until we found them. The only thing more difficult to do than help a beloved animal die with dignity is to do the same for humans. The reasons for keeping both alive are almost always selfish and cruel. I knew death for Sec would immediately bring him comfort and peace. His was the kind of death many people who live close to the land wish for—fast. Sec died with dignity—no senility, tubes, or nurses. No nostalgia. He went the way he'd have wanted to go, just like a working horse should—useful even in death.

Years later, I made a pilgrimage to the Kentucky Derby Museum and visited the shrine for the other Secretariat. I bought a Secretariat cap and a book by William Nack called *Secretariat: The Making of a Champion.* Nack writes, "All that is really known, over the passage of almost three decades, is that Secretariat's legend remains as vibrant and secure as ever, and he continues to be viewed as the modern standard against which all members of his tribe are judged. If anything, time has only enriched and embellished his name." I could have written that about my horse too, and I guess I am writing it now.

Both horses were sometimes called Hancock horses, but that doesn't seem to mean the same thing east and west of the Pecos River. In the East it seems to mean a horse that comes down through royal thoroughbred bloodlines owned by the Hancock family of Virginia, famous breeders of famous racehorses. In the West it means a big, stout, rawboned, good-looking, bighearted horse with good withers and a long sloping hip. I always thought Hancock was a nickname, but one Texas rancher said maybe there had been an old stud named Hancock, like Old Sorrel, a King Ranch stud that became a foundation horse of the quarter horse breed. One cowboy thought it was just a name for good conformation. So I kept asking. Finally, my friend Rod Flournoy, a rancher and horse breeder in Northern California, sounded definite. He had once owned what he called a Hancock stud: Penuche Dun, a son of Red Man, who was a grandson of a horse named Joe Hancock, sure enough a foundation sire for quarter horses. Joe Hancock was the son of a half-Percheron mare, grandson of a Peter McCue stud and a thoroughbred mare. Joe Hancock was bred by a Hancock family in the Texas Panhandle. The two Hancock families don't seem to be related, and neither do the horses, although maybe they are. One of my great grandmothers was a Taylor, and her family raised horses. Our Taylor family history gets lost in the 1700s. Once descendants start numbering in the millions, ancestry gets hard to track. Descendants of some Virginia Taylors, who may or may not be kin, eventually founded the old XIT Ranch in the Texas Panhandle, so maybe descendants of Virginia Hancock horses ended up in Texas too.

Anyway, one Secretariat was born in Virginia and one in Texas. The mare who produced the racehorse had lots of help, but I doubt anyone was around when Sec was born. Most ranch mares foal without assistance out in a pasture somewhere. If it is raining, they get rained on. If it is snowing, snowed on. Sec's birth pasture was often frequented by mountain lions and town dogs as well as rattlesnakes, scorpions, cactus, and barbed wire. No attentive midwives made sure his dam was put in a nice stall with plenty of water and fresh straw to lie down on. Nobody was at hand to dry off the foal, clip the umbilical, or disinfect the navel. Through it all, mare and foal fended for themselves.

One thing Sec and the racehorse did have in common was that pretty doesn't count for much in their respective worlds. Pretty might get both a racehorse and a ranch horse noticed, but in the end, what counted was how they performed, what they could do. Both were alert and could be spooky. Both could seem nervous and flighty yet be solid as a rock too. Neither one liked machines with motors, especially tractors. Alert to a fault, both sometimes stopped to watch a plane fly overhead. Both could be lazy or come dancing home, neck arched, eyes rolling white around the edges after a little excitement had gotten their blood up. Both could endure harder and more work than most other horses as long as the grub kept pouring in. Nack writes that Secretariat "never missed an oat" and "licked the tub." So did Sec. Both were also good "alley fighters": the racehorse not afraid to shove the horses next to him to open his own running room; Sec could hold his own with the backbiting remuda horses. Unlike the racehorse, Sec didn't like people much. He didn't want to be petted, didn't like little kids. But both pricked their ears when a camera shutter clicked, maybe a little vain, maybe a bit of a ham. Like Sec, the racehorse did a few funny tricks—stealing a reporter's notebook, taking a rake handle in his teeth and trying to scrape his own stall like he'd seen his groom do every day of his life. Nobody shoveled Sec's shit. It dried up in the sun, got rolled away by dung beetles or pounded into dust by horses' hooves, and eventually blew away to fertilize nearby grass.

The jockey who rode the racehorse said he let him run his own race, seldom ever corrected him, seldom used a whip. He said, "You want to make him think he's doing something, so you sit against him, take a hold of him, and make him think he's doing everything on his own. You have to build his ego. You have to give him confidence." I think that's what I was trying to do with Sec, but not make a contest out of it, not spoil him, not encourage him to think he had to "beat" me. It was a fine line though, and I'm not sure I walked it very well. Sec and I sort of bandied back and forth, with me pretending to be the boss one day and him pretending to be the boss the next. I seldom touched him with a spur, certainly never used a whip on him, although I had to threaten with the *sound* of a whip to catch him. I am pretty sure if I had ever actually raised a whip on him while horseback, he'd have run out from under it and left me sitting in the air. Sec was always about three seconds away from fire, so I didn't play with it. I was no jockey.

Nack, describing the racehorse, could have easily been describing my bay: "He had a presence to him that the others did not have, a sense of greatness, what horsemen used to call the 'look of eagles.'" Nack also quotes a description from Seth Hancock: "You want to know who Secretariat is in human terms? Just imagine the greatest athlete in the world. The greatest. Now make him six-foot-three, the perfect height. Make him real intelligent and kind. And on top of that, make him the best-lookin' guy ever to come down the pike. He was all those things as a horse. He isn't even a horse anymore. He's a legend." So who is Sec in human terms? He's all those things and more. The first human who pops to mind is Tom Selleck, but that isn't fair. Selleck is big, kind, intelligent, good-looking, and a legend, but he's a movie star who sometimes pretends to be a cowboy. Sec was the real thing. So I guess Sec's human counterpart would need to be real too. I can't think of one cowboy who covers all those bases, so I'd have to make him a composite of the best I've ever known.

Sec never had any roses draped over his shoulders, although his shoulders were dusted with rose fungicide once when the remuda caught some kind of contagious mange and passed it around like a venereal disease. I doubt Sec ever saw chiffon or diamonds, certainly not on me, but I did ride him occasionally with a silk wildrag at my throat and a wildflower or two stuck in my dusty old felt hat.

Although I think Sec was a few years younger, both horses were probably destroyed close to the same day—the racehorse in October 1989, to prevent his further suffering from laminitis, another serious hoof disease. The racehorse was buried beneath a marked grave, perhaps providing fertilizer for grass that would be grazed by future generations of racehorses.

I suppose the biggest difference between them was stardom. Millions of people loved Secretariat; only one loved Sec. Millions of young, pretty women lined up along the rail or switched on their TV sets to watch the racehorse run; only one frumpy middle-aged lady watched Sec. Maybe it's wishful thinking, but I don't believe he would have traded me for a rail full of pretty ladies. The racehorse graced the covers of *Time*, *Newsweek*, and *Sports Illustrated*, not to mention newspapers from coast to coast and around the world. Sec had only one writer, one photographer who even knew he was alive. I made him the subject of several articles, but he was never a cover boy because he packed the photographer and her cameras around. Sec did his best to teach me to be a good cowboy. He probably failed at that, but he did help me get better at writing about and photographing horses. Like Sec, I was getting lame and my physical prowess was declining. Luckily, because of my pen, I might be able to make myself useful for a few more years.

Of the racehorse, Nack said, "He had style, and when he was himself, he made it almost art." Sec actually became art. He ended up in a few paintings by western artists such as Wayne Baize, Fred Fellows, and Gordon Snidow, but I don't think Sec cared. When the racehorse retired from the track, his black groom, Eddie Sweat, retired the lucky hat he wore to the races, smashed it, and put it in a frame. I retired Sec's bridle with its handmade

Henderson snaffle, Big Bend Saddlery headstall with deer antler conchos, Randy Stowell shoofly, Indian smoke-tanned (I think from Fred Fellows) braided hobble strap, and sorrel-and-white Blind Bob McCarty. I hung it on my wall and never used it again. The soft chap-leather-lined headstall is still set for Sec's good-looking head. No other horse was as interesting to ride after Sec. No other horse made me feel so safe while at the same time helping me to look like such a dang good hand. I knew Sec was one of the last tired horses and one of the last fresh horses I would ever ride. I would never again look as good horseback without Sec, and I never felt pretty again.

CHAPTER EIGHT

Cattle

"Wild animals and even farm animals were becoming less and less the common experience of men and women in an increasingly urbanized and industrialized society. It was easy to entertain warm feelings toward animals that seemed to have no other function than as play-things."

—Yi-Fu Tuan

I WAS SITTING IN A BORING literature class one day, an idealistic undergraduate and a range animal science major at the time. My college sat on the side of a mountain, as most colleges do, so that college professors can look down upon the rest of us from a lofty perch. I was watching buzzards soar near the classroom windows, almost at eye level. The professor was asking us to decide whether Edward Abbey's narrative voice should be classified as homodiegetic or autodiegetic. Yawn.

The buzzards were putting me to sleep. Buzzards drift so aimlessly and effortlessly on thermals, especially in the hot rimrocked desert grasslands of West Texas. Just as my eyelids were drooping, the big black birds seemed suddenly to shift gears. Instead of drifting, they began to circle with more of a purpose. Is a cow dead down there on the main street? I wondered if they had put to sleep the old cowboy Nicasio Ramirez, who always sat on the corner in the sun. As the circle tightened, more and more buzzards appeared out of nowhere. First ten, then twenty. Then I was watching one hundred, then maybe one thousand buzzards circle right outside the windows. It was a once-in-a-lifetime sight!

I raised my hand.

"Sir!" I stammered excitedly. "The buzzards are gathering to fly south right outside our window! There are thousands of them!"

The professor frowned and told me to keep my mind in class. I changed my major to English that day. The professor probably thought he had inspired me, and he did. I decided right there in that classroom, as the buzzards broke their circle and headed south, that maybe *I* should be teaching Abbey, or at least writing about him and the things he wrote about, which were often cows and buzzards. But I didn't become a teacher, at least not for twenty more years.

Instead, after graduation I married, moved from ranch to ranch, moved into town for a while, and then for thirteen years lived on a big cow-calf ranch whose mountain territory enclosed more than 220 square miles of rocky desert grassland. Most of it fenced only by rimrock and canyon, perfect buzzard soaring country. The ranch raised horned Hereford cattle, and although they seldom drew blood, they hooked and horned each other unmercifully until some kind of status quo was reached, even inside corrals. I like horned cattle. I believe that if you take away their horns, like women, they become helpless. They can't defend their territories, can't protect their calves. We sometimes found the same cow in the same place, year after year, and might have found more if we had remembered better. The cows that held territory along streams that ran through the flats had claimed the easiest country, but I always liked best the ones that ranged up on the rocky points with the mountain lions. They always seemed to raise the best calves and had the longest horns, but maybe I just wanted that to be true because my territories too were easy to defend because no one else wanted them.

Eventually, a partner and I decided to try every cowboy's dream of buying some cattle of our own. We looked for leasable country that ranch owners didn't want to operate themselves. Ranchers sometimes discover a pasture within their territory where water dries up too fast and that's too remote to look after. It's usually rocky and rough, a place where cow teeth wear out and calf numbers are low because bulls are too lazy to tackle the steep terrain to get around and breed. Sometimes when country never makes a profit and along come some honest, hardworking kids who want to try to put together a few cows of their own, a benevolent rancher might lease that marginal country to them. Bankers will also sometimes loan money to young, hardworking, proud people who will somehow pay back their debts. And as the old ranchers, the bankers, and the young kids know, gambling sometimes works.

So we leased some dry, rocky, remote canyons in the Davis Mountains, and we had a plan. Young healthy heifers were too expensive and our lease too remote to husband them through their first calves. Plus, we both held full-time jobs. Prime cows were beyond our price range, so we carefully selected and bought one at a time the twenty best almost-toothless grannies we could find. Ranchers sell old cows when they probably won't survive another winter or raise another calf, and ranchers are usually right. But just maybe we could buy these old cows cheap, maybe squeeze one more calf out of them, and maybe get ourselves a start in the cow business. Maybe. We also leased some nearby state park land that had enough grass to last about a month. The park needed the grass mowed to keep down fire hazard, but it would have to pay someone to mow it. Instead we'd pay them to graze it—a win-win. We could buy our grannies, gather them up, and hold them on park grass, waiting for cool fall weather and hopefully some rain before trailing them to the lease.

By the time we struck the trail with our little herd, the lease country had grown some grass and every pocket had caught a little water. We planned to drop our grannies on a rim that bordered a big canyon and gradually graze along the rim, moving them from water to water. Eventually we'd take them down toward the most dependable spring-fed water in the bottom of the deepest canyon, saving that grass until last. Everything depended on water and rain.

We knew the fifteen-mile trail in from the park would be hard on our grannies, up and down steep mountains, mostly up, and no water until the end. But once we got them to the lease, all the drives from then on would be mostly downhill as they each got heavier and heavier with calf. They wouldn't have to—and we knew they couldn't, no matter what—climb back out until their calves could walk out beside them. It was the best gamble we could afford.

We preg-checked to ensure that each granny carried a spring calf. We wouldn't need a bull. If our venture worked, we'd have the old cows to sell, maybe at a better price than we gave for them, and their calves too. We'd pay back the bank, borrow less money next time, and make another gamble until we could get a start. My partner and I were younger than the ranchers selling the old cows. We figured we could make longer circles horseback, and we still believed in our own immortality. We still believed in luck.

We wanted only native cattle because cattle not raised in West Texas tend to crave something green to eat in the early spring and start eating loco weed. Loco must be like dope for livestock. Once horses and cattle get a taste for it, they will eat nothing else, getting crazier and crazier and thinner and thinner. Native cattle seem to know better and seldom touch it. All the cows we bought were good, native, horned Herefords, except one. She was native but muley (meaning hornless) and seemed in good shape except for being one-eyed. She evidently once had cancer eye and received a cowboy eye operation—which consisted of digging out the bad eye with a pocket knife and sewing the bloody hole shut with saddle thread. Before ranchers figured out how to breed red circles around white-faced Hereford eyes, cancered eyes were a common problem, especially for those who lived in desert country, where sunlight was intense. Because the muley had a defect and no horns, the horned cattle hooked her constantly. Consequently, she hung out at the edges.

The rocky jeep trail to the lease was only two cows wide and horse-killing country. Steep rock walls rose and fell on each side, making cowboying difficult. We couldn't afford help. Even friends expected day wages or at least a meal. Our lease was too remote to pack in groceries and equipment to cook with, so we carried lightweight burritos of dried beef rolled in tortillas. Four of us took on the job of trailing our cattle to their new home. My daughter's grandpa, more than seventy years old, rode point to lead them up and down the steep trail. Taking point usually falls to the best rider because the job entails staying in the lead no matter what. But with these old cows, we didn't figure Grandpa would need to stop any runaways. Our most patient rider, my little daughter, rode drag. We knew she would lollygag along, happily sucking on her saddle strings, looking for birds and bunnies, and let the cattle string out long and slow. Some people like a wide herd, but cows don't get as hot or as tired when allowed to trail one another in single file. The other two riders, myself and my partner, would ride swing, climbing up and down the cliffs and canyons at the sides of the herd, trying to keep the cattle strung out and trailing. But we soon discovered that two riders could ride along in front and chat, and two could ride along in the rear and chat. The old one-eyed cow, because the others picked on her, struck the lead and never stopped. The others simply followed, trying to hook her in the butt.

The one-eyed cow's habits became more interesting as the winter wore on. When we gathered the grannies to move them to the next water hole, the old one-eyed cow was already there. She had the salt and water trails well marked for her tormentors to follow. As the herd moved in, she moved out. Toward spring, we started finding dead cows and dogied calves. Although the grass held, the old cows were struggling too hard in the rough country, and the water was drying up fast. We found one cow down, still alive but covered with black lice. Her calf, still nursing, had a ring of black lice around his white nose. I thought about author Barry Lopez's theory about the "conversation of death." I wondered if the old cow had sacrificed herself to the lice for the sake of the herd, since none of the others seemed to be infested. Mother Nature has no sympathy for the weak. A few cowboys used to call me Mother Nature after I said anybody dumb enough to break a leg ought to be left there to die of thirst. We picked up the calf and shot the cow. The buzzards were enjoying our gamble.

On the morning of the last move to fresh grass and water, we rose in the dark and trailered our horses to the end of the road. The sky was turning gray as we stepped into the saddle, and the March wind had already started to pick up. Whenever we headed to the lease, I tried to be prepared. We would be miles and hours from help until long past dark. Nobody happened down the trail in these remote canyons. No photographers, no artists, no backpackers, no park rangers, nobody. Cowboys seldom carry food or canteens or first aid kits. Not because of any foolhardy attempt at heroics but because if the day is going to be long enough to need food and water, then the horse doesn't need to be carrying one more ounce of weight. If the animal doing all the work can't drink or eat, reasons the cowboy, then the human that horse is packing around sure doesn't need anything. Horses should always eat and drink first. If lightweight kids were along, we might let their horses pack a little extra. So my daughter carried our four burritos and a small canteen.

In my pocket was a tiny jar of Carmex, relief against the painful, bleeding chapped lips I knew would come after eighteen hours in the saddle on a hot, wind-whipped March day. Real cowboys grow mustaches to protect themselves from chapped lips. I can't seem to grow one. Around my neck I had tied a cotton bandana that sorta matched my shirt. I hoped my partner would think it was just fashion. In winter and fall, my neck rag is silk, but I would need no warmth today. River rafting had taught me the cooling effects of a cotton bandana soaked in water and tied around my neck, dripping. I thought that trick had saved my life at least twice. Occasionally bones break, oak limbs and yucca puncture, and bandages are hard to come by. I thought the bandana would be an inconspicuous first aid kit. Perhaps my immortality had already begun to crack.

The rest of my safety precautions were common cowboy gear. I wore high-heeled boots so my foot wouldn't slip through the stirrup if my horse fell. I wore leather leggins to protect my largest veins and arteries from thorns and sticks. I wore a long-sleeved shirt and a broad-brimmed Navajo creased hat to turn the sun. I looked at the starry, cloudless sky and chose not to pack my slicker, which would just tear up in the brush anyway. I wore close-fitting cotton jeans that would not bunch up in wrinkles to rub the insides of my knees raw, and I wore no belt to catch on the saddle horn and tie me to a horse I might want to get away from.

And I was riding a new horse, always a tense situation until his dependability and quirks are known. As we mounted and started up the steep jeep trail that led into Dry Canyon, the wind tore at my hat. I tightened the stampede string that kept it in place to protect my brain. But the wind was strong and getting stronger. Because of my thick hair, I knew it would be an all-day battle to keep my hat in place. So I rode back to the truck, threw my hat in the cab, and tied the cotton bandana around my hair to keep it out of my eyes. My head was now exposed to more danger than I usually risked, but I figured I would just lose my hat anyway as it sailed off into one of the deep canyons. If I got in a storm with my new horse, a real likely time would be when he felt me grab too fast for a wind-loosened hat and I'd be off balance and one-handed. I needed both hands to keep or regain control, at least until I started to trust the new horse.

Because of my nervousness over the new horse, my eyes and ears and all six senses searched ahead for trouble while I pretended to be relaxed and lost in thought. I knew the wind would pick up the long fringe on my leather chinks and tickle my horse's shoulders. So while chatting with my partner in the dark of early morning, I fiddled with my fringe and flipped it around, first one leg and then the other, getting my horse used to the booger. Up ahead, somewhere in the darkness, I heard the wind hit the dry leaves of a live oak and shake it like an Indian rattle. Live oaks do their fall shedding in the spring for some contrary reason known only to them. Had we been beside the tree at that moment, I'd have jumped and startled my horse. So I mentally prepared myself to remain calm when the wind rattled a live oak beside us today. There were no live oaks in my horse's home pasture.

I cleared my throat repeatedly, puffed my cheeks full of air, and shook my head violently, expelling wind like an escaped balloon to drive out the dust—pretending to cuss the weather. If I had had any money in my pocket, I'd have been jingling that too. I kept at this coughing, cursing, fringe-flipping frenzy until the wind finally rattled a live oak next to us and my horse didn't bat an eye.

After the first long uphill pull, my horse's head began to swing easily between the slack reins of my mane-hair McCarty. Neither rattling live oaks nor snapping leather fringe seemed to worry him. Perhaps because of the weather, the climb, and the early hour, my horse knew this was going to be a long, long day and that he had better save his energy. He finally convinced me to save mine too. The blowing dust and tiny rocks were already getting into my hair, eyes, and nose. This would be a black booger day.

Many hours later, when we got our surviving old grannies to the expected water hole, it was dry. We pushed on to the next—also dry. We were in trouble. Could the wobbling old cows live to reach the last water hole on the rim of the canyon? And if they lived to reach it, would there be water? Would any of them still be alive the next time we came back? This was too much stress on old cows. The gambling odds had shifted. Stumbling, staggering, stringing saliva with every agonized step, the old ladies inched their way toward the last water hole. I cussed and jerked on my horse's reins unmercifully. He traveled too fast. He pushed too hard. I had to keep us circling to keep him backed off the old cows. The more I tried to slow him down, the antsier he became. I cussed. I jerked him around. I don't think I ever treated a horse worse. My own frustration, knowing we were losing our gamble, was affecting the way I treated my horse, and he didn't understand what he was doing wrong.

When we finally reached the last water hole, the old cows just stood and drooled. They were too hot and too tired to drink. The rocky ground rose in a circle almost straight up from the water. Yearling country—no place for a granny. We looked around and knew that the next time we rode in, we'd find several of these old cows—maybe all of them—lying dead right where they stood. The buzzards would love us. But as we sat there, letting our horses drink and avoiding each other's eyes, I noticed the old one-eyed cow slip off over the rim and down a deer trail. She was pushing on to the more permanent spring-fed water and grass in the bottom of the deepest canyon. I marked the spot in my memory. We might still need that trail.

Back in civilization, another six hours later, we learned that wind gusts had clocked in at more than one hundred miles per hour in the mountains that day. A roof had blown off at the airport and trees had blown down on the college campus. I had forgotten all about the wind.

By late spring only fifteen calves and ten cows remained alive, but one of them was the one-eyed muley. She had raised a good calf and she had led us back out. I made up my mind that when shipping time came, I'd insist we keep her one more year. But she shipped with the rest. We cut our losses and finally, years later, repaid the debt. After trying yearlings with another partner, we eventually gave up that lease and never went back. But maybe we should have. That country made good horses. It helped raise my daughter horseback, and it taught me to look at a one-eyed cow with respect, something my more expensive college education never did.

Eventually I returned to college for a high school teaching certificate, still didn't teach, went back for a master's degree, and divorced. I kept my small cattle herd, by now fifty head and paid for, and found my own leases: one in the Guadalupe Mountains, one near Dryden. I had also begun free-lancing for the new *Range* magazine, whose publisher/editor claimed to want to bridge the growing divide between environmentalists and ranchers by embracing the philosophy that we actually all wanted the same end result—exactly my own opinion. Anything I thought both sides would find interesting, I sent to *Range.* About the same time, I lucked into a temporary job teaching college freshmen to write and loved it, but I needed a PhD order to hang onto it.

I had a long talk with myself, admitted that making a living raising my own cattle just wasn't possible, and reluctantly sold my cows to help finance my next degree. I headed to the University of Nevada, Reno—partly because they would let me live on the college ranch, partly because the editor of *Range* magazine was also editing their alumni magazine and offered me a job as managing editor, and partly because Reno appeared to be the headquarters for those who hated cows. I wanted to find out why. Maybe I thought I was ready to take on my version of saving the world. I knew I would need a dissertation subject, so I wondered if I could somehow connect my cowboy journalist skills to something that would interest academics, especially the hard-core environmentalists who were trying to outlaw cattle grazing. I wanted to make friends with the enemy and explain our side, so I chose a female vegetarian as my PhD committee chair. I also picked the reigning female Abbey scholar, a male cultural geographer, and a female ag professor for my four-person committee. I would either sink or swim, or maybe find common ground. Maybe.

I was especially interested in a new way to study literature called ecocriticism. All the great and not-so-great books were being newly scrutinized by looking at how race, gender, and economics were represented. Ecocriticism added nature to that mix but from an ecology point of view, meaning all disciplines could contribute. Ecocritics had already welcomed science, history, psychology, geography, and art into the conversation, and I hoped to add agriculture, especially horses and cows. I also thought kids were learning environmentalism (which at the time meant anti-agriculture in all forms) from well-meaning teachers who got their ideas from their well-meaning college professors. So if I wanted to get to the heart of the matter, I needed to figure out where those ideas were originating. The University of Nevada–Reno seemed to be ground zero.

I soon discovered that the cow was no stranger to the nature-writing canon. However, classic cow characters to compare with Hemingway's marlin, Melville's whale, Faulkner's bear, or London's dogs/wolves are nonexistent, even in books by and about cowboys. This surprised me, because everyone I knew had stories about some bull, some cow, some heifer, some steer, or some calf. A few characters showed up in cowboy poetry. In cowboy fiction I remembered only one good cow character: J. P. S. Brown's old wild steer, Sun Spot. Brown characterizes Sun Spot in such a way that I feel like I know him: how he likes to nap on south-facing slopes to warm the white spot on his side, how he manages to evade capture, where he drinks, where he grazes. The cowboys eventually catch him but then turn him loose, out of respect. The only thing I didn't like about Brown's portrait was the name. I've never named a range cow. Cows are not pets. The too-familiar relationship between person and pet seems disrespectful somehow. Not naming could be interpreted as distancing ourselves from what we will eat, but milk-pen calves or crippled heifers and steers that get penned and put on feed for slaughter usually do get named and petted. Naming an old range cow or steer just seemed like something they wouldn't like. I got to know several quite well, but I always called them respectfully "that old high-horned cow who hangs out at Last Chance" or "that old one-eyed Hereford muley."

I found many influential books beloved by the environmental movement to be full of crazy ideas. Jeremy Rifkin, for example, while writing a tirade against cows, *Beyond Beef: The Rise and Fall of the Cattle Culture*, described the bull like this: "The bull has always reminded us of our maleness—he represents generativeness, ferocious power, domination, and protection. He is the most territorial of beasts, passionate and aggressive, the embodiment of fertilizing power. The bull is pure unrestrained energy. A formidable force, he is fearless, unreconcilable, and purposeful."

I thought Rifkin was wrong enough to be hilarious. The bulls I knew spent 99.9 percent of their time napping and eating. They had no problem restraining their energy and had never protected a single thing. Cows protected their calves fiercely, but bulls? Never. Because of their size and weight, bulls did have power, but they seldom had it under control. Most of the fences they knocked over were smashed while they were scratching an itch. Fighting bulls were a joke: dust, bellowing, crashing horns—but at best only skinning up each other's forehead, seldom drawing blood. No eyes got poked out, no guts ripped open, nobody died. They just liked to make a lot of noise. Horned bulls hooked the ground when they wanted to look threatening. At the end of all this hooking, they usually had a dirt clod stuck to one horn with a flower growing in it. The biggest, most steroid-looking ones were usually sterile. During breeding season, I often found them bunched up together taking a nap while cows fifty yards away were riding each other. Passion, if they had any, lasted less than a minute.

Rifkin also described the cow: "The cow is one of the most gentle and sublime of creatures, the embodiment of patience. Her enlarged udders are available for all the world to suckle. She is nurturer and nourishment, the giver of life. She is self-contained, peaceful, a serene image, grounded and tranquil. The cow is purity, and represents the forces of benevolence and good in the world."

Where does he get this stuff? Obviously Rifkin had been looking at too many four-color calendars of cows and didn't really know the full meaning of sublime. It's also obvious that he'd never seen or tried to milk an old sublime (beauty mixed with terror-producing awe) desert range cow. First of all, she wouldn't have "enlarged udders." Second, even with two stout horses, two stout ropes, and two stout ropers who knew their business, it might not happen. Cows don't let down their milk unless they want to, and a bawlin' old cow with horse and cowboy blood on her horns—slingin' snot and stretched out on her side in the rocks and cactus—probably doesn't want to. Unless you smell like a calf, you won't get any milk, and even then you'd better smell like *her* calf.

The cow seemed to conjure for Rifkin a domestic female image as an overweight, middle-aged, bawling, slow, slothful, not-too-intelligent stomper of stream banks, dropper of dung, drawer of flies, and slinger of sagging udders. On the other hand, bulls represented manifest destiny: the powerful, oversexed, overbearing, booted and spurred white males of the American West, which reminded me again of Ed Abbey.

As I studied the authors credited as the founding fathers and mothers of "Stop the Moo in '92" or "Cattle Free by '93," I noticed more and more misinformation about livestock, and some authors seemed to be challenging one another, such as John Muir and Mary Austin. Sheep had grazed California's San Joaquin Valley for more than one hundred years by 1833, when the count was above three hundred thousand head. Yet thirty-five years later, in 1868, when Muir first saw it, his unpublished journal describes that valley as "the floweriest piece of world I ever walked." That's not what he said though in the rewritten and *published* version of that same journal when he tried to help the railroads and his wealthy friends stop sheep grazing in order to build the biggest business the world has ever seen: tourism. Muir, founder of the Sierra Club, was born in Scotland, a country where sheep, flowers, steep mountain pastures, and crystal streams had coexisted and coevolved for thousands of years. After the young Muir left his immigrant father's failed midwestern farm, one of his first adult jobs was working as a California sheepherder. He kept the journal, but he was no Scottish shepherd. Mary Austin, in her 1906 book *The Flock*, challenged Muir's portrayal of sheep as "hoofed locusts" and shepherds as "insane," almost word for word. Austin was accurate; Muir was wrong.

I knew I could publish these "book reports" as cowboy journalism in *Range*. However, I was also sure that almost everyone on my PhD committee was a card-carrying member of the Sierra Club. Did I dare expose Muir's promotion of tourism, his prejudices toward Basques and other foreign-born shepherds, his stealing of their dinners to feed himself and his hiking friends, and his lies about his own mountain hiking prowess? I did.

I first presented "John Muir and Mary Austin: Stigmatism of the Sheepherder, Risk in the High Sierras, and the Sin of False Witness" at a California American Studies Association and Rocky Mountain Studies Association joint cross-curricular conference in Reno. My professors then encouraged me to travel to a California conference focused on Muir's writing to present my findings to hard-core Muir fans. I published another version in the

San Francisco Examiner. At the time I feared for my life and my diploma, but obviously I survived.

I didn't know much about being a professional scholar, but I had been trained by cowboys. I could pay attention. I knew how to observe, remember, and compare. So I became a deeply embedded investigative journalist, interviewing authors, hunting important subjects and quotes, and fishing for solutions or new perspectives. I soon began to believe that the hatred for cattle, agriculture, and rural people had little to do with facts and was embedded deep in American stories, which were full of imagery, metaphor, and myth. One myth that began to catch my attention was the stereotypically destructive, lazy, shitty cow. One of my favorite images, which appeared in Ed Abbey's books, was a cowboy riding along, spending his life staring at a shit-encrusted, fly-clouded, jouncing cow's butt day after day. Abbey said, "Suppose you had to spend most of your working hours sitting on a horse, contemplating the hind end of a cow. How would that affect your imagination?"

The mythic Wild, Wild West, which was "no place for a lady" and attracted "lone males" to the "virgin" wilderness, had been invented by eastern fiction writers, not rural westerners or Native people. The myth always left the cow shit out. Corrals and hitching posts in movies were always spotless. Hoss and Little Joe never had to stop at the door and scrape their boots. Shit just didn't fit into the myth. So Abbey put the shit back in. Anyone who doesn't believe in cow shit would not want to brand Brammer calves—ever—even with the toe of their boot over the spout. They wouldn't want to be hit in the face by a cow tail when yuccas are blooming, wouldn't want to shove an arm up a heifer's cervix to pull out a stuck calf, wouldn't want to climb into crowding chutes when spring grass is green, wouldn't like "mud" without rain, scours, flat rocks, scared wild cows. Yup, real cows do shit—a lot. Bulls shit even more, and I've spent many years staring at their shitty rear ends. My imagination is probably ruined.

One of my fondest memories and best stories involves a hot, sleepy afternoon moving bulls, the world's slowest, most boring job. Bobbing in my saddle after a big lunch, I suddenly woke up to realize that the slowest bull had switched his tail over one of my bridle reins and had it clamped tightly under his tail. My horse, of course, wanted loose—now! Luckily, I was using split leather reins instead of a looped McCarty or rawhide reins and romal, so I quickly dropped the captured rein and let the wreck work itself out. When everything finally came loose and stopped, I was still horseback, no bones broken, and my bridle was still in one piece. My smooth leather rein had simply slid between the bull's tightly clamped tail and his shitty butt. The green sticky rein I rode with the rest of the day imprinted the cheap lesson forever on my memory.

Cow shit creates memories. When it appears between your sandaled toes, under hat brims, inside a torn shirt pocket, up a pant leg; gets into boots or eyes or hair; is embedded between your teeth or smeared all over your rope—usually you have just finished learning a cheap lesson. The cow shit sort of says, "And don't ever try that again."

So I'm not by any means claiming that cows are the world's most wonderful animals. Baby calves are cute but only for a couple of weeks. I've worked enough cattle that sometimes it is even hard for me to come up with something nice to say about them. I've been stepped on, dragged, butted, pushed, kicked, smashed, knocked down, run over by, humiliated by, and hurt—especially my feelings. I've also questioned their intelligence on many occasions. We often called cows stupid when they stepped on our feet, when they took our horses away, when they blew snot down our necks while we branded their calves. We called them stupid when we'd help a wild heifer deliver a backward calf and then she'd jump up, run off, and leave her calf unlicked because it smelled like a human, a human who had just saved her ungrateful life. We called them stupid when they got old, smooth-mouthed, and stiff-jointed and refused to get on the truck that would permanently take them away from their home pastures. We called them stupid when they silently lost a tracker in noisy, slippery shale or lay down and disappeared behind a foot-high bush. We also called them stupid when they would out-hear, out-see, and out-smell their tracker. I've heard lots of college-educated cowboys humbly admit that they had been outsmarted by a stupid cow.

However, I had also been trained by cowboys to never leave a cow behind, no matter how ornery or stupid, so I noticed when a cow was missing. For instance, I was sure Thoreau had mentioned cows in his essay "Walking." Yet the cows had vanished in a shortened version that historian Roderick Frazier Nash had included in *American Environmentalism: Readings in Conservation History*. Nash's popular textbook was already in its third edition by the time I read it in 1990. Sprinkled throughout his shortened version of Thoreau's essay were many ellipsis—dots where passages had been removed. When I looked up those ellipses in Thoreau's original, I found the cows, brushed up and hiding. Not only did I find those missing cows, but I found what I considered unethical tampering with our history and some of our best literary heritage for the sake of advocacy. I was shocked! Nash, a respected University of California–Santa Barbara history scholar, had carefully left out all references to horses, cows, farming, and pastures. His deletions and one intentionally misplaced paragraph changed Thoreau's focus from how wildness as a saving grace lurks beneath the surface of all things domestic to California-style anti-agriculture propaganda.

Talk about speaking truth to power. Did a mere wannabe doctoral candidate from a tiny border college dare to take on a Harvard graduate and one of the most well-respected historians in academia? You bet I did. My discovery became first a grad school research paper, then an academic conference paper. Eventually I published an academic version as a chapter called "Rustling Thoreau's Cattle: Wildness and Domesticity in 'Walking'" for an anthology edited by Richard Schneider (*Thoreau's Sense of Place: Essays in American Environmental Writing*, with an introduction by Lawrence Buell).

One of the first places I tested reaction from "the enemy" was at a 1993 environmental writing workshop led by Gretel Ehrlich, sponsored by the University of Montana Program in Environmental and Nature Writing and held at the Teller Wildlife Refuge in Missoula. When we workshoppers introduced ourselves, I found it very interesting that everyone except me (there were twelve of us if I remember correctly) came from an alcoholic and often abusive family. Was there some psychological connection between passionate environmentalists and dysfunctional homes? What drew them to nature rather than religion or substance abuse?

Ehrlich's comments on each page of my manuscript were very encouraging: "This is a refreshment. . . . Did he really! Did he tamper with Thoreau's prose? . . . This is fascinating! . . . Wonderful! . . . Expand. . . . Fabulous! . . . Fascinating. . . . Yes! . . . Yes! . . . Yes! Barney, this is fabulous . . . your humor and insights are wonderful—I'm so glad we met—Gretel." Obviously she didn't give me much help in improving my workshop submission, but attending was well worth my time for confidence building.

The most important thing I did with what I found was to write it as cowboy journalism. I knew my readers would consider this "news." To spice things up, in some versions I included a few personal stories about the wildness I had personally experienced in cows. *Range* ended up publishing several versions in both the magazine and their books. One version was picked up by an Ohio newspaper and maybe more that I never saw.

In all these various versions I explained how Thoreau's original essay attempts to define the word *wildness* and how important it is to the sanity and happiness of modern man. He says that wildness is imported by cities and that men plow and sail for it. But all of that may be unnecessary. He says, "We have a wild savage in us." He says the earth possesses a terrifying wildness that will be our eventual salvation.

Thoreau was rejoicing in the fact that the cow had not lost this wildness and that each generation of "horses and steers have to be broken before they can be made the slaves of men." He said, "The seeds of instinct are preserved under the thick hides of cattle and horses, like seeds in the bowels of the earth, an indefinite period." And he loved to see "the sportiveness in cattle" and "to see the domestic animals reassert their native rights—any evidence that they have not wholly lost their original wild habits and vigor" or were "not yet subdued to man."

His essay focuses on the idea that wildness is something we cannot lose. He says that civilization can hide it, oppression can stifle it, and education can tame it, but scratch the surface and wildness springs eternal. He does say that wildness can be found in the forests and in wilderness, but he also lists numerous other places: in "tawny" grammar, in less "civilized" cultures, in libraries, in architecture, underneath calluses, in the migratory instincts of birds, in the simplest and obscurest of men, in soil, in the smell on a trapper's coat, in tan skin, in both bogs and spades, in the sound of a bugle on a summer night, in the humble act of walking, and in domestic animals. He does not say that wildness needs our condescending protection; he says that wildness would protect us.

In some versions, I included a few paired paragraphs from both Thoreau and Nash so that readers could compare and decide for themselves. One vivid example of how Nash changed Thoreau's meaning occurs when Thoreau explains wildness through skin color:

> A tanned skin is something more than respectable, and perhaps olive is a fitter color than white for a man—a denizen of the woods. "The pale white man!" I do not wonder that the African pitied him. Darwin

> the naturalist says, "A white man bathing by the side of a Tahitian was like a plant bleached by the gardener's art, compared with a fine, dark green one, growing vigorously in the open fields."
>
> Ben Johnson exclaims,
> "How near to good is what is fair!"
> So I would say,
> "How near to good is what is wild."

Nash deletes Thoreau's original paragraph about skin color and replaces it with a paragraph about meadow and forest that actually appears several pages later in the essay:

> I would not have every man nor every part of a man cultivated, any more than I would have every acre of earth cultivated; part will be tillage, but the greater part will be meadow and forest, not only serving an immediate use, but preparing a mold against a distant future, by the annual decay of the vegetation which it supports. . . .
>
> Ben Johnson exclaims,
> "How near to good is what is fair!"
> So I would say,
> "How near to good is what is wild."

Through this manipulation, Nash links meadow and forest with "How near to good is what is wild" instead of skin color as in Thoreau's original. This gives Nash's version a preservationist and anti-agricultural flavor that Thoreau never intended.

Nash's moved paragraph originally appeared right after Thoreau's sentence "Not even does the moon shine every night, but gives place to darkness." Thoreau follows that with the idea that even grammar rules should sometimes be broken to allow for freedom of expression. Through comparisons between forests and cultivated fields, moonlight and darkness, proper grammar and lingo, Thoreau explained how the world needed and already contained some sort of balance between this wildness he was attempting to define and the constraints placed upon us all by society, education, government, and religion. Nash moved sentences around so that they took on the wilderness meaning Nash wanted and eliminated Thoreau's deep thinking. That is advocacy, not scholarship. Nash does American literature a sad disservice by narrowing Thoreau's classic American ideas down into preservation politics.

I'm not sure if there was a connection, but a couple of years after I had given conference papers and published on Muir and Thoreau, a very important new book by academics appeared: *Uncommon Ground: Toward Reinventing Nature.* I'd like to claim some credit, but I think once ecocriticism encouraged scholars to look at nature issues through disciplines other than science, the imagination-based foundation for environmentalism just started becoming obvious. Although the general public and especially those living in rural areas often wonder just what it is that academics really do in their ivory towers, this new book described the way the process should and sometimes does work.

Fifteen well-known environmentalists from throughout the nation sequestered themselves at the UC campus in Irvine to examine the environmental movement from the inside. Believing that the humanities could reveal perspectives that had not been considered by science, they looked at nature from psychological, historical, philosophical, and sociological perspectives and then wrote book chapters from the ideas that came out of their discussions. Nature, they decided, existed in our psyches in many imaginary forms: as demonic other, as avenging angel, as helpless victim, as seductive virgin, and as nurturing mother. Scenery had successfully replaced sex in modern advertising. While rural Americans were being demonized for valuing nature only as a resource and a commodity, these university-based environmentalists argued that wilderness had also become a lucrative big business, spawning such things as nature stores in the mall, wolves on T-shirts, ecotourism, and pricey real estate. I had long been warning my rural readers that the Nature Conservancy (in my opinion a non-tax-paying high-end real estate company for the very wealthy) seemed especially interested in buying the land that surrounded water.

Realizing their book would be perceived as "hostile to environmentalism," editor William Cronon, a professor of history, geography, and environmental studies at the University of Wisconsin at Madison, assured readers that "nothing could be farther from the truth." He said that instead, the participants strongly believed that ignoring the difficult questions their group had uncovered would be to "proceed on intellectual foundations that may ultimately prove unsustainable." Still, their book sent environmentalism into a panic. Did I dare defend academics to my rural readers? You bet

I did, when they deserved it. So I wrote "Uncommon Ground: University Environmentalists from across the Nation Do Some Serious Soul Searching" for *Range.* I began with lines from my favorite essay in the book. "Are you an environmentalist or do you work for a living?" asked Richard White, at the time a professor of history at the University of Washington. White argued that modern environmentalists either equated work with destruction or celebrated play. He concluded: "If we do not come to terms with work," we will "turn public lands into a public playground . . . equate wild lands with rugged play . . . [and] imagine nature as an escape, a place where we are born again. It will be a paradise where we leave work behind. Nature may turn out to look a lot like an organic Disneyland except it will be harder to park."

Other essays collected in the book discussed how Americans falsely perceived black-and-white divisions between "wild" nature and "ruined" nature, divisions based on "nature as Eden." The idea that before white settlers arrived, nature on this continent existed in a pure, natural, and balanced state ignored centuries of Native American land management practices that included regular burning, irrigating, farming, and grazing. To re-create this imagined state of emptiness, Indian land management was simply ignored. According to Cronon, "The removal of Indians to create an uninhabited wilderness—uninhabited as never before in the human history of the place—reminds us just how invented, just how constructed, the American wilderness really is." Wilderness and national parks were actually created by removing Indians, Basque shepherds, Hispanic ranchers, and Scandinavian farmers—which again reminded me of Abbey.

Abbey's writing often dealt with humans who for one reason or another had been kicked out of their homes. When Abbey wrote about "Cow Heaven" in the essay "Big Bend," cows had been banished from the national park "heaven." The deer, which he called "a giant rodent—a rat with antlers," had been allowed to stay, but not cows: "Everywhere deer sign, nowhere the faintest trace of man. We have stumbled into a miniature Eden." During his lifetime, Abbey watched as government agencies threw the less powerful out of Eden: Native Americans, Hispanics, ranchers, farmers, women, children, and cows. Almost the entire Mexican border consists of state and national parks, national monuments, military reservations, proving grounds, national recreation areas, wildlife refuges, dams, lakes, and wilderness areas. In one of Abbey's last books, *One Life at a Time,*

Please, he says, "Here on this international boundary, in this neutral zone, one's actual citizenship makes little difference."

When Abbey took "A Walk in the Desert Hills" across the southern Arizona desert, he claimed to be happy that the place was free of cow dung and said, "I give thanks again for the United States Air Force." However, anyone who reads much of Abbey's work can't take that sentence very seriously. Perhaps no one knew better than Abbey that the entire U.S.-Mexico border area now belonged mostly to a government against which he thought true patriots should be willing to defend their country. As Abbey walks along, with building irony he writes, "Only one animal remains conspicuous in this region, by its absence—the cow," and "nothing human" lives here or ever did. A few pages later, as his need for water becomes critical, he says, "There has got to be water at Gray's Well—a rancher named Henry Gray once lived there—and if there isn't I'll die, and what of it?" And what of the fact that Abbey probably once looked after that exact windmill when he worked as a cowboy on the Henry Gray Ranch? I believe Edward Abbey, the hiker/curmudgeon/anarchist, would trust cattlemen of any race, gender, nationality, or religion to maintain windmills in the desert but would have no such faith in bureaucracies to perform the same critical task.

In *Desert Solitaire* Abbey lists ways to impose a "dictatorial regime" upon the American people. The first step, he says, is to concentrate people into cities; the second is to "mechanize agriculture to the highest degree of refinement, thus forcing most of the scattered farm and ranching population into the cities. Such a policy was desirable because farmers, woodsmen, cowboys, Indians, fishermen and other relatively self-sufficient types are difficult to manage unless displaced from their natural environment." He hoped someday cities would be smaller, more scattered, and that across the desert "blue-eyed Navajo Bedouins will herd their sheep and horses." Someday, he hoped, we would be able to accept humans in paradise where "wilderness is not a playground but their natural native home." He said, "The American Indians had no word for what we call 'wilderness.' For them the wilderness was home." In "The Carson Productions Interview," Abbey said, "The newly-approved Tellico Dam . . . has destroyed the habitat not only of the famous little fish known as snail darter but also forced 341 farm families off their land." He did not approve.

In 1985 a cowboy friend mailed me a dog-eared copy of an anti-cow speech that Abbey had given to a packed house of Montana cattlemen.

Reading it gave me an uneasy feeling. So for the next ten years, I studied everything I could find about grass and grazing and historical land uses and predator–prey relationships and fire and Allan Savory and water tables and pampas grass and diversity and mass extinctions and mourning dove habitat and plate tectonics and soil composition and weather patterns and on and on and on and on. I had been loading ammo although I didn't yet know why. Rereading Abbey in graduate school, I began to understand.

Like Thoreau, Abbey spent considerable time thinking and writing about wildness. Like all wild animals and Abbey's ideal humans, cows risked their lives for their territories, often freely choosing some brush and prickly pear–choked flat; an island available only by swimming; the steep sides of rocky, barren mountains; or canyons subject to flash floods and carpeted with quicksand. In that anti-cow speech, when Abbey said that domestic animals, like humans, would improve if hunted, was he talking to me? When he lamented sadly in "Telluride Blues—A Hatchet Job" that cowboys "don't seem to like to fight so much anymore" but passively allowed developers to "tear up good deer- and cattle-country" and ruin little towns like Telluride, was he warning rural people that we were about to get kicked out of paradise if we didn't start fighting back? Was he talking to me? Abbey knew the best way to get action was by making people mad, and he worked hard to become a master.

Cattlemen finally began to panic when environmentalists started slapping bumper stickers that said "Stop the Moo in '92" and "Cattle Free in '93" on their vehicles. When cattlemen started hunting for the source, they found Abbey and wanted to ban his books. But to me, Abbey's "Free Speech: The Cowboy and His Cow" rant seemed a desperate final attempt to prod rural people into action. When Abbey said cowboys didn't want to fight anymore, he was definitely talking to me, even though we had never met and I doubt he knew I existed. He couldn't write fast enough and needed help, needed a small army, maybe even at least one pseudo-academic cowboy journalist. Did I dare defend one of my favorite authors against criticism from my own people? Of course I did.

So in graduate school I started interviewing Abbey even though he was long dead. Eventually I published "Edward Abbey: Friend or Foe?" in *Range* magazine. For a lead, I wrote, "Several years ago I sat in a cattleman's meeting and listened to the president encourage members to call for a ban on Edward Abbey's books. I wondered if we were thinking of the same author.

Surely the cattleman president didn't want to ban *The Brave Cowboy*, the story of a horseman's last stand against civilization, or *Fire on the Mountain*, the story of an old rancher's last stand against federal forced taking of his land, or *Good News*, the story of a future war between urban bad guys and rural good guys?"

The cattleman president objected mostly to Abbey's *Monkey Wrench Gang*, a book accused of inspiring radicals to dismantle windmills. But that was never Abbey's intention. His characters were trying to preserve "prime grazing land for sheep and cattle." His novel was about trying to stop encroaching civilization, not a tirade against ranching. Until that meeting, I had always believed that monkey wrenching was something only rural people did. I and a close cowboy friend would both be a little richer today if we had been given a nickel for every surveyor's ribbon we pulled and stuffed in our pockets.

Granted, Abbey did stand before a packed house in Bozeman, Montana, where he delivered a blistering attack on public land grazing, but Kentucky farmer and author Wendell Berry said that Abbey fans are often forced to say, "Well, he did say that, but . . ." and then try to defend his latest stunt. I find myself in that position. Abbey ended his speech with, "Keep your sacred cows and your dead horses out of my elk pastures," and gunfire supposedly erupted in that Montana parking lot. Well, he did say that but . . . I defend his speech as a wake-up call. It was from that moment on that I and many others started doing our homework so that we could better defend ranching to an increasingly uneducated public. I think that is what Abbey wanted.

On the surface, Abbey's words appeared to be political activism. But at one point in his career, frustrated over audience reaction to his writing, Abbey thundered, "I am not and never will be a god-damned two-bit sycophantic journalist for Christ's sake!" *Sycophantic* is one of those dang big words most people just skip over, but it refers to flattery. Abbey wasn't ashamed of being considered a journalist, but he did not want anyone to think that to sell books he had sold his soul to flatter environmentalists. One of his greatest frustrations throughout his life was the fact that people seldom reacted to his words as planned. When he insulted them, they loved it, and sometimes his words were taken up as weapons and used against the people he was desperately trying to defend and goad into action. When Abbey said, "Keep your sacred cows and your dead horses out of my elk pastures," I think he wanted readers to find out which animals were here first.

Similar to dogs, the cow's heritage is in fact wild. Worldwide, cattle were once the proud symbol of wildness and danger, hunted in protected walled forests by only the richest lords. The famous twenty-five-thousand-year-old Lascaux cave paintings in France depict more cattle than any other animal. The modern cow descends from extinct wild ungulates like the African, Asian, and European aurochs (*Bos taurus primigenius*). Scotland's legendary, long-extinct, wild white aurochs—which look amazingly like white bison—were also ancestors, as were India's endangered and beautiful red gaurs (*Bos gaurus*). The cow's family tree includes Caesar's *Bos urus* (an auroch), Indonesia's banteng (*Bos javanicus*), and the hairy wild yak (*Bos grunniens*). Even the European and Asian wisent (*Bison bonasus*), a small buffalo, contributed to the wild cows' gene pool or vice versa. Those cattle breeds also represent a genetic hash of world countries: England, France, India, Scotland, North America, South America, Asia, and Africa. The hides of the breeds listed come in red, white, yellow, black, and brown but do not correspond to skin colors of humans found in the same area. These cloven-hoofed, hollow-horned, humped, hairy, and grazing animals are all members of the same species. They can all interbreed, as can all humans. Bison cross with cows to become Cattalo or Beefalo, cross with Angus for Amerifax, and cross with Simmental for Simmalo. The "American breed" crosses zebu, Charolais, Hereford, shorthorn, and bison.

According to paleontologists, horses were native to North America ten million years ago. Shrub oxen and other cattle were native here two million years ago. Shrub oxen once ranged from Northern California to Mexico and east to Illinois, maybe farther. Both horses and cattle went extinct about a quarter of a million years ago when bison, wolves, and humans migrated—perhaps together—across a land bridge, or perhaps across ice, or perhaps the humans transported themselves and their livestock (bison) and animal herding partners (wolves) by canoe or raft, depending on which story is currently in favor. When Abbey demanded that a Native American drinking buddy explain why his people exterminated so many early American animals, the Indian shrugged and said, "We were hungry."

In 1610 the Virginia colonies shipped in cattle from the West Indies, but Native Americans were still hungry and ate them. A colony of Dutch settlers reintroduced cattle to New York in 1619. Four years after the *Mayflower* landed, the first British cattle arrived in Massachusetts. However, one hundred years or more before these more famous eastern imports and reintroductions began, the cow had already been reintroduced into the desert Southwest with the Spanish explorer Hernando Cortés (1485–1547). By the time white settlers finally arrived in southwestern deserts, four hundred years after the Spanish conquistadores, enough cows and horses had escaped, been turned loose, or been born wild for the animals to once again seem wild and indigenous. One of the few major sources of protein the desert has proven able to produce sustainably—most recently for more than five hundred years and anciently for millions—is beef. In his essay "Down to the Sea of Cortez," Abbey credits the Spanish conquistadores with bringing cattle back to southwestern deserts. He calls grazing "the old story" and describes Mexican scrub cattle as a mix of desert, North and South American, and world wildlife with Abbey-like affection:

> Scrub cattle ranging through the bush galloped off like gnus and wildebeests at our approach. I never saw such weird, scrawny, pied, mottled, humped, long-horned and camel-necked brutes trying to pass as domestic livestock. Most looked like a genetic hash of Hereford, Charolais, Brahman, Angus, moose, ibex, tapir and nightmare. Weaned on cactus, snakeweed and thistle, they showed the gleam of the sun through the translucent barrel of their rib cages. But they could run, they were alive—not only alive but vigorous. I was tempted to think, watching their angular hind ends jouncing away through the dust, that the meat on those critters, if you could find any, might just taste better than the aerated, water-injected, hormone-inflated beef we Americans get from today's semi-automated feedlots in the States.

In the real world, crossbred animals are usually hardier than pure breeds, so spotted, mixed-breed cattle often appear symbolically in books by mixed-blood Native American authors. Abbey's cattle description contains subtle admiration both for the hardy mixed-blood Mexican cattle and the hardy mixed-blood people who survive on so much less than the overstuffed, industrialized, helpless variety. As I unearthed all these ancient bones, I published articles in livestock magazines, trying to provide cattlemen with ammunition.

Abbey was often under fire as a racist for comments such as, "Stop every *campesino* at our southern border, give him a handgun, a good rifle, and a case of ammunition, and send him home." But this is actually Abbey's strange way of demonstrating respect for other cultures. For example, he dismisses the Peace Corps as "a typical piece of American cultural insolence." Refusing to subscribe to the condescending idea that Mexican people need our help, he said we should ask the countries we condescendingly refer to as Third World for help in learning to live lighter on the land. Abbey does, however, resist idealizing and romanticizing these hardy desert dwellers and balances any praise he might give with plenty of insults, just as he does with cows. Why does he do that? Is he just being contrary?

Who would guess that a feminist filmmaker and deconstruction theorist could help an old cowboy journalist begin to understand and better explain Abbey? Born in Hanoi, Trinh T. Minh-ha, a nonwhite female writer, described her own complicated position as a "triple bind." This triple bind, she said, came from the dilemma of trying to decide whether her loyalties should rest with her race, her gender, or a bigger picture. Although Abbey would definitely be labeled as "other" to a feminist woman of color, I think he found himself in much the same dilemma and solved it much as Trinh (she uses Trinh as her surname) did: with a plural voice. Trinh described her own writing voice as a combination of a capitalized *I* representing the all-knowing "author" and a lowercase *i*, representing herself humbly situated in a specific community. Trinh's *I/i* voice carefully tries to speak from multiple positions. In one interview, Abbey also admitted that he created a voice in his nonfiction, that he gave that character his own name, and that "some people mistake the creation for the author."

Abbey's capital *I* creation, Cactus Ed, is a cocksure white male author ready to shoot even God. Like Coyote, the traditional desert storyteller's trickster, Cactus Ed is obsessed with sex, ribald humor, and irreverence. He often sounds like a sexist, racist, anarchist, curmudgeon, and other various villains. And there's probably a grain of truth in that. However, using Trinh's system, Cactus Ed should be represented with capital letters as ED. But behind the bluster lurked a quieter, more serious voice, represented as ed with small letters. His ed voice was sympathetic, concerned, and humble. Abbey typed his way between bluster and humility as ED/ed. He was not ashamed of his own gender, heritage, or personality, yet he was not willing to assume the responsibility to be a model for society. He was no hero and had no desire to be. His thoughts were as good as the next person's, and he had a right to voice them, but he did not consider himself superior, only equal. This ED/ed perspective gives him a very postmodern voice with ancient storyteller roots—that familiar, humble *we* used by cowboys and Native Americans.

ED shouted about "Californicating" while ed whispered that he did not want nature turned into a theme park. ED called vegetarian food "pussy food" while ed worried about his beloved wild rivers—beloved by both himself and cows—becoming irrigation ditches for lettuce. His political views toward the cow are not quite so clearly negative if the reader begins to listen to ED cussing cows in one breath and ed respectfully calling them wild desert animals in the next. Trinh explains this as an author's disorienting tactic: "Never does one open the discussion by coming right to the heart of the matter. For the heart of the matter is always somewhere else." When ED shouts his message, as in his anti-cow essay, the reader can be fairly certain he is after something other than agreement; "the heart of the matter" was somewhere else. When ED shouted, he was often lying, trying to cause trouble, trying to make people think or fight back. Cactus Ed tried to poke his readers toward ed's frustratingly elusive "deeper meaning," which students and readers hate to look for because they haven't been taught to use the tools.

So. What is Cactus Ed the trickster storyteller trying to say? Again Trinh provides one way to begin to solve the riddle. She says that "every discourse that breeds fault and guilt is a discourse of authority and arrogance" and that the "language of Taoism and Zen . . . which is rife with paradox . . . is 'illogical' and 'nonsensical'" to Western readers expecting rhetoric because "its intent lies outside the realm of persuasion." Abbey's cow essay was rife with paradox. It was illogical and nonsensical, and his intent lay outside the realm of rhetoric and persuasion. As usual, he exercised his constitutional freedom of speech to the limit, attacking several sacred cows as he attacked every authoritative and arrogant discourse that bred fault and guilt: feminism, environmentalism, political correctness, motherhood, science, and religion. Under the disguise of ED's bluster, ed discussed world religions, world hunger, capitalism, art, and an author's heavy responsibility to readers. Learning to listen to the ED/ed voice, readers will find layer after layer of philosophy and ecology—with no easy black-and-white eco-rant answers and no sycophantic journalism.

On the surface, Abbey's writing often appears preachy, but he used modern environmental issues and people figuratively, as metaphor, symbol, plot, and character. He wanted to write literature. He seemed to know that "facts" were useless against centuries of deeply embedded stories. He knew that facts did not change minds but stories could. As he searched the Southwest for signs and symbols, he found that the cowboy and his horse carried too much baggage: too heroic, too tragic, too exotic, and too romantic. He found Sonoran Desert plants and animals too regional. The Gila monster, scorpion, tarantula, even the stately saguaro signified little to those who had never lived with them. Surprisingly, he did find two complex and overlooked world-class symbols in the southwestern deserts—the humble cow and her partner the even humbler buzzard.

The complex, contradictory, and symbolic cow, Abbey knew, had been quietly marbling in literary fat from Greek myth through the Bible, from India to South America, from Aesop to Darwin, paradoxically representing god, monster, disguise, sacrifice, laborer, wealth, and poverty. Io, one of the mortal women Zeus loved, was changed into a white cow by his jealous wife. Bull gods and goddesses dominated world religions from Egypt to New Guinea. Worshippers wore masks decorated with cattle horns during coming-of-age ceremonies, and cattle were sacrificed to ensure rain. In the Bible, cattle were often described as "craven images," such as the golden calf.

During the sixteenth and seventeenth centuries, both the Catholic Church and Protestant sects burned animals at the stake as witches, just as they did women. Most of these animal "witches" were domestic animals: horses, cows, pigs, and dogs. Domestic animals carry a long history of imagined villainy, as did their caretakers. Nomads whose herds of cattle grazed the Sahara, Persia, Arabia, Morocco, Kenya, and Ethiopia were often feared, hated, and thought of as expanding a destructive culture. When Abbey adopted the cow as a character in his desert writing, he tapped into a deep and complex world symbol that touched theology, psychology, anthropology, sociology, history, and more. Cow worship/fear was and is a worldwide phenomenon.

Thoreau and Abbey both used cows to write about much bigger ideas than simply advocating for preservation of leisure-class playgrounds. Thoreau admired Eastern thought and read widely among Buddhist, Taoist, and Hindu classics. Transcendentalists were interested in Americanizing races, religions, cultures, and nature into a harmonious blend to match the dream of the new country. Consequently, Thoreau's writing is full of yin/yang paradox, like finding wildness in all things domestic and the domestic in all things wild. Emerson thought Thoreau was just being contrary with his love of paradox. But by comparing wild and tame in his essay "Walking," Thoreau attempted to explain that wildness can't be bred out, beaten out, preached out, educated out, or domesticated out of any animal, including the human slave—an idea that inspired Lev Tolstoy, Martin Luther King Jr., and Mahatma Gandhi. Thoreau didn't say that wilderness would save the world; he said wildness would. Abbey agreed, and so do I.

When writers like Thoreau and Abbey use a word, they do so with careful consideration of its meaning through time and throughout the world. When Abbey calls public land grazers "sacred cows," I believe he wants the reader to find out that the cow was responsible for keeping India's soil fertile and provided cooking fuel, milk, and meat to the lowest and poorest castes. In a country where farmers couldn't afford gasoline or tractors, the cow provided the muscle to plow the fields, haul produce to market, and furnish transportation. From plaster for house walls to leather businesses, the cow supported a large percentage of India's teeming vegetarian population. What better way to explain noncapitalist democracy to a Hindu reader than via ED/ed's desire to be reincarnated, not into the rich man's caste but as a buzzard, a black feathered untouchable, one who must patiently wait until a sacred cow dies of its own volition and becomes carrion before his or her children can eat—one of the many reasons why the cow is sacred in both the American West and India.

Abbey also took his reincarnation as a croaking, obnoxious, carrion-eating buzzard seriously. Since he did not want buzzards to go hungry, he considered what a buzzard ate. As every vermillion flycatcher knows, food supply is more crucial than habitat. Tramping around the desert Southwest, Abbey noticed that while a lone buzzard might be found pecking at a road-kill rabbit, the happy gathering and feasting of the clan mainly occurred around dead cows: "Arizona is where the vultures swarm like flies about the starving cattle on the cow-burnt range." In Mexico he finds even more scavengers: "Above the cattle the vultures swarm like flies, attracted by the sight and smell of dying meat." But Abbey gives all that swarming a positive slant: "The inevitable vultures soaring overhead reminded us, though, that somewhere in this brushy wilderness was life, sentient creation, living meat." The buzzards reminded him that in the desert, the cow represented sustainable protein. The buzzards reminded him that life can't exist without death. Large carrion-eating buzzards and vultures appear worldwide and only where large grazers graze, but their feathers on other continents are usually white like angels, not black.

In the essay "Down the River with Henry Thoreau," Abbey writes, "*Walden* has been published abroad in every country where English can be read, as in India—God knows they need it there—or can be translated, as in Russia, where they need it even more. The Kremlin's commissars of literature have classified Thoreau as a nineteenth-century social reformer, proving once again that censors can read but seldom understand." Obviously Abbey, labeled as a twentieth-century social reformer, ranged beyond simply encouraging a fight between environmentalists and ranchers in his thinking and writing. Although readers examine other nature writers for literary meaning, they often regard Edward Abbey's nonfiction as activism, similar to the position Trinh finds the minority writer struggling against. When a writer is labeled as a representative of some out-of-favor, angry group, readers look not for literature but for rhetoric, and readers usually find what they are looking for. I tried hard to explain Abbey to both his rancher foes and environmentalist fans.

Of course my argument that Abbey's cow is much more than an environmental issue may be based on coincidence, conjecture, and wishful research. Truth is not only complicated; it's elusive. Sometimes is it contradictory. I don't think any of my closest friends or family members have even the vaguest idea about what I try to do on paper. Sometimes I'm not sure what I'm doing myself. I often say on paper what I don't dare say in life. And sometimes I change my mind before the ink dries. Sometimes I think writers write to try to figure out what they think. So maybe I found a side of Ed Abbey that he never felt obligated to apologize for or to explain and maybe couldn't.

Mostly I loved, studied, and defended Abbey because he was one of my favorite authors. His popular memoir *Desert Solitaire* contained several chapters where Abbey cowboyed and gathered cattle:

> As we loaded the horses into the truck for the return to the ranch I asked Mackie how he liked this kind of work. He looked at me. His shirt and the rag around his neck were dark with sweat, his face coated

with dust; there was a stripe of dried blood across his cheek where a willow branch had struck him when he plunged through the brush after some ignorant cow.

"Look at yourself," he said.

I looked; I was in the same condition. "I do this only for fun," I explained. "If I did it for pay I might not like it. Anyway you haven't answered my question. How do you like this kind of work?"

"I'd rather be rich."

"What would you do if you were rich?"

He grinned through the dust. "Buy some cows of my own."

Abbey understood. The years 1992 and '93 have come and gone and cows still graze public lands. I hope I helped contribute to that result. The biggest threat to "public" land ranching today is overgrazing by "wild" horses, another imagination-based problem being imposed on the West by those who do not live here. Abbey's "Moon-Eyed Horse" in *Desert Solitaire* might be a place to begin enlightenment.

So I rode on—only now I rode only metaphorically.

I believe we desperately need to return to teaching the humanities as wildness, not straitjackets or assembly lines, and with clear and understandable language. As I ventured deeper into academia, I discovered that what seemed "new" to them was "old" in my world. We country bumpkins had always avoided hierarchies and dichotomies. We didn't like to rank and divide anything into us versus them. We recognized gender and class differences, of course, but not in the same way academia did. Gender was about procreation, not sex and power. Class was about responsibility and earned pride, not money. We had always been wary of power structures, ideology, stereotypes, subjectivity, and objectivity, and we had been attacking the "meaning" of words, especially big fancy ones, forever. We practiced the scientific method daily, and we invented critical thinking, only we called it common sense. As soon as I read Edward Said's postcolonial theories in his book *Orientalism*, I recognized parallels with the patronizing way the East and West Coasts imagined "flyover country" and urban areas imagined the rural. "They" imagined "us" as their colonized producers; our land contained their resources and provided their playgrounds. We were backward, irrational, violent, inferior, and childlike—definitely in need of wise management by our colonizers.

Although I missed chasing real cows on real horses, as my physical prowess deteriorated, cows and horses became even more interesting when I found them in books. Cows seemed to be hiding in everything I read. In Thoreau's essay "Wild Apples," he credits the cow with inventing numerous new varieties of apples. "We have all heard of the numerous varieties of fruit invented by Van Mons and Knight," he said. "This is the system of Van Cow, and she has invented far more memorable varieties than both of them." After a cow spends the morning eating domestic varieties of apples under cultivated trees, explains Thoreau, she drifts off to "plant" the seeds in wild corners of the pastures. For several seasons the cow will then graze her little apple sprouts off into bushes, until the gnarled bush becomes so impenetrable that one central branch is finally able to shoot up out of the cow's reach. In this way, he says, the cow produces a more "independent" and "hardy" tree. Cows also keep apple trees pruned up to "about the right height" and thus produces her "own shade and food." This partnership between the cow and the apple tree allows them both to become gradually wilder as they range farther and farther out on the fringes of civilization. He says these wild cows and their wild trees produce fruit and meat far more flavorful and hardy than the cultivated varieties from which they both sprang.

Obviously, Thoreau was using wild apples as an allegory. He said in the same essay, "Poets and philosophers and statesmen thus spring up in the country pastures." He often compares himself to the wild apple: "But our wild apple is wild perchance like myself who belong not to the aboriginal race here—but have strayed into the woods from the cultivated stock." Although today Thoreau is credited with originating the idea to preserve wilderness, he actually believed that wilderness, and more importantly wildness, was in a constant state of re-creation aided by cows. Three years before his death, when he knew he was dying of tuberculosis and near the end of his journal-keeping years, he warned, "If we do not look out we shall find our fine schoolhouse standing in a cowyard at last." Scholars usually interpret this sentence as Thoreau's negative view of where education might be headed—back to the cow yard. I interpret it as positive—forward to the cow yard. But maybe I'm biased.

Eventually I combined what I found in books with my own personal knowledge and backed up my ideas with respected scholars from many disciplines.

My grad school research papers eventually became academic conference papers, academic journal articles, chapters for scholarly books on nature writers, chapters for my dissertation, and parts of my book published from that dissertation, *The Wild and the Domestic.* Some appear later in anthologies. Even in the most scholarly publications, I often used my own personal cowboy experiences as a counterargument. This chapter, as well as a few other sections of this book, is a mash-up of bits and pieces from all those publications and a condensed sample of that style. More importantly, I also sifted out numerous newspaper columns for my neighbors and articles for horse and cattle magazines, struggling to rewrite academic language into plain ol' English for cowboy journalism. I spoke truth to environmental power about wolves, 1080 poison, and overgrazing. I tried to draw a new circle around many classic nature writers and Ansel Adams's photography to include them on "our" side and to include us in the circle that loved and protected nature. On the other hand, I exposed the clay feet of heroes like John Muir, endangered species, and the Nature Conservancy. I looked for news about fellow academics who were also questioning the truth about these subjects. I exposed the imaginary differences between wilderness and home, between wild and tame, between native and nonnative, between agri-culture and hunter/gatherer-culture, between vegans and carnivores, and between grazing and overgrazing as simply ideological, romanticized, postmodern, postcolonial, dualistic power structures, blah, blah, blah—or in my own, much-easier-to-understand language: bullshit.

CHAPTER NINE

Grace

"When gods die . . . you're not sure if there will ever be another god to fill their place. Or if you'd even want another god to fill their place. You don't want the fire to go out inside you twice."

—Gary D. Schmidt

WHEN MY HARDWORKING Iowa grandmother's husband died in her lap of a massive heart attack, she thought her life was over. He left her with one final year of debt before their farm would be paid off and with a corn crop in the field that should have paid it. Then Mother Nature slapped Gram with an early frost, freezing that corn crop before it matured and ruining it for most uses. Immature and undented, it would also mold. Good neighbors harvested the damaged crop and dumped the unshucked ears in her corncrib. Her problem was what to do with it.

Cattle can eat moldy corn without harm, so Gram decided to go deeper into debt, buying steers to feed over winter and trying to pack enough extra pounds on them to make that final farm payment come spring. Cattle can't survive on corn alone. They need roughage like hay to keep their rumens working. So Gram decided to chop the whole ears into mouth-friendly disks. This would allow her steers to eat the cobs and husks, good roughage, as well as the corn, moldy or not, and require less hay. I think, though, more than the money, she needed something challenging to do, something that would keep her almost constantly busy. So through her tears and that long Iowa winter—through rain, sleet, or snow, often in well-below-zero temperatures, every day, pretty much all day—my grandmother sliced those ears of corn by hand with a machete, one ear at a time. Then she carried bucket after bucket of slices to her steers. In the spring, she paid off the farm. She said the hard work had gotten her through the worst part of her grief and helped her sleep at night. Maybe that was the most important lesson she ever taught me. A pen, lined paper, and difficult writing projects have saved my sanity several times.

When I left my beloved adobe house at Willow Springs, like my grandmother I thought the best parts of my life were over. But I still had my pen and my new full-time difficult career as a college professor. Instead of trying to apply Ray Hunt's methods to horses, I tried applying them to students. Of course, I never mastered teaching either, but it turned out to be a wonderful way to spend the next part of my life—a life that was not ending but just beginning. My biggest problem was where to live. I quickly found a grass lease for my small cow herd and didn't own any horses. Perro and I moved into a tiny duplex with a fenced backyard on the edge of a creek, which allowed us to take long walks, but I left The Lone Chicken behind at Willow Springs.

Like my grandmother, I raised chickens. I thought homemade eggs were worth the trouble, and I never had to spray for bugs or spiders. I'd order fifty little yellow chicks at a time through the post office and put them under a heat lamp. Once they were big enough to turn loose, the coons would get a few, the snakes a few, and a few would drown in the horse trough because my daughter's horse, Little Red, liked to push them in. The coyotes, foxes, and bobcats would pick off the rest. The next year I'd buy fifty more chicks and try again. After a few years, though, I gave up on raising chickens and just donated the last old hen to the coyotes. I stopped penning her at night and quit feeding her.

But every morning, there she'd be, pecking around. She started roosting in a pecan tree over the sidewalk where her humans passed regularly and where Perro always slept. Once a big norther blew in during the night and covered her with snow and ice. She stayed in her tree for a couple of days without moving and looked frozen. But when the sun came out and warmed things up, she hopped down and went back to scratching.

The cowboys started taking notice of her independent ways and named her The Lone Chicken. A few started showing up with one of her Barred Rock black-and-white feathers stuck in their hatbands. Cody Crider, at the time a good young bronc rider, tied one of her feathers in his leggin fringe for good luck. I took his picture while he did it. Once when the roundup was camped at my house, in the middle of the night the cowboys heard her squawking. A coon was carrying her off into the night. By now some of them had gotten pretty attached to her, so someone got up and shot the coon. She sat around licking her wounds for a few days and soon went back to scratching again. So, of course, I had written about her.

After I left Willow Springs and moved to town, I tried to leave the old Barred Rock hen behind. But when her people and her dog left, the critters quickly came out of the woodwork. She was not going to make it there alone, so I finally boxed her up and took her to town. She must have found some bugs that had been sprayed with poison around my little duplex because she was soon too feeble to stand and eventually died. I'd made a terrible mistake. That was not the way The Lone Chicken should have died. She should have been carried off, kicking and squawking, by a coon, a bobcat, or, better yet, a mountain lion—her meat and blood feeding future killers, her feathers dancing on the wind. The cowboys who wore her feathers would have liked that better.

Then Perro suffered what Doc Ray Allen, our local vet, called a stroke. Perro was thirteen at the time and began walking with a shuffling wobble like an old man. He had always wanted to be a cowdog when he grew up, but nobody used dogs to work cattle where he lived and I didn't know how to train him anyway. He tried to teach himself but usually just got yelled at and told to "git to the house." He tackled a calf once, brought it down, and got in big trouble. He always wanted to help load horses into trailers, but he tended to practice loading when someone was trying to unload them.

He probably trotted a million miles. He'd catch jackrabbits or just go look over the next ridge, all day while his people were horseback. Even when riding in the back of a pickup, he constantly ran circles and bit at passing tree branches. He thought he was immortal. He tried to whip everything from German shepherds to game wardens. He pulled his own burrs out of his feet. He always passed judgment on my daughter's boyfriends and would never bark when his all-time favorite would sneak her home after hours. His best adult friend was our old roundup cook, who always had enough scraps to open his own dog heaven. Perro never learned to fetch and got deafer as he aged, or at least he pretended to be. I think he really was deaf after I moved him to town, but I was never sure. If he escaped the yard where I had imprisoned him for crimes he did not understand, he wouldn't come back when I called. I had to stomp my foot and make jerky hand motions to *show* him I was mad. Even if he couldn't hear, he knew those motions meant business and that he better quit ignoring me, although nobody had ever laid a hand on him. He just wanted to be a good dog and didn't like to see one of his people frown.

After his stroke, he began to refuse to go in his doghouse, so I made him a bed in the grass. I tried a nice soft piece of foam rubber, but that didn't suit him. He liked the old ragged blanket from his doghouse best. I guess it smelled like home. One day I noticed a bumblebee going in and out a little hole under his doghouse. I had recently heard about a horse that had stepped on a piece of roofing tin, disturbing a bumblebee nest, and had almost died from hundreds of stings. In just a few seconds, I saw six bumblebees come and go from the corner of Perro's doghouse. My old dog was wobbling around at the farthest corner of the yard with a bumblebee following him. Suddenly I realized that the bees had probably run him out of his doghouse and would have run him out of the yard if he hadn't been fenced in. No wonder he didn't want to come home when he escaped.

I bought a can of poison but imagined thousands of angry bumblebees swarming out to attack us when I sprayed their hole. So I grabbed one of the S-hooks from my pot rack, grabbed my saddle rope, and carefully set to work extending my reach. I slipped one end of the S-hook through the honda of my rope and the other end under the edge of the doghouse roof. Then I threaded the rope up and over the yard fence behind the doghouse and tied it to my pickup bumper. I put Perro in the cab with me and backed up, tipping the doghouse on its side. Bumblebees swelled out from under it and stormed over the fence in a cloud of anger, but we were safe in the pickup cab. After they calmed down, I left Perro in the cab and snuck back in the house through the front door, grabbed my can of poison, and peeked out the side door next to the doghouse. Under the doghouse was a huge pile of what looked like yellow marbles with bumblebees crawling over them. I sprayed quickly and slammed the door.

After an hour or so, I peeked out again. Dead and dying bumblebees littered the ground. I saw one healthy bee, who had evidently been off on an errand, come back to view the destruction. He kept trying to go to the nest, but the fumes drove him back. Then he'd go to one of the dead bees and shake it. He crawled to the nest and back to shake the same dead bee over and over. Perhaps the dead one was a mate or relative; perhaps his kids were in the nest. I wanted to tell the frantic bee that I was sorry. I wanted to explain that I love nature, even bumblebees, but I just couldn't let them hurt my old dog.

After a few days, I cleaned up the eggs and dead bees. Once the poison dissipated, Perro began sleeping in his doghouse again. First thing every morning, I'd rouse him, help him to his feet, and make him go on a shaky walk around the backyard. I had to hold him up while he drank water, even though Doc Allen said he should start to improve after a few weeks. No one who saw Perro after his stroke would believe that he used to be able to catch jackrabbits and once trotted thirteen miles through the mountains to see a girlfriend—twice in one day! No one would believe that he once rounded up and brought me a wild aoudad ram to photograph. Shakespeare said that reputation is a false external thing, "oft got without merit and lost without deserving." That's certainly true about old dogs.

Some friends invited me and my daughter over for a cookout one night, and we decided to take Perro along. He wobbled around in the sunshine in his winter coat, panting but happy. He was so glad to get out of prison. While we cooked and ate, he hung around begging for bites of bacon or steak. When we finished eating, he cleaned up everyone's leftovers. About dark he was missing, so my daughter went to look. He was sitting patiently, close to our pickup, obviously ready to go home. We weren't, so he'd just have to nap while we roasted marshmallows, made s'mores, drank wine, told stories, and laughed until the fire burned down and everyone started to get cold. We had brought bedrolls and planned to adjourn to pickup beds for a little stargazing before we called it a night.

But the next time we checked on him, Perro was gone.

We called and whistled and searched in the darkness. No one had a flashlight. I knew in his wobbly condition, he couldn't have gone far. Because of his either real or pretended deafness, I wasn't sure he could hear us calling. I turned on the pickup motor, which usually brought him on the run, but no dog. I started to get nervous. We could hear dogs barking in the distance but too far away for our invalid dog to travel. My daughter and I were cussing ourselves for bringing him. The party broke up quickly, and I hurried back to my house to find a Coleman lantern. I knew I'd find him if I could only see better. By the time I got back to the picnic spot, there trotting down the road in my headlights like his old self was my dog, looking for his lost people. He seemed years younger. No more wobbling, strokey old dog. The outing had really helped him.

Several hours later, all safely home and tucked in bed, I had a dream about water. Suddenly I was wide awake and sitting straight up in bed. My poor dog! I had let him run around for several hours in the sun, panting, then fed him all those salty scraps and never thought about water. I guess he had finally gone in search of a drink and had to fight the resident dogs for access. I was about to turn myself over to the Humane Society, but then I remembered how young he looked trotting down the road. I guess he must have decided he could still take care of himself after all, and he could still fight for water.

After The Lone Chicken and Perro died, my daughter headed to Montana, and all I had left was my small cow herd. When I decided to sell my cows to finance a PhD, I also had to give up writing my newspaper column. I thought again that the best parts of my life were over. But I packed up and headed to Nevada for two busy years, and once again my life seemed to begin, not end.

When I returned to Texas and my teaching job, my problem again became where to live. First I rented what I called "the buzzard house." The backyard was tucked under a grove of tall pine trees, and all the buzzards in West Texas seemed to roost there. I spent evenings in the backyard watching them drift in by the hundreds and somehow disappear into the dark branches. Since I saw only two or three at a time riding thermals on miles and miles of rimrock, I wondered how far this many must have flown to roost in these favorite trees.

When the owner sold the buzzard house, I found one to rent on the side of the mountain near the college. My picture window faced a U-shaped indentation that must have been an ancient water trail, since I watched deer, javelinas, and wild turkeys thread through surrounding houses to come down that U-shaped indentation every evening on their way to Kokernot Spring. That spring had been named San Lorenzo (1684), Aguaje de San Felipe (1787), La Brocha, Burgess Water Hole (1884), and finally Kokernot. In 1930 the Kokernot family had donated the spring and property surrounding it to the college. That water had attracted conquistadores, explorers, Apaches and Comanches, early trading caravans, buffalo soldiers, the railroad, and early ranchers—all had probably used the old trail that ran past my house. I had held my outdoor wedding on some rock steps near that spring in 1971. So I called that house "the old trail house." Although I didn't see him pass, I'm sure the black bear that ended up on the golf course came down that old water trail too.

Then that house also sold.

Luckily Ike Roberts, at the time general manager of the Catto-Gage Ranches, which sprawled from Marathon through Alpine to Marfa, offered me a chance to move into a double-wide trailer on a Marfa camp. I had no duties other than keeping full the reservoir that fed both my house and a string of water tubs. I got no salary, but I paid no rent either. I kept a journal about tending that water:

> Water. People don't realize what it is worth until they don't have any. Right now I don't have any. . . . The trouble started Saturday night when, as usual, I drove up to the reservoir to turn off the water to my house and turn on the water for the cows. When the pump on the well is working at filling the reservoir, nothing comes through to my house. So once a week since I moved in, I've performed that little ritual, and it's not easy. The valve for the reservoir is in a big mud puddle. I can't reach it from the edge, so I've placed a board and a plastic milk crate in the water to give me a platform. I lie down on the board and reach out as far as I can with one hand on the milk crate. Then I take the lid off the buried can that keeps the valve somewhat free of mud and turn it on or off. Getting up is the hard part because I'm 53 years old and not as thin, nor as supple as I was in high school. So, usually on Saturday night I wash my dishes and take a bath, fill the coffee pot for morning, then go turn off my water. The next morning I eat a leisurely breakfast and go turn the water back on when I think I better flush the toilet. It usually works just fine and by the time I get back home from the reservoir, I have water. But this Sunday morning was different.

Winter was even worse because that valve puddle became hand-numbing cold.

> I broke ice off my puddle to turn my water off and let the reservoir fill yesterday. But I couldn't get the valve to turn. I cut my finger. My hand was aching from the cold and both feet soaked through until I was wet above the ankles, still couldn't get it to budge. Tried pliers, but kept slipping off. Can't see what I'm doing in the muddy water. The can surrounding the valve had filled up with mud, so I scooped out as much as I could before my hand went numb. Then I'd dry it on a towel, wait a while and go back. I quit once and said, "I can't do this." Then thought to myself, yes you can, you must, nobody is going to

help you. But I had taken some pictures of the windmillers pulling a well and knew that Cullen would want to see them. So I finally gave up and came home. Both boots poured water out. Socks were soaked. Jumped in my hot (now lukewarm) bathtub of water that I'd run before I went to turn off the reservoir and called Cullen. He came out about sundown with rubber boots and a vise grip. Even then he cried and moaned about the cold water. I told him I felt a little better hearing him whine because I get so mad at myself when I can't do what seems to be a simple chore.

So the next spring, I decided to drain the leakiest water trough and put new cement in its cracks. I hoped fixing it would at least slow how fast the reservoir drained and how often I had to fill it. None of the men connected to this water line seemed interested in fixing it. Cullen's boss, my friend Don Coleman, said windmillers were not plumbers. The ranch manager said it would just crack again next winter. But I was the one who had to keep that reservoir full, so I decided to try. Once I had the trough scooped clean and almost dry, I noticed a box turtle struggling through the mud to get a drink and realized that any animal less than four feet tall would not be able to drink once I fixed it. So I left just enough leak for the short-legged guys, which was probably the reason the men didn't fix it, but they didn't want to admit to being soft-hearted.

That old ranch camp was a classic example of how we humans are at the mercy of nature: fire and wind, rain and rust. My camp had once been a beautiful rock house surrounded by porches and trees. But the house had blown up and burned in a propane accident several years before. The ranch replaced the rock house with a cheap double-wide trailer, and pack rats had already built nests in the heating ducts. Frozen water and rust were gradually eating the water pipes, and everything leaked. But around the leaks, I often found tracks in the mud. I've always paid attention to tracks. It tells me who or what waters there. At each leak, it seemed that I found only one set of tracks per species. I'd find only one set of rabbit tracks, only one small bird's track, only one set of coyote tracks. I wondered why. Maybe because I had been living alone for more than ten years, I was fascinated with animals that lived alone. They may get together to mate and then for a while a female may travel with her juveniles, but for most of their lives, most animals live alone. Especially in the desert, animals don't seem very social.

Living with me in that burned-out camp were only one cottontail, one bull snake, one roadrunner, one lizard, and one antelope buck with no harem. Maybe they found mates, but I never saw any mates or young.

One November evening about sundown, I walked out to see if the lone peach tree, which seemed to be the only thing holding up the leaning old wooden barn, had weathered the late-spring freeze. Nope. Our usual late frost had zapped all the peaches again. The barn was a spooky place. Someone had put up a rickety fence to keep cows out of the gray pile of disintegrating hay beneath the trembling structure. Scratching an itch on one of the leaning poles could have been fatal to a whole herd. The barn was open on three sides, the rafters sagged, tin was blowing off the roof, boards were falling in. When the wind blew, the whole thing rattled like a place Ichabod Crane wouldn't go near. Since I identified more with the headless horseman, I stood my ground. But I'm not totally stupid and didn't intend to be the one to jar the last nail loose and have it all fall on my head. I felt content to lean on the fence and just look.

High in the rafters, I usually spotted one solitary female barn owl, her monkey face turned away from me as she snoozed. For a while three roosted together, but eventually her chicks flew, hopefully finding their own barns. My eyes also scanned the beautiful old gray boards, and I noticed what at first I thought were squares of wood used to patch holes. Slowly my brain recognized coon hides, six of them, nailed to the boards skin side out. The hides had faded to barn-wood silver and almost disappeared. Three still had their tails attached. Too high up to reach even with a ladder, they must have been tacked there when hay had been stacked high in the barn, maybe during a drouth. I wondered who had trapped them. They reminded me of Robert Frost's poem about an abandoned woodpile. Who would go to all that trouble—trapping, skinning (no holes either—good job), stretching, and tacking—and then forget? Did the price of coon hides drop? Did the trapper die, quit the ranch, get sick? Nobody just walks off and forgets their hides.

Years before, in the dim light of an early dawn as I drove to a job in town, I saw a car brake, hit something, and keep going. Bobcat! I slammed on my brakes, jumped out of my pickup in dress and panty hose, grabbed a hind leg of the still-kicking cat, and quickly slung him into my pickup bed. Bobcat hides were selling for $300 at the time, and I was working long hours for $500 a month. Coon hides at the time were selling for $50 and skunks for $8. I'm a trapper's daughter and have done a little myself. Like I said, nobody forgets their hides. Something must have happened to the trapper. The abandoned coon hides in their state of decay gave me an eerie feeling. They were now worthless except maybe as poetry.

Perhaps the most forlorn residents of that burned-out camp were the fire-damaged trees—standing skeletons of their former selves, with burned branches lopped off back to the trunk. A few new branches had tried to sprout but, through lack of water during years when no one lived there, had died back again. I watered the trees, and a few short tangled green branches again began to sprout, hovering like green halos around the tops of the old silver trunks. No one would have called the place beautiful anymore. But I did. When an early fall ice storm threatened to break what few limbs had grown back on the old trees, I pleaded with the storm, "Please don't hurt them anymore." Almost every evening, just at twilight, the barn owl would silently float onto a gnarled branch sticking out of one of those halos just a few feet from where I sat hidden in the black shadows of my porch. I could almost touch her.

Another aspect of Eastern philosophy that I admire is wabi-sabi: seeing beauty in the imperfect, the worn, and the used. If a pottery cup cracked during firing, instead of throwing it away, a wabi-sabi potter would fill the crack with gold to strengthen and beautify it. But wabi-sabi is not unique to Eastern cultures. Children often drag around a beloved blanket or teddy bear until it falls apart, each worn or missing part representing memories. After a pair of boots, spur straps, leggings, or a saddle begins to take on the shape of the user, it becomes harder and harder to replace. Breaking in a new hat takes months. Gloves, ropes, even jackets just don't feel comfortable until time passes. Missing or scarred parts of a saddle often represent stories. Spur tracks across the seat of a saddle were probably made while the rider was desperately trying to hang on while losing his or her grip. Rope burns, missing tie strings, bent conchos, smashed stirrups—each mark held a story that taught a memorable lesson. Silver and leather take on a soft and nostalgic patina once the engraving has worn away. Hair mecates feel more comfortable with the bristles worn off. Shirts and wildrags become favorites when threadbare and faded.

I'm an old journalist, not a new one. To me rubbed trees burnished by cattle, snubbing posts grooved and polished by roped horses, well-licked salt blocks, weathered barns, nicked and rounded anvils—all smoldered with earned beauty. I liked to photograph a cowboy working with one arm in a cast or on crutches, one wearing boots held together with duct tape or soldering wire, one whose old hat had gotten so floppy-brimmed that he'd stitched two brims together: one black, one silver belly—both probably previously worn-out favorites that he couldn't bear to throw away. I found beauty in wrinkled, gnarled, and calloused hands resting comfortably on a well-worn saddle horn or draped across the top rail of an old silvered corral. I wanted my photography and words to help the world see that perfection and newness were overrated. As Japanese photographer Kenji Toma once said, "Everyone thinks the most beautiful moment of a flower's life is the peak. But I think they are most beautiful when they are dying."

I once interviewed Martin Black, at the time a young and very handsome Nevada buckaroo who had already earned a top hand reputation. He said, "Most old men are slow and a lot of younger guys don't think they're getting anything done. But you watch them old men and they'll get more cows worked easier and never get out of a trot. Them young guys will be dashing over here and dashing over there, and they're running by a lot of opportunities to get the job done smoother. But an old man, he knows that if he gets too fast, he's going to get out of control. So he won't go fast. He'll stay slow and wait for the opportunities to come."

As Martin said, most young cowboys at best tolerate the old men and at worst make fun of them. Sure enough, one young cowboy told me years ago about an old man who wore shoes instead of boots and kept coming out to help the 06 during roundup long after the young cowboy thought the old man should have retired. The young cowboy laughed and bragged that one night he poked holes in the coffee can the old man took to bed to pee in, and that the next morning the old man rolled his bed and never came back. Everybody laughed.

Years later, I met an old man who had probably been the best cowboy West Texas ever produced and wrote a book chapter on him ("Nicasio Ramirez: Cowboying from Chihuahua to Nevada" in *Cowboys Who Rode Proudly*). When I asked old gringos who the best hand was in their day, they'd name Nicasio Ramirez. Old Mexican cowboys gave the same answer. They said he broke lots of colts, roped and dallied with either hand, tanned his own hides and built all his own gear, and could masterfully handle a team of mules or horses hitched to a fresno while building water tanks and dams. They said he could do it all. Nick was born in 1897 into a wealthy landowning family in Mexico, and while trying to defend that ranch, Nick killed one of Pancho Villa's raiders. They took the young don captive and instead of killing him, forced him to ride with them. He escaped one night, crossed the Rio Grande, and rode all the way to Nevada before he stopped. Eventually drifting around, working on ranches in California and Arizona, he ended up in West Texas on the 06 Ranch, where the owner selected him as a cowboy teacher for his grandson Chris Lacy. As a six-year-old, Chris rode in the salt wagon while Nick drove the mules, learning the rough country and how to handle long days, leaving at 6 A.M. and returning about 4 P.M. At age eight the young cowboy began doctoring screwworms with Nick, who started teaching the future manager of the ranch how to rope by roping broom weeds.

Nick went back to Mexico only long enough to persuade his childhood sweetheart to marry him and brought many old vaquero traditions north. He could tail down a steer like a charro and used his chaps like a matador when sorting in the pens. He could tie down calves with their own tails or rope a deer for fresh meat. If he roped a cow by the horns, he could throw slack in his own rope to catch her heels. He was a master at riding a bucking horse, counting fast-moving cattle, and stripping calves off their mothers. He would step off a tired horse and walk beside it, throwing rocks out of the road or trail while the horse rested. In less than forty minutes he could skin a steer with just his pocket knife for fresh beef. When he lost a thumb while dally roping, he finished cutting it off himself with that same pocket knife.

Nick never wore boots, only shoes.

After retiring from full-time work, he still enjoyed helping the ranches during branding season, eating at the wagon, and sleeping in a bedroll. As he aged, he started taking a coffee can into his bedroll so he wouldn't have to get up to pee. One night, one of the young cowboys took a horseshoe nail and poked tiny holes his can. Nick rolled his bed the next morning, left the 06 Ranch wagon, and never returned. After his wife died, Nick lived alone, cooking on a woodstove, chopping his own wood. He spent his final days sitting in the sunshine on a bench in downtown Alpine watching traffic go by.

I knew who poked those holes in Nick's coffee can, but I have never revealed his name. I often wondered if that hole puncher ever found out who that old man really was. If so, did he remember and regret what he had done those many years before. Now that he's an old man himself, I wonder if some upstart kid will pay him back someday.

I liked to write about aging cowboys. The most interesting men I knew were old, weather-beaten, sometimes broken, and usually living alone. I especially looked for and liked to profile the elders of our tribe. Those who stayed, who survived the life, had their rough edges worn away by wind and rain and hooves and horns. They had been humbled and mellowed, their short fuses lengthened. Once in a while I was lucky enough to find one who would talk to me. When that happened, my job was easy. I'd just turn on my tape recorder and listen. Often the stories came off the tape and onto the page without much effort on my part. I might juggle them around for a little order, maybe throw in a sentence to join one story to the next, but mostly I just tried to stay out of their way. One of those tribal elders was Tom Blasingame.

The first time I ever saw him he was standing next to the JA Ranch chuckwagon at the 1985 Texas Ranch Roundup in Wichita Falls. He was eighty-seven at the time but looked timeless. Something about the way he stood or the way he looked out from under his hat or the way his clothes fit or the way his muscles held him together—something, I'm not sure what, made me stop to watch him. He stood alone. The day was sweltering hot. Tom was wearing a white long-sleeved shirt, dark gray wool vest, and a red silk scarf around his neck, yet he didn't look uncomfortable as he watched the crowd. Other men who had the same look stopped to shake his hand. I've heard it said that a good cowboy can't be judged until the judge sees him horseback and watches him work, but I sometimes disagree. People who work with animals learn to read body language. They know what to expect long before they actually ask an animal for a response: the way a cow raises her head when she sees a rider approach, the way a horse looks at or ignores an approaching human. This man looked like a cowboy, and the people stopping to say hello treated him like a good one.

So I walked up and introduced myself. He stuck out his hand and said, "Tom Blasingame." I tried to maintain a poker face, but I'm sure my eyes bugged out a little. I had heard of Tom Blasingame for years. I thought he was just a legend, doubted he was real—or figured he was long dead if he was real—never dreaming I'd meet him. He was the subject of one of my favorite songs, by Canadian singer-songwriter Ian Tyson. As a reporter working the ranch rodeo for stories, I had my tape recorder under my arm.

I also had with me a recording of that song. I asked Tom if he had ever heard it. No, he hadn't. So I played, "Tom's the name, Tom Blasingame, eighty-five years in the saddle," and watched his face while Tyson sang the legend I was so familiar with. Tom watched the tape player until the song ended, registering no emotion. Then he looked up and said simply, "I guess that must be me."

"Will you talk to me?"

"Why, sure," he grinned.

Tom began by telling me that he had always been a gentleman, even in his youth: sincere, quiet, and a nondrinker. Then someone walked up and said, "Yeah? Tom, tell her about that dance"—the time some pretty girl danced past him, and Tom took off his hat and asked her to "shake a little of that in there." Tom blushed. I laughed.

The next story Tom told was about working on the lower Matadors where, he said, "they used to run two wagons. Had two crews, two remudas; quite an outfit. I remember the fall of twenty-eight. They put all the men with one wagon. We went to where all the wild cattle and big steers was running. We worked down in there two weeks, and on the last day we made a big drive and took them north out on open country, heading for a two-section holding pasture. We got them out of the brush, and cattle were coming from every direction, trying to break back, and men running and turning them. Them boys knowed what to do too! Cattle on the outside was runnin' full speed in a mill, and them big steers was trapped in the middle, standing three foot higher than the cows. We got a hundred and two big steers in that drive, and some of them was sixteen years old. We took the fence down about fifty yards wide and just eased that roundup into the holding pasture. Ol' Claude Jeffers had been there nearly all his life, and he said that was the best drive they ever made on that country."

At the time, I'd been a published cowboy journalist for fourteen years. But I never heard a story like that one before or since. Thus we began a friendship that would last the rest of Tom's life. He invited me to visit him at his camp on the JA Ranch. So my daughter and I showed up with our saddles, bedrolls, a Dutch oven, and my sourdough starter. I rode with Tom two days, one prowling a big circle and one gathering cattle. My daughter also rode with him and the JA crew one day to move some cattle while I took pictures. He gave her a nickname, Slim. Never in my wildest dreams did I think I'd someday even meet Tom Blasingame—but my daughter and I got to ride the Red River with him.

He'd been the wagon boss for the Matadors and the old JA Ranch before it broke up. "Old Charlie Goodnight," Tom explained, "filed on all the choice country where the water was and left the rough bad country for the settlers. Then, as the homesteaders starved out, he put the JA together." Tom lived alone on a Red River camp he called Gobbler City because wild turkeys roosted outside his bedroom window. In his late eighties, he was still starting his own colts. After his wife, Eleanor, moved to town for health reasons, Tom went to see her on weekends but kept his camp. In his youth, he'd worked for the big Double Circles, Chiricahua, Cross S, and Five L Ranches on the Apache Reservation, "biggest outfits in the Southwest," said Tom. "I was one of them stockman bosses over several Indian families for a while on the Carrizo division of the Apaches. Whenever you throwed a roundup together, you had to drag that calf out and call out the brand on his mother. That was a slow, tedious job. Every Indian family had a different brand, and I had sixty different brands."

Then he worked for the Bell Ranch in New Mexico, went back to the Matador in Texas, back to Arizona, and back to the JA. Of course, Tom didn't like "new" ways of ranching. He said, "They talk about all this technology and stuff. Well it ain't nothin' but just a big fancy word. Actually, what makes a good manager is good men and plenty of good grass and water. That'll make technology for you!"

Toward the end of our second day, Tom asked if I'd like to see the old wagon. When the cowboys lifted the old patched-canvas fly into the cold Panhandle air, it wasn't cold anymore, because our cowboy blood started pumping and kept us warm. Someone headed back to headquarters to get wood and coffee makings and I headed for Tom's camp to get my sourdough. Eight gates times two later, we were having a regular cowboy party. Tom walked around the old wagon pointing out where the stakes were to be driven and where to build the fire. "I miss the wagon," said Tom. "The JA pulled in their wagon in fifty-five. They had so much trouble keeping wagon cooks. The old ones wore out, and the new ones didn't want to fool with these pot rack outfits. It's a lot handier to work with the wagon camped close to your work." Everyone, even his boss, knew who our wagon boss was. While I tended my sourdoughs, Tom curtly instructed one cowboy not to stand between the cook and the fire.

"I was the wagon boss of that same wagon," said Tom. "Right here on this ranch. We had ten thousand cows and a heck of a lot more country. Yes, sir, that's the same wagon."

I read them a poem about Charles Goodnight and the chuckwagon he invented more than one hundred years ago—maybe that exact wagon and chuck box. I took a photo of Tom and "Slim" standing beside it. Then, after a couple of hours, we all scuffed our boot toes in the dirt and put the wagon back in its shed. I ended one of my two-part articles on him with this: "Once the wagon was put away, Tom didn't look quite as young. Great flocks of geese were honking over our heads on their way north, but Tom hadn't seen them because he didn't hear very well. I touched him on the arm and pointed to the geese. He looked up and nodded, 'I guess they think it's spring.'"

That February, I invited Tom to come for a tour of the 06 and be my guest for the Texas Cowboy Poetry Gathering, which I had founded and still ran at the time. I liked to line up something magical for the closing moment of the gathering and that year had persuaded Red Steagall to learn the song about Tom. Cowboys loved the song, but almost none of them had ever met Tom. Tyson had written about an old cowboy he'd heard about—but never met either. Nobody seemed to know if Tom Blasingame really existed. Maybe he was just another myth.

When the emcee announced the song at the end of the final performance, suddenly an old man stepped up to the edge of the stage. The emcee bent down to hear him. He explained to Steagall that the old man was having trouble hearing and wanted him to please turn up the microphones because he liked this song. Well, being a nice guy, Steagall did even better. He quickly asked someone backstage to bring out another chair and invited the old-timer to come up and sit with him on stage while he sang. The gatherings used to be quite informal and accommodating. We were not professionals. Everyone squirmed a little, but oh well—the old man was obviously a cowboy. Toward the end of the song, after we'd heard Red sing about Tom Blasingame's eighty-five years in the saddle and how he'd worked for all the big outfits, how he'd never sold his saddle and was still looking at the world through a cow horse's ears, Red leaned over and stuck the microphone in the old man's face.

"What's your name, old-timer?" asked Red.

"Tom Blasingame," he said and looked down at his hands.

I still get chills when I remember the reaction of the crowd and the poets. For a long moment there was complete silence. Then the packed auditorium seemed to be on its feet in one motion, like a stampede was about to begin. Hats disappeared like we were in church. Tom would never in a million years have interrupted the emcee or walked up on that stage to sit beside Red Steagall if I hadn't set it all up and begged and pleaded. Tom agreed only after I explained how nobody knew if he was real or not and how much it would mean to the other aging cowboys in the audience. His brief appearance was a small personal gift from Tom. He would not accept any pay. He was not entertainment. That long-ago night in Alpine, Texas, he proved to seven hundred people that Tom Blasingame was not a myth. I would call that moment pure cowboy poetry.

After I revealed his whereabouts, more and more stories were written about him. He was photographed, interviewed, filmed, put on stage, sung about, and paraded around like a zoo animal. I felt very guilty, but Tom tolerated it well, maybe even enjoyed it. One of the few projects that impressed me, and that I had nothing to do with, was a photo cover for a magazine called *Texas Celebrates.* It was published at the beginning of the Texas bicentennial. They wanted Tom on the cover, horseback at sundown, against some glitzy mirrored widows of a high-rise building in Dallas. The idea was to juxtapose the old and new Texas in one photograph. I thought it was a hokey idea. But the story about taking the photograph is classic Tom Blasingame at his best. Tom hadn't been to Dallas since 1909 and wasn't too crazy about the big city even then. However, he understood that the photographer couldn't find glitzy windows in his Red River country, so he agreed to fly to the land of tall buildings. The photographer had borrowed a very gentle four-year-old horse, but it grew progressively more and more skittish as the late evening Dallas traffic zoomed past: horns honking, sirens blaring, trains; even a helicopter appeared on the scene. The photographer worried that putting such an elderly man on a now nervous young horse was foolhardy. At one point the crew decided maybe the old and new Texas were hopelessly mismatched and considered scrapping the shot.

But as soon as the helicopter settled down, Tom approached the horse and "something magical" took place, said the photographer. The horse seemed to trust Tom immediately and began to relax. In just a few minutes, the white was gone from around the horse's eyes, his ears perked up, and his tail blew easily in the breeze. Tom mounted, trotted a couple of circles, and brought the horse into position for the picture the magazine wanted—an old cowboy at sunset silhouetted against the mirrored golden windows of downtown Dallas.

Click.

Then, one night just after Christmas 1989, my Willow Springs phone rang. Tom's wife, Eleanor, was on the other end. She wanted permission to use my poem about rain for Tom's funeral. She said it was his favorite. Tom, at ninety-one, had been out prowling along the Red River not far from his camp on a new three-year-old colt he'd named Ruidoso. The JA cowboys found him lying peacefully in the grass, his colt grazing a few feet away. There was no sign of a struggle; the colt hadn't bucked him off. It looked like Tom had just quietly stepped off, lay down, folded his hands across his chest, and died.

The only wish I ever heard Tom utter was to die with dignity, as a cowboy, with his boots on. He hoped he'd never have to retire, never have to ride in a wheelchair. He got his wish. I wrote several articles about Tom, and I'm probably not finished yet.

I had written both Tom and Nick's stories years earlier, but that burned-out Marfa camp made those memories come calling, reminding me of old men and tribal elders. I often wondered why the end of Tom Blasingame's life and the end of Nicasio Ramirez's life were so different. The only thing I can think of is that Tom had better storytellers who reached the right audiences. I wrote about Nick too late, after the damage had been done.

The Catto-Gage manager, Ike Roberts, was also becoming a tribal elder. When he retired, the owners of my old, burned-out Marfa camp hired a new young manager, who decided he wanted a real cowboy living there again, so I had to move back to town. When I had to leave still another place that was becoming home, all the lights seemed to go out at once. Secretariat, Perro Pinto, The Lone Chicken, and Tom Blasingame were already gone. Soon Ramón Hartnett died, then Nicasio Rameriz, Ray Hunt, Tom Dorrance, Bill Dugan—although I've forgotten the exact order. The Ponderosa coffee shop in Alpine and the old Marfa coffee shop Carmen's Café, both closed, and Marfa no longer belonged to ranchers. I emailed the offices of *Western Horseman* one day and they wrote back to "Mr. Nelson."

Almost sixty, I was tired of having "home" depend on someone else's decision, so I found a little house on the outskirts of Alpine and bought it cheap because other buyers were scared off by its water system: big black storage cistern, noisy pressure pump, and pipes and gauges headed every which way. My closest neighbor would be Doc Allen, our local vet. A little dirt road lined with white brush on both sides leads to the first home I ever owned, and I'm sure it will be my last because I'm fast becoming a tribal elder too. My north windows look out toward a West Texas rimrock where buzzards soar. To the northeast I can see the 06 rimrock and top country, the same view I had from the Willow Springs porch bed. Just outside some glass doors where I can watch, I provide a pan of water for birds, red racers, gray foxes, raccoons, skunks, javelinas, mean ol' roadrunners (which eat my baby birds), and whatever else needs a drink. I can't go to them anymore, but they come to me because they know that little "spring" will always be full of water. I fill it with a bucket, never let it dry up, and never let it stay frozen for more than a few hours. Blue quail and ten-point mule deer follow my little dirt road to my water-pan spring.

One of my favorite pieces of home decor is a basket of pinecones that sits on the cedar chest that my grandfather had a neighbor make for my grandmother in 1922. The pinecones bring back memories of a sundown supper at the Padlock Ranch wagon in Montana, somewhere on the Crow Reservation, limestone rock jutting out of the expanse of grass like small islands. I picked up pinecones there for reasons I no longer remember and packed them home. Those old pinecones have topped that cedar chest for almost fifty years. Frozen in plaster, real tracks of wolf, cougar, jaguar, and bobcat decorate the mantel of my wood-burning fireplace. On one wall hangs a No. 4½ Newhouse wolf trap and digging tool used in Mexico to catch the last of the lobos. On another wall is a windmill tail, Aermotor, made in Argentina. Scattered on other walls are my bridles and hackamores.

A few years after moving in, the time came to retire from my college teaching job. I felt adrift again, like I'd lost or outlived my purpose. Years before, when I saw my chapter as wife and mother coming to a close, I soon headed back to college for a PhD. I deepened my cowboy journalism by studying novels, autobiographies, biographies, memoirs, plays, and poetry about cowboys, horses, and cattle. I started editing magazines and journals. Eventually my purpose became teaching what I had learned to college students. But now facing retirement, I was again losing my purpose. So I did what I always did when I felt scared—I picked up my pen.

My daughter had married a cowboy and fixed up and lived in one old falling-down camp house after another, and I had become a grandma. Readers are probably thinking that the cowboy lifestyle I've been describing is history, over, gone. That's not true. We "last of a dying breed" are hard at work raising our own replacements, teaching them how to live like this and do this rewarding work. So one of the last magazine articles I published was on how to raise kids. I'd been noticing how urbanites seemed to be clashing with nature once they moved to what they thought would be a rural utopia. They feared for their pets, their children, and their property. California bikers, Colorado athletes, and Arizona backpackers, even undefeated Florida Indian tribes, had become so fearful of cougars that they were demanding their removal from ceremonial grounds. I had lived with cougars always and don't doubt that one occasionally watered at the little pan outside my glass doors. So I wrote about my grandchildren and called my article "The Beast in the Garden vs. Redneck Kids." This is the ending:

> Well, people, welcome to redneck country! We've always had beasts in our gardens. You talk about human encroachment into wildlife habitat as though you invented it. Instead of making fun of us, maybe you should humbly ask how on earth we raise children in these dangerous places.
>
> Easy. Redneck kids are always armed.
>
> I was seldom outside without a rock or BB gun in hand. One redneck kid can reclaim and secure a yard in short order. Got a mountain lion sleeping under the hedge? No problem. Ping! Deer eating the petunias? Ping. A duck in the swimming pool? Ping. In ten minutes, the poor kid will be completely out of targets. No blood. Nothing dies. Territories just get moved around. Sometimes days pass before another target wanders into BB gun range. Because of that wait, a BB gun also increases attention spans. A redneck kid can sit in one spot for hours without moving a muscle. Your kids' teachers will appreciate that and maybe you can reduce their Ritalin dosages. . . . House cat stalking your quail? No problem. Ping. Dog digging in the rose bushes? Horses chewing the paint off the BMW? Ping. Ping. No problem. Certain things can even be declared off limits, like siblings and windows, but that takes discipline. So BB guns can also force parents to discipline their kids. Teachers will appreciate that too.

Don't like guns? Can't afford a BB gun? Make a slingshot. I'm a redneck mama. If I was trying to raise twelve kids in a trailer house full of rats and cockroaches, with hungry pit bulls and drug dealers sneaking around outside, you can bet I'd find something to make thirteen slingshots out of. Take back the neighborhood. We need to stop turning responsibility and control over to the government or the police or pest control services. Why produce kids if you don't have a job for them?

Slingshot-raised kids just walk around in the world differently. They'll pick up a rock or a stick if they sense danger. Aggression can turn some individuals into bullies, but not normally, and usually only when combined with unusual abuse. Normal kids will just learn to stick up (pun intended) for themselves. Bullies like to pick on the weak and unarmed. Cowboys say that horses sense fear. I think the same is true of all animals, humans included. A mean rooster will chase only the kids who aren't roping it. Even mice seem to know who they can intimidate into screaming and jumping on a chair and who will calmly set a trap. The pesky fly that has been trying to crawl up my nose for half an hour will disappear as soon as I grab a fly swatter. . . . I know one part pit bull that only comes out of hiding for a drink of water when my three-year-old grandson is taking his afternoon nap. His parents live in prime mountain lion habitat, and I can already imagine his little sister banging through the screen door someday, her gimmie cap on backward, and whispering, "Hey, Dad, Barky found a mountain lion and chased it up the apple tree. Where'd you hide my BB gun?"

Want to live in the garden? Then raise redneck kids.

Illustrating the article were several cute photographs, taken by my pretty daughter, of my cute grandchildren climbing a dirt bank, fishing, climbing trees, and making faces, and one especially adorable one of them all dressed up, my granddaughter in a rare dress with her hair semi-combed. She's looking at her older brother with a mean look, so I captioned it, "Watch it, Buster. You call me 'Ma'am' when I'm wearing a dress." As I write these words, they are teenagers helping with branding at one of their parents' grazing leases. They're both good hands. My granddaughter day works for some of the big local ranches, although my grandson—so far—has chosen a future career teaching music instead of horseback. As a family, they're operating more than 250 of their own mortgaged cows on leased country the owners don't want to use. It's been raining, so far. But a few months with no rain and my heirs—chuckle—could be out of the cow business. They could, of course, probably get rich much faster if they put their money in a zero percent savings account. But what fun is that? As the old poet Badger Clark wrote, they'll be "poor of course, but astride a horse."

Since their old grandma was not of much use anymore either horseback or afoot, I couldn't go back to putting in sixteen-hour days to either help them cowboy or chase stories. But my pen had always saved me from feeling worthless, so I began to hunt for a project I could still do, and that hunt reminded me of my farmer grandmother again. As she aged, Gram's world too got smaller and smaller. She went from driving teams of workhorses in the fields to raising a huge garden, then to a smaller garden, and then to flowerbeds. Just before she died, I visited her assisted-living apartment. Near her east window she had a dozen tiny pots of soil where she was raising African violets. In one was a leaf with its stem buried, in another a leaf just lying flat on the soil, in another a half leaf stuck edge down—each a different situation and each with tiny new plants emerging around it. She was still farming, still experimenting, still learning. She was probably raising those little sprouts to give to her neighbors in the assisted-living building. I kept thinking about her and those African violet leaves as I searched for a retirement purpose.

I soon found myself on the steps of the tiny little *Davis Mountain Dispatch* office in Fort Davis, asking my old friend and editor Bob Dillard if I could restart my old "Switchin' Flies" column again. Sure! Owner, editor, and publisher, Bob mainly wanted to fill up empty inches in his four- to six-page weekly newspaper. Column inches are scarce in our village, so he gave me free rein, no grief, and no wages. But I could write about anything as long as I produced about eight hundred words and met his weekly deadline. He thought I should be able to spell and figure out commas by then, so I doubt he even read it before he slapped it on the opinion page. I tried to steer clear of politics, but I've tackled everything else, from how to take care of cast-iron skillets to baseball. My usual subjects are nature (buzzards, bugs, weather), self-sufficiency (fighting grass fires, preparing for power outages), and education (overrated grammar, one-room schools). I do a lot of cowboy humor (obituaries, education, anti-technology), defending small-town culture (fund-raising, volunteers), and encouraging respect for real work (rock layers, fence builders, plumbers, cooks). My favorite people to pick on are myself and my brother, who likes being a villain. I meet a group of little ol' ranch ladies for lunch every week, and sometimes I write about our adventures (picnics, road trips, genealogy, baby goat season). Once in a while I get a compliment, and once in a while I get in trouble. Both soon blow over. If not—well you can't please everybody.

Every week I treat that column like a letter to a friend or neighbor because it is. If I wrote for a New York audience, no telling what kind of crazy BS I'd write. So when tempted to get carried away with my own intelligence, sharp wit, and sick humor, I remind myself: "OMG, I can't say that because [fill in the blank; you know who you are] will probably read this!"

I suppose writing for a tiny small-town newspaper in hicksville West Texas doesn't sound like much of a purpose. The people who read that little newspaper may not seem like a very important audience, but they're the real deal. They often serve on boards of directors or as cattleman association presidents, get elected to the Texas or U.S. Congress, work for or advise federal and state agencies, or have friends who do. I never know who might be on the other end of their conversations. Sometimes they might be standing next to the U.S. president when he signs a bill into law. I consider writing for my neighbors the most important writing I have ever done or could ever aspire to. According to the American Press Institute, the purpose of journalism is "to provide citizens with the information they need to make the best possible decisions about their lives, their communities, their societies, and their governments." Editor Dillard and I tried hard to live up to that purpose.

I think all humans have a secret desire and need to feel useful and help others, most of it probably misguided. Too much help or the wrong kind produces bossiness, busybodies, dictators, spoiled children, addicts (always codependent on someone who helps them). So I try to make sure my column is mostly entertaining. Any inspiration I try to give is designed to help my local readers help themselves and appreciate the way we do things out here in the middle of nowhere.

In one column, for example, I wrote about building and putting out a fire in the desert. I wrote it because the state and national parks around here had banned campfires. They said fires were dangerous and made messes. So I reminded my local readers of our fire-building habits. First of all, a good desert rat uses just enough wood to cook, boil coffee, or warm up their hands—no more, because desert wood is rare and precious. If the fire is still burning when the person is ready to leave, they used too much wood.

I said I'd built little fires to boil coffee all over these mountains but had never built a fire circle. Maybe, if inspectors looked close, they'd find a flat rock with a little soot on one side where I had balanced a coffee pot, or if I had cooked Thanksgiving dinner, maybe they'd find the two holes where I hammered my pot rack poles into the ground, but they'd have to look awful close to find those holes, and even then they might be looking at tarantula burrows instead. If the wind was blowing hard, I might have piled up a small hill as a windbreak for my Dutch oven to keep from burning my biscuits, but I've never found one of my windbreak hills after a rain.

I said our camp cooks had been feeding cowboys at the same cooking spots for more than a hundred years. The cooks built huge fires in long trenches, three times a day, and shoveled out a dozen piles of coals for their Dutch ovens and pots. In rainy years, the grass might be stirrup deep, yet I've never heard of a ranch cook starting a grass fire. Their fires had also burned to ashes by the time they drove off. In a day or two, the wind would scatter those ashes and critters would have cleaned up any scraps, leaving not a trace, except maybe a stick or two of leftover bullshit wood where a big live oak woodpile used to be.

I said the idea that fires make messes comes from people who have been taught the wrong way to build and put out fires. Yes, if you use too much wood and pour water on it and stir it up to put it out, you'll make a big mess. The Girl and Boy Scouts and Smokey Bear have done considerable damage to campgrounds with their campaigns to stir campfires into mud that turns into charcoal-embedded concrete mounds. The next camper can't build a fire in that dirty, black, sloppy, wet spot, so they'll build a new rock circle. Pretty soon dozens of nasty, sooty mounds and circles cover the ground. I've never poured water on a fire to put it out. Fires are good for the country, good for the soil, and good for the soul. Fire is even good for grass. I advised my readers to just sit there and tell stories until a campfire dies a natural death, let the wind scatter the ashes, and then let it rain.

My little column provides me with just enough deadline, responsibility, purpose, and practice. I look for and publish the good stuff about my people and this place, and when I do find a crack, I try to fill it with gold.

Acknowledgments

WRITING A BOOK is like raising a kid: you need a village, and I've got a good one. No way can I ever thank everyone who contributed to this project—the cowboys, cooks, and ranch owners who either willingly or under duress let me tag along, and especially those who let me take their photographs and publish their words. Thanks to those who wrote letters to me through the years, helping to educate me, whose words I may or may not have used anonymously. I've done my best to represent you honestly. If I have failed, then I have truly failed.

Special thanks to Chris Lacy (great-grandson of o6 Ranch founder H. L. Kokernot Sr.), general manager and longtime boss of the o6 Ranch, for periodically inspecting my dusting above doors and behind the fridge at Willow Springs, which was my home for thirteen wonderful years. Thanks for letting me "help," even though it was like two good men riding off. Thanks to his wife, Dawn, for patiently reading an early draft of this manuscript to him while they carried on with their very busy schedules and lives. Thanks to both for their encouragement and support.

I could never thank enough all the editors who published my words, all the teachers and friends and family who influenced my thinking through the years, and all those who read bits and pieces of early versions of this manuscript. But I do want to single out a few. Thanks especially to Betty Tanksley, another H. L. Kokernot Sr. great-grandchild, for thoughtful advice and counsel throughout the process. Also thanks to Sissy Schoenfeldt and Jodye Stone, two more West Texas ranch women who patiently read or listened to parts and gave helpful feedback and encouragement. Thanks to West Texas windmiller Don Coleman for reading several chapters while holding a red pen that he never used. Any mistakes in this book are his fault. Also thanks to Ronnie Scott, Bob Blackwell, Billito Donnell, Hal Cannon, Randy Witte, and Gary Morton for reading various selections.

Thanks to my smart grandson, Riley Spencer, who caught numerous errors that his granny missed. Thanks also to my frat boy, non-cowboy brother Richard DeGear for his brutally honest feedback from outside the cowboy world and to my daughter, Carla Spencer, who refused to read a single word until published, I hope because she "trusted" me to get it right but maybe to avoid blame. Thanks to my granddaughter, Jorey Spencer, for carrying on the female cowboy heritage that runs deep in her blood, and thanks to her dad, Chris Spencer, for making that possible.

Thanks to those who tried sometimes successfully and sometimes unsuccessfully to track down old articles: Ty Holland, Don and Linda Coleman, Ronnie Scott, Susan Morrison, and Macy Molsbee.

Thanks to Jay Dusard, who took the cover photo of me many years ago in Arizona and granted permission for its current use. Jay was one of America's all-time great large-format photographers and one of my personal role models. I feel very honored to have one of his framed originals hanging on my office wall. His books and prints are destined to become classics.

Thanks to Herb Mignery for not only giving permission to use the clever cartoon of me that appeared many years ago in *Western Horseman* but also for sending the original to me. It is now framed and proudly hanging on my office wall above my retired saddle.

I also want to acknowledge and thank the many publications mentioned in the text and listed in "Selected Publications"—newspapers, magazines, literary journals, and anthologies—where various versions of bits and pieces of this mash-up from my writing career were originally published. I especially want to thank the University of Nevada Press for permission to use pieces from my book *The Wild and the Domestic* and Tate Dillard, current editor of the *Mountain Dispatch* of Fort Davis, Texas, for permission to use bits and selections from my "Switchin' Flies" column, published for thirty years by his late and beloved father, Bob Dillard. I never told Bob how much writing a column for him meant to me. I planned to just hand him a copy of this book, but I just didn't write it fast enough. I can only hope that somehow he knew.

A special thank-you goes to my thirty-year friend and Northern California horseman and rancher Rod Flournoy for helpful suggestions on the text and for firing off an encouraging letter in his beautiful Spencerian script handwriting when I told him the press wanted me to cut the original manuscript for this book in half. His words kept me from jumping off the nearest bridge:

> I have been wanting to write for weeks but will answer here in haste to say, do not let a wretched editor cut material out of your precious book. . . . Mark Twain hated editors, had he turned 'em loose on his work, we would not have his wonderful prose to read and enjoy. Benjamin Franklin told about a feller he knew that had a grocery store. Some fishermen brought him in a catch of fish to sell and the man hung up a sign that said, "Fresh fish for sale here."
>
> An editor stopped by and said, "If you've got fish to sell anyone knows it's here, so cross off 'here.'"
>
> "Okay," said the grocer and he drew a line through "here."
>
> Then said the editor, "Anyone will know the fish are fresh, so cross it off."
>
> So, he done it.
>
> Then another editor came along and said, "If you've got fish here, anyone knows they are for sale, so cross off 'for sale.'"
>
> So, due to editors, "Fresh fish for sale here" became "Fish."

Thanks, Rod. All those who read that sign probably went home, grabbed their tackle boxes and fishing poles, and headed out to do just that.

And finally, a big thank-you to the University of Oklahoma Press editors. Acquisition editor James Kent Calder was the one who insisted that I cut the manuscript in half. Anything you readers don't understand, that seems chopped up, or that you wish I had said but didn't is Kent's fault! Seriously, his patience as I stubbornly resisted his suggestions was Job-like. Once I finally started listening to him, the manuscript improved considerably. Thanks, Kent! And big thanks to copy editor Peg Goldstein for catching my many embarrassing errors and making my writing sound better than I deserve. Any mistakes that remain are probably because I talked her into letting my lingo slide. Thanks, Peg!

And finally, thank you, coffee.

Selected Publications

Copies of most articles, published photography, and more complete publication lists are available in the Barbara "Barney" Nelson Collection, Archives of the Big Bend, Sul Ross State University, Alpine, Texas.

Books

God's Country or Devil's Playground: An Anthology of Nature Writing from the Big Bend of Texas. Austin: University of Texas Press, 2002.

Here's to the Vinegarroon! Alpine, Tex.: Territorial Printer, 1989.

The Last Campfire: The Life Story of Ted Gray, a West Texas Rancher. College Station: Texas A&M University Press, 1984.

Voices and Visions of the American West. Austin: Texas Monthly Press, 1986.

The Wild and the Domestic: Animal Representation, Ecocriticism, and Western American Literature. Reno: University of Nevada Press, 2000.

Magazine Articles

Appaloosa News

"Gentling a Horse the Jefferey's Way." Sept. 1979: 30–33.

Arabian Horse Express

"The Grey Finds a Home on the Range." May 1984: 41–43.

Arabian Horse World

"The Grey." July 1984: 126–29.

"Hothouse Flowers to Texas Bluebonnets." July 1985: 257–63.

"Land of the Buckaroo." Sept. 1985: 254–55.

The Cattleman
"Branding Time." May 1985: 88–91.
"Electronic Marketing: Ultramodern Answer to an Old Problem." March 1988: 132–38.
"Elmer Kelton and All the Times It Never Rained." Sept. 1986: 90–102.
"Owen Womack: Dedicated to Brangus." April 1985: 70–78.
"Public Trust at Stake Over Endangered Species." March 1991: 74, 76–84.
"Ten Good Men and the Highland Cattle Supermarket." Oct. 1985: 172–78.
"20 Commandments for a Cowboy's Wife." June 1982: 114–15.
"West Texans Take a Look at Poisonous Plant Control." May 1980: 84–88.

Country People
"Men Who Run the Range." Sept./Oct. 1985: 4–5.

Cowboy
"The Hat Band." Summer 1990: 18–20.
"Ronnie Scott: New Mexico Horse Trainer." Summer 1990: 44–45.
"Two-Legged Colts." Summer 1991: 32–34.
"Wally Wines: A Man of Tradition." Fall 1992: cover story.

Horse and Rider (a few dates are unknown)
"Able Hands." n.d.: 25–26
"Choice Not Chaos," Part I, Sept. 1985: 10–13+; Part II, Oct. 1985: 10–14+; Part III, Nov. 1985: 10–14+.
"A Day in the Saddle." n.d.: 34–37.
"Getting Ready to Learn." n.d.: 16–29.
"Hansen's Handmade Spurs." Nov. 1985: 34–36.
"Leg and Rein Cues." n.d.: 14–17.
"Montana's CA Ranch." Nov. 1985: 40–42.
"Okay, Let's Try It Again." Oct. 1986: 40–43.
"Taking Ray Hunt Home." April 1987: 22–25.
"Texas Ranch Round-Up" n.d.: 16–19.
"Youth Clinic." Dec. 1986: 1–15.

Horseman
"Are You Saddlewise?" Aug. 1978: 72–76.

Persimmon Hill
"The Durable Harley May." Autumn 1979: 58–67.
"El Fotografo: W. D. Smithers." Autumn 1987: 50–59.

Ranch
"That Time of Year." June 1987: 8–9.

Range
"Ansel Adams." Summer 1995: 32–35.
"The Beast in the Garden vs. Redneck Kids." Summer 2006: 18–21.
"Butchering Thoreau." Fall 1995: 50–53.
"Butchering Thoreau." Summer 2012: 60.
"Cowboy Haiku." Summer 2013: 78–79.

"Demonizing Cowbirds: Too Many Political Agendas Are Hiding behind the Skirts of the Endangered Species Act." Fall 2000: 20–21.
"Edward Abbey: Friend or Foe?" Spring 1996: 46–47.
"Fighting Hell with a Bucket." Fall 2012: 24–27.
"Ground Hog Day at the Wolf Wars." Summer 2003: 57–59.
"Ivory-Billed Woodpeckers, UFOs and Elvis." Winter 2006: 22–23.
"Last Resort: Wild Geese Are Destroying Arctic Ecosystems." Fall 2006: 26–29.
"Natives and Invaders, Wild Cows Came before Bison." Fall 1999: 64–67.
"Nature Faking." Spring 2002: 12–15.
"Out on the Range in Jess Valley, CA." Spring 2010: 6–7.
"Out on the Range in Texas." Winter 1995: 34–35.
"Poison Propaganda: Compound 1080's Greatest Threat to Wildlife Occurs When Defenders of Wildlife Uses It to Raise Funds." Fall 2004: 48–50.
"Sheepherders and the Sierra." Summer/Fall 1993: 13–15.
"Solace for Wyoming Sheepherders." Spring 1998: 40–41.
"Subdividing America with the Nature Conservancy." Winter 2004: 70–73 (cowritten with Bob Dillard).
"Thoreau was a Cow-Boy." Summer 2001: 12–13. Reprinted as cover story in the *Short North Gazette* (Columbus, Ohio). July 2001: 1, 18–19.
"Uncommon Ground: University Environmentalists from across the Nation Do Some Serious Soul Searching." Winter 1998: 52–53.
"The Way I See It." Spring 2005: 65.
"The Way It Was and Is." Summer 2010: 72–73.
"Well, They Did Say That, but . . . : Famous Nature Writers Often Wrote Passages That Enraged Their Friends and Comforted Their Enemies." Spring 1995: 12–13.
"Why Would a Cowboy Protect a Blind Salamander?" Spring 1997: 43–45.

Texas Monthly

"All the Pretty Horses." August 2012: 96–101+.
"Cowgirl Up!" August 2011: 90–103.

Western Horseman

"Abilene's Western Heritage Classic." April 1988: 90–92.
"The Art of Wayne Baize." Aug. 1981: 30–34.
"Bear Paw Mountain Cowboy." Nov. 1984: 84–87.
"Beto Muzquiz: Raising Horses in Mexico." Dec. 1984: 52–55.
"Big Bend Ranch Rodeo." July 1987: 40–42.
"Bill Black, Cowbossin' on the MC." April 1986: 15–20.
"Bob Eidson, Cowboy Cowman." Part I, April 1984: 78–86; Part II, May 1984: 16–21.
"Born a Charro." Jan. 1986: 128–31.
"Braider Bryan Neubert." Dec. 1989: 56–59.
"Branding with Charlie Daniels." Dec. 1984: 14–16.

"Breaking Colts with Donnie Slover." July 1982: 26–33.
"Camp Mitre." Jan. 1978: 82.
"Carla's Saddle." April 1981: 6–7.
"Carlos Ochoa: Today's Mexican Rancher." Nov. 1984: 30–32.
"Catching Horses in the Remuda." Nov. 1983: 64–67.
"A Cocinero's Life on the Open Range." June 1982: 12–15.
"Cody Crider, Colt Breaker." Feb. 1990: 127+.
"College National Finals: Even the Losers Are Winners." Sept. 1982: 73–75.
"Cortés Joyeros: Mexico's Fine Silversmiths." March 1985: 43–44.
"The Cowboy and the Kid." June 1980: 91–93.
"Cowboy Christmas: Pecos Style." June 1983: 88–94.
"Cowboy Customized Spurs." June 1981: 104–5.
"Cowboy Poet, Waddie Mitchell." Jan. 1987: 46–47.
"Cowboy Poetry Gathering." May 1985: 91–93.
"Cowboy Thanksgiving." Nov. 1987: 98–99.
"Cowboy Trade Party." June 1987: 106–07.
"Cowboying in Codfish Hollow." Feb. 1984: 14–18.
"Cowboys and Christmas Cards." Dec. 1983: 33–39.
"Day Working for Day Wages." Dec. 1981: 14–19.
"Don Davies, Rawhider." June 1982: 16.
"Double E Day and Reunion Rodeo." June 1977: 82–84.
"Drifting with the Dugan Wagon." July 1986: 42–46.
"The Dugan Wagon." May 1985: 40–43.
"Editorial Letter." June 1980: 7.
"Fall Gather on the 06." Nov. 1979: 97–99.
"Fran Locke: Cowboy's Wife." Sept. 1984: 26–30.
"Free-lancing for Horse Magazines." Sept. 1988: 51–54.
"Gary Morton, a Cowboy's Artist." Sept. 1982: 58–60.
"Gear of the Working Cowboy." March 1981: 88–90.
"Goin' to College on an Anvil." Feb. 1971: 40+.
"Hackamore Tip." Aug. 1981: 121.
"Happy Birthday Craig." Feb. 1982: 85–86.
"History of NIRA." Jan. 1979: 6–9.
"A Homecoming in Elko." May 1986: 72–76.
"Horse Employment Agency." Dec. 1988: 58–62.
"Horse Sculpture." Feb. 1982: 114.
"Horseman's Holiday without a Horse." Feb. 1985: 37–38.
"How to Make a Range Tepee Tent." June 1980: 101–103.
"Knives from the Anvil." July 1983: 14–15.
"A Little Museum's Big Idea." June 1982: 93–94.
"Mark Dahl: Self-Made Silversmith." May 1986: 100–101.
"The McIvor U Up and U Down Ranch." May 1983: 43–47.
"Mike Capron: Artist and Cowboy." April 1986: 124–25.

"Morris Bray and Fido Henderson." Oct. 1981: 97.
"Note in Horses and People." Nov. 1980: 74.
"The Odd Couple . . . Cowboy Style." June 1985: 35–39.
"Of Stockwhips and Friends." June 1986: 62–64.
"Old Timers' Album." June 1974: 200.
"On Length of Stride." April 1982: 56–57.
"Packing into Jubilee." April 1982: 72–77.
"Pasture Loading." June 1987: 100–101.
"Ranching on the Reservation, Part 1: The Crows." April 1993: 94–97.
"Ranching on the Reservation, Part 2: Northern Cheyennes." May 1993: 10–13.
"Ray Hunt Horsemanship Clinic." Oct. 1984: 144–51.
"Regarding the Cowboy." Aug. 1983: 16–21.
"Restraining Horses." Oct. 1980: 89–94.
"Riding the Big Bend." Feb. 1981: 35–38.
"A Rodeo for Ranch Cowboys." Aug. 1983: 52–55.
"Rodeoin' in Town and Punchin' Sheep at Home." March 1982: 93–95.
"Ross Knox: Brush-Hand Buckaroo." Oct. 1987: 38–40.
"Shoeing the Rodeo Horse." Nov. 1981: 30–35.
"Silver for Poor Folks." Jan. 1982: 28–30.
"Silver Rein Keeper." Dec. 1981: 8.
"Something Special in Rodeo: College National Finals." Sept. 1981: 41–45.
"The Sore Backed Horse." Nov. 1982: 55–57.
"Sul Ross State's Animal Health Technician Program." July 1977: 160.
"Texas Outfit: The X Ranch." March 1982: 14–21.
"Tom Blasingame: Still at Home on the Range." Part I, March 1987: 24–30; Part II, April 1987: 30–35.
"Tommy Vaughn: His Horses Get on the Job Training." July 1984: 28–33.
"Training Colts with Ray (Hunt) and Barry." Aug. 1983: 8–14.
"Trappings of the West." Aug. 1986: 29–30.
"Two Sides of 'Lady Luck' at the College National Finals." Sept. 1983: 68–72.
"Victoria: A Charra of Mexico." Dec. 1984: 87.
"The West Isn't Just Blue Jeans Anymore." Aug. 1984: 48–50.
"A Working Cowboy's Hobby." July 1974: 84+.

Related Professional Publications

"The Coyote Nature of Cowboy Poetry." In *A Companion to the Literature and Culture of the American West*, edited by Nicolas Witschi, 297–315. Malden, Mass.: Blackwell Publishing, 2011.

"Cowboy Poetry." In *Princeton Encyclopedia of Poetry and Poetics*, 4th ed., 313–15. Princeton, N.J.: Princeton University Press, 2012.

"Dana Gioia Is Wrong about Cowboy Poetry." *Western American Literature* (Winter 2006): 404–22.

"Edward Abbey's Cow." In *Coyote in the Maze: Critical Essays on Edward Abbey,* edited by Peter Quigley, 206–225. Salt Lake City: University of Utah Press, 1998.

"Every Educated Feller Ain't a Plumb Greenhorn: Cowboy Poetry's Polyvocal Narrator." *Heritage of the Great Plains* 3, no. 2 (2000): 49–64.

"Exploiting Mexican Wolf Science and Story as Material for Wild Books." *Interdisciplinary Studies in Literature and Environment* (Winter 2006): 91–109.

"The Flock: An Ecocritical Look at Mary Austin's Sheep and John Muir's Hoofed Locusts." In *Exploring the Lost Borders: Critical Essays on Mary Austin,* edited by Melody Graulich and Betsy Klimasmith, 221–42. Reno: University of Nevada Press, 1999.

"Jinete." *RE Arts & Letters* 17, no. 1 (1991): 66.

"Marion Otis 'Bug' Means: Stretching and Taking Risks." In *Cowboys Who Rode Proudly: Carrying Cattle—and the Methods of Handling Them,* edited by Evetts Haley, 103–9. Midland, Tex.: Nita Stewart Haley Memorial Library, 1992.

"Nicasio Ramirez: Cowboying from Chihuahua to Nevada." In *Cowboys Who Rode Proudly: Carrying Cattle—and the Methods of Handling Them,* edited by Evetts Haley, 167–71. Midland, Tex.: Nita Stewart Haley Memorial Library1992.

"Predators in Literature." In *Teaching North American Environmental Literature,* edited by Frederick O. Waage, Laird Christensen, and Mark Long, 256–68. New York: MLA, 2008.

"Rustling Thoreau's Cattle: Wildness and Domesticity in 'Walking.'" In *Thoreau's Sense of Place: Essays in American Environmental Writing,* edited by Richard Schneider, 254–65. Iowa City: University of Iowa Press, 2000.

"That One-Eyed Hereford Muley." In *Pride of Place: An Anthology of Texas Nature Writing,* edited by David Taylor, 69–89. Denton: University of North Texas Press, 2006.

"Tom Blasingame: A Legend in His Own Time." In *Cowboys Who Rode Proudly: Carrying Cattle—and the Methods of Handling Them,* edited by Evetts Haley, 31–37. Midland, Tex.: Nita Stewart Haley Memorial Library, 1992.

Permissions and Credits

Giving proper credit to previously published sources becomes almost impossible when writing a memoir about a writing career! The material and stories that I mash up in this book come from all over the publishing map (livestock magazine articles, scholarly conference papers, scholarly journal articles, book chapters, books, anthologies, and a newspaper column). Various versions of the same stories and my cowboy thoughts on particular subjects appear again and again in almost all those publications. Some later appeared in anthologies. Untangling which previously published source should get credit for similar material has been complicated. Most of the material has been completely reorganized and rewritten; sometimes just a sentence or a paragraph has been used. Quotation marks have been used when appropriate. Hopefully, the following gives proper credit to the most important and fully quoted sources.

Earlier versions of some commentary and stories were published in the *Jeff Davis Mountain Dispatch* between 1990 and 2020 and are used here by permission.

Earlier versions of material on wildness, Edward Abbey, and Henry Thoreau, and excerpts from personal cowboy stories, were previously published in *The Wild and the Domestic: Animal Representation, Ecocriticism, and*

Western American Literature (Reno: University of Nevada Press, 2000) and are used here by permission.

Earlier versions of parts of chapter 8 were previously published as "That One-Eyed Hereford Muley" in *Pride of Place: An Anthology of Texas Nature Writing*, edited by David Taylor (Denton: University of North Texas Press, 2006), 69–89, and are used here by permission.

The poem "Jinete" was previously published in *RE Arts & Letters* 17, no. 1 (1991): 66, and is used here by permission.

www.ingramcontent.com/pod-product-compliance
Lightning Source LLC
LaVergne TN
LVHW091110080826
845145LV00008B/1868

* 9 7 8 0 8 0 6 1 6 8 4 5 6 *